Romania

GW00696163

In brief...

- **Position**: South-east Europe, north of the Balkans.
- **Neighbouring countries**: Bulgaria, Serbia, Hungary, Ukraine, Moldava.
- **Time zone**: GMT + 2 in summer, GMT + 3 in winter.
- **Surface area**: 238,391 km^2
- **Climate**: continental (hot summers, cold winters).
- **Capital**: Bucharest, population 2,016,131.
- **Language**: the official language is Romanian.
- **Currency**: the leu ('lion'); plural, lei.
- **Religion**: 86.8 % Orthodox; 5.1 % Catholic; 1 % Uniate; 3.5 % Protestant. ●

HACHETTE

This guide was written and researched by **BERNARD HOULIAT**,

with the collaboration of the Romanian Ministry for Transport, Construction and Tourism.

Specialist in Eastern Europe and the culture of Roms, BERNARD HOULIAT is a regular contributor to Hachette publications. Having lived for several years in Romania, where he has worked for international organisations, he is the author of two books which are well know and respected by travellers who love this country: Tsiganes en Roumanie (Rouergue, 1999) and La Roumanie au petit bonheur (Quelque Part sur Terre, 2000).

The author would like to thank Philippe Etienne, the French Ambassador in Romania, for his warm support. As well as all those who have offered information, research, advice, friendship and compassion throughout this project: Octavian Arsene, from the Ministry for Transport, Construction and Tourism and all who work for him in the country; the friends of western embassies in Bucharest; the Centre culturel français in Iaşi (Paul Elie Levy, Selma Toprak); ; the Centre culturel français in Timişoara (Monica Selariu and Emmanuel Sapet); the Maison de l'Ille et Vilaine in Sibiu (Florentina Chidu); the Botiza association (Muntean, Pasca, Costinar, Bobocea and Trifoi families); Mother Tatiana (Moldoviţa Monastery); the nuns at Dragomirna, Probota and Suceviţa; Aurelian Albut, Irina Balea, Miruna Beindei, Ioan Borlean, Trandafir Cazac, Maylis Cazaumayou, Doinita Derevlean, Franz Dizmacsek, Fabio Di Pietro, Miki Dungeanu, Hermann Fabini, Caroline and Walter Fernolend, Cristina Gheauş (Romanian Tourist Office in Paris), Félix Houliat, Florin Istrate, Eftimie Luchian, Andrei Mahalnischi, Cristina Maier, Paula Mihailov (Antrec-Tulcea), Familie Morar, Arlette Novak, Constantin Pauna, Istvan Plajas, Hugo Schneider, Stefana Totorcea, Cornelia and Ionel Ureche, Petre Vasiliu.

Photography was produced especially for this guide by **Pierre Soissons**.

Cover photograph: interior frescoes at Probota Church, Moldavia (© Pierre Soissons).

Exclusive advertising rights: **Hachette Tourisme**, 43, quai de Grenelle, 75905 Paris Cedex 15. Contact : Valérie Habert ☎ +33 (0)1.43.92.32.52.

Write to us:
Hachette Tourisme, 43 quai de Grenelle, F-75905 Paris Cedex 15
< **bleusevasion@hachette-livre.fr** >.
© **Hachette Livre (Hachette Tourisme)**, 2004.

Romania

HACHETTE

Time to explore?

Human, sensual, excessive, down-to-earth: all these attributes, and more, apply to Romania which thrives on its complexity. No less complex is its wild landscape and its outstanding variety of natural habitats.

Romania has been at the thick of all the invasions and empires that have shaped Eastern Europe, but its people have somehow managed to maintain a unique identity whilst living amidst a host of different cultures, rarely found elsewhere. Above all, Romania is an old, wise civilisation, as its exceptional cultural heritage clearly shows.

Misunderstood, probably; little known, certainly. Perhaps it is time to explore this friendly, generous, inexhaustible country. ●

Detail of a fresco from Suceviţa Monastery, Bucovina.

contents

Context

Itineraries

© Pierre Soissons

Itineraries

contents

© Pierre Soissons

contents

Basics

In brief

© Pierre Soissons

Maps

context

Majestic nature

© Bernard Houliat

The Carpathians and the Danube have shaped the geography and history of Romania, crowning and carving the landscape. The country boasts a wealth of landscapes home to species now extinct in the rest of Europe, dotted with charming villages where time has stood still for centuries.

Geography: the rule of three

The land is split into three roughly equal parts: mountainous regions, rolling foothills, and lowland plains. These three geographically distinct regions in fact form a series of concentric circles. In the centre lie the rolling hills of the **Transylvanian**

Previous page: on the foothills of the Carpathians, some families have been farming the vast pastures for centuries.

Above: village huts basking in the sun on the cheerful slopes of the Apuseni Mountains.

plateau. The mountainous peaks of the **Carpathians** ring the plateau, flanked on one side by the Moldavian and Wallachian **foothills**. The plains of the **Banat** and **Crişana** stretch to the horizon in the west, while the vast expanses of **Wallachia** and **Dobrogea** are the gateway to the Balkans and Asia.

Mountains: the snowy peaks of the Carpathians

More than half of the Carpathian mountain range *(p. 91)* belongs to Romania. The range stretches from beyond the northern border in the Maramureş region, crossing the lands of Bucovina. The range then turns sharply to the south. The part of the chain to the north of Bucharest is known as the Moldavian Carpathians. There, the chain curves to the west and its peaks continue to climb. The highest summit is Mount Moldoveanu at 2,544 metres. The Danube *(Dunărea)* carves a deep swathe through the range, forming a truly stunning spectacle. In the west of the country lie the Apuseni Mountains. This region offers a remarkable variety of flora and fauna and is home to many traditional villages. The Apuseni range is sometimes steep and craggy, but more often the summits are gently rounded and covered in thick forest, cleared in part for vast tracts of lush pastureland.

A natural amphitheatre of hills

Transylvania is a smiling land of gently sloping valleys. Protected by the sheltering Carpathian ramparts, the region has played a key role in forging Romania's historical and cultural identity and has also left its mark on traditional Magyar mythology and German folk culture.

Also known as *Țara românească* (the Romanian county), **Wallachia** is the name of the land that lies between **Muntenia** in the east and **Oltenia** in the west. The Carpathian foothills are a tangle of aromatic valleys dotted with meadows, orchards,

economy

A generous land

Romania is extremely rich in natural resources. It is the second largest producer of oil in Europe, although its reserves are limited. It also has vast amounts of non-ferrous **minerals**, including **rare** and **precious** resources such as silver, lead, and gold. These metals have been mines since Dacian and Roman times.

The country is the world's 15th largest **gas** producer and the 11th biggest producer of **lignite**. Industry centres on specialised sectors such as metallurgy, mechanical construction, and petrochemicals.

Forestry remains a vital, but sadly overexploited, resource. **Agriculture** has yet to reach its full potential despite recent progress. Lush and fertile, the farmlands of Wallachia and the Banat are **among the richest in Europe.** ●

A backpacker's paradise

With such an amazing variety of landscapes, an ancient rural tradition of hospitality, and numerous places to stay, Romania is ideal for hikers. But to explore the country in depth, you will need a guide. Hiking trails are only signposted in the mountains near larger towns. Elsewhere, signposts may be unreliable or even absent altogether. Maps are rarely very detailed. Although better maps are beginning to appear on the market, they can be hard to get hold of. Finding your way around alone can be hard going, but well-trained guides can be easily be hired, even in the more inaccessible regions, which are often the most interesting. Some little-known mountains and ranges to tackle might include Apuseni, Mehedinti, Maramureș, Bucovina, Bârgaeu, Neamț and Ceahlău or Vrancea *(see regional address books and p. 307)*. ●

© Bernard Houliat

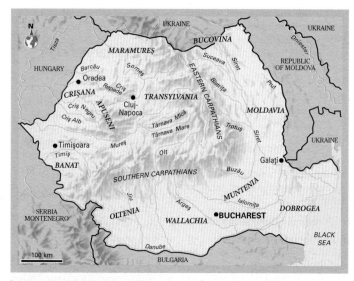

ROMANIA'S MOUNTAIN RANGES

and forests. These become immense plains, scattered with trees, which gradually slope down to the Danube. Historically speaking, **Moldavia** includes the regions of **Bucovina**, **Bessarabia** (now divided between the Ukraine and the Republic of Moldova, *p. 244*) and Moldavia. Nowadays, the term refers to the whole eastern half of the country, from the Prut River to the peaks of the Carpathians, and from the Ukraine to the Danube. The lush green forests that cloak the mountains form a sharp contrast with the rather harsher landscape of the Moldavian hills and the monotonous plains of the Siret valley.

Winter Sports

Most of the mountain ranges in Romania offer skiing facilities. The Carpathians are home to high quality resorts, much cheaper than those in Western Europe, which offer a full range of services and places to stay. Among the better resorts are those in the Prahova valley (Predeal, Azuga, Bușteni, Sinaia), around Brașov (Poiana Brașov), or in the Banat region (Semenic). Borșa in Maramureș has magnificent natural scenery, although the resort itself is far from appealing. Cross-country skiing is not very well established, although the country seems ideally suited to the sport.

Potholing

Romania is also one of the best places in Europe for caving and **potholing** thanks to its abundance of caves, primarily situated in the **Banat** *(p. 87)* or in **Oltenia**. There are great caving opportunities in the Apuseni Mountains as well, home to one of the biggest karst landscapes in Europe. Further afield, the plateau of Padiș and especially the **caves of Scărișoara** *(see inset p. 130 and facing)* are also worthy of exploration. ●

© Diane Dufresne

© Victor Bortas

© Pierre Soissons

© Pierre Soissons

Top: the Fargaras mountains. Centre: the Moldavian plains. Bottom: the Danube delta.

Rich, rolling plains

Dobrogea is not just a bare landscape of steppes and steep escarpments. Vineyards and deciduous forests bring a pleasant softness to the countryside, which extends gently down to the beaches along the **Black Sea coast**. The **Danube** reigns over this region, its course carving out side-streams and losing its way in marshes before ending on the very edge of Europe in a broad delta which is constantly expanding into the Black Sea thanks to its sediment-rich waters.

The Banat and **Crişana** are backed by the Carpathians. Their geography and history makes them very much part of Central Europe. **Maramureş,** cut off in the north-west by the Carpathians, has retained traditions that originated in Roman times. The region is verdant and crowned with wooded mountains.

Flora and fauna

Romania has a wide range of biotopes and has a great variety of flora and fauna. The vegetation is abundant and incredibly diverse. Some species of plant are endemic to Romania, while others are found in the Caucasus and central Asia.

The forests

Roughly twenty-six percent (6.3 million hectares) of the country is covered in forest. The forests of the northern regions are predominantly coniferous (spruce, fir), but broadleaved trees such as beech and birch are also common. In the centre and the south (excluding the mountains), broad-leaved species and oak dominate. At higher altitudes, beech and spruce give way to great swathes of cembra pine. These Romanian forests are a great treaure, but sadly over-exploited.

Wildlife

Romania's **wildlife** is among the richest in Europe. There are an estimated 3,000 **wolves**, nearly 40% of the European population. Despite their vicious reputation, wolves present little danger. Romania is also home to nearly 60% of Europe's **bears**, with about 5,000 animals. They roam the mountains and the Transylvanian hills. Bears and stags play an impor-

Nature conservation

The exceptional **Danube delta** was officially declared a " biosphere reserve " in 1992 *(see inset p. 280)*. Since 2000, the law has provided a framework for protecting the environment. The protected areas represent 5.18% of the country.

Eleven national parks have been planned in addition to the Retezat national park *(p. 140)*, created in 1935.

The proposed national park sites are Rodna, Căliman, Cozia *(p. 99)*, Retezat, Ceahlău *(p. 267)*, Măcin, Piatra Craiului *(p. 96)*, the Semenic mountains *(p. 110)*, the gorges of Bicaz *(p. 267)*, Nera, and the Cerna Valley. **Six natural parks** have also been planned. These are the Bucegi and Apuseni Mountains nature reserves *(p. 121)*, the Iron Gates on the banks of the Danube *(p. 108)*, the Brăila ponds, also on the Danube, and Vânatori Neamţ. Though there are hundreds of **natural and scientific reserves**, there is a lack of funding to enforce regulations. The country is also proud of its "natural monuments", which are birds and other fauna, plants, and rare sites of special environmental interest protected by law.

Floating hotels

On the main channels of the Danube, large barges pulled by tugboats have been transformed into hotels *(p. 280)*. Each hotel has a dozen or so comfortable cabins, often with restaurants offering panoramic views *(see inset p. 296)*.

These floating dormitories can simply drop anchor at places of interest. Small skiffs are available for guests and prove the perfect way to glide along the canals and explore the lakes. It is the ideal way to discover what the delta has to offer, all in stylish comfort, of course. ●

© Pierre Soissons

There is nothing like a local train for getting to the heart of the countryside.

tant role in Romanian folk culture, particularly during the winter folk rituals *(p. 36)*. Roughly 1,000 **lynx** inhabit the deep forest, along with stags, deer, wild boar, wild cats, badgers and martens. The emblem of Moldavia *(p. 222)*, the **aurochs**, is now extinct in the wild, but a few European bison from the Bialowieza reserve in Poland have been re-introduced to the **Vânatori Neamț** reserve. In the mountains, chamois and marmots live alongside many **bird species** including golden eagles, western capercaillie, and hazel grouse.

The Danube delta is home to at least 300 bird species *(p. 276)*. It is a resting place for many migrating species, making it one of the best places for birdwatching in the world. The delta also has interesting mammal species such as mink and raccoon dogs from Siberia.

The iron trail

People who love the romance of train travel have the perfect opportunity to indulge their passion in Romania *(p. 317)*. Travelling by train, you will get to know the real Romania. Fellow passengers might even strike up a conversation in English, French, or

German, and often have useful tips on things to do and places to visit. On longer journeys (from Iași to Timișoara, for example), it is customary to share a glass of *țuică* (brandy) with fellow passengers.

The most beautiful journey is definitely from **Oravița** to **Anina** *(p. 109)*. Elsewhere **local trains** in **Bucovina,** Vama to Moldovița *(p. 231)* or Rădăuți to Putna *(p. 235)* wind past houses and gardens. Smaller lines in the **Banat**, round Timișoara, are a delight to ride in, full of the poetry of a bygone age. Or you could spend 14 hours travelling from Bucharest to Sighetu Marmației, relaxing in the sleeping cars that are a relic of the railway's golden age. Crawling through the **Maramureș** mountains in the early morning at 20 kilometres an hour, it is magical watching the dawn light pick out painted wooden houses tucked away in the landscape and ancient villages alive with activity. Last but not least, along the **Vaser valley** in Maramureș, the famous narrow-gauge track *(p. 215)* for the use of foresters carries the last **steam engines** in operation in Romania. ●

Rural traditions

During haymaking, the countryside is a riot of noise and colour.

© Pierre Soissons

Visitors to Romania can expect many surprises. The most beautiful of these is the countryside itself, full of generous energy and colour. In certain mountainous or hilly regions, the landscape is nothing short of a picturesque paradise. It is also a hive of bustling activity, of women singing and calling out to each other, men whistling or shouting commands to their horses and dogs, swishing scythes, giggling children, jingling sheep bells, and creaking carts piled high with tottering bales of hay. These picture-postcard villages strung out along the valleys are delightful. Charming pastel-coloured villages huddle round a fortified church. Hamlets are scattered on hilltops or tucked away in secret valleys. Life is vibrant and colourful in the countryside, where children play with cats and geese in the tracks of bare earth that pass for roads.

Traditional farming

If rural Romania has managed to keep its traditions alive, it is because the villagers have learned to rely on their own strengths in times of trouble. During the communist era, about 90% of farmland was under state control. The remaining 10%, mostly in mountain areas, was all that remained for private cultivation. In 1990, the land was handed back to its former owners. Some 5 million people had claims, so the land was divided up into miniscule plots. During this transition period, farmers rediscovered the benefits of the old farming ways, sowing a number of small fields with different crops. This looks pretty and is great for tourism, but this farming technique requires a great deal of effort for a yield that is often disappointing.

On the brink of change

The rural economy is currently based on a combination of self-sufficiency and neighbours lending a helping hand when needed. Nevertheless, having resisted change for so many centuries, this system is on the brink of disappearing for good. The rural economy is set to expand rapidly over the next 20 years. Romania's entry into the European Union (*see inset p. 324*) could be the death knell of ancestral but low-yielding farming traditions. Romanian peasant farmers have already practically been excluded from the European agricultural development programme SAPARD.

In reality, life in the countryside is far from idyllic. While life in the villages is not too hard, resources are limited and hugely dependent on the weather and economic conditions. The average peasant farmer cannot afford the luxury of debating whether his traditions are worth saving. He is more likely to want to leave this difficult, physically demanding lifestyle behind. If he had the money, he would not hesitate one moment before knocking down the old wooden hut much beloved of tourists and putting up a modern house, all in concrete, instead.

An extraordinary folk heritage

Numerous traditions have been passed down over the years, particularly in the Romanian countryside. As always, it takes time to discover a country's true nature. It would be a shame to come away with a superficial impression gleaned from carefully staged displays of folk culture. All you need to do is share the daily life of a village for a short while, perhaps somewhere in Oltenia, in the Moldavian hills or in Bucovina. There, you will witness a slower, more hospitable lifestyle which Western Europe seems to have forgotten. Rediscover the taste of real fresh eggs or elderberry jam. Remember how it feels to dawdle. Take the time to explore the country's remarkable heritage. In Romania, culture thrives outside the muse-

B & B in Romania

The gradual introduction of **bed and breakfasts** has proved successful and is beginning to catch on. The majority of these establishments are in houses approved by the Ministry of Transport, Construction, and Tourism. Unfortunately, these establishments can sometimes be modern and somewhat lacking in charm. You might be lucky enough to find a **traditional home** which has been restored and equipped to welcome tourists, in regions such as Maramureș (p. 216), the Saxon citadels (p. 174), Count Kalnoky's residence in Transylvania (p. 192), or the fringes of the Apuseni Mountains (p. 142). It is worth taking half-board, not only because it can be tricky finding a place to eat nearby, but also because it is always good to explore traditional cuisine through home, rather than restaurant, cooking. The evening meal and breakfast are copious and often make use of fresh farm produce (*see regional address book*). ●

© Pierre Soissons

economy

Investors take note

Political stability, a well-trained, affordable workforce, and the emergence of new markets have enticed many international investors to Romania. The principal sectors are now construction, cars, petrochemicals, hotels, banking, telecommunications, and agro-business. The country's biggest trading partners are members of the European Union. In 1999, Renault took control of the **Dacia** factories in Pitești (Wallachia). It was these factories that produced the copies of Renault's R12 model that are everywhere on Romanian roads. Following the German **Metro** supermarket chain, the French have also introduced their own **Carrefour** chain. Both have contributed to the development of a modern consumer society.

Foreign businesses can employ a keen and highly skilled workforce. **Information technology** is a key strength. Increasingly, however, graduates are being lured away to work in the United States, Canada, or Germany. •

ums. Folk music and traditional medicine play an important role in daily life. Skilled craftsmen are still a vital part of the village. Even everyday objects are highly decorated, reflecting the vitality of the rich folk culture.

The place of wood in folk lore

The Carpathians and their foothills are thickly wooded. The immense forests provide a seemingly unlimited supply of raw material. It is perhaps unsurprising, therefore, that in the traditional Romanian home, everything from religious objects to kitchen utensils are made of wood. Woodwork requires a delicate touch, technical skill, and a hint of spirituality. The simple yet elegant wooden churches are carved with ancient country symbols in Bihor, Oltenia

Manners

Although modern Western culture gains more ground each day, Romanian manners still hold a touching key to the past. It is a good idea to bring your hostess flowers. The bouquet should contain an odd number of stems, as even numbers are associated with funerals. Ladies should expect a kiss on the hand, a practice particularly present in rural areas. You will be warmly greeted with exclamations of "Bine ați venit" ("welcome"), to which you should respond "Bine v-am găsit". Don't forget to take your shoes off when entering an apartment or house. What you wear is just as important. A dishevelled or untidy outfit is seen as showing a lack of respect towards your host. In the countryside, smoking inside someone's home is not polite.

© Pierre Soissons

Among family

Staying in a village with a Romanian family and joining in the activities of the local boys and girls is an unforgettable experience for children. Certain travel agencies offer packages tailored especially for families (p. 307). Farm stays can be organised directly through villagers. Here is the ideal opportunity to potter around villages in a wooden cart, to get back to making huts in the forest, baking bread, picking wild raspberries and blueberries, herding cows, baling hay, or even, as in Maramureș, studying bear tracks. •

(p. 128), Salaj (p. 190), or Maramureş (p. 196). These decorations are technically perfect and richly symbolic. The houses themselves are often veritable works of art carved with infinite attention to detail, while the fence round the little patch of garden might be a weave of delicate hazel boughs.

The villagers delight in transforming everday objects into works of art: the handle of a scrubbing brush or scythe might be embellished with rosettes or flower designs carved with a simple pocket-knife. Unfortunately much of the traditional carved furniture has long since vanished from the Saxon and Hungarian villages, finding its way to antiques shops in western Europe. Sadly, traditional woodcarving is a dying art. The chests, wardrobes, chairs, and benches which were for centuries decorated with sumptuous floral designs may soon no longer exist.

Village crafts

Many families do still make a living from their craftwork (see inset this page). The quality of their work is often remarkable. Craftsmen still use traditional materials such as flax,

society

Plea for a dying art

Many Romanian families looking for a little bit of extra income are quick to part with objects such as traditional clothing, furniture, icons, and so on, some of which can be real finds. This trading for cash has increased greatly since 1990. Rather than buying such objects direct from locals, travellers should be encouraged to purchase similar objects from local artisans instead. Naturally, buying locally is an excellent way of boosting the local economy and supporting the work of traditional craftsmen (see regional address book). ●

hemp, clay, copper, reeds, wood, animal hides, wool, and vegetable dyes. They make hand-made embroidered table cloths, floral-patterned rugs, boots, astrakhan caps, decorated belts, saddles, violins, casks, sledges,

© Antoine Schneck

Souvenirs

Decorated eggs from Bucovina (inset p. 241); icons painted on glass, woollen blankets, carpets in Maramureş (inset p. 217); ceramics and hand-woven rugs in Oltenia (p. 106); carved wooden utensils in the Apuseni Mountains; embroidered table cloths in Transylvania and

Moldavia; painted furniture in Rupea. All make delightful traditional souvenirs, locally made, that will provide warm memories of your visit to Romania.

Local Colours

In the cities, go on a tour of the **market** (see regional address books). Hardware, clothing, crockery, religious figurines, pirated music cassettes, spare car parts, tools — here you will find an unlimited supply of bric à brac, enhanced with a heady whiff of grilled sausages and folk music.

You should also visit a târg, the **weekly fairs** (see

regional address books) which are held on the outskirts of villages in the heart of rural areas as well as in the main market towns. Horses, cattle, materials, and tools are bought and sold in a lively and cheerful atmosphere.

Each year, at the beginning of the month of June, a big **pottery fair** is held in Horezu in Oltenia (see inset p. 117). ●

© Antoine Schneck

In praise of Romanian villages

In Maramureş, Sundays are a good opportunity to wear traditional costumes.

© Pierre Soissons

The rich folk traditions of the rural villages have always been at the heart of Romanian identity. United by the church and its age-old rituals *(p. 32)*, the villagers have always been fiercely protective of their traditional culture, as only people who have often seen their way of life under threat can be. For example, in the Maramureş region, the villagers have decorated their exquisite wooden churches in the traditional manner *(p. 196)*. Each village takes pride in its own songs and costumes, while architectural details such as the way garden gates are carved also vary from place to place *(p. 204)*. Of course, rural communities throughout Europe have always developed their own rich folk traditions. However, nowadays it is becoming rare to find such a flourishing rural tradition. The ancestral way of life in local villages has also inspired the writing of talented authors such as **Ion Creangă** *(see inset p. 264)* or **Lucian Blaga**, who wrote a much celebrated essay entitled *In Praise of Romanian Villages*. ●

sculpted chairs, and so on. They call on the blacksmith to make door hinges. They bake bricks and ceramic tiles for their wood-burning stoves. They build their homes in raw earth and roof them with reeds or shingles, decorating the roof with zinc lattices.

Craftsmen brighten up homes with stencilwork on the walls and floral designs on furniture. Brightly painted Easter eggs are popular *(p. 241)*. One craft has become rarer: the artists who paint icons on wood or glass now mostly lead retired lives in monasteries.

At home in the countryside

Romanians pour their hearts and souls into their homes *(p. 24)*. On a sunny day, the villages are a blaze of colour, with bright blue window frames on a background of dazzling white walls, dark green boards nestled against yellow shingles, wooden walls slowly ageing to a golden patina. In some Saxon villages, the walls are painted with a pastel wash. Colour is everywhere: red or yellow casseroles by the dozen hanging on a wall, earthenware tiles in rich hues arranged in charming patterns. The care that has gone into these touches is enchanting, revealing a lively and fresh folk tradition. Even the poorest farmhouses have elaborate wall decorations, maybe a row of stags hewn from wooden planks, a pattern of leaves or the silhouette of a pine tree. You might see a rooster and a bouquet of flowers carved in stucco on a ceiling. Often, traditional motifs are painted directly onto the walls.

The heart of the home

Beyond the cities and large towns, rural houses all over Romania follow the same familiar pattern. The home is traditionally a place of work as much as a place of rest, with a well, workshops, a wood pile, stables, chicken coops, a bread oven, a vegetable garden, orchard, and close by, the family's fields. Scenes of village life are often depicted on the large wooden gates that guard the entrance to villages *(p. 204)*. These gates, carved and painted with symbols traditionally held to bring good luck, are a source of great pride to villagers in Maramureş *(p. 196)*, the Szekler region *(p. 180)*, the Moldavian mountains, and the hills of Oltenia.

The layout of the home hardly varies from region to region. Outside is a covered porch. Inside there will be one or two rooms and a storeroom opening off a hallway.

Depending on the region, the covered porch is called *satra*, *cerdac* or **prispa**. It protects the house from rain and sun. In the summer, meals are cooked here on a cast-iron stove. Women and children sit on benches, sorting lime-tree leaves or shelling beans in the shade. Bunches of medicinal plants and onions hang from the walls. The porch is the perfect place to sit and enjoy the sun on a late summer afternoon.

The other main room in the Romanian home is the cosy **winter kitchen,** where the focal point is the **soba** *(see inset p. 242)*. The *soba* is a large tiled stove which is wonderfully comforting during the long, dark days of winter. Each home also has an elaborately decorated "**parlour**", reserved for receiving honoured guests or for special occasions such as the traditional display of a bride's dowry. ●

During the summer months, meals are cooked outside in the prispa, or covered porch.

© Pierre Soissons

Traditional homes

Although traditional rural architecture is a major tourist draw in Romania, there are no laws in place to protect it. Traditional homes are still plentiful in more isolated regions such Moldavia, Maramureş, parts of Oltenia and the Apuseni Mountains, the far reaches of the Danube delta, and Bucovina. Unfortunately, there is nothing to prevent you from buying a house in Maramureş or Bucovina, dismantling it, and rebuilding it as a charming little chalet in your own garden.

A number of open-air museums in various parts of the country now offer exhibitions of traditional house-building styles. The best-known of these is the Bucharest village museum (p. 80), but there are similar exhibitions close to Sibiu (p. 157), Sighetu Marmaţiei (p. 202), Curtişoara (p. 104), and Cluj-Napoca (p. 190).

In Bucovina

Maramureş

Characterised by the ingenious use of space and impressively sophisticated architecture, the traditional Maramureş home is made of round or square beams piled horizontally and dovetailed on the outside. The door and window frames are decorated with plant motifs. The main building material is wood, of which there are abundant local supplies.

Saxon towns

The walls are made of stone or brick and given a lime wash in delicate pastel colours, while brightly coloured window frames add a fresh touch. The gables are often ornamented with stuccowork motifs, while the roofs are covered in rows of flat tiles. The beds, benches and wardrobes will often be decorated with beautifully intricate floral motifs (p. 50).

Moldavia

Here you will see lime-washed houses, with white walls enhanced by brightly coloured doorways and windows, which are often also elaborately carved.

Apuseni Mountains

Here you will find some of the most basic and plain homes in the whole country. Their high thatched roofs bring to mind the astrakhan caps worn by their owners.

Saxon facade

Bucovina

The majestic houses with roofs with four sloping sides are still common. In Bucovina, even the most mundane homes show a flair for decoration. The striking use of colour, the superbly detailed wood carvings, and the widespread use of traditional motifs show that local folk customs are still well respected.

Danube Delta

Homes in the delta are made of earth with reed roofs. Their ornamentation is very basic, with just the doors and windows being painted blue. ●

In Maramureş

Gateway to a farm in Maramureş

Oltenian house

© Bernard Houliat

© Pierre Soissons

© Pierre Soissons

Saxon house

© Pierre Soissons

© Bernard Houliat

Moldavian houses

© Pierre Soissons

Apuseni farm buildings

© Pierre Soissons

© Pierre Soissons

Moldavian house

House in the Danube delta

© Pierre Soissons

Flavours of Romania

© Pierre Soissons

Villagers mark religious feast days, weddings, and funerals by sharing a meal.

Romanians hold the arts of the table in high regard. They honour guests with a host of delicious dishes, the table groaning with food. Romanian cuisine, developed by generations of farmer's wives who had to make the best of often scarce ingredients, is generally solid and nourishing. Over the centuries, it has adopted ingredients from the Oriental and Slavic culinary traditions. Just a few basic ingredients are now used in an astonishing variety of dishes, with each region boasting its own specialities.

Comfort cooking

In the countryside, everyday cooking is plain, solid, and nourishing. Farmers, shepherds, and woodcutters need a full stomach to do a long day's work, but money is limited. A family will produce most of what it needs for itself: cabbages, potatoes, beans, onions, wheat, fruit, pigs, cattle, poultry, and dairy products. In many regions, corn is also grown. The flour ground from corn is used to prepare a dough similar to polenta called *mămăliga*, which often replaces bread in the countryside. It might even be served as the main course in robust dishes such as *mămăliga cu brânză*, served with cheese and bacon, in Maramureş. As a staple foodstuff, it perfectly reflects the simple and often harsh nature of rural life. That said, cooking here also takes great inspiration from nature, just as nature influences its inhabitants in so many other ways in their daily lives.

Wild flavours

In the countryside, people still pick fresh natural ingredients for use in cooking and in medicine. The traditional use of plants is still a fundamental part of life in the mountains.

One of the finest examples of this folk wisdom is found in **Moldavia**. Alongside more common ingredients, the locals still often use plants found growing wild. Tender young nettles are prepared and served with an accompaniment of cream or cheese. Acacia flowers are used in jam or in crepes, while spruce buds are transformed into syrup. The leaves of coughwort, a forest plant, are used to wrap the national dish, *sarmalé (p. 29)*. Elderflowers are used in *socată*, a sort of sour lemonade, while the berries are turned into jam. Dandelion flowers are prepared in the same way. Blueberries, bilberries, wild cherries, wild strawberries, and raspberries are used to sweeten desserts. There are also ten or so species of mushrooms and dozens of ways to prepare them. It would be a shame to visit Bucovina and pass up the chance to taste cep mushroom soup *(hribi)*, sautéed russulas *(vinețele)* or chanterelles with dill *(gălbiori)*. However, it must be said that Romanian cuisine would be rather dull without the influence of the Slavic and Oriental culinary traditions.

The Oriental influence

If you share a meal with a family in Dobrogea, Muntenia, or Moldavia, you will immediately be struck by the **Turkish influence** on Romanian cuisine, especially on feast days. You will be offered starters made with aubergine, peppers, or other vegetables *(mezeluri)*, various spiced meat dishes *(chiftele, mititei)*, mutton marinated in spices then smoked and dried *(pastrama de oaie)*, and vegetable stews *(ghiveci)*. Such savoury delicacies are accompanied by Turkish-inspired desserts. Try the pastries smothered in honey and walnuts *(baclava, sarailie)*, Turkish delight, often used in cakes, sorbets (the word *șerbet* is in fact Turkish), or rose-petals and waterlily preserves. Taste these delicacies with a cup of steaming, super-strong Turkish coffee.

---

tradition

A paradise for soup-lovers

In Romania, soups offer a host of unusual, surprising, and often remarkably delicate flavour combinations. Served in the middle of a meal, the soup course follows the starter and is followed by cheese and salad. You might be offered a smooth, velvety broth called **supă** or **ciorbă**, pronounced "tchorba".

Borș , pronounced "bortch", is the name of both the soup and the wheat-bran stock which gives it its characteristic sour taste. It is prepared in oak barrels or in ceramic pots.

Borș is a wholesome, nourishing soup, reputed by **Moldavian peasants** to revive an invalid's appetite. In **Bucovina**, you must try tasting beetroot *borș (borș de sfeclă)* which contains four or five different vegetables, various herbs, and a spoonful of sour cream. Delicious fish soup *(borș de pește)* is eaten in the **Danube delta**. In **Transylvania**, try the excellent soup made with beans sprinkled with paprika *(supă de pastei)*. Heavenly. ●

Hearty produce

The **seasons** still play a part in Romanian cuisine, as ingredients become available at different times of the year. Beginning in May, farmers' wives sell home-grown produce outside their homes. In late August, the streets are pungent with the scent of roasted and peeled aubergines *(vinete)*, while the market stalls groan with ripe watermelons. September is the season for red peppers *(gogoşari)* and the long, thin onions sold by farmers in Buzău *(cepe)*. These are key ingredients in *zacuscă (see inset p. 299)*, the winter favourite. The farms are bursting with hearty, flavourful produce. Veal *(viţel)*, lamb *(miel)* and chicken *(pui)* are fattened for the winter. Egg yolks here are a healthy orange and the butter *(unt)* has a rich taste.

Dairy products

In the mountain regions, where cow, ewe, and water-buffalo milk *(lapte)* is readily available, dairy consumption is high. A good example is the sour milk *(lapte acru)*, a sort of **yogurt** found mostly in Bucovina, which is mixed with bitter cherry or rose petal preserves. Cream *(smântână)* is also used generously in many recipes. However, most milk still goes to make cheese *(brânză)*.

Romanian cheeses often look very similar, although they vary in taste a great deal. **Caş**, pronounced "cash", is found throughout the country. It refers to a large, while, round cheese made with cow's or ewe's milk. Its taste varies depending on the pasture, the season, and the way the shepherd prepares it. If the cheese is conserved in salt water, it is called **telemea** and is very much like Greek feta. After draining the cheese following its first cooking, shepherds reheat the whey and skim off the **urdă**, a cheese with granular texture and a smooth taste. The best way to taste **urdă** is on a sheep farm, with a pinch of salt and a bit of green onion.

The Braşov Mountains *(p. 170)* have an interesting range of cheeses, some of which come carefully wrapped in curls of spruce bark. The large round

Hospitality

Regardless of a family's economic status, hospitality is sacred. The desire to share one's home and blessings without expecting anything in return is a fundamental part of the rural nature and religion: "Those who give to others receive from God". In a sense, it is a part of the culture and a form of social obligation. This generosity is inseparable from the Romanian identity and is best displayed at the dinner table.

Table manners

At the table, do not feel obliged to finish your plate, as your hosts will presume you are still hungry. The same goes for wine glasses, which will be refilled when empty. At the end of a meal, it is polite to thank the hostess by saying "*Sărut mâna pentru masă*" (literally "I kiss your hand for this meal"). She will respond "*Să vă fie de bine*", which means "May it bring you blessings").

Home cooking

Romanian home cooking can be marvellous! It is a pity that many restaurants serve tasteless, fatty dishes that are not all representative of the true culinary culture of the country. While the cuisine of certain regions can be heavy at times (in the Banat, Maramureş, or Transylvania), it is certainly not lacking in heart or flavour.

If you choose to stay in someone's home *(p. 311)*, you are in for a treat. Traditionally, the hosts rarely sit down to eat with the guests, because they are so busy making sure the meal runs smoothly. ●

© Pierre Soissons

tradition

The national dish

No feast would be complete without the Romanian national dish, served in all parts of the country. *Sarmalé* are rolls of cabbage or vine leaves stuffed with minced forcemeat, cooked in a broth on a bed of tomatoes or chopped cabbage. The rolls may be wrapped in cabbage, vine leaves, black radish leaves or other leafy greens. The stuffing is usually made of minced meat such as beef or pork, mixed with rice, onions and other condiments. During the Lenten season, or *post (see inset p. 34)*, the stuffing must be vegetarian. The meat is replaced by mushrooms, carrots, rice, walnuts, onions and garden herbs. The vegetarian version is just as delicious and a lot lighter than the original version! ●

© Pierre Soissons

brânză de burduf cheeses, made with cow's or ewe's milk, are fermented in the stomach of a pig or sheep to give it its seasoned flavour. Home-made fermented cheese (*brânză frământată*) is matured in a pine cask.

When staying in shepherding villages in the Sibiu region (*p. 146*) you will have many opportunities to sample the local cheese, as each family produces its own stock. One highly aromatic variety, called *nasal*, is refined in the Ţaga caves in the heart of the Transylvanian hills. It can now also be found on sale in the Metro chain of supermarkets. The dairy industry also produces a cheese much like Emmental, but with a pleasant spicy taste, called *şvaiţer* (the Romanian spelling of "Swiss" cheese). You could also sample *caşcaval*, a hard cheese made with cow's or ewe's milk, which can be found everywhere, although be warned that it tastes rather bland.

Alcoholic drinks

Romanian **brandy** (*ţuică*) is an institution that is served on every conceivable occasion, even as an aperitif, and is always accompanied by a resounding "*Noroc, sănătate, la mulţi ani* " ("To luck, health, and a long life!").

Home distillation is still tolerated in Romania, although recent laws have toughened the rules as they come into line with European Union regulations. The most common sorts of brandy are plum, apple, grape, and pear. They can range from pleasantly aromatic to downright pungent. In Moldavia they have an industrial-strength beetroot version. In Maramureş, *ţuică* is called **horincă**; the Transylvanians call it **palincă**, from the Hungarian *pálinka*, while the Saxons say **schnaps**. When buying *ţuică* in a shop, it is definitely a good idea to taste before purchasing. Far better still would be to taste and buy direct from a producer.

In Moldavia, *secărică*, *țuică* mixed with cumin and warmed through, is served in generous shots. In the Bucovina and Apuseni Mountains, they have a sweeter version called *afinată*, made with blueberries and sugar steeped in brandy. Elsewhere, cherries are used to make the brandy known as *vișinată*.

Be wary of other alcoholic beverages sold in markets. These so-called vodkas, rums, and other unappealing chemical cocktails are generally undrinkable and may even be dangerous for your health.

The beer tradition

Romania produces and consumes beer *(bere)* that is generally of good quality. The country is currently the world's twenty-fourth largest producer, totalling more than 10 billion hectolitres per year, compared to the United States which produces 238 billion hl, France 20 billion hl and Belgium 14 billion hl. Major international brewers such as Brau Union (Aus-tria), Carlsberg (Denmark) and Efes (Turkey) have already bought up a large number of Romanian breweries.

Draught beer is the most readily available. Pale, sweet, and light, it is served in a half-litre stein *(o halbă)* or in a 25 cl glass *(un țap)*. Some bottled brands such as Ciuc, Ursus, Bergenbier, Reghin, and Suceava are deservedly popular. Beer lovers will appreciate beer festivals such as the ones held in Timișoara in May and Brașov in October.

...and wine

Planted with 270,000 hectares of vineyards, two-thirds white *(vin alb)* and one-third red *(vin roșu)*, Romania is a country with a **long tradition of wine-growing**, vines having been cultivated here since Roman times.

The country is the world's twelfth largest wine producer, behind other European countries such as Germany (9th) and Portugal (11th). The wide variety of soils and grape varieties produces unusual wines of high quality. There are some **home-grown grape varieties**, including

Reading the labels

Wine can be found in all grocery stores and many supermarkets offer a good selection of vintages. The label gives the name of the region of origin, for example Odobești, Murfatlar or Jidvei, followed by the name of the dominant grape, e.g. Murfatlar merlot. Wine connoisseurs may be surprised to see reds described as dry or semi-dry.

The producers

Many small vineyards are hoping to develop good quality wines almost from scratch. The best places to sample the produce of these family-run vineyards are Târgu Jiu or Șegarcea in Oltenia, Lechința and Jidvei in Transylvania, Focșani, Odobești and Huși in Moldavia, around Niculițel in Dobrogea, and Dealu Mare or Buzău in Muntenia *(p. 88)*. Even better, book a **stay with a wine producer** in Cotnari (Moldavia; *p. 268)* or near to Buzău. To find out more, visit "Discovering Romanian winemakers" at < www.transylvania.be >. ●

© Pierre Soissons

In Sorești, the Pauna family are keen to welcome visitors to their vineyard. (Address book p. 118).

A land of vineyards

Romanian wines have enjoyed an enviable international reputation since the 1920s, and even for hundreds of years before that in the case of certain prestigious vineyards such as Cotnari *(see inset p. 250)*. During the communist era, the policy of agricultural rationalisation led to a decline in the quality of the wine. The situation began to improve in the 1990s, however, when the land was handed back to the farmers. Today, 81% of vineyards remain privately owned. These are generally small plots averaging less than 1 hectare each. The wine produced in these vineyards is primarily for domestic consumption. The old state-run farms, which are in the process of privatisation, still control 17% of vineyards. The majority of these are working to improve their wines and to conform to international standards. Romanian vineyards are developing fast, showing superb potential. Two sectors have emerged, the first targeting the mass-production of medium-quality wine, and the second aiming to cultivate high-quality wines capable of rivalling other fine European vintages. In the last few years, some remarkable wines have come from Romanian vineyards. Some of the former cooperatives and a few independent wine-growers are making giant strides in the quality of their production *(see opposite)*. ●

some unusual suprises like *grasă* from Cotnari *(see inset p. 250)*, *fetească albă*, *zghihara* from Huşi, and *cramposia* from Drăgăşani. After the 19th century phylloxera epidemic devastated the vines, fresh ones were imported from France, Germany and Italy, bringing in grape varieties including pinot gris, pinot noir, chardonnay, Italian Riesling, merlot, sauvignon blanc, cabernet-sauvignon, and Muscat Ottonel.

Tea and coffee

Black tea is not commonly drunk. Instead, you will often be served a glass of *ceai* (pronounced "tchai"), which is green tea infused with plant extracts. On the whole, it is delicious. In populated areas, everyone drinks endless cups of **coffee**. Coffee machines have conquered the bars and espresso is on sale everywhere. In smaller places that are farther afield though, don't hold your breath for anything but instant coffee. ●

Rites and rituals

Frescoes in the church of Poienile Izei, Maramureş.

© Pierre Soissons

ituals and traditions still play a major part in daily life in the rural reaches of Romania. Many of the centuries-old customs relating to key moments in village life are still widely respected. If you get the chance, attending a rural **wedding** or **funeral** is an unforgettable experience. Woven into the fabric of these events are strands of ancient magic. Many activities such as house-building, sowing the fields, and folk medicine include elements that reveal a deeply held belief in the supernatural.

Most surprising, perhaps, is the deep **religious faith** *(see inset p. 22)* of the villagers. The great majority follow the church calendar, especially the periods of fasting and abstinence *(see inset p. 34)*. Rare are those who dare to break a holiday fast or work on the day of rest. The majority of homes possess at least one icon or holy image bought at a local market.

Local celebrations

To this day, the departure of the herd for the summer pastures and their return at the end of the season are cause for celebration. These are key moments in the life of the village, when young and old come together and celebrate with food, music, and dancing until the early hours. In early May, in **Hoteni** (Maramureş), the farm labourers have their own celebrations to thank them for all their hard work *(Tănjeaua de pe Mara; p. 207)*. In the same region in May, the festival of *ruptul sterpelor* marks the separation of the milk sheep from the barren ones and of lambs from their mothers *(p. 199)*. The villagers measure the quantity of milk each animal produces to calculate how much cheese each owner should receive over the summer.

In the Apuseni Mountains, fairs and festivals are held in the pastures. The festival of **Mount Găină** and the more traditional one held in **Călineasă** take place in July.

The shepherds of **Marginimea Sibiului** *(p. 147)* give thanks for their ewes on September 19 in **Poiana Sibiului**. Although the two events have little in common, the **Prislop Hora** (the Prislop dance) is held on the second Sunday in August in the Prislop pass between Maramureş and Bucovina. This is a chance to see beautiful costumes and listen to enchanting music.

Village festivals and pilgrimages

Local celebrations are often spectacular. On the feast day of the patron saint of the local church, for example, everyone invites their family and friends to share a copious meal.

Every October 14th, large numbers of pilgrims remember Saint Paraschiva, whose relics are preserved at the metropolitan cathedral in **Iaşi** in Moldavia *(Sfânta Paraschiva, p. 256)*. In **Dragomireşti**, in Maramureş *(p. 211)*, the feast of Saint Elijah (Sfântu Ilie; July 20), is celebrated by a procession of local people in traditional costume. Pilgrimages for Assumption on **August 15th** are impressive, particularly at the Putna monastery in Bucovina *(p. 236)*, in Moisei or Rohia in Maramureş, and in Nicula in Transylvania.

Where they are still celebrated, the magnificent parish feasts held by the **German** populations in Transylvania or the Banat are occasions for those who have left to come back and visit those who have stayed behind. The **Magyars** of Transylvania also have their own festivals which are particularly bright and colourful. **Szekler** festivals are linked to the Catholic calendar, marking feast days like **Pentecost** in **Miercurea Ciuc** *(p. 183)*.

Winter festivals

Between December 24th and January 7th, Carpathian villages are bathed in a magical Christmas glow — harness bells jingling, smoke rising from wood fires, boots crunching through freshly fallen snow.

When the Christmas fast *(Postul Crăciunului, p. 34)* is finished, families gather around the tiled stove and mountains of food are prepared ready for neighbours and relatives to drop round. Local children go

---

The Orthodox calendar

The Orthodox calendar begins on September 1 and the twelve feast days centre on **Easter**, which is considered to be the most important of them all. The date of Easter Sunday is calculated following the Council of Nicea, held in 325, falling on the Sunday after the first moon after the Spring Equinox (March 21). It can fall a week after the Catholic Easter, or the two dates may be separated by a month.

The twelve holidays

● Nativity of the Virgin (September 8)

● Exaltation of the Cross (September 14)

● Entrance of Mary into the Temple (November 21)

● Nativity of Christ (December 25)

● Epiphany or Theophany (baptism of Christ, January 6)

● Presentation of Christ in the Temple (February 2)

● Annunciation (March 25)

● Palm Sunday (Christ's entry into Jerusalem)

● Ascension (40 days after Easter)

● Pentecost (50 days after Easter)

● Transfiguration (August 6)

● Dormition of the Virgin (Assumption, August 15) ●

Bucovina church, Tree of Jesse.

© Pierre Soissons

tradition

Post

Post ("fasting" or "Lent") is a time for meditation, calm reflection, and abstinence. Two long Lenten seasons set the rhythm for rural life: the fast for **Easter** *(Postul Mare)* and for **Christmas** *(Postul Crăciunului)*. The feast day of the apostles Peter and Paul (June 29) is also preceded by a period of fasting which can last anywhere between three and fifteen days, depending on the date of Easter. Assumption, which falls on August 15, is likewise preceded by two weeks of fasting. Finally, Wednesdays, Fridays and certain other days of the Orthodox calendar are also days for fasting. The Orthodox *post* forbids all animal products, whether meat, eggs, or dairy.

During the Easter fast, which is the strictest, fish is permitted twice. Fasting does not mean starving, and meals can be delicious. *Post* dishes are often more refined and healthier *(p. 28)*. You may have the opportunity to taste such delicacies in someone's home or in a monastery. •

from house to house singing *colinda* (Christmas carols) and come home with bags of candy, apples and maybe some money. A few people may recite *urături*, long, often satirical, poems, accompanied by a bell, a flute or the gloomy sound of the *buhai*, a sheepskin drum played by plucking on a tuft of moistened horsehair that pokes through the skin. On **New Year's Eve**, most Moldavian villages still have a few surprises in store *(p. 36)*.

On January 1st, **Saint Basil** is celebrated. It is customary to offer congratulations to everyone bearing the saint's name, Vasile in Romanian, which is very popular. On this day, guests must be warmly welcomed, mo matter what time of day or night. On January 6th, for the feast of **Boboteaza**, the baptism of

Funerals...

If you should pass by a funeral, don't be surprised if you are invited to share a meal after the service. It is an honour for the family to invite guests. They might even show you the deceased and ask you to take photos. Pictures of deceased family members in their coffins often decorate homes.

© Pierre Soissons

...and weddings

Do not be offended if at some point during the wedding meal, you are handed a basket and invited to make a donation. Each guest (normally there are between 200 and 600 at a wedding) gives generously so that young newlyweds can afford to build a home or buy a car.

Birthdays

Romanians are very fond of birthday or saint's name day celebrations. The hero of the day is showered with gifts and flowers and wished *mulți ani*, or "long life". He must in turn treat all his friends and

Christ, crosses and altars are sculpted in ice and put up near rivers where they are decorated with fir branches. A priest then blesses the buckets of water brought forward by the faithful.

Easter

Crowning the 48 days of Lent, known as *post (inset opposite)*, **Easter** *(Paşte)* is the biggest event of the Orthodox calendar and is known as the "Feast of feasts".

Spring cleaning is part of the preparation. Homes are cleaned from top to bottom, exteriors are repainted and gardens are tended. During the "Holy Week" leading up to the feast, old clothes and rubbish are burned. In Bucovina, fires light up the night sky from Wednesday to **Holy Thursday** or *Joia Mare* – "Great Thursday".

For **Good Friday** *(Vinerea Mare)*, housewives cook *pasca*, a crown of brioche stuffed with cream cheese flavoured with raisins and cinnamon.

On the evening of **Holy Saturday** *(Sâmbătă Mare)*, baskets are filled with victuals to be eaten the following day with red-dyed eggs *(see inset p. 241)* and *pasca*. Traditionally, the faithful gather at churches at 11 pm with their baskets. At midnight, the priest proclaims *"Hristos a înviat"* – "Christ has risen", to which the congregation responds *"Adevărat a înviat"* – "Christ has risen indeed". Bearing candles, the priest and congregation then circle the church three times. Mass ends around four or five in the morning with the blessing of the baskets. Back home, the dyed red eggs, representing the Resurrection and health, are placed in receptacles, along with a coin (strength and power). They are covered with clean water, which those present then use to wash their face and hands, symbolising the purity of the soul. The meal then begins. Everyone toasts each other by bumping eggs instead of glasses. The feasting, interrupted by regular church services, lasts three days. The meals traditionally serve up lamb in the form of soup, pâté, and a roast, symbolising the sacrifice of Christ and our redemption through Him. ●

colleagues, maybe planning a generous meal, which often takes place in the workplace. Clients are often exasperated to find offices suddenly shut all afternoon because of these birthday celebrations, with the unmistakeable sound of laughter and clinking glasses, not to mention mouth-watering aromas, coming from behind the closed office doors. ●

Left: a funeral in Maramureş, held according to an ancient ritual.

Right: At leud in Maramureş, newlyweds are accompanied by "marital sponsors" (naşi, pronounced "nache").

© Bernard Houliat

Dances with bears

The obsessive rhythm of drums, whistles and firecrackers echoes out in a village huddled in the snow. It is New Year's Eve in Moldavia and in an ancient ritual, hordes of terrifying apparitions wander the countryside. The apparent mayhem in fact follows a strictly defined ritual whose original significance is lost in the mists of time. Such ancestral folk customs have died out in most of Europe, and are sadly under threat here as well.

A battle between Good and Evil

Accompanied by eerie music, the procession splits into two groups, the "devils" and the "angels". The two troupes roam through the villages, stopping in front of each house to perform ritual dances. The devils, representing **Evil**, are made to look as ugly as possible. Their costumes and dances symbolise disorder and chaos. They dress as bears, goats, or monsters with red horns jangling with bells. Some play the role of grasping merchants or menacing policemen. One man is chosen to play the *mosneag*, a dirty-minded old thief, and another the *baba*, a foul old woman, who, every so often, lifts her skirts and squats in an imitation of childbirth. Some, blacked up and dressed in multi-coloured skirts in imitation of the gypsies, drag a battered cauldron through the streets. They are known as *caldarari*. The devils hold cars for ransom, steal sausages, and tease any cats and dogs that cross their path. They catch girls, smear them with soot, and force them to dance. A character dressed as an Orthodox pope lashes out at passers-by with a cudgel.

The **angels** represent the forces of goodness. Their procession is much calmer. They are dressed in white, including the mythical horse-man. They dance like ghosts in the night. The *irozii* wear gaudy approximations of military uniform with epaulettes made of tin cans or paper. Some wear bishop's mitres or caps decorated with baubles and mirrors. Their chests are pinned with trinkets, beads, and coins, like so many medals.

Right: The *caldarari* dress up like gypsies to take part in the festivities.

© Bernard Houliat

© Bernard Houliat

Past and present

These rural rituals have an important social function. They re-tell the story of the Orthodox pope and denounce the scheming of local worthies. The key character is the *haidouk*, a sort of Balkan Robin Hood. These rituals were tolerated during the communist era and were even imitated in the larger towns and cities. Nowadays the ritual has lost

Left and above: Each devil chooses a girl to dance with. *Irozii* wearing a gaudy imitation of military uniform accompany the "bride".

© Bernard Houliat

much of its original subversive character, and it is rather sad to see the best troupes from rural villages being invited to perform for the television cameras in a parade which has lost all its joy and spontaneity.

Universal rituals

Calling on the mythical forces that long governed the lives of peasants throughout Europe, such celebrations were believed to bring fertility, health for both farmers and their livestock, good harvests, and a tight-knit village community. This cycle of winter festivals was found throughout Europe. From Cyprus to the Pyrenees, from Galicia to Bavaria and Bulgaria, the rituals involve figures that are the focus for ancestral fears—bears, monsters, or lubricious old women. One of the most widespread is the horse-man dressed in white, found in Moldavia, the Basque country, Cornwall, and even Greece.

© Bernard Houliat

A dying breed

These festivals still take place in Romania, but sadly there is little room to doubt they will soon disappear, as they have elsewhere. Rural communities are changing fast. The centuries-old rituals still followed in villages throughout Romania are a remarkable relic of the past, although the origins of the rituals are shrouded in the mists of time. ●

The role of the bride is always played by a man.

Romania, between unity and diversity

© Pierre Soissons

Prince Petrus Rareş decorated Moldavian churches with frescoes at a time when his country was threatened by Turks, Poles, and the Reform. A votive painting in Probota church (p. 246).

Romania's tormented past stems from its geographical situation on the cusp of the Balkans and the Orient, between western Europe and the Slavs. Nevertheless, the people of Romania have managed to forge their own identity: in spite of successive invasions and occupations, they have preserved their own traditions and, in particular, their own language. Proud of their Latin culture and of being able to trace their civilisation back to its Daco-Roman roots, Romanians have always felt they belonged to one nation. They are bound by a common ethnicity, language, culture, and religion. This identity was perpetuated during the course of history even when the land was divided into three provinces called Wallachia, Moldavia and Transylvania. Romania was only united in its current borders less than a hundred years ago. Much of the richness of Romanian culture results from the presence of various ethnic minorities.

Today, more than ten percent of the population belongs to one of nineteen ethnic minorities recognised by the state. Each minority has its own representative in Parliament, which has a special parliamentary group for national minorities. The status of minorities is in fact better in Romania than in a number of western democracies. The languages of the larger minorities are even taught in school alongside the official language, Romanian.

Geto-Dacia

Beginning in the first millennium B.C., the Getos and the Dacians, descended from the Thracians, established communities in the land between the Carpathians, the Danube, and the Black Sea. Fierce and resourceful, they kept up resistance to invasions from early on. However, they gradually began to integrate with the Greek colonies of Histria (p. 287), Tomis (**Constanţa**, p. 289), and Callatis (**Mangalia**, p. 292), which were flourishing on the shores of the Black Sea. In Wallachia and Transylvania, they built well-defended fortresses from the third century B.C. Two centuries later, the various tribes began to unite under King **Burebista**, who declared **Sarmizegetusa** (p. 138) in the south-west to be his capital.

Detail of Trajan's Column depicting the emperor setting out on the Dacian expedition.

© Phototheque Hachette

Roman Dacia

The Romans decided to invade the region at the beginning of the second century A.D., drawn by the lure of gold in the Carpathians. It took them five years to defeat King **Decebal**. The military exploits of Emperor Trajan (53 – 117 A.D.) were immortalised in 109 on a triumphal monument in the village of Adamclisi. The Roman Empire had a new province, Dacia, which eventually was to prove one of its richest. In fact, the Romans called the region *Dacia Felix*, or blessed Dacia. Large numbers of Roman colonisers settled in the region to mine gold in the Apuseni Mountains, where the vestiges of the Roman mines can be seen (p. 121). The Romans integrated well with the local population. The new Daco-Romans spoke Latin, whose influence is obvious in modern-day Romanian. But in 271 – 275, barbarian tribes from the East overran the province, causing the Emperor Aurelian to retreat. He left Dacia to the invaders and retreated to the other side of the Danube.

A long silence

There are no records dating from the Dark Ages. Very little is known of these centuries, as there are no written sources and archeological finds are rare. We do know that hordes of Goths, Huns, Gepids, Slavs, Avars, Pechenegs, Cumans and Tatars set up nomadic settlements. Only the **Slavs**, who arrived in the 6th century, left their trace on the Romanian language, without, however, changing it significantly.

●●● See the **Chronology** p. 320. ●

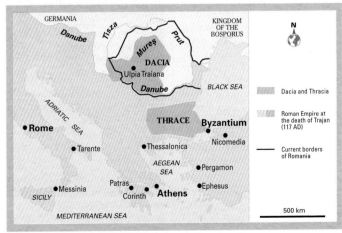

LANDS OCCUPIED BY THE GETO-DACIANS AND THRACIANS

population

Romania in the tenth century A.D.

After centuries of the Geto-Dacian, then Daco-Roman civilisations, many families withdrew to the Carpathians in order to seek refuge from invasions. These isolated groups maintained their Latin culture and eventually formed the basis for the modern Romanian population. A recognisably Romanian people re-emerged in the tenth century, although with some foreign influence. For instance, they spoke a Latinate language, but practised Byzantine Orthodox christianity. Led by local chieftains, they were beginning to form a nation. ●

If modern-day Romania is able to contribute to stability in the Balkans, it is doubtless because the country has succeeded in integrating such diversity into its extremely complex history. It has grown into a mature civilisation with a rich and fertile culture.

Invasions and principalities

Of all the invaders who were tempted by Romania's riches, only the **Magyars** from Pannonia in what is now Hungary were able to establish permanent settlements, at the end of the ninth century. In the tenth century, their king, **Arpad**, founded settlements in the land "beyond the forest" (*trans silvania*). In 1003, King Stefan I included **Transylvania** in the Hungarian territories. It was to remain under Hungarian influence for many centuries.

The three provinces

One of the priorities of the Magyars was to reinforce the territories that the Tatars crossed (*p. 42*) on their regular incursions into Hungary. The local populations were thinly scattered and poorly organised. In the mid-twelfth century, the Hungarian kings brought in **German colonists** called Saxons (*see inset p. 147 and p. 150*) to fortify defences and to farm the lands in southern Transylvania. Another group of Hungarian settlers, called **Szeklers** (*p. 180*) or Szekelys, were charged with defending the eastern fringes of the kingdom in exchange for self-governance. Thus Transylvania opened up to western influence. Local confederations began forming in the eastern reaches of the Carpathians, along trade routes between Byzantium and Poland to the east and Asia and Central Europe to the south. To begin with, the Hungarian rulers supported the emergence of these, but then decided to subjugate them. However, they failed to foresee the growing thirst for independence in these two regions, Wallachia or **Ţara Românească** ("the Romanian county") and **Moldavia**. These two provinces, along with Transylvania, now form the modern state of Romania.

Infidels massacring the monks of the monastery of Saint Catherine of Sinai. Detail from an exterior fresco at the Suceviţa monastery (p. 232).

© Pierre Soissons

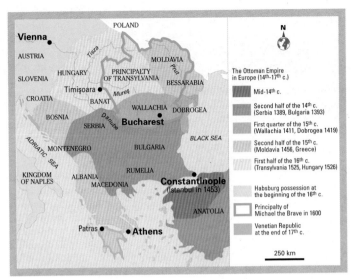

THE OTTOMANS IN CENTRAL EUROPE

The development of Wallachia and Moldavia

In the south, Wallachia was the first province to achieve independence under the authority of **Basarab** (1310-1352), who defeated Charles Robert, King of Hungary, in Posada in 1330. At around the same time, prosperous markets developed on the eastern flanks of the Carpathians, in areas such as Baia, Siret, and Suceava. But the **Tatars of the Golden Horde** swept across from the Russian plains bringing chaos in their wake. In 1352, the King of Hungary ordered an expedition to impose **Dragoş**, Voivode (governor) of Maramureş, as leader. He was charged with restoring stability to the kingdom.

After a few years, the new province grew in autonomy. **Bogdan**, Dragoş' successor in Maramureş, fell out with the Hungarians, crossing the Carpathians and seizing power in 1359. He became the first true voivode of **Moldavia**, a principality that, at its height, reached from north of the Carpathians to the Black Sea and the Dniestr. But just as these two provinces finally freed themselves from Hungarian domination and became independent principalities, a far greater threat emerged.

The **Ottomans** occupied Bulgaria in 1393 and had designs on Wallachia. In 1394, the Sultan **Bayazid I** crossed the Danube for the first time. Towards the end of his reign, in 1411, **Mircea the Old** (1386-1418) signed a treaty with the Ottomans who recognized the freedom of Wallachia in return for an annual tribute. This Ottoman influence over Wallachia was doubled in 1419 when Mehmet I cut off access to the sea by annexing **Dobrogea** *(p. 274)*. This state of affairs was to last for four centuries.

Within a few decades, Moldavia suffered the same fate. In 1456, **Mehmet II** threatened the territory following his sack of Constantinople. The Voivode Petru Aron agreed to pay an annual tribute. Moldavia began a long period of dependence.

Transylvania: Three nations and four peoples

In Transylvania, the Romanians were sidelined by the Hungarian kings who wished to impose Catholicism on their subjects. No

invasions

Descendents of Genghis Khan

The **Tatars** (or Mongols), related to the Turks, came from central Asia. In the thirteenth century, Batu Khan, the grandson of Genghis Khan, extended his rule over the northern and western territories of the Black Sea and as far as Dobrogea. He founded a state centred in Crimea, the **khanate of the Golden Horde**. For centuries, Tatar hordes ravaged central Europe. After the peninsula was annexed by the Russian Empire in 1783 and again after the Crimean War (1854-55), some two-thirds of the Tatars (about 200,000 in all) emigrated to the Ottoman Empire, many of them settling in Dobrogea. ●

orthodox Romanian could hope to join the Magyar nobility, one of the "three nations" in Transylvania, along with the Szeklers (Szekelys) and the Saxons *(p. 180 and inset p. 147)*. Many did choose to convert, such as the family of Iancu of Hunedoara *(see inset p. 137)*, who ruled Transylvania under the name of János Hunyadi (1441-1456). His son **Matei Corvin** *(see inset p. 190)* became one of Hungary's greatest kings, reigning from 1458 to 1490.

Resisting foreign influence

By paying an annual tribute to the Ottomans, Wallachia and Moldavia escaped direct rule and the threat of mass conversion to Islam. This domination, which was later to extend to Transylvania, coincided with a period of political instability marked by episodic acts of resistance. Yet the period also witnessed the emergence of a culture which produced some magnificent architecture.

The principalities

Each principality was ruled by a prince (voivode or hospodar) from the capital—**Suceava** then **Iaşi** in Moldavia, **Târgovişte** then **Bucharest** in Wallachia. The prince was elected

The Tatars today

The Tatar population today numbers between 29,000 and 55,000 people, mostly living in Dobrogea. They have a representative in the Romanian Parliament and try to keep their culture flourishing.

The Hungarians

Hungarians make up the largest minority in Romania, with just over 1.4 million people, representing 6.6% of the population. They mainly live in the West, along the Hungarian border, and in Transylvania, where they form a large proportion of the population. The Covasna and Harghita regions also have

Remetea, a Magyar village in the Apuseni Mountains.
© Pierre Soissons

a notable Magyar population, the **Szeklers** *(p. 180)*, who have their own culture and traditions.

The Hungarian minority is represented by the UDMR (Democratic Union of Romanian Magyars) which has 27 members of parliament. The UMDR participated in the Constantinescu government (1996 – 2000) and its relations with the ruling party are generally positive. ●

legend

Vlad, alias Dracula

Legend has it that Vlad was so ruthless that after decapitating several of his nobles, he used their heads as bait for crayfish. He then invited their friends to the palace, offered them crayfish to eat, and then told them: "You are now eating your friends' heads". The story ends with Vlad impaling his guests alive.

This is just one of the anecdotes spread round Europe in the fifteenth century by **Matei Corvin**, king of Hungary, to discredit Vlad. The legend which has grown up around Vlad the Impaler is indeed horrific. However, while some elements of the story are undoubtedly true, the legend has its roots in a campaign of slander. The name **Dracula**, which has become synonymous with terror, simply means "son of Dracul", the dragon. Vlad's father, Vlad II Dracul, was in fact an honourable member of the Christian Order of the Dragon, founded by Sigismund of Hungary. The Irish writer Bram Stoker drew on this ancient Romanian legend when, in 1897, he created one of the most famous characters in literary history. The character of Dracula has spawned a multi-million-dollar industry in films and books. Unfortunately, some holiday operators have capitalised on this success by offering tours in decidedly bad taste. ●

by **boyards** or local barons from among the male heirs of the ruling families, the Basarabs in Wallachia and the Musats in Moldavia. This was an unreliable system which fostered political instability and hampered economic and cultural growth until the 19th century. Given this political instability, it is little short of remarkable that religious architecture in Wallachia and Moldavia soared to such splendid heights.

Wallachia under Vlad the Impaler (1456 – 1476)

Like other princes of his time, the accession to the throne of **Vlad III Tepes**, also known as **Dracula**, caused a bloodbath. As he refused to pay the tribute to the Ottomans, the sultan sent emissaries ostensibly with an ultimatum, but with secret orders to chop off Vlad's head. Vlad outwitted the sultan and had them impaled alive. Though impaling was a common practice at the time, Vlad was particularly keen on it as a method of execution. It is not for nothing that he was known as Vlad the Impaler.

However, although he was also known as Dracula, he was not a vampire *(see inset above)*! He waged a long campaign against the Turks, their allies, and the brigands that plagued his lands. He was later taken prisoner by Matei Corvin, king of Hungary.

Moldavia from Stefan the Great to its decline

In 1457, Vlad the Impaler travelled to Moldavia to help Stefan oust his father's murderer from the throne. The long reign of Prince **Stefan the Great** (Stefan cel Mare, 1457-1504) was marred by wars and treason. Nevertheless, Moldavia enjoyed a period of relative prosperity. Armenians from Suceava and German merchants encouraged trade. Stefan built fortresses, churches and monasteries, of which 24 remain standing today. In 1475 and 1476, the sovereign fought courageously against the Ottomans, aided by Hungary and Poland. The Catholic pope named him "**Athlete of Christ**" for his brave struggle. His

Stefan the Great was a great strategist who made Moldavia one of the great European states of the fifteenth century.

son, **Petru Rareş** (1528 – 1538, *p. 223*) set out to rekindle the national flame. He crowned his father's achievements by founding new monasteries in Moldoviţa (*p. 231*) and Probota (*p. 246*). He also decorated churches in the north of Moldavia with stunning frescoes which are today famed all over the world. This tradition of building was kept alive by his successors, such as Alexander Lapuşneanu, the Movila family, and Vasile Lupu (Basil the Wolf). But during this time, the province became increasingly dependent on the Ottoman empire. The era of local princes drew to a close in 1711.

Transylvania: between East and West

Transylvania fell under Ottoman control after the Turks defeated the Hungarians at the battle of **Mohacs** in 1526. Since the eighteenth century, the region has been influenced by Saxons (*see inset p. 147*) who contributed greatly to the development of Braşov (*p. 170*), Sibiu (*p. 152*), and above all Sighişoara (*p. 163*). They built more than 300 villages that are superb examples of traditional European architecture (*p. 150*).

The region was also influenced by the Reform, introduced by the Hungarian and Saxon elite. Economic, cultural, and political exchanges with Wallachia and Moldavia continued. There was even a brief reunification of the three territories in 1600 under **Michael the Brave**, the Wallachian

German minorities

What would Transylvania be without its nine centuries of German influence? The Saxons built superb towns and a great many fortified villages, thereby playing an enormous role in the stability and prosperity of the region (*p. 150*); they were there at the birth of modern Romania and would have continued to be so if the Second World War had not intervened, leading to an exodus of the German population (*p. 156*).

The Swabians who were brought to the Banat by the Austrian emperor at the beginning of the eighteenth century never outnumbered the Saxons. Nowadays, very few of the Sudetes who settled in Bucovina or the Zipsers in Maramureş remain.

Romanian Germans are represented by their own political party, the German Democratic Forum (Demokratisches Forum des Deutschen). •

The Viscri citadel, in southern Transylvania.

king. In 1699, the Ottomans ceded the region to the Habsburg empire following the Treaty of Karlowitz.

Obscurity and Enlightenment

The **Age of Enlightenment** cast a shadow over the Romanian principalities which slowly lifted towards the end of the century with the birth of the more progressive ideas that marked the 19th century. This period also saw the emergence of the **Uniate Church**, "united" with Rome.

Wallachia and Moldavia: the end of independence

Gradually, the Ottomans tightened their grasp on Wallachia, imposing their own voivodes. During the 17th century, the region experienced a brief cultural revival under **Matei Basarab** (1632-1654) and **Constantin Brâncoveanu**. The latter became prince in 1688, but was beheaded in Constantinople on March 24th, 1714, along with his sons and his adviser. The man who betrayed him for his throne suffered the same fate the following year. These were the last local Wallachian princes, the end of a line begun by Basarab four centuries earlier.

Moldavia suffered a similar fate. Prince **Dimitrie Cantemir** (1693 and 1710-1711), a great Greek scholar, tried to establish a hereditary monarchy. He sided with Tsar **Peter the Great** in a coalition that was swept aside by the Turks on the river Prut on July 11th, 1711. He fled to Russia where he continued his brilliant intellectual pursuits, travelling throughout Europe and writing reference works including a *Descriptio Moldaviae*.

Exiled in Russia, he could only watch as the Turks heightened the pressure on Moldavia and Wallachia. The Ottoman sultan selected princes from **Phanar**, a district of Constantinople that was home to to the Greek elite. Many Phanariot families had already settled in the area, and a few noble Byzantine families such as

heroes

Michael the Brave (1593-1601)

In 1593, Mihai Viteazul (Michael the Brave) acceded to the Wallachian throne. He joined forces with Cardinal Sigismund Bathory, prince of Transylvania, to drive out the Ottomans. In 1599, after the abdication of Bathory and with the support of the Austrian emperor, he conquered Transylvania. He then moved on to Moldavia and stole the crown from Jeremy Movila. From May to September 1600, he was the prince of Wallachia, Moldavia and Transylvania, the first time the three Romanian provinces were united. However, he quickly lost Wallachia and was faced with an revolt by the Magyar nobility in Transylvania. On August 19th, 1601, he was assassinated by his ally, General Basta, commander of the Austrian emperor's army. ●

the **Paleologues** and the **Cantacuzenes** were already part of the aristocracy in the principalities.

The Phanariots

Becoming a hospodar in the days of the local princes involved a series of tried and tested rituals. The candidate paid to obtain the *firman*, the nomination decree. Before that, he had to offer gifts to the sultan and his vizier, not forgetting any number of intermediaries. The hospodar then had to pay a large tribute known as *harac* or *karadj*. He would pay the majority of this tribute by selling off local resources such as silver, grain, livestock, honey, wax and other products. The tribute would be handed over to the Turkish army to finance its campaigns in Wallachia and Moldavia. The hospodars were often very unpopular. Some governed the two regions on several different occasions, squandering local resources to pay the tribute. As a result, the countryside was deserted as large numbers of farmers sought refuge in Transylvania and Russia. Some even settled south of the Danube, in the heart of the Ottoman empire where life seemed more tolerable! Travellers crossing Wallachia were alarmed to see the villagers living in fear, fleeing at the sight of anything resembling an official procession. Land lay fallow as villagers rebuilt their communities far from the main thoroughfares.

A time for reformation

Despite their limited powers, several hospodars did undertake reforms, laying the foundations of the modern state. **Constantin Mavrocordato**, for example, who reigned in Wallachia and Moldavia on ten separate occasions starting in 1740, took back power from the boyards. He successfully abolished serfdom in 1746. Unfortunately this had little effect on harsh peasant life. In 1776, **Alexander Ypsilanti** set up an education system in Wallachia and founded the Saint-Sava school in Bucharest.

In the last decades of the eighteenth century, the influence of the Enlightenment reached Moldavia and Wallachia. The phanariot elite were influenced by **enlightenment philosophy** which reached Iaşi and Bucharest. Out of this intellectual context grew an awareness of the need for a united **Romanian identity**, whose values were propagated by the church and academies in the three provinces.

The desire for national unity

Romania's emergence as a nation took place against the backdrop of the "Oriental question", which shook the Balkans during the nineteenth century. The European powers used it as a bargaining card. While the Ottomans were seeking to consolidate rather than expand, the Russians wanted access to the Mediterranean via the Bosphorus and Dardanelle straits. Austria hoped to control the Danube, and the English, masters of the Mediterranean, were prepared to do whatever it took to maintain their grasp on the region.

The Romas

The Romas came to Romania in about 1000 A.D. The last census recorded 535,000 Romas, representing less than 2% of the population. But it is thought that they actually outnumber Magyars and that the true figure is somewhere between 1.5 and 3 million. The discrepancy between these two sets of figures is due to the fact that many Romas, fearing persecution, declared themselves to be Hungarians if they spoke the language, or else Romanians. In the public arena, the Roma population is represented by numerous organisations, including "Aven Amentza" ("Come with us" in Romany), a dynamic group which promotes freedom and dignity for the Roma people. ●

© Pierre Soissons

Roma women from Târgu Mureş in Transylvania.

Awaken Romanians!

Taken from a poem by Andrei Muresanu (1816 – 1863) and set to music by Anton Pann (1796 – 1854), the text which was to become the Romanian national anthem was written during the 1848 Revolution.

Wake up, Romanian, from your deadly slumber,
In which barbaric tyrants kept you so long by force!
Now or never is the time for you to have a new fate,
Which should command respect of even your cruel enemies.
Now or never is the time for us to prove to the entire world
That in these arms Roman blood still flows,
And that in our hearts we proudly keep a name
Triumphant in all battles, the name of Trajan.
Behold, glorious shadows, Mihai, Stefan, Corvin,
This is the Romanian nation, your own great-grandsons,
With weapons in their hands, your fire in their veins,
All shouting, "We want to live in freedom, or else die!
Priests carry the cross on high! Our army is blessed,
Its banner is called freedom and its ideal is sacred,
We'd rather die in battle, and in a blaze of glory,
Than live again like slaves in our beloved land!" ●

The fledgeling nationalist movements throughout the region were used as pawns in this chess game.

Support from Russia

Ending nearly six years of war between Russia and Turkey, largely fought on Romanian soil, the treaty of **Kutchuk-Kainardji** (1774) revealed the fatal weakness of the Ottomans. It gave the Russian Tsar access to the ports of the Black Sea, which crucially didn't ice over during the winter, which in turn meant that Russia became the dominant economic and political power in the region.

Thus began Romania's long involvement with Russia. This bond was strengthened in 1812 when Tsar Alexander I again defeated the Ottomans, annexing **Bessarabia** and a vast tract of Moldavia between the rivers Prut and Dniestr. In 1775, the Ottomans were forced to hand **Bucovina**, the historic heart of Moldavia, to Austria. It was to remain in Austrian hands until 1918.

The end of the phanariots and the People's Spring (1821 – 1848)

In 1829, the treaty of Andrinople ratified Greek independence and granted Serbian independence. It also brought Moldavia and Wallachia under Russian control. Russian officials supervised the drafting of a constitution called the Organic Regulations. Modernisation had arrived.

The region was open to influence from the West, and the influx of new ideas led to a popular insurrection in 1821 *(see inset p. 105)*. Despite its failure, it fanned the flames of the nascent nationalist movement. The nationalists demanded the unification of all parts of Romania, national independence, and the distribution of land to poor peasant farmers, among other things. However, their hopes were soon dashed. When the flames of revolution which swept across Europe in **1848** reached Bucharest and Iaşi, the revolt was quickly crushed by Russian and Turkish troops.

In Transylvania during this time, the Romanian population shared the popular enthusiasm that fed the Hungarian revolution led by Louis **Kossuth**, which tore through Vienna in March 1848. Their confidence was soon betrayed as it transpired that Hungary intended to annex Transylvania without the participation of the Romanian population who had long been fighting for their political and religious rights.

A young lawyer from Cluj-Napoca, **Avram Iancu**, stirred up thousands of peasants from the Apuseni Mountains. The intervention of the Russian army against the Hungarian revolutionaries, coupled with the restoration of imperial authority, put an end to their hopes.

In 1867, when it was still part of the Austro-Hungarian Empire, Transylvania became part of the kingdom of Hungary, shrouded in blind nationalism. Exasperated and humiliated minorities were faced with forced **Magyarisation**. This put paid to any remaining hopes for possibility for peaceful and harmonious cohabitation in the region.

From independence to unification (1854 – 1866)

Only a split between Russia and Turkey would enable the Romanian principalities to progress towards independence. Their chance came with the **Crimean War** (1854 – 1855) during which Great Britain, France, the kingdom of Sardinia, and the Ottoman Empire joined forces to oppose Russia. It enmeshed western European powers in the affairs of south-eastern Europe. The **Treaty of Paris** in 1856 confirmed the principle of Ottoman sovereignty, but in reality Russian influence in the region was simply replaced by European domination. In early 1859, Romanians took an important step towards their goal of unification thanks to clever use of the constitution, when the Moldavian and Wallachian assemblies both elected Prince **Alexander Ioan Cuza**.

In 1861, the Moldavian-Wallachian union was recognised by the Ottomans. In 1863, Mihai Kogalniceanu, Cuza's prime minister, rapidly launched a series of widespread reforms. For example,

Slavic minorities

Several cultural minorities of Slavic origin make up approximately 1% of the Romanian population.

© Bernard Houliat

Russian Lipovanis, descendants of the Old Believers.

● **Ukrainians and Poles.** Ukrainians live in the northern regions. Hutsuls *(inset p. 241)* live in Bucovina, alongside Polish villages (p. 227) which have managed to keep their traditional ways alive.

● **Russians.** Nearly 40,000 Lipovanis *(p. 284)* live in Moldavia and in Dobrogea in the Danube delta.

● **Other slavic peoples.** Some 30,000 Serbs *(p. 107)* live in the Banat, where there are also Czech, Slovak, Croatian and Bulgarian villages.

Other minorities

The other minorities recognised by the Romanian government are Greeks, Albanians, Armenians, Italians, Turks, Macedonians, and Jews. ●

© Photothèque Hachette

The Romanian royal family in 1922. Queen Maria and King Ferdinand are in the centre.

he secularised the lands belonging to the monasteries of Mount Athos, Sinai, and the Holy Land, which over the centuries had received princely donations amounting to a quarter of the Romanian territory. The Patriarch of Constantinople challenged this move. The ensuing dispute led to the independence of the church of Romania *(p. 51)* - a significant event considering the major role of Orthodox christianity in developing the national identity.

Independence and the Monarchy (1866 – 1881)

Cuza was overthrown in 1866. The progressive Bratianu, who sought refuge in Paris after 1848, was charged with finding a prince to rule. He succeeded in persuading Charles of Hohenzollern-Sigmaringen, a 27-year-old Prussian and scion of one of Europe's great families. In May 1866, he was made ruler of the United Principalities by the parliament. From then on, the least dependence on Constantinople, however symbolic, became intolerable. In 1876, Charles lined up alongside Russia in the war in which the Tsar's empire was finally to defeat the sultan. In 1878, the Berlin Congress ratified **Romanian independence** and

returned Dobrogea, occupied since 1419 by the Turks, to Romania. In 1881, **Romania** officially adopted the tricolour blue, yellow, and red flag. On May 22 of that same year, Charles became the first King, Carol I.

Modern Romania

The kingdom of Romania began the twentieth century in a difficult international context, struggling to find its place in a volatile Europe involved in its own power struggles. At first close to Austria-Hungary, Romania's identity crisis ended when the country chose to side with the allies in the middle of the First World War. This conflict was to further shape its destiny.

Between neutrality and expansion (1912 – 1918)

Romania chose to abstain from military action during the Balkan Wars (1912–1913) which freed the Balkans from the Turks. King Ferdinand I succeeded his uncle Carol at the end of 1914. The country chose to remain neutral again at the beginning of the First World War, in spite of territorial incentives promised by both sides in exchange for their support. Finally, under pressure from the liberals, Romania joined the Allies –

Great Britain, France, Italy, and Russia – in August 1916, declaring war on the Central Empires. Despite numerous military setbacks, the country was still on the winning side on November 11th, 1918.

On December 1, 1918, in Alba Iulia, the "Grand Assembly of Transylvanian and Hungarian Romanians" was convened, comprising 600 officials elected by universal suffrage as well as 628 institutional representatives. Delegates from the Banat, Transylvania, Crişana, and Maramureş voted unanimously for a united Romania. They wanted a democratic country that guaranteed equality for citizens, regardless of nationality or religion. Euphoria swept up thousands of patriots, reaching nearly 100,000 in all, who took to the streets in support of their delegates. On December 24, King Ferdinand ratified the unification. On January 8, 1919, it was the Saxon Assembly's turn to declare its union with Romania.

The birth of modern Romania (1918 – 1922)

In 1919, Romania signed the **Treaties of Saint-Germain** and of **Neuilly** which granted her possession of Bucovina and the south of Dobrogea (the "Quadrilateral"). In June 1920, according to the terms of the **Treaty of Trianon,** Hungary handed over Transylvania, along with Crişana, Maramureş, and the area north of the Banat. In October, Romania finally received Bessarabia, despite protests from Russia and the United States. The brand new state of **Greater Romania** (România Mare) was seemingly fragile, with an area and population which had suddenly more than doubled. It inherited serious social inequalities in the various regions, each with a different past, but hopes were high after Alba Iulia. Minorities now form one third of the population, a potentially destabilising factor which has become one of Romania's great strengths. ●

FROM THE PRINCIPALITIES TO A UNITED ROMANIA

Orthodox Romania

The magnificent ornamentation of Orthodox churches is often breathtaking.

© Antoine Schneck

The only country with a Latinate culture but an Orthodox religion, Romania is deeply marked by the spirituality of its people. The Church is still influential in all spheres of society, particularly in the simple and often touching way rural villagers express their faith in their daily lives *(p. 32)*.

More striking still are the extraordinary examples of the Church's cultural influence, particularly in the unparalleled architectural splendour of the churches and monasteries in many parts of the country. The history of Romania, which embraced Christianity in the first centuries A.D., is inseparably bound with the Orthodox faith. Over the course of centuries and despite the influence of foreign powers, the Church has come to lie at the heart of Romania's culture and national identity.

The Romanian Orthodox church

Unlike the Catholic church, Orthodox Christianity does not obey one single central authority. Nor does it have monastic orders. Alongside the four major **patriarchates** *(see inset p. 55)*, a number of **Autocephalous Churches** (literally self-headed, i.e. self-governing) appeared. Some of these were led by a patriarch, in Russia, Serbia, Georgia, Bulgaria and Romania, others by an Archbishop, in Greece and Cyprus, or a metropolitan, as in Poland.

In 1885, after Romanian independence in 1877 and the establishment

Other religions

Church in a Hutsul village in Bucovina.

© Pierre Soissons

The Romanian constitution drawn up in 2003 guarantees religious freedom. According to official figures, approximately 86% of Romanian citizens declare themselves to be of the Orthodox faith.

These include members of many minority communities, including Serbs, Greeks, Ukrainians, Hutsuls *(see inset p. 241)* and Russian Lipovanis, who follow the Julian calendar.

Romania also has Roman Catholic, Protestant, and Greek Catholic or Uniate communities.

Until the 1940s, Romania had a large Jewish population of approximately 800,000 people, mostly Ashkenazi Jews who followed the Hassidic tradition. Today, the Jewish population is at most 20,000.

Armenians have their own churches in Bucharest *(p. 65)*, Gherla, Iași *(p. 258)*, and Suceava *(p. 238)*.

Dobrogea *(p. 286)*, under Ottoman control for centuries, has a number of mosques now used by the Turk and Tatar communities. ●

of the monarchy in 1881, the Church of Romania became autocephalous. Its independence was strengthened by the creation of the **patriarchate of Bucharest** in 1925. The link between the national identity and the Orthodox faith was such that the Church's autonomy was equated with national independence. The patriarchate today comprises 7 metropolises (equivalent to a bishopric) and 28 dioceses. The current patriarch is His Beatitude **Teoctist Arăpașu** (born in 1915). The tradition of orthodox monasticism *(see inset p. 265)* is maintained in the *skites* (hermitages) and monasteries all across the country, numbering more than 300 in total.

From the Apostles to the fall of Constantinople

According to popular tradition, the apostles Andrew and Philip came to spread the good word in Scythia, part of which is now Dobrogea. The region boasts numerous inscriptions and more than 30 sanctuaries dating from the fourth to sixth centuries A.D. *(see inset p. 274)*. Lying within the sphere of influence of the Byzantine Empire (the eastern part of the Roman Empire, founded in 330), Dacia *(p. 39 and p. 136)* was slowly Christianised. Slavonic, the language used for liturgy, was first introduced in the ninth century from Bulgaria.

In the 14th century, the first Wallachian and Moldavian princes *(p. 41)* made the emancipation of the Church their priority. Their own independence benefitted from the creation of metropolises in the Wallachian town of **Curtea de Argeş** *(p. 97)* in 1359 and in **Suceava** *(p. 238)* in Moldavia in 1401.

From the fourteenth to the early sixteenth century, many parts of Romania struggled to limit the expansion of Islam, providing a buffer between Christian Europe and the muslim Orient. The siege and defeat of Constantinople in 1453 led to the **fall of the Byzantine Empire.** After the fall, members of the Church of Constantinople sought refuge with the Romanian princes, who gave financial support to the monasteries of Mount Athos and the Holy Land.

Romanian Orthodox culture

After the shock wave of the fall of Constantinople in 1453, the Orthodox world closed in on itself, except in Romania, where from the 15th to 17th centuries, the cultural legacy of the Byzantine Empire was perpetuated and combined with other cultural influences. For example, in addition to the essential Byzantine heritage, religious art was enriched through contact with the Serbian and Armenian traditions, as well as western European Catholicism and later the Protestant Reform via Poland and Transylvania.

Fifteenth-century **Moldavia** witnessed a wave of original artistic creation which, in a period lasting just over a half a century, saw the churches decorated with magnificent frescoes *(p. 224)*. At the same time, religious architecture in **Wallachia** was drawing on Oriental and Serb architecture. The cathedral of **Curtea**

Visiting the monasteries

Amongst the 300 monasteries and *skites* (hermitages) in Romania, some thirty are happy to accommodate visitors overnight, many in Neamţ *(p. 271)* and Oltenia *(p. 118)*. There is a nominal fee of around ten to twenty euros for room and board. During religious festivals, however, space is limited. It goes without saying that you should respect the rules of the monastery and the monks who live and pray there. Travellers should make their presence as discreet as possible. Note that all meals will be vegetarian.

Appropriate dress

In order to visit churches and monasteries, appropriate dress must be worn. This means no shorts or revealing outfits. Women should wear a headscarf. It is forbidden to smoke anywhere in the monastery grounds. ●

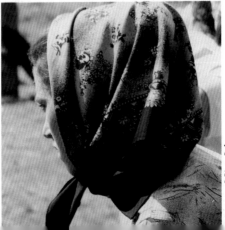

© Diane Dufresne

de Argeş is without doubt the most exquisite example of its kind.

At the end of the seventeenth century, the Italian Baroque style reached Wallachia. The region blended this new influence with its own style, producing an amazing synthesis, named after Prince Constantin Brâncoveanu *(p. 102)*. The Hurez monastery is the best example of this style.

In the seventeenth century, the Church, the focal point of cultural life in the principalities, facilitated the use of Romanian as a literary language. In Iaşi, the metropolitan Dosoftei ran a printing press which produced some of the first texts in Romanian *(p. 255)*.

Uniate dissidence in Transylvania

After the failure of the **siege of Vienna** by the **Ottomans** (1683), the **Habsburgs** imposed their protection on Transylvania in 1691. They recognized rights for the "three nations", Magyars, Szeklers and Saxons, but ignored the rights of the Romanians, even though they were the majority population in the region. The emperor promised Orthodox christians who agreed to switch their allegiance to Rome the same rights as Catholics and preservation of their Orthodox rituals. In 1697, the synod of Alba Iulia accepted the offer. In 1701, Atanasie, formerly Metropolitan of Alba Iulia, became the first bishop of the Uniate Church of Transylvania. This step represented a step towards greater equality for the Romanian elite, but was considered an act of treason by Orthodox Romanians, who revolted against the move. An uprising was crushed by General Bukow's Austrian army in 1761. Many Orthodox priests were killed and more than 150 hermitages and monasteries were destroyed.

Bishop **Inocentiu Micu Klein** and most of the signatories of the *Supplex Libellus Valachorum*, a petition sent to the emperor in 1791 demanding rights for the Romanian population, were members of the **Greek Catholic** elite who were the most vocal supporters of equality of rights for the Romanian people. This continued to be the case until

The tolerance of the Turks had its limits. Detail of the martyrdom of Saint Jean the New, Voroneţ *(p. 229)*.

© Bernard Houliat

Tolerance of the Sublime Porte

The Turkish occupation of **Moldavia** and **Wallachia** *(p. 42)* was accompanied by a remarkable degree of religious tolerance. The Ottomans did not begin attacking churches until 1821 when it quelled the hetairist movement.

Under the Habsburg yoke

In **Bucovina**, annexed from 1775 to 1918, the Austrians sought to limit the Orthodox Church's influence and simply closed the majority of its monasteries. Some churches, such as the one in **Humor** *(p. 228)*, saw their religous heritage suffer, with precious frescoes ruined due to lack of maintenance or vandalism.

Hungarian dominance

In **Transylvania**, controlled by Hungary from the tenth century to 1918, Orthodox culture proved a strong bond uniting the Romanian population. In Maramureş *(p. 146)* and in the Apuseni Mountains, they built elaborate churches out of wood, often decorating them with intricate and stunning wall paintings. The art of painting icons on glass comes from the same tradition. ●

The great schism

From the first century A.D., the Christian church founded communities led by bishops, successors to the Apostles. These communities or patriarchates formed five major regions, also known as the pentarchy: Constantinople, Alexandria, Antioch, Jerusalem, and Rome. The bishop (or patriarch) of Rome, the Pope, was *primus inter pares* ("first among equals"), a title that was above all honorific in nature. In the fourth century, Rome claimed power over the Universal Church (*katholikos* means universal in Greek) and sought to impose the Pope's supremacy. This was unacceptable to eastern Christians. This was the principal reason for the schism, while different interpretations of Christian dogma deepened the split over time. These disagreements resulted in the great schism of 1054, bringing an end to a thousand years of spiritual unity. The pope and the patriarch of Constantinople, who represented Orthodoxy ("just opinion" in Greek), excommunicated one another. The schism deepened after crusaders sacked Constantinople in 1204. The extreme violence of the crusaders left an indelible scar on the Orthodox world. Over the course of the following centuries, the Eastern Orthodox Church was deeply distrustful of Rome. It was not until 1965 and the Second Vatican Council that the first major steps were taken towards reconciliation and Orthodox and Catholics were no longer excommunicated by each other's church. ●

Transylvania was eventually reunited with the other Romanian territories in 1918 (p. 50).

From communism to democracy

In 1948, the communist powers eliminated the Uniate church and killed many members of the church hierarchy. The churches and their congregations returned to the Orthodox Church. Even then, the state attempted to reduce the Church's influence even further by nationalising monastery lands, forbidding men to begin their novitiate before reaching retirement age, and shutting down and demolishing a number of monasteries and churches. Later, Ceauşescu recognised the importance of the Orthodox church, using it to further his nationalist policies. After freedom of worship was re-established in 1990, the Uniate Church was no longer an underground movement. But despite this, it had difficulty in reclaiming its confiscated possessions. The dispute dragged along for a while but seems to have lost intensity since John Paul II's visit to Bucharest on May 9, 1999. The Pope was most warmly received by His Beatitude Teoctist, Patriarch of the Romanian Orthodox Church. The attitude of the Orthodox church under communist rule was a subject of great debate. According to the Romanian press, the Church was not keen for the files kept by the Securitate, Ceauşescu's secret police, to be released. Certain members of the church hierarchy (as well as some of other faiths) were suspected of having collaborated. Yet such reservations did little to tame the religious fervour which arose following the fall of the dictator. The 1990s witnessed a large rise in the number of novitiates and the foundation of a number of new monasteries throughout the country. ●

Bucharest

Apart from Parliament Palace, Bucharest does not have many impressive buildings or monuments. The city's charm derives from its eclecticism, from **Lipscani**** *(p. 72)* to **♥ Stavropoleos Church***** *(p. 73)*. You must visit the fabulous **♥ Museum of the Romanian Peasant***** *(p. 80)* and the **Mogoşoaia Palace**** *(p. 81)*.

Map "What to see" inside from cover.

© Antoine Schneck

Wallachia and the Banat

Oltenia and Muntenia, the two provinces of Wallachia ("land of the Romanians"), lie in the shadow of the Carpathian Mountains. A mountain road connects **Târgovişte*** *(p. 92)*, ancient residence of the princes, to **Sinaia*,** where the royal family used to spend their summers at **Peleş Castle*** *(p. 95)*. Ancient trade routes lead to **Bran Castle**** *(p. 96)*, Queen Maria's particular favourite. **Curtea de Argeş**** *(p. 97)* and **Horezu Monastery***** *(p. 101)* played an important role in the history of Wallachia. In Oltenia, there is a constant pilgrimage to **Brâncuşi's Endless Column**** in Târgu Jiu. The **Tismana Monastery**** *(p. 106)* is situated in a gorge in the Vâlcan foothills where the magnificent Danube cuts a **narrow passage**** *(p. 107)* between Romania and Serbia. Deep in the Banat Mountains, you can explore the **Nera Gorges**** *(p. 108)*. Wandering around the streets of **Timişoara*** *(p. 111)* with its Baroque architecture, it is easy to understand why the town is called "little Vienna".

© Pierre Soissons

The Apuseni Mountains

Cut off from the rest of world, the landscape and traditions have remained relatively untouched in this massif. A medley of architectural styles is found in **Oradea*** *(p. 122)*; wooden churches in the meadows of the **Beiuş Valley**** *(p. 127)*; in the **Arieş**** highlands *(p. 129)* and on the **karstic Padiş plateau**** *(p. 129)*, hamlets inhabited by the Moţi mountain people. The area between the eastern foothills of the **Apuseni*** and **Transylvania** has much to offer of historic interest: remains of **Dacian citadels*** *(p. 136)*; **Alba Iulia*** *(p. 129)* where the Unification of Romania was signed; and **♥ Rimetea**** *(p. 131)* with its Magyar people and traditions.

© Pierre Soissons

Southern Transylvania

Centuries of occupation by German peoples has left its mark on Transylvania. The towns of **Sibiu★★★** *(p. 152)*, the former Saxon capital, and **Mediaş★★** *(p. 159)* both feel like medieval German towns. **Marginimea Sibiului★★** *(p. 147)*, the rural region in the Cindrel foothills, on the other hand, has remained resolutely Romanian. All around, the **tributary valleys of the Târnava★★★** *(p. 161)* contain fascinating Saxon citadels, such as at **Biertan★★★** *(p. 162)*. **Sighişoara★★★** *(p. 163)* with its ramparts and steep cobbled streets, is probably the best preserved old town in Romania. **Viscri★★★** *(p. 169)* is full of old-fashioned charm. **Braşov★★** *(p. 170)*, a town which once traded with Constantinople and Vienna, has also preserved much of its former glory. The citadels of **Prejmer★★★** *(p. 173)* and **Hărman★★** *(p. 173)* nearby are not to be missed.

© Pierre Soissons

© Bernard Houliat

The heart of Transylvania

In the imagination, Transylvania is tinged with mystery and intrigue. The misty mountains and picturesque old towns full of nostalgia do not disappoint. In the **land of the Szeklers** (Szekely Land, *p. 180)*, the **Vârghiş Gorges★★** and the forests of ♥ **Harghita★★** have a strong romantic appeal. **Târgu Mureş★** *(p. 184)* with its Secessionist ♥ **Palace of Culture★★** still has a *mitteleuropa* feel to it. In **Cluj-Napoca★** *(p. 187)*, a young student population lives amongst the remains of history.

Maramureş

Wood in all its forms and uses is at the heart of everything in Maramureş. To get some idea of its significance, visit the **Maramureş Village Muscum★★** before exploring the villages themselves. In ♥ **Sapânţa Cemetery★★★**, you will not need an interpreter to understand the comic quatrains engraved on the headstones. The fields and villages of the **Mara★, Cosău★★★** and **Iza★★ valleys** *(p. 210)* encapsulate life in Maramureş, as the wooden churches of ♥ **Deşeşti★★** *(p. 206)* and ♥ **Poienile Izei★★***(p. 212)* encapsulate the piety of the peasants. Finally, take a trip on the ♥ **Vaser forest railway★★** *(p. 215)* and its steam locomotives...

© Pierre Soissons

Moldavia: Bucovina

Famous for its churches, this region also offers the visitor some spectacular mountain landscape and intriguing rural communities. On the ♥ **monastery trail***** (p. 226), the ♥ churches of **Suceviţa*****, **Voroneţ*****, **Humor*****, **Moldoviţa***** and **Arbore***** vie with the beauty of their exterior frescoes. Visit the **wooden church**** in the pretty village of **Putna*** (p. 236) on the **northern edge of the Carpathians** (p. 235). Near **Suceava*** (p. 238), two fantastic sites: ♥ **Pătrăuţi Church**** and **Dragomirna Monastery*****.

© Pierre Soissons

Mountains and hills of Moldavia

The beautiful hills of Moldavia take on an added mystery in the manastery region. Visit **Probota Monastery***** (p. 246) where some superb frescoes have recently been uncovered. From the vantage point of **Galata Monastery*** (p. 260), **Iaşi**** (p. 251), the dynamic capital of Moldavia, appears full of churches including the **Church of the Three Hierarchs**** is covered with intricate stone sculpture. The **Jewish Cemetery***** (p. 259), a terrible and poignant reminder of the horrors of the 1940s. Nearby, **Dobrovăţ Church**** stands unadorned and mystical, amidst lush greenery. Monasteries and hermitages flourish in the **Neamţ Mountains**** (p. 266) and the **Bicaz Gorges**** (p. 267) cuts a spectacular route through to Transylvania.

© Bernard Houliat

Dobrogea

Between the Danube and the Black Sea, a region of steppes, marshland and forest has offered refuge for many an outcast of history. The **Danube Delta***** (p. 275), nature sanctuary and biosphere reserve, is home to over 300 species of bird. Explore this network of rivers, canals and wetlands aboard a floating hotel (p. 296).

The Ottoman Empire is still present at **Babadag*** (p. 286) in the oldest **mosque*** in Romania; the ruins of **Histria**** (p. 287) recall the ancient Greek colonies; and the remains found at **Constanţa*** (p. 289) are Roman. Although highly developed and built-up, the **Black Sea coast*** still has many beautiful beaches. ●

© Pierre Soissons

© Pierre Soissons

© Pierre Soissons

© Pierre Soissons

History

Romania is jam-packed with evidence of a rich and fascinating past. The **Dacian citadels** of Hunedoara show the level of organisation and development of this civilisation which, for so long, resisted Roman invasion *(p. 136)*.

The ruins of **Histria★★** and **Cape Dolosman★★** illustrate the extent of Greek and Roman presence in Dobrogea *(p. 273)*, further documented in the **National Museum of History and Archaeology★★** in Constanța. This was also one of the first regions to be Christianised.

Unique in Europe, the Transylvanian **Saxon citadels** *(p. 150)*, dating from the 12th century, provide a masterclass in regional planning and reveal the extraordinary development of this German civilisation in the region. The medieval towns of Sibiu, Mediaș, Sighișoara and Brașov are good examples.

In Maramureș, the **Memorial to the Resistance and to the Victims of Communism★★** in Sighetu Marmației *(p. 201)* tells the tragic story of the first decades of this period. **Parliament Palace★** *(p. 76)* in Bucharest and the avenues around it remind us of Ceaușescu's urban policy in which entire districts were destroyed to make way for his grandiose schemes. You can also learn a lot about the history of Romania, past and present, by chatting with your Romanian hosts.

Religious heritage

The only Latin country of Orthodox faith, Romania is an immensely spiritual country and belief here is still as strong as it ever was. The best and most extraordinary illustration of the cultural influence of the Church are the remarkable churches and monasteries – masterpieces of religious art – that dominate the country. This is especially true in **Bucovina**, where the churches of **Moldovița★★★**, **Humor★★★** *(p. 228)*, **Voroneț★★★** *(p. 229)*, **Sucevița★★★** *(p. 232)* and **Arbore★★★** *(p. 226)* have fresco-covered facades. For stunning monasteries, go to **Curtea de Argeș★★** *(p. 97)* in **Muntenia** and **Horezu★★★** *(p. 101)* in **Oltenia**. In **Bucharest**, the **Stavropoleos Church★★★** *(p. 73)* is a gem. The wooden churches of **Maramureș** *(p. 196)* are more modest but spiritually uplifting nevertheless. Surrounded by ramparts, the churches of the **Transylvanian** Saxon villages contain superb altarpieces *(p. 164)*.

Traditional music

No other country in Europe has a folk music tradition to match Romania's and yet it is in danger of disappearing. The best place to hear traditional music is at weddings. Spirited **violin playing** can still be heard in Transylvania and especially in Maramureş *(p. 219)*, where it is often accompanied by the *zongora* (five-stringed guitar) and the *doba* (large drum). In Bihor, or in the Apuseni Mountains, you may be lucky enough to catch the nasal sounds of the **vioara cu goară** (Stroh violin). Roma weddings in Oltenia and the Banat are set alight by **intense wild rhythms**. The traditional instrument around Buzău and in Dobrogea is the **bagpipes**, and Moldavian **brass bands**, such as in Ciocârlia *(p. 249)*, are quite extraordinary.

© Bernard Houliat

The country and its festivals

You can take part in **Orthodox festivals**, pilgrimages and **village festivals** *(p. 33)*. Do not miss the music and feasting at the **pastoral festivals** *(p. 32)*. Try to visit Romania at **Easter**: the celebrations are sumptuous, poignant and accompanied by lavish feasts. **Christmas** is a special time for the family and, at New Year, lively masquerades take over Moldavian villages. To find out more about rural life in Romania, visit one of the open-air ethnographic museums, where peasant houses and buildings have been reconstructed in authentic settings. The ♥ **Dumbrava Open-air Museum**★★ *(p. 157)* near Sibiu is, without a doubt, the best of its kind. Do not miss the Szekely Land gateways in the **Sfântu Gheorghe Museum**★★ *(p. 181)*. The ♥ **Museum of the Romanian Peasant**★★★ *(p. 80)* in Bucharest has a wealth of exhibits and information to elucidate the richness of Romanian peasant life.

© Pierre Soissons

Wildlife

Among the reeds and marshlands of the labyrinthine **Danube Delta**★★★ *(p. 275)*, the Dalmatian pelican, glossy ibis, and white-tailed eagle are just some of the great ornithological sightings to be made.

It is not unusual to find traces of bear activity in the **Carpathian Mountains**. In Maramureş and Bucovina, although common, wolves and lynxes are more discreet. Wild boar, roe deer, red deer and wild cats populate forests, whereas marmots, chamois and golden eagles can be found in the mountains.

© Victor Bortas

© Antoine Schneck

© Antoine Schenck

© Bernard Houliat

Food and drink

Romanian cuisine offers something for everyone starting, logically enough, with **soup** *(see inset p. 27)*: each region has its own special version. Do not miss the **wild flavours from the hedgerows** *(p. 27)* such as young nettle shoots, acacia jam, or spruce bud syrup. Try a bilberry dessert or one of the many wild mushroom dishes that Bucovina has made its speciality. There is a distinct **Turkish influence** in dishes from Dobrogea, Wallachia and Moldavia. There are, of course, national dishes, available throughout Romania such as *mămăliga (p. 26)*, made with maize flour, or *sarmalé*, leaves stuffed with rice, meat and vegetables. The country also produces wonderful beer, wine and strong spirits *(p. 29)*.

Folk art and crafts

Romanian craftsmen produce an impressive range of crafts. In Maramureş, the wool used to make the **rugs** is dyed with natural plant extracts *(p. 217)*. Nuns from the **Tismana** *(p. 106)* and **Râmeţ** *(p. 133)* **monasteries** decorate their rugs with floral patterns, superb examples of which you can buy in the streets of **Humor** *(p. 228)*. There are beautiful **icons on glass** in Vadu Izei (Maramureş). Elsewhere, in Bucovina, the Hutsuls *(p. 241)* produce **decorated eggs**; Oltenia *(p. 217)* is famous for its **pottery;** Apuseni for its **woodcraft** and Transylvania and Moldavia for their **embroidered tablecloths.** Further treasures can be found in town bazaars and village markets *(târg)*. Do not miss the great **pottery festival** *(p. 117)* in Horezu, in Oltenia.

Potholing and hiking

There are some fantastic caves for potholers in Romania, mainly in the Banat massif, Oltenia and the Apuseni Mountains. One of the best karstic regions in Europe is found on the **Padiş Plateau★★** *(p. 129)* and around the **Scărişoara★★** caves *(p. 130)*. The country is also a hiker's paradise, offering a great variety of landscape and terrain with a good choice of accommodation in the hills. Natural wonders abound in the **Semenic Mountains★★** *(p. 110)*, the ♥ **Nera Gorges★★** *(p. 108)*, the ♥ **Harghita Mountains★★** *(p. 182)* and the **Ceahlău massif★★** *(p. 267)*. Less-frequented areas such as Apuseni, Maramureş and Bucovina are no less fascinating, especially in terms of rural culture. ●

How long to stay

If you only stay for a week you should visit the monasteries of **Bucovina** and some **Saxon citadels.** In two weeks, you could also get to **Maramureş** and the **Apuseni** Mountains. **Three weeks** is the ideal length of stay as Romania is best explored at a more relaxed pace. Consider visiting the complexities of the **Danube Delta** on a separate trip. You will need two or three days to explore the ancient quarters of **Bucharest.**

Romania in 8 days from Bucharest

- **Days 1 and 2**: from the airport, make for **Braşov** (*p. 170*) and the **Rupea Saxon citadels** (*p. 169*).

- **Day 3**: through **Szekely land** (*p. 180*) and the **Neamţ monasteries** (*p. 262*) to **Bucovina** (*p. 221*).

- **Days 4 and 5**: villages and monasteries of **Bucovina** (*p. 226*).

- **Day 6**: through the **Bârgau** and **Târgu Mureş** Mountains (*p. 184*) to **Sighişoara** (*p. 163*).

- **Day 7**: **Târnava** Saxon citadels (*p. 158*) and **Sibiu** (*p. 152*).

- **Day 8**: return to Bucharest *via* **Horezu** Monastery (*p. 101*) and **Curtea de Argeş** (*p. 97*).

Romania in 20 days from Hungary

- **Day 1**: over the border to **Oradea** (*p. 122*). Drive for a further 2.30 hrs into the heart of the **Apuseni** Mountains. Stay in the **Albac forest** (*p. 142*).

- **Days 2 and 3**: recover from your journey by taking a stroll around the **Scarişoara** caves (*p. 130*). Stay another night here.

- **Day 4**: before moving on from the mountains, visit **Rimetea** and the surrounding valley (*p. 131*).

- **Day 5**: start early and spend the whole day exploring **Alba Iulia** (*p. 133*) and the **Marginimea Sibiului** villages (*p. 147*). The best

guesthouses in the region are in **Tilişca** (*p. 178*).

- **Day 6**: **Sibiu** (*p. 152*) and the surrounding area. Stay in Tilişca.

- **Day 7**: **Vâlcea monasteries** (*p. 100*). Stay the night near Horezu (*p. 101*).

- **Day 8**: **Argeş** hills, the **Dâmboviţa** Valley. Stay the night in Moeciu (*p. 117*).

- **Day 9**: visit **Bran** Castle (*p. 96*), **Braşov** (*p. 170*) and some Saxon villages.

- **Day 10**: half-way through your journey indulge yourself with a whole day in **Viscri** (*p. 169*).

- **Day 11**: explore the citadels of **Rupea** (*p. 169*) and the **Hârtabaciu** Valley (*p. 168*) before driving on to **Sighişoara** (*p. 163*).

- **Days 12 and 13**: **Sighişoara** (*p. 163*), the **Mediaş** citadels (*p. 159*) and Szekely Land (*p. 180*).

- **Day 14**: pass through the Harghita Mountains (*p. 182*), the **Bicaz Gorges** and the **Neamţ** region (*p. 262*) to **Suceviţa** (*p. 232*), an ideal base camp for the **Bucovina monasteries** (*p. 226*).

- **Days 15 and 16**: the **churches and monasteries** of Bucovina are a must; *en route* take in some villages and the market at **Rădăuţi** (*p. 235*).

- **Day 17**: start very early over the Prislop pass for a 4hr drive to the **Iza Valley** (*p. 210*). After exploring **Ieud**, try the guest houses in **Poienile Izei** (*p. 218*).

- **Day 18**: visit the churches at **Poienile Izei** (*p. 212*) and **Şieu** (*p. 211*). Stay the night in the same place.

- **Day 19**: back among the carved gateways of the **Cosău Valley** (*p. 207*). After visiting the open-air museum in **Sighetu Marmaţiei** (*p. 202*), you arrive in **Sapânţa** with its famous cemetery (*p. 197*).

- **Day 20**: in two hours you are at Satu Mare and back at the Hungarian border. ●

Bucharest

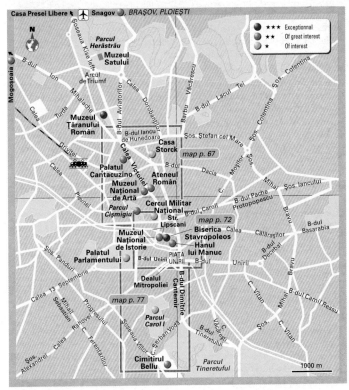

Casa Presei Libere ✈ Snagov, BRAȘOV, PLOIEȘTI

● ★★★	Exceptionnal
● ★★	Of great interest
● ★	Of interest

Parcul Herăstrău
Muzeul Satului
Arcul de Triumf
Muzeul Țăranului Român
B-dul Iancu de Hunedoara
Casa Storck
map p. 67
Palatul Cantacuzino
Ateneul Român
Muzeul Național de Artă
Cercul Militar National
Parcul Cișmigiu
map p. 72
Lipscani Str.
Biserica Stavropoleos
Muzeul Național de Istorie
Hanul lui Manuc
Palatul Parlamentului
PIAȚA UNIRII
Dealul Mitropoliei
B-dul Dimitrie Cantemir
map p. 77
Parcul Carol I
Cimitirul Bellu
Parcul Tineretuful

1000 m

GENERAL MAP

You can only really enjoy the countless pleasures offered by this city by strolling around the streets on foot. One could even say that Bucharest purposefully misleads the newcomer to increase the element of surprise when you finallt do uncover her innumerable hidden treasures.

With a population of two million, Bucharest is not really like other European capitals: major historical landmarks and prestigious monuments are rare. Apart from the pharaonic palace that was the brainchild of Ceaușescu, nothing really dominates the urban landscape. It's fair to say that it's all a bit of a mess, the town has a kind of jumbled eclecticism that lends an inexplicable charm to a city that likes to think of itself as modern and westernised but which in fact cannot

© Antoine Schneck

shake off a sensuality and nonchalence which are particularly eastern. From its very beginnings, Bucharest was a link between east and west, a city of transit and trade, full of street markets. Around the caravanserai inns, Transylvanian merchants would meet with Turkish traders, as well as Wallachian, Greek, Jewish and Armenian businessmen. Bucharest can be exhausting, but it can also be endlessly stimulating. It is one of the last cities in Europe to favour adventure and poetics above urban uniformity. Today, the town centre is becoming more westernised, but the unknown and unexpected are still never far away. ●

Calea Victoriei★

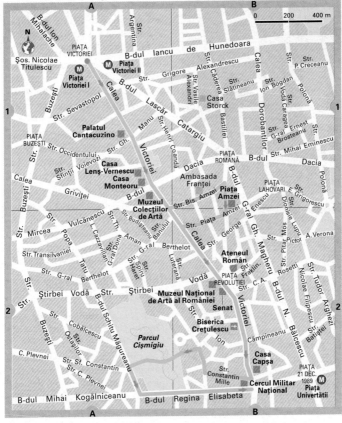

MAP I

In 1692, Constantin Brancoveanu built this road for direct access to Mogoșoaia, his residence from 1705 *(p. 81)*. Instead of stone, the road was paved with oak and named "Mogoșoaia Bridge" *(Podul Mogoșoaiei)*. It winds for 2.7 km between piața Victoriei in the north and piața Națiunilor Unite in the south, passing a varied panorama of 19th- and 20th-century architecture, where each building tells a story. In 1878, after the Russo-Turkish war, Romania's independence was consolidated and the huge avenue down which the triumphant soldiers marched became known as the *calea Victoriei* (road of Victory).

From piața Victoriei to piața Revoluției

> *Set off from piața Victoriei (S). Metro Piața Victoriei (M2).*

The upper end of this famous street has many opulent late 19th-century and early 20th-century residences.

♥ Cantacuzino Palace: the George Enescu Museum★★

> **A1** *Palatul Cantacuzino, Muzeul George Enescu. From piața Victoriei, take calea Victoriei (S). Calea Victoriei, 141* ☎ *659.63.65. Open daily except Mon. 10am-5pm. Admission charge. Allow 30 mins.*

Cantacuzino Palace typifies Bucharest's late 19th-century architectural whimsies.

Grigore Cantuacuzino, also known as "the Nabab" commissioned Ion Berindei to build this palace (1898-1900) in a style combining Neoclassical elements with Art Nouveau. The entrance is particularly flamboyant: steps, flanked by two lions, lead up to an elegant wrought-iron gateway, with a shell-shaped awning. Above, some angels climb a generously-decorated pediment.

Just behind the palace is the little house where **George Enescu** once (p. 327) lived; he was related to the family by marriage. Here, as in the the palace, music lovers can see some of the great composer's pianos, photographs, musical scores and original furniture. Do not miss his portrait painted by **Corneliu Baba**.

The Mansions along the Calea Victoriei

Just beyond the museum, on the same side of the street, the **Casa Lenș-Vernescu** (n° 133; access for clients only) was built in 1820 for the family of Filip Lenș, whose father, Jean-Baptiste de Linche de Moissac, was secretary to **Prince Ypsilanti**. The building was renovated in 1889 by **Ion Mincu** (see inset p. 79).

Today, this magnificent residence is occupied by the "casino-palace" and a restaurant where pseudo luxury attempts to recreate pre-War splendour.

A bit further, the **Casa Monteoru** (n° 115, restaurant and entrance hall open to public), renovated by Ion Mincu in 1887-1889, has preserved its magnificent **interiors★**.

The building now houses the Romanian Writers' Union (Uniunii Scriitorilor ☎ 212.58.29), and there is a restaurant on the ground floor (Il Gattopardo Blu, **Address book** p. 85).

The Art Collection Museum (Casa Romanit)★

> **A1** **Muzeul Colecțiilor de Artă**. Calea Victoriei, 111 ☎ 212.96.41 and 650. 61.32. Closed for renovation until June 2004.

This early 19th-centruy building was enlarged, decorated and finally completed around 1840, by the very rich Grigore Romanit who made it into one of the most luxurious mansions in the street, hosting a series of lavish balls. The museum houses several different collections, including Oriental art and works by European and Romanian artists.

●●● **To see nearby:** opposite the Art Collection Museum, the str. Biserica Amzei leads you past the French Embassy, to the interesting **Amzei market★**, (piața Amzei, open daily 7am-6pm).

Around piața Revoluției

The calea Victoriei leads one of the rare monumental areas of town where you'll find the imposing hotel Bucureşti and the Athénée Palace (now the Hilton Hotel).

♥ The Romanian Athenaeum**

> **B2 Ateneul Român** *On the corner of str. Franklin and calea Victoriei. Str. Franklin, 1-3* ☎ *315.00.25 or 313.90.60. For information and reservation phone Mon.-Fri. 9am-3.30pm, until 7pm on a Thur. (concert night).*

A small park leads you to the entrance of this magnificent building, now used for classical concerts.

The façade and its mighty columns are swamped by the domed rotunda. The French architect Albert Galleron was responsible for this top-heavy colossus, opened in 1888.

A line of medallions representing illustrious figures from Romanian history sits above the entrance. The concert hall (1,000 seats) with its opulent domed ceiling is covered in frescoes illustrating important moments in Romanian history.

The National Museum of Romanian Art**

> **B2 Muzeul Național de Artă al României.** *Calea Victoriei, 49-53* ☎ *615. 51.93, 313.30.30 and 314.81.10. Open Wed.-Sun. 10am-6pm. Admission charge. Allow at least 2.30 hrs.*

The **Golescu Palace** used to stand on this site. Despite being only one storey high, this was one of the most prestigious palaces in Bucharest. In its place the Royal Palace was built, according to designs by the Frenchman Paul Gottereau. Then in 1927, a fire ravaged the building and it was completely rebuilt. The inauguration of the new building by **Carol II** *(inset p. 323)* in 1935 is documented in Paul Morand's *Bucharest*. Following the exile of King Michael in 1948, the palace became national property and was turned into a museum. Collections include Romanian art up to the 18th century, modern and contemporary Romanian art, European art and Oriental decorative arts.

The right wing houses the Gallery of Medieval Romanian Art on the first floor and the Gallery of Modern Romanian Art on the second.

● ♥ **The Gallery of Medieval Romanian Art** *(Galeria de Artă Românească Medievală). Allow 30 mins.* Superb collections of icons, parts of iconostases, illuminated manuscripts and silver and gold platework from all over Romania. The museum is perfect preparation for visiting the rest of the country.

Famous for the quality of its acoustics, the Athenaeum has played host to some famous names such as George Enescu, Dinu Lipatti, Maurice Ravel, Richard Strauss and Yehudi Menuhin.

© Victor Bortas

● **The Gallery of Modern Romanian Art** (*Galeria de Artă Românească Modernă*). *Allow about 1 hr.* The collections are mainly on the second floor, spread out over eleven rooms. Highlights include:

Room 3: the artistic trends of the 1900s, with work by Ştefan Luchian (1858-1916), Cecilia Cuţescu-Storck (1879-1969), Octav Băncilă (1872-1944) and others.

Room 6: Romanian avant-garde represented by Hans Mattis-Teutsch (1884-1960), Marcel Iancu (1895-1984), Victor Brauner (1903-1966).

Room 7: several works by Constantin Brâncuşi (1876-1956).

Room 11: paintings by the remarkable Corneliu Baba (1906-1997).

● **The Gallery of European Art** (*Galeria de Artă Europeană*). *Allow about 1 hr.* Housed on the first and second floors of the palace's left wing, the Gallery brings together the private collections of the Romanian Royal family and other notable Romanian personalities (all pre-1940). You'll find works by Antonello da Messina, Tintoretto, El Greco, Cranach, Rembrandt, Rubens, Delacroix, Renoir, Monet, Sisley etc.

The Senate*

> **B2** *Senat. Opposite the National Museum of Romanian Art. Piaţa Revoluţiei, 1.*

This Neoclassical building, completed in 1948, once housed the **Central Committee of the Communist Party**. The balcony in the centre was made famous by television news broadcasts across the world when **Ceauşescu** gave his final speech at noon on 21st December 1989 and was cut short by the crowd. Crosses, candles and flowers remind us of the Romanians who lost their lives here during the revolutionary fighting.

Bucharest: General map p. 65
Address book p. 83

Around Cişmigiu Park

Creţulescu Church*

> **B2** *Biserica Creţulescu. Calea Victoriei, 47. Open Mon.-Fri. 8am-6pm; Sat.-Sun. 7am-3pm.*

This elegant church was built between 1720 and 1722 by the boyard ↪ Iordache Creţulescu and his wife Safta, Constantin Brancoveanu's daughter. The building has been restored, exposing the original brickwork. A finely sculpted frieze surrounds the entire facade dividing it into two ; the upper part is punctuated with blind arcades.

A little further on the left, you can have a drink in a café which is emblematic of pre-War Bucharest: *Casa Capşa*.

Casa Capşa*

> **B2** *Calea Victoriei, 36.* **Address book** *p. 85.*

In 1874, the four sons of the Macedonian merchant Capşa opened a café-patisserie. One of them, Grigore, had just returned from Paris, where he had worked for a famous café owner. In 1881, the family opened a restaurant and a hotel. It was not long before the establishment became the meeting place for politicians, businessmen, writers, journalists and diplomats, including Paul Morand, the French Ambassador to Bucharest from 1943-1944. The restaurant is still open and although the food may not be top-notch, the atmosphere is faultlessly *fin de siècle*.

♥ The National Military Circle*

> **B2** *Cercul Militar Naţional. On the corner of str. Constantin Mille and calea Victoriei. Str. Constantin Mille, 1.* **Address book** *p. 85.*

This enormous structure, built in a style somewhere between Neoclassical and Neo-Baroque, opened its doors in 1912. On the ground floor is a restaurant, where, for a modest

Chess players meet in Cişmigiu Park.

© Pierre Soissons

price, you can treat yourself to a decent meal in the vast, spectacular dining room. The building is also a regular exhibition space.

♥ Cişmigiu Park★★

> **B1** *Parcul Cişmigiu. From the Military Circle, str. Constantin Mille leads to the park. Open daily 6am-8pm. Free admission.*

Before 1779, this site was just a copse surrounding a lake fed by two nearby springs Prince Alexandre Ypsilanti decided to build a fountain here to ensure a decent supply of drinking water for the town. The person in charge of the fountains had his house here. He was known as Mare Cişmigiu (big Mr Fountain-keeper), from whence the park takes its name. In 1854, Prince Bibescu transformed the wasteland into an 17-hectare public garden, designed by the Viennese landscape architect

Meyer. Two tree-lined avenues cross the park from north to south, opening up a great vista towards Schitu Măgureanu Church.

On the edge of the lake, in the centre of the park, the architect Ion Mincu *(see inset p. 79)* built the *Monte Carlo* **restaurant**. Reconstructed after being bombed in 1944, it has lost its pre-War magic but you can still enjoy a refreshment on the terrace overlooking the lake. In a corner of the park, **16 busts of Romanian writers** form a circle in the grass, complete with benches.

●●● **To see north of the park**: Creţulescu Palace *(str. Ştirbei Vodă)*, is currently the UNESCO office. Take bd Regina Elisabeta *(south of the park)* to calea Victoriei, which will lead you south to the Lipscani district. ●

The Lipscani District★★

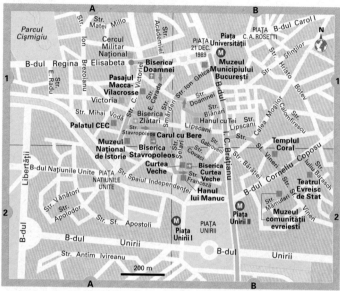

MAP II

The heart of the town used to beat around the old princely court founded by Vlad Tepeş in the 15th century *(see inset p. 43)*. Intense commercial activity took place in the surrounding streets. The name Lipscani derives from the **Leipzig** (Lipsca in Romanian) merchants who traded there, while those from Gabrovo (Bulgaria) have also given Bucharest a street name: Gabroveni. Other streets nearby are named after the tradespeople who frequented the area: Covaci (blacksmiths), Şepcari (hat-makers), etc. This vast enclave of urban harmony with its abundance of cafés, clubs and restaurants has recently become popular with a trendy, young crowd.

The southern end of calea Victoriei★

> **B**1 *Metro Piaţa Universităţii (M2) or Piaţa Unirii (M1, M2, M3).*

Once opposite the Military Circle, follow bd. Regina Elisabeta towards piaţa Universităţii for about 50 m and turn right into str. Academei. About 50 m down, you'll discover the tiny ♥ **Biserica Doamnei★** Church *(str. Biserica Doamnei; open Mon.-Fri., 8am-5pm, Sat.-Sun., 9am-3pm; free admission)*. Built in 1683 at the request of Maria Doamna, wife of Prince Şerban Cantacuzino, the church provides a refreshing and intimate haven of peace. Note the richness of the floral decoration surrounding the main doorway. Take str. E. Carada to the back entrance of the glass-roofed **Macca-Vilacrosse passage★** *(Pasajul Macca-Vilacrosse)*, built in 1891. Head back to calea Victoriei.

Further down the street, an imposing academic-looking 19th-century edifice stands out. This is the **Savings Bank building** or **Palatul CEC★** *(Casa de Economii şi Consemnaţiuni; calea Victoriei, 13; closed to the public)*. Designed by the French architect, Paul Gottereau, with a monumental arched entrance, domed ceiling and majestic staircases.

●●● **To see and hear:** just opposite, the **Zlătari Church** (1715) is renowned for its excellent choir.

The National Museum of Romanian History**

> **A1** *Muzeul Național de Istorie a României*. *Calea Victoriei, 12* ☎ *614.90.78. Open Wed.-Sun. 9am-5pm. Admission charge; free on the last Friday of the month. Allow 1 hr.*

Another huge Bucharest building on the banks of the **Dâmbovița** dominates the river end of the calea Victoriei: the former "Post Palace", completed in 1900, became the History Museum in 1971. Despite its wealth of documents, archaeological finds and armory, the museum is, unfortunately, somewhat unkempt.

In the basement, the **National Treasure** room *(Tezaurul Național)* has over 2,000 gold and silver objects, and precious stones. The highlight is the "**Hen with the Golden Chicks**" *(Cloșca cu puii de aur)*, a 4th-century Visigoth treasure, discovered in Pietroasa, near Buzău. You can also see copies of the metopes of Trajan's column which recount the Roman conquest of Dacia *(p. 108)*.

♥ Stavropoleos Church***

> **A1** *Biserica Stavropoleos. From the History Museum take str. Stavropoleos. Str. Stavropoleos, 6. Open daily 8am-6pm, free admission. Allow 30 mins.*

This masterpiece, between calea Victoriei and the Lipscani district, was founded by Ionachie, a Greek monk from Epirus, at the request of the Greek merchants in Bucharest. Built in 1724, it was originally the chapel of a caravanserai since disappeared. Although small, the church is typical of Brâncoveanu architecture *(p. 102)*. The best example is the open **porch**: four columns of delicate yet opulent ornamentation, capitals blooming with sculpted foliage, support polylobed arches decorated with painted motifs. The **balustrade** is covered with finely sculpted floral undulations: panels on the right and left show lions fighting among the leafy spirals. On the middle panel, Samson struggles with a lion. The carved **main doorway** is framed by a magnificent floral frieze similar to those around the church's side windows. The incense-filled interior is covered in beautiful frescoes. The **icono-**

The Macca-Vilacrosse passage with its magnificent glass dome is a haven of peace and tranquility in the hectic centre of Bucharest.

© Pierre Soissons

stasis ↪ is chiselled with a festival of vines and leaves. Branches grow out of the body of a recumbent man: this is the Tree of Jesse ↪. Check out the collection of ancient stones in the pretty **garden** near the church. After 1990, a small monastic community, led by Father Iustin Marchiş, took up residence in the church's outbuildings. Don't miss the Saturday evening mass: this is the only church in Bucharest where the psalmodic chant is performed according to Byzantine tradition *(cassettes are on sale in the gift shop of the Museum of the Romanian Peasant, p. 80).* The oriental charm of the setting coupled with the meditative chanting leaves an indelible impression.

Carul cu Bere*

> **A1** *Str. Stavropoleos, 3.*

Opened in 1879, the *Carul cu Bere* restaurant ("the Beer Cart"; *address book p. 85)* is one of the few Neo-Gothic buildings in Bucharest. Designed by a Polish architect, the main room has a very high ceiling supported by pillars with a gallery halfway up. The decoration is rich: murals, highly-polished wooden panelling, and stained glass windows. By 1900, it was one of the most popular meeting places for Bucharest's literati, rivalling the *Capşa (p. 70).* The famous playwright, Ion Luca Caragiale *(p. 327),* was a regular customer, finding inspiration for his plays in the faces and personalities around him.

Curtea Veche

> **B2** *Take the str. Smărdan on the left.*

The 15th-century foundations of this former **princely court** are attributed to Vlad Tepeş *(see inset p. 43):* a few walls, vaults, tombstones and a column can still be seen. The site has revealed evidence of some of Bucharest's earlist inhabitants: Dacian pottery, Roman coins and 14th century fortifications.

The Princely Court Church*

> **B2** *Biserica Curtea Veche. Str Franceza. Open daily 8am-7pm. Free admission.*

Follow the str. Franceza alongside the ruins. On the left appears the Church of the Princely Court, the oldest in Bucharest, built in 1559 and added too many times since. For two centuries, this is where the coronation ceremony of the Romanian voivodes ↪ took place. Opposite you is a massive building: Manuc's Inn.

♥ Manuc's Inn**

> **B2** *Hanul lui Manuc. Str. Franceza, 62-64* ☎ *313.14.11 and 313.14.12, <www. hanulmanuc.ro>. Address book p 84.*

In the 17th century, Bucharest was a city of trade and transit between Istanbul and Central Europe. In the Lipscani district, where commerce flourished, several caravanserais offered travelling tradesmen places to rest. For security, the inns were surrounded by walls. In 1808, the Armenian merchant, Emanuel Mârzaian, known as Manuc and nicknamed Manuc Bey by the Turks *(see opposite),* built this inn. The buildings form a square around a vast interior courtyard.

On the upper floors, wooden walkways, lead to the bedrooms. The courtyard would have been a bustle of men and carriages: one can imagine the 19th-century cosmopolitan throng that would have met here. This inn is one of Bucharest's landmarks and the only remaining caravanserai still visible. The others have either disappeared or are, like Hanul cu Tei, in ruins.

The streets of old Bucharest

From Hanul lui Manuc, you can venture down the oldest streets in Bucharest which have retained their quaint charm. Here run-down old shacks sit alongside the capital's hippest bars, restaurants and antique shops.

portrait

Manuc Bey, adventurer

Not content with having accumulated a colossal fortune, Manuc Bey (1769-1817) was an influential figure who spoke about ten languages. He seems to have been as talented in matters of business as he was in intrigues, be they amorous or political. It was in his inn, the Hanul lui Manuc, in 1812, that delegations from Russia and Romania prepared the Peace of Bucharest which put an end to the Russo-Turkish war. Threatened by the Turks, he settled in Paris, where his elegance immediately opened the doors of Parisian society. The Turks, however, eager for his head, put pressure on Napoleon. So he exiled himself again, this time taking refuge in Russia where, rumour has it that he was poisoned. ●

Şepcari, Covaci and Gabroveni are great streets to wander around. The famous Lipscani street has preserved several authentic Art Nouveau facades (nos. 72-74). At n° 63, a gateway entices you down a long courtyard, a remnant of the caravanserai Hanul cu Tei B1, where you'll find antique shops and art galleries. The courtyard opens onto str. Blanari.

Suțu Palace, Bucharest City Museum*

> B1 *Muzeul Municipiului Bucureşti. Turn left down str. Blanari, then right (str. Ion Ghica) to get to the big boulevards. Where these meet the piaţa 21 Decembrie 1989. bd I. C. Brătianu, 2 ☎ 310.35.51 Open Wed.-Sun., 10am-6pm. Admission charge. Allow 1 hr.*

In 1835, the *postelnic* Costache Suțu had Viennese architects draw up plans for this stylish Neo-Gothic residence. Inside, a monumental staircase designed by the famous architect Karl Storck (*p. 80*) rises up, dividing in front of a huge mirror from Murano which reflects a clock, the face of which only tells you the right time if you look at it in the mirror. Elegant balls were held here while, outside, chicken clucked and buffalo grazed. In 1959, Suțu Palace was transformed into a museum where you can see how the 19th-century boyards ↪ would have lived.

Memories of the Jewish district

> B2 *From piaţa 21 Decembrie 1989, take bd I. C. Brătianu south then turn right down str. Vineri. M° Piaţa Unirii (M1, M2, M3).*

The tragedy of WWII put an end to centuries of strong Jewish presence in Bucharest (since the 16th century). The urban landscape owes something to the Jewish elite (doctors, lawyers and businessmen) who between 1900 and 1930 commissioned avant-garde architects such as Marcel Iancu, Horia Creanga and Henriette Delavrancea, to construct private homes and buildings.

The heart of the Jewish quarter was bulldozed by Ceauşescu. Some buildings escaped, however, such as the Coral Temple, a working synagogue (*Templul Coral*; str. Sf. Vineri, 9 ☎ 312.21.96). Nearby, a former synagogue houses the Jewish Community Museum (*Muzeul Comunităţii evreiesti*; str. Mămulari, 3 ☎ 311.08. 70; open daily except Tue. and Sat. 9am-1pm; admission charge). In a neighbouring street, the Jewish State Theatre (*Teatrul Evreiesc de Stat*; str. Dr Iuliu Barasch, 15 ☎ 323.39.70 and 323.45.30) perpetuates the Goldfaden theatre company (*p. 258*) with regular performances in Yiddish. ●

From Civic Centre to Bellu Cemetery★

The 1977 earthquake gave Ceauşescu the opportunity to construct a monument in celebration of his reign, the **Civic Centre** (*Centrul Civic*). Under the rather doubtful pretext that buildings had been made unsafe by the quake, a huge demolition programme was set in motion, which not only left a gaping hole in the town centre, but also uprooted 70,000 people. The area was once a peaceful enclave of greenery and pretty, almost provincial streets built between 1850 and 1930: bourgeois residences and houses with surrounding gardens, cubist villas and modern bungalows. This whole world, which included twelve churches, three monasteries and two synagogues was completely swept away, leaving an indelible sense of suffering. In its place Ceauşescu erected a series of huge buildings along the 4 km stretch of bd Unirii. One of these constructions is ranked among the largest buildings in the world. As you wander south, *via* Metropole Hill, you can get an idea of how Bucharest was before this disaster. The trees in the huge park and the cemetery provide welcome shade after this beautiful city walk.

From piaţa Unirii, head back up the large boulevard Unirii (*Metro Piaţa Unirii, lines M1, M2, M3*).

The most famous and controversial of Bucharest's monuments came into being between 1984 and 1989. 400 architects and 20,000 workers were mobilised in its construction, literally exhausting the country's resources. It is 84 m high and covers 60,000 m². Everything about it is oversized: there are a thousand rooms, 440 offices, dozens of conference rooms (some over 2,000 m²), corridors so long that the end cannot be seen, kilometres of carpet and tons of crystal for the chandeliers.

Nowadays, the surrounding area seems to have melded in with this colossus. From the boulevards it really does look impressive. Initially called "The People's House", it was intended to concentrate all the government departments on one site, within easy reach of the dictator, who would also lived there. After 1990, it became the Republican Palace and then the Parliament Palace, once the latter took up its residence there.

Return to boulevard Unirii (south side) and take the first passage you see on the right. There you'll find a quite different world, including a somewhat unexpected church.

Parliament Palace★

> **A1** *Palatul Parlamentului*. Metro Izvor (M1, M3). Access from the south (calea 13 Septembrie) and the entrance "A3" ☎ 311. 36.11. Open daily 10am-4pm. Admission charge. 45-minutes guided tours.

Bucharest General map p. 65
Map I (Calea Victoriei) p. 67
Map II (Lipsnani: District) p. 72
Map III (Civic Centre) p. 77

Antim Monastery★

> **A1** *Mănăstirea Antim*. Str. Antim Ivireanul, 29. Open daily 8am-6pm. Free admission.

Overshadowed by big tower blocks, this oasis of elegance and tranquility seems to withdraw into itself. Georgian by origin, **Antim Ivireanul** (1660-1716) was an erudite and multi-talented artist (calligrapher, painter, sculptor) as well as being a man of the cloth. Having become a metropolitan ↪,

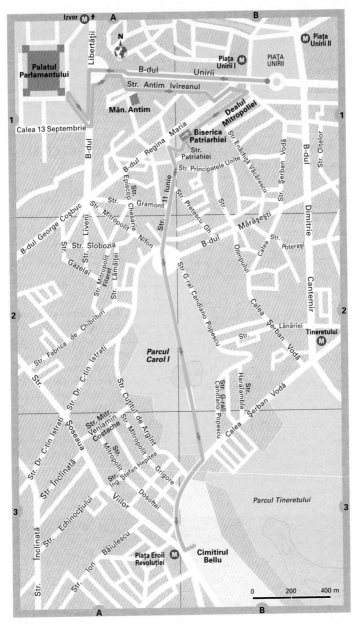

MAP III

he built this church in the style developed by **Constantin Brâncoveanu** *(p. 102)*, of whom he was a close advisor: some beautiful stonework decorates both the openings and the capitals within the porch. Antim himself would have been involved with the work, sculpting the double doors for the main entrance.

Metropolis Hill★

> **B1** *Dealul Mitropoliei.*

The hill had barely been named before the metropolis ↝ of Wallachia (which still exists) became part of the patriarchy ↝ of Romania in 1925. The best approach to this ensemble, which emerged unscathed from the earthquake and subsequent demolitions, is to head towards the piața Unirii. In the south-west, a beautiful tree-lined alley leads to a group of pretty buildings where you can see the bell-tower of the Patriarchal Church and a remnant of the former surrounding wall.

● **B2 The Patriarchal Church★** (*biserica Patriarhiei*). *Str. Mitropoliei, 1. Open daily 8am-6pm. Free admission. Allow 15 mins.* Founded by Constantin Șerban Basarab, the voivode ↝ of Wallachia between 1656 and 1658, this church became the Metropolitan church in 1668 and the Patriarcal church in 1925. Inside, there is a soft ambiance of Byzantine splendour, which bestows great beauty on the services presided over by the Patriarch. The analogy with Constantinople does not stop there: the church is dedicated to the emperor-saints Elena and Constantine. A huge crowd gathers here on Easter Eve; at mid-night, the faithful leave the church with candles lit and walk around the church three times. It is also worth visiting on other festival days such as the feast of Elena and Constantine (21 May) or Saint Dimitri the New of Bessarabia (27 Oct) whose remains are preserved here.

From Patriarchal Church to Bellu Cemetery★

If you enjoy walking, a pleasant hour-long trip takes you from Metropolitan Hill through Carol I Park to Bucharest's most epic cemetery.

● **AB2/3 Carol I Park★** (*parcul Carol I*). *Permanently open; free admission.* Str. Patriarhiei goes down the south-west side of the hill. At the point where it joins boulevard Regina Maria, turn left onto str. 11 Iunie. At the bottom is the entrance to one of the capital's best parks: Carol I Park. Cross it from north to south to join calea Șerban Vodă.

● **B3 ♥ Bellu Cemetery★★** (*cimitirul Bellu*). *Metro Eroii Revoluției (M2). Open daily 8am-6pm. Free admission. Allow about one hour.* Cross calea Șerban Vodă and continue southwards to the piața Eroii

Only the Pentagon in Washington is bigger than Parliament Palace.

architecture

Ion Mincu and the "Neo-Romanian" style

In the middle of the 19th century, Romanian artists studied either in France or in Germany. At the same time, a national feeling was emerging with the birth of the Romanian state. Artists began to glorify the achievements of the Romanian people – architects, for example, looked for a new path midway between national tradition and Western influence. Ion Mincu was one such person. Following his studies in Paris, he developed a modern style in Bucharest which tried to keep alive the spirit of traditional construction. After a period of excessive academism, his work began to reflect Wallachian buildings and the art of the Brăncovean era *(p. 102)*: ogee arches, porches supported by pillars... Despite a tendency towards pomposity, the result is original and Bucharest has him to thank for several curious buildings: Casa Lahovary (str. Ion Movila, 5-7), the superb Bufet Kişeleff, the Casa Doina (şos. Kişeleff, 4). Further examples can be seen on calea Victoriei: Casa Monteoru, (n° 115, *p. 68*) and Casa Lenş-Vernescu (n° 133, *p. 68*) as well as the **Bellu Cemetery** *(see opposite)*. His disciples (Petre Antonescu, Nicolae Ghika-Budesti and Cristofi Cerchez) were to fill the town with buildings influenced by this "Neo-Romanian" style. ●

Revoluţiei where you will find the entrance to the cemetery. Established in 1858, it became the preferred burial ground for Bucharest's wealthy families. Wandering among the tombs, you will be altenately surprised and delighted by a dizzying display of funerary lyricism. Well-known artists were commissioned to construct Pharaonic mausoleums as well as moving and even humourous tombs. One architect stands out: Ion Mincu *(see above)* who ran riot here creating a terrifying crematorium and some extravagant family vaults such as for the Gheorghieff, Lahovary and Stătescu families. He too lies here, among his own creations. This graceful cemetery has been badly vandalised over the past few years and many valuable sculptures have unfortunately disappeared. ●

Hidden Treasures beyond the City Centre★

The poetry of everyday life resonates through the many cultural intrigues dotted about this town. There are museums, cemeteries, street bazaars, markets, little squares, parks, gardens, and some stunning modern art. Uncovering all the hidden treasures within the city would take weeks, not to mention the manifold marvels found just ouside...

Beyond the bustling centre of Bucharest are sights equally rich in history and culture. They provide the perfect excuse to escape the city for a few hours.

The Museum of the Romanian Peasant★★★

> **General map A1** *Muzeul Ţăranului Român. Metro Piaţa Victoriei (M2). From piaţa Victoriei, go back up the şos. Kişeleff (North). Şos. Kişeleff, 3* ☎ *650.53.60, fax 312.98.75, < www.itcnet.ro/mtr >. Open daily except Mon. 10am-6pm. Admission charge. Allow 1-2 hrs.*

Since 1990, this building has been the site of a ground-breaking project, kicked off by the artist **Horia Bernea** (1938-2000): a space entirely devoted to peasant life. This is a fascinating and complex museum, unlike any other. Here the universe of the peasant is not simply presented, it is brought to life in all its nobility. Particularly moving are the rooms containing religious icons and crosses that display both naïvety and sophistication. Just near the entrance, a village school has been reconstructed. Below ground, an astonishing exhibition, " The Plague " (*Ciuma*), is dedicated to the Communist era. You can understand something of the regime through the items of protocol or simple everyday objects on display.

Thanks to its stunning conception and the great team who run it, the museum won the 1996 prize for **European Museum of the Year.**

The Storck Museum★

> **General map A1** *Colecţia de Artă Plastică Frédéric Storck et Cecilia Cuţescu-Storck. Metro Piaţa Victoriei or Piaţa Romana (M2). From piaţa Victoriei, take str. Grigore Alexandrescu (E) and turn right to str. Vasile Alexandri, 16* ☎ *211.38.89. Open Wed.-Sun. 9am-5pm. Admission charge. Allow about 1 hr.*

The Museum was created in 1951 to pay tribute to the work of the Storck family, the founders of the Romanian school of sculpture and, in particular, to the works of Cecilia Cuţescu-Storck. Their house, built in 1913 by a French architect according to plans by Frederic Storck, is stunning with it's red brick exterior and stained glass windows. No less than 150 paintings, 250 sculptures and a mass of other archives are kept here, as well as some astonishing, voluptuous **murals★** painted by Cecilia adorning the walls.

The Village Museum★★

> **General map A1** *Muzeul Satului. Metro Aviatorilor (M2), then a 15-minutes walk. Follow boulevard Prezan and, at the Triumphal Arch, go right. Take bus 783 (piaţa Unirii-Otopeni Airport) getting off at the Triumphal Arch. Şos Kişeleff, 28-30* ☎ *222.91.10. Open daily except Sun. 9am-6pm. Admission charge. Allow 1-2 hrs.*

© Victor Bortas

Mogoşoaia Palace, masterpiece of the Brâncoveanu style, was designed as the prince's summer residence.

Created in 1936 on the initiative of Dimitrie Gusti (1880-1955), founder of the Romanian School of Sociology, the Village Museum was one of the first of its genre in the world.

Nearly three hundred buildings (churches, cottages, outbuildings and workshops) from the four corners of the country have been installed here in verdant surroundings, on the banks of Lake Herăstrău.

The aim of the museum is to receate faithfully the atmostpere of each building. Every barn, stable and outbuilding is surrounded by its own wooden fence (often in hazel wood) and gateway, sometimes modest and sometimes monumental.

Mogoşoaia Palace★★

> **Off general map, by A1** *Palatul Mogoşoaia. 13 km N-W of Bucharest. Calea Valea Parcului, 1* ☎ *490.42.37. Open daily except Sun. 10am-6pm. Admission charge. Allow 1 hr.*

In 1680, Constantin Brâncoveanu (1655-1714; *p. 102*) bought the estate of Mogoşoaia and founded a settlement consisting of a church, a palace, large kitchens, greenhouses and a park.

● **The church**. Situated just outside the enclosure, the church was built in honour of Saint George (1688). It is an excellent example of early Brâncoveanu architecture with ogee arches, a sculpted band separating the walls into two distinct registers, stone surrounds with plant motifs, and a vaulted porch. The **votive painting** is original and shows Constantin Brâncoveanu next to his wife, holding a model of the church. Behind him, his four sons are pictured, and behind his wife, his seven daughters.

● **The palace**. The palace buildings were constructed between the late 17th century and the beginning of the 18th century. Following the tragic death of Brâncoveanu and his sons, the property fell into disrepair until 1860, when it was bought by Nicolae

Bibescu who, with the help of a French architect, began the first restoration. The architect raised the entire structure, reworking the north facade, adding four columns taken from Polovragi monastery *(p. 82)* and modifying the dimensions and shape of the windows. In 1912, a second renovation dealt with the external stonework, exposing the brickwork which constrast harmoniously with the stone details. Despite all this, the palace is impressively proportioned and remarkably finely decorated: the original paintwork has been partially preserved and the stone balustrades, capitals, columns and surrounds are carved with floral and animal motifs.

Snagov Monastery★

> **Off general map by A1** *Mănăstirea Snagov. About 40 km N of Bucharest towards Ploiesti on the DN1.*

In Ciolpani, turn right towards the Snagov-Sat holiday complex on the banks of Snagov lake *(6 km from the DN 1)*. Boats take you to the monas-tery which is on an island on the far side of the lake. Founded in 1364, it is dominated by a beauti-ful church, completed in 1517, containing an empty tomb which, according to legend, was the burial chamber of Prince Vlad Tepeş *(see inset p. 43)*. ●

Address book

Fin-de-siecle residences have preserved their old-fashioned splendour.

> *Dialling code* ☎ *021.*

Guide p. 65. Maps: Gen. p. 65; Map I: p. 67; Map II: p. 72; Map III: p. 77.

Getting there

● **By air**. Daily connections with most European capital cities and major Romanian towns (Tarom and Angel Airlines). **Otopeni International airport Off map by A1** ☎ 204.10.00. Car hire *(p. 86)*. Transfer to the town centre *(see inset p. 84)*.

● **By train**. **North station** *(Gara de Nord)*, N-O of the centre **Gen. map A1**. Railways agency *(Agenţia CFR)*, 10-14 str. Domnita Anastasia, (near calea Victoriei) ☎ 313.26.43. *Open Mon.-Fri. 7.30am-7.30pm; Sat. 8am-noon. Closed Sun.*

● **By bus**. Bucharest has connections with European capital cities. Daily connections with western Europe (Atlassib and Eurolines), Istanbul (Toros), Sofia and Athens (Anesis). Buses and maxitaxis serve Romanian towns. Departure points for international coaches and maxitaxis to the big Romanian towns are usually found near the Gara de Nord station, although they change regularly. Check with the company. Bus stations are also used by regional buses. Main bus stations: **Autogara Filaret**, piaţa Garii Filaret, 1 ☎ 336.06.92. **Autogara Obor**, bd Garii Obor, 3 **Gen. map B1** ☎ 252.76.46.

Accommodation

▲▲▲▲▲ **Athénée Palace Hilton**, str. Episcopiei, 1-3 **I-B2** ☎ 303.37.77, fax 315.21.21, < www.hilton.com >. *272 rooms.* The most prestigious hotel in Bucharest, opposite the Royal Palace and the Athenaeum.

▲▲▲▲ **Duke**, bd Dacia, 33 **I-B1** ☎ 212.53.44, fax 212.53.47. *38 rooms.* In a district which typifies 1900-1940s architecture.

▲▲▲▲ **Residence ♥**, str. Clucerului, 19 **Gen. map A1** ☎ 223.19.78, fax 222. 90.46, < www.residence. com.ro >. *30 rooms.* One of the most attractive hotels in Bucharest.

to the town centre

Many hotels will organise your airport transfer to the town centre. Check when you reserve your room.

● **By taxi**. There are ranks of metered taxis at the airport exit. The cost of the journey is often over-priced (and varies according to the customer). Agree on a price before getting into the cab to avoid a nasty shock later. Never pay more than €20.

● **6-seat limousines**. Limousines are often not much more expensive than a taxi! **Sky Services** ☎ 204.19.17 and 0723.33.89.24 (mobile), fax 204.19.17, < www.e-sky.ro >.

● **By bus**. Going by bus is a quick and cheap option. **Express 783** runs between the aiport and the town centre (piaţa Victoriei, piaţa Romana and piaţa Unirii). It operates from 5.30am to midnight, every 15mins (Mon.-Fri. in the day) and every 30 mins (Sat.-Sun.). The journey takes about 40 mins. The ticket desk is on the right of the bus stop. You do not buy your ticket from the driver. Beware of pickpockets. ●

▲▲▲ **Continental**, calea Victoriei, 56 **I-B2** ☎ 313.36.94, fax 312.01.34. *53 rooms.* Between piaţa Revoluţiei and bd Regina Elisabeta. *Restaurant.*

▲▲▲ **Euro Hotels International**, str. Gheorghe Polizu, 4 **Off map by A1** ☎ 212.88.39, fax 212.83.60. *30 rooms.* Of excellent quality.

▲▲▲ **Flanders** ♥, str. Ştefan Mihăileanu, 20 **Gen. map B2** ☎ 327.65.72, fax 327.65.73. *8 rooms.* Excellent Belgo-Romanian hotel. Friendly atmosphere. Restaurant with a very pleasant terrace area.

▲▲▲ **Helvetia**, piaţa Charles de Gaulle, 13 **Gen. map A1** ☎ 223.05. 66, fax 223.05.67. *29 rooms.* A peaceful and charming hotel north of town. Near the Herăstrău park and only 15 mins from the airport.

▲▲▲ **Ibis**, calea Griviţei, 14 **I-A1** ☎ 222.27.22, fax 222.27.23, < www. ibishotel.com >. *250 rooms.* Typical quality and price of the Ibis chain. Near the *Gara de Nord* station.

▲▲ **Doina des Carpates**, str. Maica Alexandra, 9 **Gen. map A1** ☎ 223. 70.14. *3 guest rooms,* shared bathroom. In a quiet street (piaţa 1 Mai).

▲▲ **Hanul lui Manuc**, str. Franceza, 62-64 **II-A2** ☎ 313.14.11, < www. hanulmanuc.ro >. *31 rooms.* You reach the rooms along a system of staircases and wooden walkways. Staying in such a great caravansérail is an wonderful experience, just don't expect it to be too clean. Avoid the restaurant, take a drink in the courtyard instead.

▲▲ **Vila 11**, str. Institutul Medico Militar, 11 **Off map by I-A1** ☎ 0722.49.59.00. *20 beds in a room,* shared bathroom. A small but clean and welcoming guesthouse near the *Gara de Nord* station. One double room en suite. It would be hard to find cheaper in Bucharest.

Restaurants

♦♦♦ **Amsterdam Grand Café**, str. Covaci, 6 **II-B2** ☎ 313.75.80. A friendly, relaxed place, right at the heart of the Lipscani district.

♦♦♦ **Angel's**, str. Paris, 52 **Off map by I-A1** ☎ 231.90.44. Bar and *restaurant.* A relaxing spot surrounded by 1920-1930s- style villas. Nice terrace.

♦♦♦ **Balthazar**, str. Dumbrava Roşie, 2 **Off map by I-B1** ☎ 212.14.60. Italian, French and Japonese influenced menu.

♦♦♦ **Basilicum Pub**, bd Schitu Măgureanu, 16 **I-A2** ☎ 315.47.93.

A pleasant, tastefully decorated pub, opposite Cişmigiu park.

♦♦♦ **La Bastille**, str. Căderea Bastiliei, 72B **I-B1** ☎ 212.49.14. This excellent French restaurant uses the best Romanian produce.

♦♦♦ **Carul cu Bere**, str. Stavropoleos, 3 **II-A1** ☎ 313.75.60. With the neo-Gothic backdrop, this is a great place for drinks (p. 74).

♦♦♦ **Casa Capşa**, calea Victoriei, 36 **I-B2** ☎ 313.40.38. Nostalgia is the dish of the day here: take a coffee and savour the atmosphere of Paul Morand's "quartier général". Food is disappointing.

♦♦♦ **Cyprus Taverna**, str. J. L. Calderon, 41 **Off map by I-B2** ☎ 311.11.03. Mediterranean flavours influenced by Turkish and Balkan cooking.

♦♦♦ **Il Gattopardo Blu**, calea Victoriei, 115 **I-B2** ☎ 659.74.28. Come for the Casa Monteoru backdrop.

♦♦♦ **Mesogios**, str. J. L. Calderon, 49 **Off map by I-B2** ☎ 313.49.51. *Excellent fish restaurant.*

♦♦ **Bistro de l'Institut Français** ♥, bd Dacia, 77 **I-B1** ☎ 212.08.53. The menu changes daily in this relaxed dining spot. A good choice of French and Romanian dishes.

♦♦ **Burebista**, calea Mosilor, 195 **II-B1** ☎ 210.97.04. Hearty and tasty Romanian cooking.

♦♦ **Casa Oamenilor de Stiinţă**, piaţa Lahovari, 9 **I-B1** ☎ 210.12.29. This "scientists" dining room is an original and cheap option for eating out.

♦♦ **Cercul Militar Naţional**, str. Constantin Mille, 1 **I-B2** ☎ 314.37.35. A spectacular dining room with opulent decor. Reasonably priced (p. 70).

♦♦ **Deja-vu**, bd Nicolae Bălcescu, 25 **I-B2** ☎ 311.23.22. Portions are generous at this *Moldavian and Russian restaurant.*

♦♦ **Hanul Hangitei**, str. Gabroveni, 16 **II-B2** ☎ 314.70.46. In the heart of the Lipscani district.

♦♦ **Moara Mariei**, str. Blănari, 14 **II-B1** ☎ 315.64.94. "Mary's mill": one of the best restaurants in the area.

♦♦ **Sahara** ♥, splaiul Independentei, 7-9 **II-A2** ☎ 315.04.31. The best restaurant for middle-eastern cuisine.

♦♦ **Taverna La Butoaie II**, str. Mihai Eminescu, 171 **I-B1** ☎ 211.58.99. The brick walls and wooden furniture give this place a homely feel. Not far from bd Dacia.

♦♦ **Tokay**, str. Oltetului, 30 ☎ 242.14.93. Excellent and well-priced *Hungarian restaurant.*

♦♦ **Vama Veche km 0**, str. Cristofor Columb, 13 **I-B2** ☎ 211.64.46. Near the piaţa Lahovari, this is a friendly restaurant serving generous portions. Balkan dishes.

♦ **Paradis 2**, str. Hristo Botev, 10 **II-B1** ☎ 315.26.01. Excellent Libanese cooking at an unbeatable price.

Bars and clubs

Green Hours 22, calea Victoriei, 120, **I-A1/B2**, < www.green-hours.ro >. Live jazz concerts on a Thu. In summer you can sit in the courtyard.

Lăptăria Enache, bd Nicolae Bălcescu, 2 **I-B2**. At the National Theatre, in summer, the roof terrace offers an amazing view of the city. Large wooden tables and excellent beer. In winter, you sit in the theatre's attic room. Live jazz.

Terminus Pub, str. George Enescu, 5 **I-B1/2**. A cosy bar decorated with antique curios and wooden tables.

Shopping

● **Antiques**. Craii de Curtea Veche, str. Covaci, 14 **II-B2** ☎ 314.83.04. One of the many antique shops.

● **Bazaars**. The **Vitan market** is in the S-E of town. From piaţa Unirii, head along the north bank of the Dâmboviţa to calea Vitan. There is another market (**Voluntari**) in the N-E of town along şos. Colentina, towards Urziceni (DN 2). There are many other good little bazaars and markets dotted around town.

city travel

• **Taxis**. Taxis are still relatively inexpensive and plentiful. To save bargaining at the end of your journey, ask the driver to turn on the meter as soon as you get in. The most trustworthy companies are: **Cobălcescu CrisTaxi** ☎ 9461 and **Perrozzi** ☎ 9631.

• **Metro**. Opened in 1979, the Bucharest underground has 4 lines and 45 stations. The main line M2, crosses town. Trains circulate between 5am and 11.30pm. At peak times they arrive every 4 to 7 mins, at other times frequency can drop to every 15 mins. The direction panels are not always entirely clear. Tickets are on sale in the stations. The underground map features on most city maps on sale at newspaper kiosks.

• **Tramway, bus and trolleybus**. The town is served by a complicated network of tramway, bus and trolleybus routes. Tickets are on sale in kiosks at the main tram and bus stations. Daily, weekly and fortnightly ticket are available. Make sure you stamp your ticket when you get on the bus or tram (machine near the door). •

• **Books**. **Librăria Noi**, 18 bd Nicolae Bălcescu **I-B2** ☎ 311.07.00. Old, new books and maps on Romania.

• **Markets**. **Piaţa Amzei I-B1**. *Open daily 7am-6pm.* Near the French Embassy, this attractive food market overflows with fruit and vegetables. **Piaţa Obo**, şos. Colentina, 2 **Gen. map B1** Obor metro (M3). *Open daily 10am-8pm, Sun. 10am-2pm.* A food market and mini-bazaar. **Piaţa 1 Mai**, bd Mihalache **Gen. map A1** *Open daily from morning to evening.* North of piaţa Victoriei. A popular and lively market.

Useful addresses

• **Embassies**. **Belgique**, bd Dacia, 58 ☎ 210.29 69, fax 210.28.03. Consulates ☎ 212.35.78. **Canada**, str. Nicolae Iorga, 36 ☎ 307.50.00. **France**, str. Biserica Amzei, 13-15 ☎ 303.10.00, fax 303.10.87. **Suisse**, str. Pitar Moş, 12 ☎ 307.92.47.

• **Airline companies**. **Air France**, str. General Praporgescu, 1-5, étage 1, app. 1 ☎ 210.11.76, fax 210.16.51. **Alitalia**, calea Victoriei, 224 ☎ 210.41.11, fax 210.41.09. **Angel Airlines**, şos. Bucuresti-Ploiesti, 40 (Băneasa airport) ☎ 201.17.01, fax 201.17.04, <www. angelairlines.ro>. Many connections with Iaşi, Suceava, Tim-

işoara, Arad. **Austrian Airlines**, bd Magheru, 16-18 ☎312.05.45, fax 312.02.11. **British Airways**, calea Victoriei, 15 ☎ 303.22.22, fax 303.22.11. **Czech Airlines**, str. Batistei, 3-5 ☎ 311.09.86, fax 312.08.84. **KLM**, aleea Alexandru, 9A ☎231.56.19, fax 231.56.22. **Lufthansa**, bd Magheru, 18 ☎315.75.75, fax 312.02.11. **Malev**, calea Victoriei, 26 ☎ 312.04.27, fax 312. 04.28. **Swiss**, bd Magheru, 18 ☎312.02.38, fax 212.57.74. **Tarom**, splaiul Independentei, 17 ☎ 337. 04.00; str. Buzesti, 59 (S-W of the piaţa Victoriei) ☎204.64.64.

• **Bus companies**. **Anesis**, 20-22 str. Poterasi ☎ 330.91.76. Connections with Athens. **Atlassib** 4 bd Gheorghe Duca ☎ 222.47.35; 4 str. Ankara ☎ 230.79.80. **Eurolines**, 5A bd Al. Ioan Cuza ☎ 210.08.90. Many connections with western Europe. **Toros**, 136-138 calea Grivitei ☎223.18.98. Connections with Istanbul and further transfers to Syria, Iran and Irak.

• **Car hire**. **Avis**, Otopeni airport ☎ 201.19.57. **Budget**, Otopeni airport ☎ 204.16.67. **Sixt**, Otopeni airport ☎201.46.26.

• **Post Office**. Postal office n° 1, 10 str. Matei Millo.Near the Military Circle **I-B2**. *Open Mon.-Fri. 7.30am-8pm; Sat. 8am-2pm; closed Sun.* •

Wallachia and the Banat

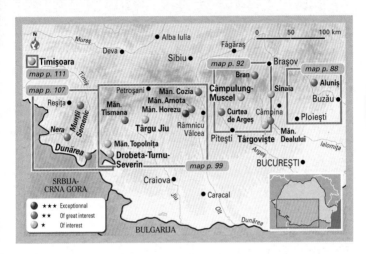

The territory once inhabited by the Vlach or Wallach people used to be quite simply known as the "**land of the Romanians**" *(Țara Românească)*. Wedged between the Carpathian mountains and the Danube river, it is today known as **Wallachia**, a territory split into two regions: **Muntenia** to the east and **Oltenia** to the west.

The Carpathian mountain range creates a natural frontier to the north, pierced by the River **Olt**. A diverse landscape of forest-covered peaks interspersed with meadows, deep gorges and secret valleys gives way to rolling hills and plains which peter out on the banks of the Danube. Wallachia does not have the same cultural mix as Moldavia, Dobrogea or Transylvania. A pure seam of Romanian culture is found here, closely linked to ancient Orthodox traditions such as mountain hermitages. There is also a eastern feel to the region, which is the natural result of centuries of Turkish presence.

Oltenia's western border lies where the Carpathian mountains and the Danube river meet, and **the Banat** begins. Resolutely anchored in Central Europe, the Banat has little in common with Wallachia; its multi-ethnic society shares neither a similar history nor any common origins. Even on the map it seems to face the other way.

© Pierre Soisson

The Secret Mountains of Buzău ★

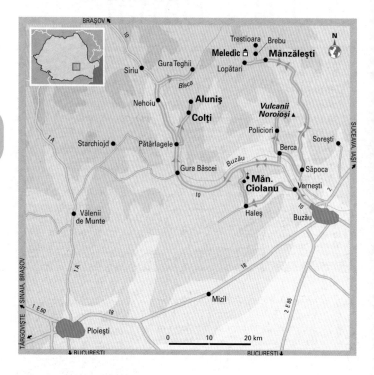

Those travelling from Bucharest to Moldavia will pass through the harsh, stark landscape of Buzău. Venturing west from the great plain, villages with luscious gardens, vineyards and heaving orchards abound. There are also many rupestrian churches and monasteries in the area which are still tourist free. Further into the mountains, you will witness some strange natural phenomena such as mud "volcanoes", seams of amber, oil springs and deep canyons cut in to the salt rock. Continue higher into mountains and you will discover a sumptuous landscape of gorges and forests providing some great hiking ground. Apart from the town hall and the streets around the station and market, there is little of interest to see in the massively modernised town of Buzău.

Ciolanu Monastery ★

> **Mănăstirea Ciolanu.** 32 km N-W of Buzău. From Buzău, take the DN 10 towards Verneşti (N) then turn left. In Haleş, turn right. Open daily 9am-5pm. Free admission. Allow about 15 mins.

This 16th-century monastery stands sleepily in a large, grassy courtyard, shaded by a few trees and an air of deep tranquility.

The **church** contains some beautiful wooden sculptures and the window surrounds show the clear influence of the Brâncoveanu style (p. 102).

In the surrounding forests and clearings is a scattered open-air exhibition of some 200 sculptures by young artists.

The Berca mud "volcanoes"★

> *Vulcanii Noroiosi. 30 km N-E of the Ciolanu Monastery, 22 km N of Buzău on the DN 10. The visit (approx. 20 mins) is not dangerous. Boots advisable. There is a nice bar serving snacks nearby.*

From the Ciolanu Monastery, descend the valley and take a right towards Buzău, then left towards Berca. After the bridge, the first left, and the first right leads into a valley. In Policiori, turn right down a badly-surfaced road for 3 km, before taking a left fork. After a climb of about 1 km, you will come to the region's most interesting site: **Pâclele Mari**.

Several of these "volcanoes", which are barely 2 m wide and 1.5 m high, can be active at any one time. A greyish mud sits in the crater, disturbed every now and then by rising gas bubbles accompanied by a thick liquid – a mixture of clay and water pushed to the surface by the pressure of the gas. The liquid sometimes overspills, forming miniature lava flows which can spread out over a hundred metres.

agenda

Approximately 200 km from Buzău on roads of varying condition; some tracks are not surfaced. You will need 2 days. If you are staying in Bucharest (just 2 hours drive away), this region is a great place to come for a **weekend visit**: arriving on Friday evening at the **Soreşti** vineyards (p. 118) for wine tasting and a night in this quiet spot. The next day, drive on to **Ciolanu** (p. 88), stopping off to visit the mud "volcanoes" and exploring the depths of the Mânzăleşti valley (p. 90). You can spend the night in the Meledic cabin (p. 117). On Sunday, return to the Buzău valley. After a visit to the rupestrian churches (p. 90), return to Bucharest via Vălenii de Munte.

Accomodation in Buzău (p. 115), Colţi (p. 116), Gura Teghii (p. 116).

Address book p. 115. ●

© Pierre Soissons

The mud "volcanos" create a lunar landscape without vegetation (the water is too saline for most local plantlife) in the heart of a luscious green area.

A little mud track climbs to the **Meledic plateau** where, near a lake, a converted refuge will give you a warm welcome.

Colți, the amber kingdom★

> *65 km N-W of Buzău, 43 km N-W of Berca. Return to Berca, cross the river and turn left onto the DN 10. In Pătârlagele, follow the little country lane which leads to Colți. Address book p. 116.*

This valley is known for its seams of amber which are occasionally still exploited today.

To the left upon entering the village, lies the **Museum of Amber** (*Muzeul Chihlimbarului; open daily except Mon. 9am-5pm; admission charge*), situated at the mouth of a disused amber mine. If the museum is closed, enquire at Mme Nica's house on the Aluniș road. This little museum displays blocks of amber and the tools used by prospectors and craftsmen.

© Victor Bortas

Some of the hermitages in this Romanian Cappadocia are notoriously difficult to get to.

The Mânzălești Valley★

> *Mânzălești: 67 km N of Buzău, 45 km N of Berca. From the Berca "volcanoes", return by the same route towards Berca, then follow the minor road along the south bank of the river in the Buzău valley. Continue for 8 km, then in Săpoca take a left. Address book p. 117.*

To get to Romania's more hidden locations you have to journey along this extraordinary valley. On the road between Mânzălești and Lopătari, look to your right at the salt mountain which has been slashed through by 30 m deep gorges. At the bottom of some cliff faces a dark liquid can be seen seeping out: an oil spring! The surrounding area offers a diverse landscape: within a few metres dry salt crevices give way to soggy grass, then abundant orchards.

Before you get to Lopătari, take a right towards Brebu and Trestioara.

Aluniș and the rupestrian churches★★

> *About 6 km N of Colți. Ask Dumitru Nica in Colți for information on access to the churches. Address book p. 116.*

In the 4th century, Christianity became more widespread in the Danube (*see inset p. 108*) and Carpathians regions (*see opposite*), mainly due to the work of preachers and hermits in the more inhospitable locations. In the highlands between the towns of Mlăjet, Aluniș and Bozioru, there is an exceptional and little known site: the remains of a group of around 20 churches and hermitages dating from the 13th and 14th centuries.

The sites are named after the hermits who once occupied them and most require one to three hours'

geography

The Carpathians

© Victor Bortas

The Carpathians form the spine of Central and Eastern Europe. They stretch in a mountainous arc over nearly 1,500 km (of which 910 km, 60% of the range, are in Romania) from north-eastern Austria to Slovakia (where Mount Gerlach, the highest point in the Carpathians, reaches 2.665 m), Poland, the Ukraine, Romania and Serbia, from where the Balkan mountains take over.

They are the eastern continuation of the Alps. Their intricate relief conceals many sanctuaries. Huge forests and the relative absence of human activity has created an outstanding repertoire of **European flora and fauna**: the main European populations of bears, wolves and lynxes are found in the Carpathians, the only sizeable habitat where they still live "naturally". These mountains and their enclosed valleys are also of great ethnological interest since their near inaccessibility has maintained a variety of cultural traditions such as the **Moți** (p. 130), the **Szekelys** (p. 180), the **Hutsuls** (p. 241) and the people of **Maramureș** (p. 195) in Romania alone. ●

walk to get to. Some can only be reached with the help of a ladder.

♥ **Aluniș Church*** (open for church services: Sun. morning and festival days) is the only easily accessible sanctuary. It is half built into the rock, the other half constructed from wood, painted an intense blue.

●●● **Possible trips**: from the Buzău mountains you can get to Szekely Land (p. 180) and Brașov (p. 170) by the DN 10.

Alternatively you can head in the opposite direction and cross the jagged southerly slopes of the Carpathians, where they peter out in a curve. Come off the DN 10 after the village of Gura Bâscei and make for Vălenii de Munte, Ploiești and Târgoviște. ●

Princes and Carpathians★★

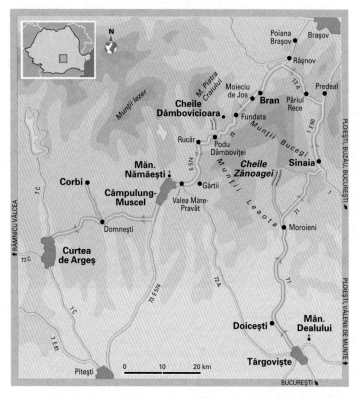

You can learn a lot about the history of the "**land of the Romanians**" (or Wallachia) from a visit to its three main cities **Câmpulung**, **Curtea de Argeş** and **Târgovişte**, which lie in the protective shadow of the Carpathian foothills. In more recent times, the kings of Romania would come to Sinaia for their holidays. Queen Maria loved visiting Bran Castle in its idyllic setting on the doorstep of Transylvania. Surrounded by some of the biggest mountains in Romania, a journey here follows ancient trade routes, meandering through the chalk cliff faces of the Bucegi mountains dazzling in the sunshine and the elegant Piatra Craiului ("King's stone") range.

Târgovişte★

> *78 km N-W of Bucharest, approx 130 km S-W of Aluniş via Vălenii de Munte.* **Address book** *p. 119.*

The town had a prestigious past as the capital and artistic heart of Wallachia from 1385 to 1559, during which time it endured 33 separate reigns. In the 16th century it was a major cultural centre which produced builders, sculptors and painters, such as the Dobromirs who decorated the interiors of many churches in the region. These churches, such as Stelea and Dealului *(see opposite)* stand as evidence of a bygone glory.

Wander around the town and you can't miss **Stelea Church★** *(Biserica*

Stelea; open daily 7am-7pm; free admission; visit lasts about 15 mins). Founded in 1645 by the great Moldavian prince, Vasile Lupu *(see inset p. 256)*, it is subtly decorated with enamel disks. The shape of the tower is similar to those on Moldavian churches. But the most remarkable church is the Princely Church in the court of the former Wallachian voivodes ↪.

The Princely Court**

> *Curtea Domneasca. On bd Bălcescu. Open daily except Mon. 9am-5pm. Admission charge. Allow 1 hr.*

The voivodes' residence is mentioned in documents as early as 1396 and contains important remains which tell a lot about their political and cultural influence. It was once surrounded by a double circle of ramparts, part of which survives. Between the 14th and 17th centuries, the palace was continually embellished. The palace was built by Mircea cel Batrân, but was extended by Petru Cercel and modified by Matei Basarab and Constantin Brâncoveanu *(p. 102)*. The perimeter of the court is dominated by the 15th-century **Chindia Tower*** which was once a lookout post. Nearby stands the Princely Church, a masterpiece of Wallachian art.

♥ The Princely Church** *(Biserica Domneasca)* was founded in the 1580s by **Petru Cercel** and added to by **Constantin Brâncoveanu** in 1698. The building is in the form of a Greek cross ↪, with one tower over the naos ↪ and two smaller ones over the pronaos ↪. The most recent renovation uncovered the original brick walls. To best appreciate the harmonious volume, stand to the west of the church and look back at the vast porch with its two rows of three windows on either side. Their elongated form is echoed in the blind arcades of the three towers. Inside are some **murals** dateing from the modifications of 1698: Brâncoveanu and Petru Cercel (right) feature in the

agenda

Approx. 280 km from Târgoviște *(p. 92)* to Curtea de Argeș *(p. 97)* via Sinaia *(p. 94)*, Bran *(p. 96)* and the Argeș hills. There are endless walks to do in the Bucegi mountains *(p. 96)*, to Piatra Craiului *(p. 96)* and Leaota *(p. 96)*. Lots of castles and churches to visit. You will need 2 days. **Accommodation** at Târgoviște, Sinaia, Bran, Moeciu de Jos, Câmpulung Muscel, Curtea de Argeș.

Address book p. 115. •

votive picture (pronaos) bearing a model of the church. They are accompanied by a number of Wallachian voivodes, including Matei and Neagoe Basarab (left), and Mihai Viteazul (right). On the tribunal balustrade, south-west of the naos, there is a scene of the **Feeding of the Five Thousand**, rarely used in Byzantine iconography. An **iconostasis** ↪ dating from 1697 illuminates the richness of the naos with its richness. Left of the doorway there is a superb icon of Mary and Child. Saint Nicholas is on the left.

♥ Dealului Monastery**

> *Mănăstirea Dealului. From Târgoviște, take DN71 towards Sinaia. After Târgoviște turn right for Ploiești (DN72); after 1 km, take a left. Open daily 8am-6pm. Admission charge. Allow about 30 mins.*

In 1501, the voivode **Radu the Great** (Radu cel Mare; 1495-1508) completed the modifications to this monastery which apparently holds a curse *(see inset p. 94)*. Only the **church*** (1501) now remains, but it is one of the most elegant in Romania. Its spatial clarity enhancesthe decor which is modest yet refined in its details: the towers and the west facade (notably the two panels framing the entrance door) contain highly complex sculptures of eastern

history

Nifon's curse

In a quest to reinforce his own prestige and that of his principality, the enlightened prince **Radu the Great** (1495-1508) surrounded himself with well-respected individuals. He gave the Metropolitan of Wallachia's seat to **Nifon**, former Patriarch of Constantinople, who had been driven out by the Turks. **Târgovişte** thus became a leading town in Orthodox Europe; but not for long. Nifon soon left the post due to internal scheming, first putting a curse on Radu and his country. Radu fell seriously ill and rebellious uprisings brought disorder to Wallachia. Radu pleaded with Nifon to return but he died just a few weeks before the voivode himself, and is buried in the monastery he founded. Radu's successor, **Neagoe Basarab**, spent a small fortune acquiring a part of Nifon's remains in an effort to expunge the curse and bring peace to the troubled country. These are buried near to Radu himself as if in posthumous reconciliation. In August 1517, Nifon's head and hand were buried alongside the rest of him and he was canonised at the same time. **Saint Nifon**, Patriarch of Constantinople and Metropolitan of Wallachia is still commemorated annually on 11 August. ●

inspiration. This ornamentation is Armenian in origin and was widespread throughout Byzantium before reaching Romania *via* Serbia.

These **oriental influences** spread over the following two centuries culminating at Curtea de Argeş (p. 97) and the Church of the Three Hierarchs in Iaşi (p. 255). The strip of stone which runs around the exterior walls (*brâu*) was later copied in Wallachian and Moldavian buildings. It separates two rows of blind arcades of the utmost purity which break up the proportions of the church. Six voivodes ↪ are buried inside including **Mihai Movila**, son of Simion Movila (p. 44), and **Mihai Viteazul** (inset p. 45), who's head lies under a tombstone, on the right in the pronaos.

♥ Doiceşti Church★

> *Biserica Doiceşti. 8 km N of Târgovişte by the DN 71. Open for church services: Sun. morning and main festival days. Free admission. Allow about 15 mins.*

Constantin Brâncoveanu (p. 102), who had a residence here, commis-

sioned the church in 1706 dedicating it to the birth of Mary. Standing in the middle of its cemetery, it has a simple beauty. The cabled columns in the porch have sculpted leaf bases and the windows are decorated with foliage (see the south facade), emphasised by painted floral motifs.

●●● **In the area**: towards Sinaia, beyond Moroeni, there is a road to the left leading to the **Zănoaga gorges**★★ (*cheile Zănoagei*). There is a fantastic view from the top just before the descent to Sinaia, with the rugged landscape of the **Bucegi Mountains** rising up on your left.

Sinaia★

> *62 km N of Târgovişte, 54 km N of Doiceşti by the DN 71. **Address book** p. 118.*

Surrounded by the forests and slopes of the **Bucegi Mountains**, this health resort owes its reputation to King Carol I who established one of his residences here in the 1870s. Notable families from Bucharest subsequently populated the slopes with glorious villas which today lend an air of romantic past grandeur. Apart from the castles, is the excellent network of **hiking trails** throughout the most spectacular massif of the Romanian Carpathians.

Sinaia Monastery*

> *Mănăstirea Sinaia* ☎ *31.49.17. Open daily 9am-6pm. Free admission, except the museum. Allow about 15 mins.*

The monastery (1690-1695) was named after Mount Sinaï where its founder, Mihai Cantacuzino, once spent some time during a pilgrimage to the Holy Land. Resplendent in its fir tree setting the church is of modest dimensions and constructed on a Latinate cross plan unique to Wallachia at the time. Do not miss the scultural details.

♥ Peleş Castle*

> *Castelul Peleş* ☎ *31.09.18. Open Wed.- Sun. 9am-3pm. Admission charge. Allow 1 hr.*

Built in two stages between 1875 and 1914 this castle was commissioned by Carol I as a holiday home for the royal family. After King Michael lost the throne in 1947, the castle became a museum exhibiting paintings, furniture, weaponry, tapestries, etc. Without quite reaching the exuberant style of Louis II of Bavaria's residences, Peleş provides a pot-pourri of styles dominated by the influence of German Neo-Renaissance with a touch of Italian Baroque. A medley of finely sculpted woodwork, stained glass, marquetry and carpets are found throughout the castle's 160 rooms. A superb park surrounds the castle.

♥ Pelisor Castle*

> *Castelul Pelisor. Joint entrance ticket with Peleş Castle (allow an extra hour).*

Built for the royal family in 1902, this castle is less grandiose than its neighbour, but houses a fine collection of decorative works of art. Queen Maria was a keen patron of young Romanian artists, expressing

The 19th century saw the building of some truly fantastic royal residences throughout Europe: Peleş Castle features highly on this list.

© Pierre Soissons

her own penchant for Art Nouveau, peppered with Byzantine and Celtic influences.

Casa George Enescu*

> *Casa George Enescu.* Str. Yehudi Menuhin ☎ 31.17.53. Open daily except Mon.-Tues. 9am-3pm. Admission charge.

In the greenery of the Campatu district lies the elegant Luminis villa where, in 1927, the famed composer, George Enescu, gave violin lessons to the young Yehudi Menuhin.

Bran country★★

> *From Sinaia, take the DN 1 towards Braşov. Before you get to Predeal, turn left on to the DN 73 A, towards Pâriul Rece and Râşnov.* **Address Book** p. 115.

Native Romanian communities have inhabited the highlands around Bran for centuries while the nearby plains were colonised by German immigrants. The splendour of the mountain landscape and the presence of the **Bran Castle** attract the crowds in summer, but there are many quiet spots just off the beaten track.

The striking Bran Castle will stay forever linked to the memory of Queen Maria.

© Pierre Soissons

Bran castle★★

> *Castelul Bran.* 51 km N-W of Sinaia by the DN 1, DN 73 A and the DN 73. On entering Râşnov, take the DN 73 left towards Bran. Open Tue.-Sun. 9am-5pm. Admission charge. Allow 1 hr.

Perched on a rock, the romantic profile of the most famous castle in Romania is surrounded by forests, villas and a happy crush of tourists. Built in the 13th century by the Teutonic Knights it was pledged to Braşov in 1377-1378 (p. 170). Holding a strategically important position, the castle overlooks the southern ridges of Bran which link Braşov to Târgovişte and Wallachia. At the time of the Austro-Hungarian Empire, Bran was a frontier post. Although it seemingly had nothing to do with Vlad Tepeş (see inset p. 43), over the past thirty years, the castle has become associated for commercial reasons with the myth of Dracula.

In 1920, long before talk of vampires, it became the second residence of Queen Maria of Romania who brought her own inimitable touch to the restoration of the castle; beyond the superb interior courtyard, you can find opulently furnished rooms evoking the world of medieval knights.

●●● **Possible itinerary:** from Bran, you can return to Braşov (25 km N-E) and travel through southern Transylvania (p. 145).

A spectacular journey through the Carpathians★★

> *From Bran, continue on the DN 73 (S).*

From Bran to Rucar (37 km S-W of Bran), the road slices across one of the most stunning stretches of landscape in Romania. Across the Carpathian mountains with the **Bucegi** and **Leaoto** ranges on the east side and the **Piatra Craiului** range to the west, you journey through deep valleys, along mountain ridges, and a landscape dotted with woods, fir trees, farms and shepherds' huts.

Its design and decor make the Curtea de Argeş Church one of the most unusual in the country.

●●● In the area: in Podu Dâmbo-viţei *(29 km S-W of Bran)*, a road on the right descends deep into the ♥ **Dâmbovicioara Gorges★★** *(cheile Dâmbovicioara)*. Just before you get to Câmpulung Muscel in Valea Mare-Pravăţ, turn right towards the **Nămăeşti Monastery★** with its church built into the rock face.

Câmpulung Muscel

> *21 km S-W of Rucăr by the DN 73.* **Address book** *p. 115.*

In the 14th century, this town was the first capital of the Wallachian voivodes ↪, at a time when **Basarab I** and his son **Nicolae Alexandru** were founding the Basarab dynasty which was to produce so many great Romanian princes. A handsome tower (1647) marks the entrance to the 13th-century **Negru Voda Monastery★**, rebuilt several times, notably by **Matei Basarab** in 1635, and later in the 19th century.

●●● In the area: take the DN 73 C towards Curtea de Argeş. In Dom-neşti, turn right. Continue for 10 km to ♥ **Corbi★**, where there is a **hermitage** built into the rock face.

Curtea de Argeş★★

> *61 km S-W of Câmpulung Muscel. 12 km after Câmpulung Muscel by the DN 73, turn right and take the DN 73 C.* **Address book** *p. 116.*

The history of this site is closely linked to the beginnings of the Wallachian state, who's capital was transferred here from Câmpulung Muscel. The **Princely Church** is one of the oldest surviving 14th-century buildings and is particularly inter-esting as a record of the main char-acteristics and evolution of Wal-lachian religious art.

♥ The Princely Church of Saint Nicholas★★

> *Biserica Domneasca Sfântu Nicolae. Open Tue.-Sun. 9am-6pm. Admission charge. Allow approx 40 mins. Elena Teodorescu gives a passionate and fascinat-ing guided tour.*

A collection of ruins, a surrounding wall, the entrance door, is all that remains of the very first residence of the Wallachian voivodes ↪. Apart, that is, from the **Church of Saint Nicholas**. It was the first in a long series of voivodal foundations, the

tradition

The legend of Master Manole

Prince **Neagoe Basarab** entrusted the construction of the church to a team of nine stonemasons led by the **Master Manole**. Every time they were on the point of finishing the church, it collapsed. They decided a human sacrifice would be the only way to get the project finished. The builders vowed together that the next person to arrive on the building site would be walled into the building alive. The fate fell to Manole's wife, who had turned up bringing food. When the magnificent building was finished, the prince fearing that Manole would take his building talent elsewhere, withdrew the ladders and scaffolding with him still on the roof. Refusing a slow death, the master builder fashioned some wings out of planks and attempted to fly down, but he crashed not far away. The legend follows that, on that spot, a spring gushed forth. ●

first time the prestige of a prince had been associated with the Church, hence strengthening his legitimacy within the country and beyond. A masterpiece of Romanian religious art, it is the oldest monument to survive intact in Wallachia. Destroyed in 1330 it was quickly rebuilt in the shape of a Greek cross ↪, a form in vogue in Constantinople at that time. Sober and bare, the exterior walls are covered in alternate bands of brick and shingle which emphasise the harmony of its proportions. The window frames were added in the 18th century.

The church, designed as the princes' crypt, consists of three sections in accordance with Orthodox ritual. The composition of the **naos** ↪ respects the Byzantine tradition of the "Greek inscribed cross" with four pendentives supporting the tower.

Of special note are the **wall paintings** inside. Drawing on the Byzantine art of the Paleologues, it was the first time such **richly thematic iconography** had used in Romania. Far more than simple decoration conductive of prayer and meditation, these paintings contain references to the liturgy and are populated by figures of saints. The aim of this profusion was to pro-

mote the strength and complexity of the church. And the prince was its guarantor.

The Monastery★★

> *Mănăstirea Curtea de Argeş*. Cross town to the north. A large park indicates the monastery. Open daily 8am-6pm. Admission charge. Allow about 30 mins.

One of the most curious **Episcopal churches★★** in Romania stands at the heart of this monastic complex. It was built between 1512 and 1517 by the voivode ↪ Neagoe Basarab. The pronaos, wider than the naos, has 12 columns supporting a tower. Another tower adorns the naos and, on the western section of the pronaos, there are two spiral turrets.

The walls inside are luxuriously decorated and draw heavily on eastern influences coming from much further afield than Byzantium. Ever since the creation of the Kingdom of Romania (1881), kings have been buried here in the pronaos alongside voivodes such as Neagoe Basarab and Radu de la Afumaţi. The remains of the unconventional King Carol II *(see inset p. 323)*, who died and was buried in Portugal in 1953, were moved to the crypt on 14 February 2003. ●

Monasteries of Oltenia★★

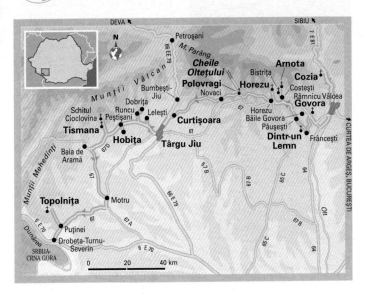

The many delights of Oltenia's complex winding landscape cannot be savoured in a rushed visit. Take it slowly and make lots of detours into the countryside where you will find monastery gardens, small churches decorated with naïve scenes, houses overgrown with vines,

agenda

Approx. 250 km from Curtea de Argeş to Drobeta Turnu Severin. You will need 3 days to visit all the monasteries. A weekend break from Bucharest is great way to visit the region. Monasteries have guest rooms which are often pretty basic but sometimes very pleasant (see inset p. 118). Further **accommodation** is available in Râmnicu Vâlcea (p. 118), Târgu Jiu (p. 119), Drobeta-Turnu-Severin (p. 116) and in Horezu (p. 117), with the potters.

Address book p. 115. ●

and heaving orchards. In any village, you will encounter the charm of the Oltenian peasant, inspiration to **Brâncuşi** (p. 327).

If religious art here does not have the same vigour as in Bucovina (p. 221), the churches and monasteries are evidence of the long-standing, solid presence of Romanian Christianity in the southern Carpathians. Different princes made their improvements, notably **Constantin Brâncoveanu** (p. 102), whose cultural ambitions are seen in **Horezu Monastery**.

Cozia★★

> **Mănăstirea Cozia**. 51 km W of Curtea de Argeş, 20 km N of Râmnicu Vâlcea. From Curtea de Argeş, get on Râmnicu Valcea and follow directions for Sibiu ☎ 75. 02.30. Open daily 8am-7pm. Admission charge. Allow about 30 mins.

The river Olt flows at the foot of this monastic complex in a spectacular setting. The church (1387-1391), was founded by the voivode **Mircea cel Batrân** and is dedicated to the Holy Trinity. Carefully and

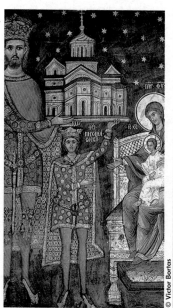

© Victor Bortas

The church founder and his son present a model of the church to Christ through the intermediary of the Virgin. Detail from Cozia Church.

masterfully constructed by Serbian builders, it was a model for the Romanian triconch ↪ form. Across the road is an elegant **Hospice Church★** (*bolniţă*).

The monasteries of Vâlcea★★

> *Pass through Râmnicu Vâlcea and take the DN 64. After 10 km, take a right towards Băile Govora (DN 67).*

Within just a few kilometres, several monasteries and hermitages can be found dotted around the orchards, gorges, forests and mountain slopes. Each one has a unique and always utterly peaceful atmosphere.

Govora Monastery★

> *Mănăstirea Govora. 84 km W of Curtea de Argeş, 33 km S of Cozia, 13 km S of Râmnicu Vâlcea. Open daily 8am-6pm. Admission charge. Lodging available (see inset p. 118).*

There has been a monastery on this site since the 14th century. In 1645, **Matei Basarab** (*p. 45*) rebuilt it to house the printing press he had been given by **Petru Movila,** the Metropolitan of Kiev. During **Brâncoveanu's** era (1701-1702) further changes were made, giving it its present elegance: look at the finely painted mouldings. Surrounded by flowers this site is a haven of calm; the even spacing of the windows and doorways create a peaceful play of light and shadow.

♥ Dintr-un Lemn Monastery★

> *Mănăstirea Dintr-un Lemn. 90 km S-W of Curtea de Argeş, 20 km S of Govora. Get back on the DN 64 for 3 km, take a right turn towards Frânceşti, once in this market town the monastery is on the right. Open daily 8am-6pm. Admission charge. Lodging available (see inset p. 118).*

The path which leads to this monastery is surrounded by trees, hedges and gardens, as are the two interior courtyards. According to legend, a hermit found an **icon of the Mother of God** in the hollow trunk of a old oak tree. A voice told him to build a church with the wood from this tree, hence the name *Dintr-un Lemn*, which means "from one wood". Built where the tree once stood, the little church (mid-16th century) is made from huge dovetailed beams. A wide porch entices you into the beautiful interior, where there is an **iconostasis** ↪ made of yew and several icons on wood. Generously sized (150x110 cm), the famous Mother of God icon hangs in this great church, founded by Matei Basarab (1640). It is said to have been made on Mount Athos or in Constantinople, following an ancient archetype.

●●● **In the area:** take the DN 67 (N), coming off at the exit for Costeşti, 6 km before Horezu. Follow the valley, passing by the late 15th-century **Bistriţa Monastery ★** (*Mănăstirea Bistriţa; open daily 8am-6pm; free admission; lodging available, see inset p. 118*).

♥ Arnota Monastery★★

> *Mănăstirea Arnota. 120 km W of Curtea de Argeş, 30 km N of Dintr-un Lemn Monastery. From Bistriţa Monastery, take the badly surfaced, winding road for 4 km. Open daily 8am-6pm. Admission charge.*

According to legend, **Matei Basarab** fled here to escape the Turks before acceding to the throne. Convinced that his life had been saved by this wild and impenetrable place, he built a monastery here on taking power. The church (1633) is at the centre of the complex and contains some well-preserved wall paintings (1644). Partly renovated by Brâncoveanu *(p. 102)*, it was substantially modified in the middle of the 19th century. Matei Basarab is buried here next to his father.

Horezu Monastery★★★

> *Mănăstirea Horezu. 123 km W of Curtea de Argeş, 86 km E of Târgu Jiu, 43 km W of Râmnicu Valcea, 56 km E of Târgu Jiu, 15 km S-W of Arnota Monastery. From Arnota, take the DN67. 1 km from Horezu, turn right. Open daily 8am-6pm. Admission charge. **Lodging available** (see inset p. 118).*

Rising up amid a luxurious green landscape are the white walls of Oltenia's largest monastic complex. This region is renowned for its many monastic establishments and the two Princely crypts, **Cozia** *(p. 99)* and **Arnota** *(see opposite)*, however **Constantin Brâncoveanu** *(p. 102)* wanted to add one final complex to his magnificent reign. He founded the Horezu Monastery, perhaps the most accomplished example of the building style associated with this great prince. Dozens of skilled artists were called upon to create the project (1688-1697): Horezu consequently became a hive of artistic activity which soon spread to nearby monasteries.

The site comprises no fewer than five churches, a hospice and numerous other buildings, making it the largest and most complex monastic settlement in Wallachia. An immense courtyard welcomes you, impeccably looked after by nuns. The two level arcaded living quarters lend a peaceful rhythm to the building, while large open spaces complement the whiteness of the walls.

© Victor Bortas

The Arnota Monastery overlooks the gorges of Bistriţa from wooded heights.

Brâncoveanu and the cultural awakening

The name Prince Constantin Brâncoveanu remains associated with an extraordinary cultural revival which took place in Wallachia at the end of the 17th century and in particular with the spectacular and original artistic movement which so marked the history of Romanian culture.

A westernised prince

Wallachia had two great rulers during the 17th and early 18th centuries: **Matei Basarab** (1632-1654) and **Constantin Brâncoveanu** (1688-1714). The latter was an enlightened humanist who modernised the role of prince and took inspiration from government systems in Western Europe that he and those around him knew well. Thanks to his diplomacy, he managed to maintain a fragile balance between the Ottoman, Austrian and Russian empires, allowing his country 26 years of relative peace.

Cultural ambition

The name Brâncoveanu is especially linked to the surge of cultural activity unprecedented in Wallachia: never before had the arts, teaching and printing known such rapid development. Following the example of the Italian, Germanic and French courts, the prince developed a taste for pomp and splendour which resulted admittedly in heavy taxes but also in a prestigious building programme: palaces sprung up all over the country while churches and monasteries were founded or restored. Eastern and western influences came together in his architecture: a synthesis of Byzantine tradition and the Italian Renaissance with a scattering of Baroque touches.

Balance and refinement

This movement particularly affected religious buildings: using a classic plan (triconch ↪), builders experimented with weight distribution resulting in more graceful forms. The Renaissance spirit is apparent in the spacious and well-defined interiors and the balanced structure of the facades. Venetian-style loggias and delicate porches began to appear scanned by cabled and fluted stone columns with delicately ornate capitals and pierced stonework balustrades. Lavish yet never excessive decoration adorned window and door frames.

A crucial period in the history of Romanian art

WhileHorezu Monastery (p. 101) is the archetype of this style, other fine examples include Govora (p. 100), Doicești (p. 94) and Mogoșoaia palace (p. 81). The style can also be found further afield, notably in two Bucharest churches: Colțea and Antim (p. 76). Also in Bucharest, both Crețulescu (1722; p. 70) and Stavropoleos (1724-1730; p. 73) Churches use this model which would inspire Wallachian art for a long time and was taken up again in the late 19th century by the Neo-Romanian movement. ●

Examples of Brâncoveanu style:
Govora (top);
detail of a balustrade, Horezu Monastery (centre left);
detail of doorway, Stavropoleos Church, Bucharest (centre right);
Horezu Monastery (bottom).

© Pierre Soissons

Domed ceiling in the porch of the main church in Horezu.

The church (1693) stands in the centre of the courtyard and is dedicated to the Emperor-Saints Elena and Constantine (feast-day 21 May). Sculpted wreaths frame the **entrance door** where the lintel carries the emblem of Wallachia, not unlike the two-headed eagle of Byzantine emperors. In the pronaos ↪, Brâncoveanu's tomb remains empty. On the 15 August 1714, he and his fours sons were decapitated in Istanbul as punishment for conspiring with Austria and Russia against the Sultan.

From Horezu to Brâncusi country★

> *Approx 155 km from Horezu to Topolnița.*

Inhabited since Paleolithic times, western Oltenia was strategically important for the Romans: having crossed the Danube by the Droberta bridge, the most direct route into present-day Translyvania, the heart of the Dacian kingdom and Apulium (Alba Iulia), was, at the time, through the Jiu valley. This area controls one of the best and most spectacular passes through the Carpathians, harbouring a multi-

tude of mountain refuges in nearby tributary valleys around the Parâng, Vâlcan and Mehedinți mountains.

♥ Polovragi Monastery★

> *Mănăstirea Polovragi. 23 km W of Horezu, 53 km E of Târgu Jiu. Head west from Horezu. In Polovragi, turn right for the gorges. Open daily 8am-6pm. Admission charge.* **Lodging available** *(see inset p. 118).*

Situated downstream from the **Olteț Gorges★** *(Cheile Oltețului)*, this monastery was founded in 1643 and completed in 1703 during the reign of Brâncoveanu *(p. 102)* who had the interior repainted by the painter Constantinos' assistants.

♥ Curtișoara : Gorj Museum of Architecture★★

> *Muzeul Arhitecturii Populare din Gorj. 46 km W of Polovragi, 10 km N of Târgu Jiu. Follow the road which follows the Carpathian range, then, on entering Bumbești Jiu, take a left towards Târgu Jiu. The museum is 10 km along the road ☎ 22. 38.90. Open daily except Mon. 8am-5pm. Admission charge. Allow about 1 hr 30.*

This fascinating open-air museum is laid out on 13 hectares of countryside. A collection of around twenty barns, wine stores, mills and houses surround an 18th-century Cornoiu manor house *(cula)* and a little church *(1820).* Furniture and other household objects (some great carpets) are on display.

Return by the DN 66 to Târgu Jiu.

Târgu Jiu★

> *290 km W of Bucharest, 5 km S of Curtișoara. Join the DN 66 (S) at Curtisoara.* **Address book** *p. 119.*

On the banks of the River Jiu, this former market town *(târg means "market")* and capital of the Gorj region, is associated with the sculptor **Constantin Brâncuși** *(p. 327),* who created one of his masterpieces here. From the north take bd Ecatarina Teodoroiu to the centre where you can leave your car parked. Cross bd Brâncuși and the large park bordered to the west by an alley *(aleea Parc)* parallel to the Jui. Calea Eroilor (Heroes' Street) starts from here.

● **The Brâncuşi trilogy****. The calea Eroilor, a massive 1,653 m in length, traverses the town from west to east and acts as a structural support to Brâncuşi's sculptures, erected between 1936 and 1938. The artist designed a route of perfect vistas through town, where distances and proportions were minutely calculated according to the rules of the golden section. Sadly, this axis has been built upon, breaking the perspective and sequencing desired by the artist. Nevertheless, one can still admire the purity of the work and its references to Romanian peasant symbolism. The circuit begins with the **Table of Silence** *(Masa Tăcerii)*, surrounded by 12 seats. Nearby is the **Gate of the Kiss** *(Poarta Sărutului)*.

One kilometre away, at the other end of the calea Eroilor, the **Endless Column** *(Coloana Infinitului)* stands on a raised mound, 29 m high: a succession of modules reminiscent of the sculpted pillars in peasant houses.

●●● **In the area**: from Târgu Jiu, take the DN 67 D west. Vegetable and fruit growing villages such as **Leleşti**, **Runcu** and **Dobriţa***, which inspired the ethnologist Jean Cuisenier, nestle in the valleys off to the right of the road. At Peştişani, turn left and, after 2 km, you will reach the village where Brâncuşi grew up.

Hobiţa*

> *26 km W of Târgu Jiu by the DN 67 D. From Târgu Jiu, take the DN 67 D.*

Constantin Brâncuşi *(p. 327)* was born in this village in 1876 and spent his first few years surrounded by ancestral objects and values. It was his grandfather who constructed the village church on the edge of the forest, and his father who, in 1862, built the family home. This house, the sculptor's birthplace, is one of the few things to have survived from a world that has all but disappeared. It is

---

history

The tragic fate of Tudor Vladimirescu

Greek traders from Odessa founded the **Hetairia** secret society in 1814, which organised the uprising of Balkan Christians, hoping to liberate Greece. Ypsilanti, son of a Wallachian Hospodor ↪ of Greek origin, relied on the support of Tsar Alexander. To initiate the rebellion in Wallachia he solicited the help of the Oltenian military chief **Tudor Vladimirescu**. Leading the **Pandours**, a troop of militiamen, he made the most of his position to bring to light the rights of an exasperated peasant population. Tudor entered Bucharest at the end of March 1821. A few days later a revolt broke out in Epirus which led to the independence of Greece in 1830. Ypsilanti left for Wallachia dressed in a Russian general's costume but without the support of the Tsar. When the coalition collapsed Tudor found himself hostage for a project in which he had only played an instrumental part. On 9 June 1821, Ypsilanti's men assassinated Tudor as Ottoman armies moved into Wallachia and the **Neamţ** mountains *(p. 266)* beginning a ferocious reprisal against the conspirators. An independence movement nevertheless got underway in the Balkans. Tudor Vladimirescu remains the symbol of the awakening of the Romanian people. ●

now a **museum★** (*Casa-muzeu Constantin Brâncuşi; open daily 9am-5pm; admission charge*). As well as the family's belongings, you can see just how much Brâncuşi 's art was influenced by the everyday aesthetics of Oltenian peasants: note the sculpted columns of the entrance gallery and the images of the large wooden gateway.

Return by the DN 67 D and head south. Take a right to Tismana after 10 km.

Tismana Monastery★★

> *Mănăstirea Tismana. 37 km W of Târgu Jiu, 29 km N-W of Hobiţa. From Hobiţa, get back on the DN 67 D and turn left. 9 km further on take a right turn. Open daily 8am-6pm. Admission charge.* **Lodging available** *(see inset p. 118).*

In an overgrown valley, one of the oldest monastic settlements in the southern Carpathians stands on a ledge 40 m above the River Tismana, a waterfall gushing nearby. According to legend, the original church was built by the monk **Nicodim** (*see inset below*) from yew wood in the late 14th century. Radu cel Mare rebuilt the site in the early 16th century and in 1651, **Matei Basarab** reinforced its fortifications. **Tudor Vladimirescu**

established his headquarters here in 1821 when he mobilised the Pandours (*see inset p. 105*). The complex was further modified in the mid-19th century. A community of some sixty monks are kept busy here weaving the famous traditional Oltenian carpets and painting icons on glass. The monastery's feast day, **Assumption** (*Adormirea Maicii Domnului*; 15th August), attracts worshipers from all over Oltenia.

●●● **In the area**: a forest road takes you 7 km north of Tismana to **Cioclovina Hermitage★** (*Schitul Cioclovina*) built in 18th century.

Topolniţa Monastery★

> *Mănăstirea Topolniţa. 105 km S-W of Târgu Jiu, 89 km S-W of the Tismana Monastery, 27 km N of Drobeta-Turnu-Severin. From Tismana, take the DN 67 D and get back on the DN 67 at Motru. Turn right to Puţinei. Open daily 8am-7pm. Free admission. Allow about 30 mins.*

Founded in the 16th century on the site of a church apparently built by disciples of Nicodim of Tismana, this monastery huddles in the wilderness of the Mehedinţi mountains.

Drobeta Turnu Severin on the banks of the Danube, is the next town. ●

Saint Nicodim and Tismana Monastery

Saint Nicodim is venerated throught the Orthodox world as one of the founding fathers of **Hesychastic** ↪ and Romanian monasticism, as is **Païsie**, three centuries later at **Neamţ Monastery** (*p. 263*). Of Greek or Macedo-Romanian origin, he lived with the monks on **Mount Athos** who, at the time, were involved in the great revival lead by Gregory Palamas of the Hesychastic tradition. He became a monk at Hilanda Monastery, quickly becoming its **higoumena** ↪. He left Athos to establish a community in northern Serbia (Kladovo, near Drobeta-Turnu-Severin), before crossing the Danube and founding **Vodiţa Monastery** in 1372. Between 1377 and 1386, he oversaw the building of **Tismana Monastery**. A great theologian and unequalled in his work for monasticism, Nicodim made Tismana the spiritual centre of Oltenia, from where Hesychasm spread throughout Romania. He died on 26 December 1406 which became, after his beatification, his feast day. ●

From Oltenia to the Banat★

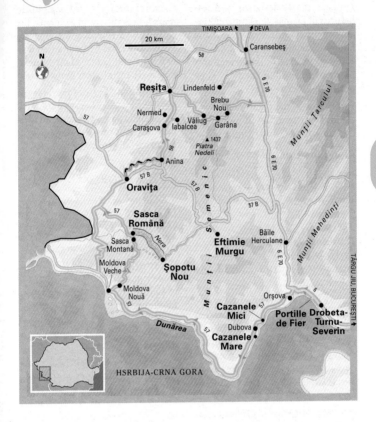

Oltenia ends on the banks of the Danube where Emperor Trajan built a bridge to consolidate his conquest of the Dacian kingdom. From Drobeta-Turnu-Severin, once a Roman camp, the **Danube** cuts a deep passage over nearly 150 km between Romania and Serbia. It is a **spectacular drive** alongside this treacherous stretch of river. Upstream, you emerge into the Banat, *via* an overgrown road. The Banat offers far more than fertile land and the city of **Timişoara**: there is, in fact, a great diversity to be found between the Danube river and the great hiking terrain in the **Semenic mountains**. German, Serbian, Czech and Croatian communities live side by side, reminding us that this is a **multi-cultural land**.

agenda

Approx. 400 km from Drobeta - Turnu-Severin to Timişoara, along the Danube taking in the Nera Gorges and the Semenic Mountains. Allow 2 or 3 days. Good roads except along the river and the Nera Gorges.
Accommodation at Drobeta-Turnu-Severin, Dubova, Sasca Montană, Garâna, Văliug.

Address book p. 115. ●

Drobeta-Turnu-Severin★

> 343 km E of Bucharest, 84 km S-W of Târgu Jiu. **Address book** p. 116.

To facilitate the passage of Roman troops, a bridge over the Danube was built between 103 AD and 105 AD at Drobeta. It was designed by **Apollodorus of Damas**, the Emperor Trajan's architect and designer of the famous Trajan Column in Rome. At 1,200 m in length, the bridge was made of a wooden roadway supported by 20 stone piers.

Part of one of the pillars is still visible in the eastern part of town, near the ruins of the Roman camp.

Along the Danube**

> *Orşova: 25 km W of Drobeta-Turnu-Severin. Approx. 150 km from Drobeta-Turnu-Severin to Moldova Veche. From Drobeta-Turnu-Severin, take the DN 57 (W).*

The road follows the Danube, which has hollowed out a giant valley separating the Carpathians from the Balkan mountains.

Just 10 km from Drobeta-Turnu-Severin is the massive **Iron Gates dam** (*Portille de Fier*), built between 1964 and 1972, which engulfed, amongst other places, the river island **Ada Kaleh**, an enclave of Turkish civilisation between Romania and Serbia.

In nearby **Orşova** and **Dubova**, you can take a boat tour of the river (***address book** p. 116 et 117*). The gorge becomes very narrow between **Cazanele Mici**★ and **Cazanele Mare**★. In Serbia, as in Romania, the chalk hills surrounding the river are uncultivated and harbour a rich natural flora and fauna. Many birds of prey make their homes in the cliffs.

In **Moldova Veche**, take a right towards Moldova Nouă and continue for 28 km to **Sasca Montană**, an ideal base for exploring the Nera Gorges which are only accessible on foot.

♥ Hiking in the Nera Gorges**

> *Sasca Montană: 166 km W of Orşova, 191 km N-W of Drobeta-Turnu-Severin. 22 km walk. Info available in the Sasca Montană lodging houses. Accommodation available in Orşova and Sasca Montană.*

If you stay in Sasca Montană, a guide can drive you (*approx. 20 km of bad road*) to **Şopotu Nou**, where the gorges begin.

From here, a path accompanies the River Nera right to **Sasca Română**. At very narrow points, the path has been cut into the rock 15 m above the river. Six tunnels are in use as well as several wooden suspension bridges. This route offers some incredibly spectacular walking and, although it is long, it can be completed in a day. Two days is perhaps

geography

The Danube

The River Danube begins in Donaueschingen, in the Black Forest (Germany). Thousands of years old and 2,860 km in length, it is the second longest river in Europe, after the Volga.

Known as the **Ister** in Antiquity, it unites Western and Eastern Europe, flowing successively through Germany, Austria, Slovakia, Hungary, Croatia, Serbia, Romania, Bulgaria and the Ukraine.

Two fifths (1,075 km) of the river is in Romania. It is fed by waters from 17 countries (containing over 80 million inhabitants) who do not all share the same environmental considerations. Today, the river is navigable between Regensburg in Bavaria and the Black Sea, and is connected by the Rhine-Main-Danube canal to the whole river network of Western Europe. •

In the 1970s, the fashion for ceramic decoration was adopted to enliven the facades of Swabian houses in the Banat.

© Pierre Soissons

more reasonable but you will need to carry food and a tent (there are bivouac sites).

●●● **Beware**: in stormy weather the gorges can become dangerous and the path is inaccessible during the snowy season. The best time to go is in spring or autumn when the horned adders are hibernating.

You emerge from the gorge at the Sasca Română suspension bridge, 4 km from Sasca Montană.

The Oravița railway*

> *Oravița: 217 km N-W of Drobeta-Turnu-Severin, 26 km N of Sasca Montană. From the bridge, head north (right) on the DN57.*

The **oldest theatre in Romania**, built during the Habsburg Empire (1817), is found in the industrial town of Oravița. This marvellous building now houses the **Museum of Theatre History** (*Muzeul de Istorie a Teatrului; str. Eminescu, 8; open daily except Mon. 10am-5pm; admission charge*).

One of the most beautiful stretches of **railway line** in Romania meanders between Oravița and Anina. Three trains a day make the 33 km journey in just over 2 hours! Sometimes steam trains use the tracks too.

You can also get to Anina on the DN57B then the DN58. This route continues northwards, passing through a region populated with traditional communities of Croatians (Carașova, Iabalcea, Nemed). Once in **Reșița**, a mining and industrial town, traverse it to the southwest to start your ascent into the Semenic Mountains.

40,000 settlers from Lorraine in the Banat

The Habsburgs officially appropriated the Banat ceded by the Ottomans at the signing of the **Passarowitz Treaty** in 1718. The **Count of Mercy**, originally from Lorraine, was sent from Vienna to get this ravaged land back onto its feet. To repopulate the Banat, the Count encouraged German settlers into the region along with Serbians and Romanians. With the promise of fertile land and other privileges, thousands of peasants and craftsmen flooded in from Swabia (hence the German name *Schwaben*, and *Şvabi* in Romanian, which was applied to the entire population), Wurtemburg, **Lorraine**, **Alsace** and Northern Italy.

From 1764, **Emperor Franz-Joseph**, the last Duke of Lorraine, incited a new wave of settlers to take up home in the Banat. Amongst them were some 3,500 families (nearly half the total) from Alsace or Lorraine. Little by little these migrants from Lorraine, the majority of German origin, became indistinguishable from the rest of the Swabian in the Banat.

Today, a few French surnames survive, bearing witness to this human migration which rebounded after the Second World War, when tens of thousands of Swabians fled to the West. Many settled in France, mainly back in Alsace, but they also repopulated abandoned villages in Provence. ●

The Semenic Mountains★★

> *Munţii Semenic. Garâna: 276 km N-W of Drobeta-Turnu-Severin, 85 km N-E of Sasca Montană, 59 km N-E of Oraviţa, 29 km E of Reşiţa. From Oraviţa, take the DN 57 B then the DN 58 towards Reşiţa, then turn right.*

This mountain range, emblematic of the Banat, has a gentle relief (Piatra Nedeli, 1,437 m) covered with forests, meadows and a few dammed lakes. There is an excellent network of tracks and footpaths (some marked) and explore the ancient German villages of **Garâna** and **Văliug**, Brebu Nou and Lindenfeld.

The only main road in the Semenic Mountains drops down to the **Caransebeş hollow** where it joins the DN 6. Turn left for **Timişoara** *(approx. 123 km).* ●

Timişoara★

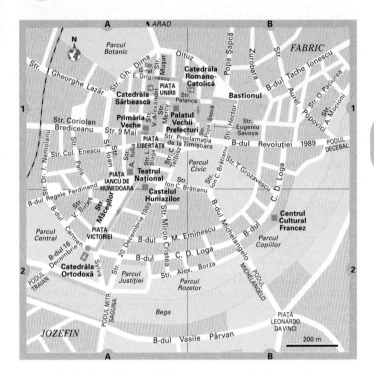

I t is no surprise this town, the most Westernised in Romania, has been dubbed "little Vienna". Pastel-coloured Baroque and Neo-classical buildings abound in the town centre, especially in piaţa Unirii. Its name is irrevocably linked to the events of December 1989: the Timişoara uprising precipitated the downfall of the Ceauşescu regime. Sited at the cross roads of the Balkans and Central Europe, this cosmopolitan university town of 333,000 inhabitants has a dynamism envied by the rest of Romania. There are plenty of quiet spots in the many parks, but to get a feel for Timişoara, you should wander around the Jozefin (established in the 18th century; S-W of the centre) and Fabric (embellished at the end of the 19th century; E of the centre) districts.

Piaţa Victoriei

> **A2** *Between bd 16 Decembrie, bd Carmen Sylva and str. Alba Iulia.*

Near the Bega canal and parks, this square, 300 m long was named Victory Square after the December 1989 revolution. Large town houses dating from the 1900s line the square, which also contains lots of shops and services. On the west side there is a row of grandiose buildings mostly designed by the Hungarian architect **Laszlo Szekely**.

● **The Orthodox Metropolitan Cathedral *(Catedrăla Ortodoxă)*.** At the southern extremity of the square, this monumental cathedral, built between 1936 and 1947, displays a mix of stylistic influences from Byzantium and Northern Moldavia. Built on marshy ground, tons of concrete and over a thousand pil-

getting around

● **Position**. 560 km W of Bucharest, approx 530 km E of Vienna, 35 km from the Serbian border and 150 km N-E of Belgrade. Less than 100 km S-E of the Hungarian border and about 300 km from Budapest.

● **Getting your bearings**. The town centre, surrounded by ancient ramparts, is comprised of mainly 18th- and 19th-century architecture. The centre of the city, its streets and three main squares, **piaţa Victoriei A2**, **piaţa Libertăţii A1** and **piaţa Unirii A1**, are laid out on a grid pattern. This is surrounded by a ring road with artery roads leading off it the former suburbs (Fabric, Elisabetin, Jozefin, Mehala). South of the town centre huge parks surround the Bega canal.

● **Programme**. You will need at least half a day to explore the city centre. With good bars, restaurants and night clubs, Timişoara can guarantee a good night out.

Address book p. 119. ●

lars were needed to produce stable foundations.

There is a **museum** in the basement (*Colecţia Muzeală a Mitropoliei Ortodoxe*; str. 30 Decembrie, 9 ☎ 19. 09.60; *open daily except Mon. 9am-5pm; admission charge*) which exhibits iconostases ↪, and precious icons on wood and glass from the 16th to the 19th centuries.

● **National Theatre (Teatrul Naţional)**. Opposite the cathedral, this vast building was completed in 1875 by Viennese architects Hellmer and Fellner (who also designed the Oradea Theatre; p. 124). The present edifice, twice destroyed by fire (1880 and 1920), owes its current look to the architect Duiliu Marcu who added the Neo-Byzantine elements.

Piaţa Iancu de Hunedoara

> **A2** *North of piaţa Victoriei.*

Hunyadi Castle (Castelul Huni-azilor), was erected in this square by Charles Robert of Anjou at the beginning of the 14th century. It was later modified by Iancu de Hunedoara (*see inset p. 137*) in the 15th century and then destroyed

several times over the following centuries. Today's facade dates from the last reconstruction in 1856. In front of the castle, a sign in the form of a street lamp tells you that Timişoara was the first town in Europe to have electric street lighting (1884).

Piaţa Libertăţii

> **A1** *North of the piaţa Victoriei, take str. Alba Iulia.*

The most remarkable building is without a doubt the **former Town Hall (Primăria Veche)**, constructed between 1731 and 1734 and now used as the university's music faculty. Pietro Del Bonzo's design is Baroque in essence, toned down by latter, more classical additions. The pediment displays the town's insignia and an Arabic inscription recalling the Turkish baths on top of which the building was built.

●●● **Towards piaţa Unirii**: have a look at the **Hotel Trompette** (1747) on the corner of Eugeniu de Savoya and Augustin Pacha, and at **Emmer Palace (Palatul Emmer)** built by Laszlo Szekely around 1900, with its splendid stone ornementation and Secession wrought ironwork.

Piaţa Unirii★★

> **A1** *From piaţa Libertăţii, take str. V. Alexandri, then str. Eugeniu de Savoya to the right, then turn left.*

One of the most beautiful squares in Romania. In the 18th century, this was the commercial centre and assembly point for military processions and religious ceremonies. Come here today simply to appreciate the splendid architecture and relax.

● **The north side of the square**. The **Nicolas Lenau College**, built in 1761 but later modified, houses the earliest theatre in Timişoara. Liszt was a pupil here. Attached to it is a series of typically 18th-century two-storey buildings which add further colour to the square.

● **The west side**. Extravagant decoration, typical of the early years of the 20th century, singles out the Serbian curacy with its fascinating **collection of religious works★★** *(Colecţia Muzeală a Vicariatului Ortodox Sârb; piaţa Unirii, 4 ☎ 11. 34.26; open daily 7.30am-3.30pm; admission charge)*. These include imperial doors, portraits and superb 18th-century icons by the Serbian painter **Nedelcu Popovici**. Behind an ornamental gateway, lies the **Serbian Cathedral★** *(Catedrăla Sârbească; open daily 7am-6pm; free admission)*. Baroque in style, it was built between 1745 and 1748 by the Serbian community on the site of an earlier wooden church. In 1865, it became the official Serbian Orthodox Cathedral, proof of the importance of this community in the Banat.

● **The south side**. The massive 18th-century **Baroque Palace★** *(Palatul Vechii Prefecturi)* was the governor's residence at the time of the Empire. It has since housed various civil and military offices and is known as the "old police station". Next door, the Secession style *(see inset p. 125)* **Brück Palace** *(Palatul Brück)* brings a touch of fantasy to the square: it is one of Laszlo Szekely most innovative works. In the south-west corner of the square, is the equally original work (1906-1908) of architects **Komor and Jakab**, better known for their creations in Oradea *(p. 124)* and Târgu Mureş *(p. 185)*. Note the glazed ceramic details inspired by Hungarian folklore.

● **The east side**. The **Romano-Catholic Cathedral★** *(Catedrăla-Romano Catolică; open daily 8am-4pm; free admission)*, built between 1736 and 1773, is a Baroque inspira-

---

The mark of the Count of Mercy

One of the earliest urban planning projects of Banat's first Austrian governor was to remodel Timişoara. Work began on the Vauban-style fortress in 1723. In the centre of town, old wooden houses were demolished to make way for brick constructions. An ordered street plan was put in place and housing facades were aligned. New areas of town grew up in the E and S-E (Fabric and Jozefin).

The Count of Mercy is a name which remains associated with the layout of the city. For a long time there was even a village named after him, **Mercydorf** ("Mercy village" in German), situated approx. 20 km N of the town, where immigrants from Germany and Lorraine settled at the end of the 18th century. Today, it is known as **Carani** but there is still a street called Frankengasse ("French Street"). ●

© Pierre Soissons

Baroque perspectives in piaţa Unirii, in Timişoara.

tion designed by Viennese architect **J.E. Fischer von Erlach**. Framed by its two towers, the facade is particularly elegan.

● **In the centre**. The **Column of the Holy Trinity** is an emblem of the town. It was erected in 1740 by survivors of the 1739 Banat plague epidemic. The square's fountain is supposed to have curative qualities and has a constant stream of human traffic. Exit the square to the east.

The bastion

> **B1** *Bastionul. Found between piaţa I.C. Brâtianu, str. Hector and str. Popa Şapcă.*

The 14th-century citadel and two quadrilateral city walls were built to replace earth fortifications from the previous century. In 1716, these ramparts were demolished following the Austrian conquest of the town, and replaced by a Vauban style city wall, in the form of a nine point star. The bastion (1730-1733), a former food store, is one of the rare remaining sections of these ramparts. Spread over several streets, his massive brick construction is nicknamed the "Mary Therese" after the Empress Mary Therese, the mother of Joseph II.

On str. Popa Şapcă, the **ethnographic section of Banat Museum** (*Muzeul Banatului, Secţia de Etnografie; str. Popa Şapcă, 42* ☎ *19. 13.39; open daily except Mon. 10am-5pm; admission charge*) resides in a section of the bastion. The multicultural heritage of the Banat is displayed through textiles and richly coloured furniture. The rest of the bastion contains bars, restaurants and a good library.

●●● North of Timişoara (*57 km on the DN69*) the town of **Arad**, close to the border with Hungary, is one of the country's main entrance and exit points. Situated on the banks of the river Mureş, which surrounds the 18th-century citadel, Arad is worth a short break before you head off for the city of Oradea and the Apuseni Mountains. *(p. 122).* ●

Address book

The Eftimie Murgu watermills are found some 30 km along the Nera gorges.

© Pierre Soissons

Bran

> *Dialling code ☎ 0268. Visit p. 96.*

Accommodation

▲▲ **Pensiunea Dan**, str. Dr Iancu Gontea, Şimon, 344 ☎ 23.67.04 and 0744.79.16.88 (mobile). *3 private guest rooms*. Take the DN 73 towards Câmpulung and, at about 1.5 km from the centre of Bran, turn left just after the bridge over the river Moieciu. Continue for a further 1 km. This peaceful modest home is on the left (signed). *Meals provided on request.*

▲▲ **Pensiunea Laura**, str. Dr Iancu Gontea, Şimon, 48 ☎ 23.66.84 or 0722.70.70.16 (mobile). *8 private guest rooms*. Directions as above. The house is on the right. An excellent guest house in the heart of the mountains. *Meals provided.*

Buzău

> *Dialling code ☎ 0238. See p. 88.*

Accommodation

▲▲ **Hotel Crâng,** str. Spiru Haret, 6 ☎ 71.05.40, fax 71.29.65. *47 rooms.* Situated between Bucharest and Moldavia, this ordinary hotel makes for a good stopping off point when travelling through the Buzeau mountains. Reasonably priced. *Restaurant.*

Câmpulung Muscel

> *Dialling code ☎ 0248. See p. 97.*

Accommodation

▲ **Hotel Muscelul**, str. Negru Voda, 117 ☎ 21.92.49. *87 rooms.* Looking a bit dated now this hotel is nonetheless incredibly good value and is in pretty decent order. A good stop over point. *Restaurant.*

Colţi

> Dialling code ☎ 0238. See p. 90.

Accommodation

▲ **Casa Nica**, n° 64 ☎ 52.25.55. *5 basic rooms*. Owner Dumitru Nica is a historian, gardener and beekeeper. His wife is also responsable for the guided visits around the Amber museum.

Curtea de Argeş

> Dialling code ☎ 0248. See p. 97.

Accommodation

▲▲▲ **Hotel Posada**, bd Basarabilor, 27-29 ☎ 72.14.51, fax 72.11.09, < www.posada.pa.ro >. *132 beds*. A good quality hotel in the centre of a little rural town with very friendly staff. Situated half-way between the Princely Church of Saint-Nicholas and the monastery. *Restaurant*.

Drobeta-Turnu-Severin

> Dialling code ☎ 0252. See p. 107.

Accommodation

▲▲ **Hotel Traian**, bd Tudor Vladimirescu, 74 ☎ 31.17.60, fax 31.02.90. *170 rooms*. A huge and reasonably priced hotel that makes a good stop-over point. *Restaurant*.

Dubova

> Dialling code ☎ 0252. See p. 108.

Accommodation

▲▲ **Pensiunea Drina Costescu**, n° 58 ☎ 36.80.27. *3 private guest rooms and meals provided*. The Costescu family has several small boats and can take you for day trips on the Danube River. There are other host families in this village which is ideally situated along the most spectacular part of the Danube.

Garâna (Wolfsberg)

> Dialling ☎ 0255. See p. 110.

▲▲ **Pensiunea Agroturistică Briza Muntelui**, n° 36 ☎ 22.51.82. *9 basic rooms* with a wooden décor.

▲▲ **Pensiunea Agroturistică Peczi ♥**, n° 33 ☎ 22.75.37. 6 attic rooms, with a view of the mountains. Restaurant and terrace.

▲▲ **Pensiunea Gotschna**, n° 177 ☎ 22.51.74. *6 rooms*.

▲▲ **Pensiunea La Rascruce**, n° 195 ☎ 22.67.88. *14 rooms*. A comfortable hostel, renowned for its food.

Festivals

Garâna jazz festival. In August, this village deep in the mountains becomes a hive of activity and conviviality.

Gura Teghii

> Dialling code ☎ 0238. See p. 88.

Accommodation

▲▲ **Hotel Varlaam** ☎ 54.29.13. *14 rooms with en suite lavatory*. On the edge of the village this farm is surrounded by enchanting views. *Restaurant*.

Horezu

> Dialling code ☎ 0250. See p. 101.

Accommodation

▲▲ **Casa Mocanu Sorin**, sat. Ursani, str. Principala, 3 ☎ 86.03.35. *2 rooms* in a pleasant hamlet on the outskirts of Horezu. *Meals provided*.

▲▲ **Pension Ceramica Palosi ♥**, str. Tudor Vladimirescu, 15 ☎ 86.16.34. *1 room*. A convivial reception, with a potting family who will take you to visit their workshop. *Meals provided*.

▲▲ **Pensiunea Constantin Frigura**, str. Olari, 15 ☎ 86.01.13, < www.pensiunefrigura.go.ro >. *4 rooms*. A welcoming home in a pottery hamlet. Meals provided.

craftwork

Horezu pottery

Horezu is the pottery capital of Romania. Instead of wasting your time looking around the shops near the monastery, head for the hamlet of **Olari** (which means "potters") towards Urşani on the N-W border of Horezu. Here, a dozen workshops along the one and only street maintain the millenium-old tradition, only sometimes veering towards a more kitsch style. Most belong to old pottery families (Vicsoreanu, Iorga, Palosi, Popa, Bâscu, Mischiu) and are open to the public.

Designs taken from wooden sculptural detail are echoed on plates, jugs, and vases. Complex spirals, stars, circles and solar symbols are replayed. Plant (tree of life) and animal motifs such as the cockerel, symbol of Horezu, are also used. The iridescence found in some decoration is due to the manipulating of the colours, brushing from the centre of the plate outwards while it is still on the wheel. A typical palette includes browns, ochres and greens, and occasionally blue on a white or yellow background. Every year, on the first Sunday in June, potters from all over Romania gather in the town for the **annual pottery fair**. •

© Pierre Soissons

▲▲ **Pensiunea Fartat Ilie**, str. Pietii, 6 ☎ 86.08.62 and 0745.68.57.72 (mobile). *3 rooms*. A large, pleasant house. *Meals provided.*

▲ **Casa Hangiu Sorin**, str. Olari, 10 ☎ 86.03.47. *2 rooms*. In a pottery hamlet *(see inset above)*. *Meals provided.*

Festivals, shopping

Potters fair *(Târgul de Olarit)*: 1st Sunday in June.

Mânzăleşti

> Dialling code ☎ 0238. See p. 90.

Accommodation

▲▲ **Cabana Meledic** ☎ 54.86.48. *14 basic but decent rooms*. An exceptional setting deep in the countryside just a stone's throw from a lake

and nearby salt canyons. Friendly staff. *Meals.*

Moeciu de Jos

> Dialling code ☎ 0268. Map p. 92.

Accommodation

▲▲ **Pensiunea Camelia**, n° 436 ☎ 23.62.33 and 0745.03.94.58 (mobile). *7 rooms*. A farm with a fabulous orchard in a pretty valley. *Meals provided.*

Orşova

> Dialling code ☎ 0252. See p. 108.

▲ **Hotel Dierna**, str. 1 Decembrie 1918, 18 ☎ 36.18.75. *36 rooms*. Fairly basic but it is cheap and the staff is friendly.

Staying in a monastery

This is a recommended experience. Some do not take reservations, so you may have to try your luck on site. At the entrance, ask if it is possible to get lodging *(cazare)* and a meal *(masa)*. Conditions vary between monasteries but prices are always reasonable. You are expected to be reasonably quiet and wear appropriate clothing.

● **Bistriţa** ☎ (0250) 86.33.27. *Sixty beds* in rooms for 4 or 6. Meals on request.

● **Dintr-un Lemn** ♥ ☎ (0250) 76.52.24. *Nine twin rooms.* Comfortable. Booking is necessary. The monastery also has more modest rooms for 2 and 4 people. Meals on request.

● **Govora** ♥ ☎ (0250) 77.03.42. *Ten beds.* Booking is necessary.

● **Horezu** ☎ (0250) 86.00.71. *Ten double rooms, 3 rooms* with 4 beds.

● **Polovragi** ♥ ☎ (0250) 47.61.96. *Eight rooms.* An excellent place.

● **Tismana** ☎ (0250) 37.43.17. *Twenty rooms.* ●

Râmnicu Vâlcea

> *Dialling code* ☎ *0250. See p.100.*

Accommodation

▲▲ **Hotel Alutus,** str. General Praporgescu, 10 ☎ 73.66.01. *101 rooms,* Of average quality this hotel has most things you could need and is well-situated near Oltenian monasteries and the Bucharest-Sibiu motorway. *Restaurant.*

Sasca Montană

> *Dialling code* ☎ *0255. See p. 108*

Accommodation

▲▲ **Pensiunea Neraland**, n° 730 ☎ 0723.52.99.51. *8 rooms.* Your hosts will drop you off at hiking trails in the Nera gorges and will even lend you with a guidebook. *Meals provided.*

▲ **Pensiunea Dora.** *6 rooms.* No telephone, but if there are no vacancies they will find you accommodation in the village set deep in the Nera gorges. *Meals provided.*

Sinaia

> *Dialling code* ☎ *0244. See p. 94*

Accommodation

▲▲▲ **Hotel Caraiman,** bd Carol I, 4 ☎ 31.35.51, fax 31.06.25. *71 rooms.* An authentic belle-epoque style hotel. *Restaurant.*

▲▲▲ **Hotel Palace,** str. Octavian Goga, 8 ☎ 31.01.22, fax 31.48.55, < www.palace.ro >. *149 rooms.* Another example of early 20th-century hotel architecture, nostalgic for a past glory. *Restaurant.*

▲▲ **Casa Noastra,** bd Republicii, 9 ☎ 31.45.56. *4 rooms.* A convivial spot and affordable prices.

Sorești

> *Dialling code* ☎ *0238. See p. 88*

Accommodation

▲ **Casa Pauna** ♥ ☎ 51.05.34. *3 rooms.* From Buzău, head towards Suceava. Near the exit for Poşta Câlnău (opposite the *Neptun* inn), take a left towards Blăjani. After a few hundred metres and beyond the valley bottom, take a left towards Sorești. The house is found on the left near the centre of this village. A family of vine growers, involved in the revitalisation of the local viticulture. Look for the green door opposite a roadside shrine. Excellent food.

Starchiojd

> *Dialling code* ☎ *0244. Map p. 88.*

Accommodation

▲▲ **Familia Paraschiv**, str. Grui ☎ 42.01.54. *4 rooms.* Hosts Dorin and Maria Paraschiv, can tell you all about the Orthodox faith. *Meals provided.*

Târgoviște

> *Dialling code* ☎ *0245. See p. 92.*

Accommodation

▲▲ **Hotel Valahia**, bd Libertăţii, 7 ☎ 63.44.91. *108 rooms.* Very reasonable. *Restaurant.*

Târgu Jiu

> *Dialling code* ☎ *0253. See p. 104.*

Accommodation

▲▲ **Hotel Brâncuși**, str. Constantin Brâncuși, 10 ☎ 21.59.81. *40 rooms.* Close to the famous sculpture by Brâncuși. *Restaurant.*

Timișoara

> *Dialling code* ☎ *0269. Map p. 111.*

❶ **Centre of French Culture♥**, bd C. D. Loga, 46 **B2** ☎ 49.05.44, fax 49.05.43, < www.ccftimisoara.ro >. Tourist information on Timișoara and events in the surrounding area.

Getting there

● **By plane**. Daily flights to Bucharest (Tarom and Angel Airlines) and other large towns in Romania: Cluj, Sibiu, Bacău (Carpatair). Daily flights to Vienna (Austrian Airlines), Budapest (Malev), Germany and Italy (Carpatair); 2 flights per week. (Tarom) to Frankfort *(Mon. and Fri.).* **Timișoara international airport** (off the map), approx. 12 km N-E; info. ☎ 49.36.39. **Tarom agency**, bd Revoluţiei 1989, 3-5 **B1** ☎ 49.35.63, fax 49.01.50. *Open Mon.-Fri. 8am-7pm.* **Carpatair**, at the airport ☎ 20. 27.01, fax 49.31.80. **Austrian Airlines,** bd C. D. Loga, 44 **B2** ☎ 49.46. 00 or 49.03.20. **Malev** ☎ 49.31.94.

● **By train**. Daily links to Bucharest (long route), Budapest and Vienna, Cluj and Iași Station, str. Garii 2 **Off map by A2** *(S-W from centre).* **Info:** Informatii CFR ☎ 49.38.06. **Railways agency** *(Agenţia CFR)*, str. Macesilor, 3 **A2** ☎ 22.05.34 or 49.18.89. *Open Mon.-Fri. 7.30am-7.30pm.*

● **By bus**. Daily links with Bucharest, Arad, Cluj, Belgrade, Budepest, Western Europe. **Bus station** *(Autogara)*, bd Iuliu Maniu, 54 **Off map by A2** *(S-W from the town, towards the railway station)* ☎ 49.34.71.

Accommodation

▲▲▲▲ **Hotel Perla III,** str. Paltinis, 14 ☎ 49.78.58. *18 rooms.* S from Bega, this modern and pleasant hotel is in a complex with two other hotels. *Restaurant.*

▲▲▲ **Hotel Central,** str. Nicolaus Lenau, 6 **A2** ☎ 49.00.91. *87 rooms.* Despite the stiff appearances, this is a good hotel. Right in the centre.

▲▲ **Hotel Silva**, str. Victor Babes, 25 **A2** ☎ 20.14.06. *15 rooms.* 10 minutes by foot from the town centre. Excellently priced and a good reception. *Restaurant.*

▲ **Casa Universitarilor**, bd Mihai Eminescu, 11 **A2/B2** ☎ 49.45.07. *15 rooms.* This university building is not a student halls; it was built to cheaply house short-term students. Cheap and modest place to stay near the town centre.

Restaurants

♦♦♦ **Rustic**, bd Mihai Viteazu, 1 bis **Off map by A2** ☎20.10.58. Romanian fish specialities.

♦♦ **Cucina Moderna**, str. Socrate, 12B **B2** ☎20.24.05. The cuisine is rustic: *sarmalé* and baked potatoes are recommended. In a pleasant setting.

♦♦ **Maestro**, str. Janos Bolyai, 3 ☎29.38.61. International and Banat cuisine.

♦♦ **Mioritic**, str. Cluj, 27 **B2** ☎49.75.21. Do not be put of by the fantastically rustic decor (chairs covered in animal skin!). Large portions and reasonably priced.

♦♦ **Zanoni**, str. Ciprian Porumbescu, 29 **Off map by A2**. The best icecream parlour in town.

♦ **Club XXI**, piața Victoriei **A2**. An annex to the beer producer Timișoreana. In summer, it is a good place to have a cheap drink or meal on the terrace. In winter, do not miss the lively *manele* singers in the cellar room. Guaranteed atmosphere…

Timișoara: Map p. 111

♦ **Fabrica de bere Timisoreana 1718** ♥, piața Mitropolite Alexandru Sterca Sulutiu. This beer producer has a large solidly furnished dining room where you can try the house beer accompanied by hearty Romanian dishes.

♦ **Lussam-Celentano**, str. Nicu Filipescu **B1**, behind the police headquarters. You can get a snack here at any time of day. Try the garlic baguettes *(baghete cu usturoi)*. Open 24/24.

Cafés and clubs

Art Club ♥, str. Hector, 2 **B1** ☎29. 42.24. At the centre of the bastion area this is a lively place with a pleasant decor. Regular jazz and classical concerts, exhibitions and theatre.

Café d'Arc, str. Ialomita, 14.

Club 30, piața Victoriei, 7 **A2**. A nice jazz club, which hosts evenings of dance and dance competitions.

Eclipse Café, piața Unirii, 8 **A1**. An unbeatable view of piața Unirii.

Lemon Club, str. Alba Iulia, 1 **A1**. Piano recitals, guest DJs and Serbian evenings.

The Note, str. Mehadia **B2**. Regular programme of jazz, pop and classical concerts and other shows, etc.

Văliug *(Franzdorf)*

> *Dialling code* ☎ *0255. See p. 110.*

♦♦ **Pensiunea Hubertus** ♥, Iac Gozna ☎ 0721.42.64.20 (mobile). *6 rooms. Open June-Sept. and during the Christmas period.* Stay with Anca and Benno Loidl. In the heart of the Semenic mountains. A wooden house on the edge of lake Văliug. A relaxed dining room. ●

The Apuseni Mountains region

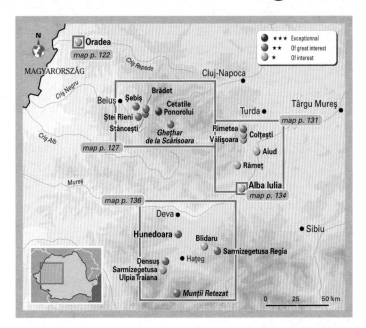

I solated in the mid-west of the country, on a map the **Apuseni Mountains** seem to be hiding themselves away between the mountains of Transylvania and Crişana, on the Hungarian border. This mountain range joins the Metaliferi Mountains (*Munti Metaliferi*), Trascău and Bihor and culminates at Curcubăta Mare peak (1,849 m).

The Apuseni captivate you with a succession of picturesque landscapes, some gentle such as the **Moţi** area, some with harsher terrain. The Romans exploited the gold mines in the **Arieş Valley** and established their capital at Apulum (Alba Iulia). Many of Romania's key historical events took place here, such as the peasants' revolt of 1784 and the assembly in **Alba Iulia** which consecrated Romania's unification in 1918. On the western side of the mountains, the lively town of **Oradea** is also historically important, being the junction point between the great western plains and the Carpathian Mountains.

© Pierre Soissons

Oradea★

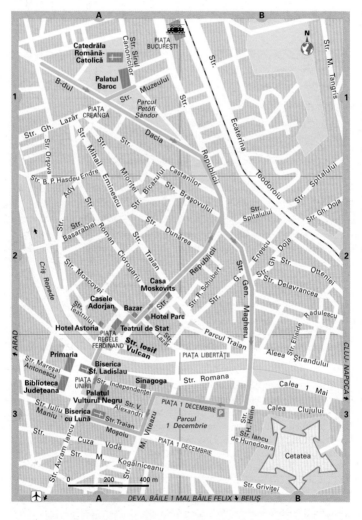

To the west, the Apuseni Mountains, flanked by the hills and valleys of **Crişana** (named after the rivers Criş Repede, Criş Negru and Criş Alb), meet the Hungarian plains. These massively different regions converge in one of the most beautiful towns in Eastern Europe. Occupying a geographically strategic position, **Oradea** has developed a distinct personality of its own. A few

dozen kilometres from the glow of the city lights, Romanian village communities still keep their ancient culture alive and worship in the intimacy of their tiny wooden churches. The Oradea region is also a great base for exploring the many marvels of the Apuseni Mountains.

With a population of about 225,000, Oradea, is the natural crossroads for the main routes into the heart of

Translyvania *(p. 179) via* Cluj-Napoca. After the fall of the Habsburg Empire, it languished in the extreme west of Romania. But the opening up of western boundaries and European perspectives since 1990 has brought back to the banks of the Crişul the creative energy that so marked the mast and culminated in the architectural fever of the 1900s *(see inset p. 125)*. Oradea has regained a sense of pride in its history and ethnic diversity. Both this and the capital's location means it will play an important part in the country's future membership of the European Union.

Baroque quarter

> **A1** *From the border, turn left off bd Dacia when you reach the park. Str. Muzeului.*

The park and the handsome Baroque quarter, which includes the Episcopal Palace and Catholic Church give a certain caché to the town.

● **The Roman-Catholic Church★** *(Catedrăla Română-Catolică). Open daily 8am-7pm. Free admission.* Built between 1752 and 1780, the cathedral is Romania's largest Baroque religious edifice.

● **The Baroque Palace★** *(Palatul Baroc). Next to the cathedral* ☎ *41.27.24. Open daily except Mon. 10am-3pm. Admission charge. Allow about 30 mins.* The construction of this Baroque Bishop's Palace began in 1762 and was completed in 1770. It is composed of three main two-storey buildings surrounding an inner courtyard. Columns with ionic capitals punctuate the facade.

It was the residence of Catholic bishops until 1971 and today houses the **Museum of the Crişana Region** *(Muzeul Ţării Crişurilor)* which contains an **ethnographical department★** with a good collection of ceramics, carved doorways, painted glass icons and furniture, including some chairs from the Beiuş region.

Piaţa Unirii★★

> **A3** *From the Petőfi Sándor park, go towards Cluj-Napoca (S). Just after the river, turn left towards Beiuş and Deva and continue straight on until you reach piaţa 1 Decembrie. Parking available. Three streets lead off 1 Decembrie to W, take str. Traian Moşoiu.*

● **The Church of the Moon★** *(Biserica cu Lună). Open daily 8am-7pm. Free admission.* This late-Baroque church was completed in 1790. In the church tower there is an interesting **mechanism**, installed in 1793: a sphere of 3 m diameter, half gold, half black, is maintained in perpetual motion, reproducing the phases of the moon and lending the church its name.

Architectural fever

Until the construction of flood-banks along the length of the Criş Repede river in the mid-19th century, Oradea was regularly devastated by **floods**. In 1836 part of the town was also completely destroyed by **fire**. The resulting urban landscape is thus relatively young, the most interesting parts dating from between the mid-19th century and the First World War. Oradea now offers a complete catalogue of the architectural styles prevalent in Central Europe at the time: the town is an eclectic mix of Baroque, Classical pomp and the Secessionism *(see opposite)*. ●

● ♥ **Black Eagle Palace**★★ *(Palatul Vulturul Negru)*. The palace, consisting of two buildings was built between 1907 and 1909 by architects Komor and Jakab. A glass-roofed shopping arcade in the form of a "Y" runs through the two main buildings of the palace connecting three streets; inside are shops, a hotel, cafés *(p.144)* and a cinema.

The building exemplifies the hesitancy of Transylvanian architects, caught between Viennese rigour and a thirst for freedom. A prime example can be seen on the facade of the left-hand building. Here the three registers, or levels, of the facade start off with geometric lines and shapes on the ground level, softening towards the middle level before becoming exaggeratedly curvaceous at the top. Contrasting with the sober patterns lower down, sinuous forms enlace the first floor balcony while a sea-shell cradles the second floor one. Windows and doorways are framed by motifs that paraphrase the embroidery from Apuseni's traditional costumes. The undulating gabled roof edge is lined with stone scrolls that open out in a floral rosette on the street end of the building.

● **The City Library**★ *(Biblioteca Judeţeana)*. Opposite the Church of the Moon. Piaţa Unirii, 3 ☎ 13.12.57. Open Mon. noon-7pm, Tue.-Fri. 8am-7pm, Sat. 9am-1pm. Free admission. In 1903, the local archi-tect **Kalman Rimanoczy Jr** built this operetta house for the Greek Catholic Bishop: his exuberant imagination juggles with intermingled Renaissance and Baroque references. During the Communist era, a library replaced the episcopacy.

● **The town hall**★ *(Primaria)*. On the right of the city library. **Kalman Rimanoczy Jr** also designed the robust, asymmetrical town hall building that was completed in 1903. It has a 50 m-tall clock tower.

● **The Church of Saint Ladislas** *(Biserica Sfântu Ladislau)*. Near the Criş Repede river, on piaţa Unirii. Open daily 8am-6pm. Free admission. Built in 1773 in a Baroque spirit, the church seems out of place, stuck between piaţa Unirii and the bridge over the Criş river.

King Ferdinand Square★★

> **A2** *Piaţa Regele Ferdinand. From piaţa Unirii, cross over to the north bank of the Criş Repede.*

The **State Theatre** *(Teatrul de Stat)* dominates the square. Founded in 1900, it is the work of Austrian architects Fellner and Helmer, who designed the Vienna Opera House. On the left, on the corner of the square, Ferencz Sztarill designed the extravagant building in 1902 which today contains the **Astoria Hotel**★ *(str. Teatrului, 1)*. Along one side of

Transylvanian architecture in 1900

In 1897, various nonconformist artists began to group themselves around **Gustav Klimt** (1862-1918), creating the Viennese Secession. This art movement favoured geometric ornamentation, pre-empting the stripped-down forms of modern architecture. As many of its Central European architects were Hungarian, this new wave of influence was soon brought back to Transylvania. But here it differed from the more rigourous Viennese version by merging with the sinuous forms of Magyar culture. As well as references to the mythology of their people, the architects were inspired by local folklore which, after centuries of co-habitation, was an indissociable mix of Romanian and Hungarian traditions. Around 1910, the architects began to seek a compromise: geometric forms began to frame their sensual flights of fancy, often in a somewhat hesitant fashion, creating buildings that were symptomatic of the contradictions inherent in the last days of the Empire. The most blatant examples of the Secession Movement in Transylvania can be found at **Târgu Mureș** (the Prefecture and the Palace of Culture; *p. 184*) and **Oradea** (the Vulturul Negru complex, Parc Hotel, and the Adorjan and the Moskovits Buildings). Other large cities in western Romania (Deva, Cluj, Satu Mare, Arad and Timișoara) also contain examples of this short-lived and little-known movement. ●

© Pierre Soissons

© Pierre Soissons

Black Eagle Palace.

the square, the ♥ **Adorjan buildings**★★ (*Casele Adorjan*, *str. Patriotilor, 4-6; closed to public*) were constructed between 1907 and 1908 by Jakab and Komor, architects of the Black Eagle Palace. Curves and counter-curves dance across the pediments while undulating festoons and floral decorations scan the facades.

Strada Republicii★

> **A2** *Begins behind the State Theatre (Teatrul de Stat).*

This central pedestrianised shopping street in Oradea has a luxurious, *fin de siècle* palatial appeal.

● **The bazaar**. *Str. Republicii, 2.* Completed in 1908, the first building down the street on the left once housed the bazaar. A spectacular porch opens onto a pedestrian passage that leads back to the Theatre square.

● **Parc Hotel★**. *Str. Republicii, 5. Guests only.* Opposite the bazaar, this hotel, though somewhet rundown, has managed to retain its 1900s wrought ironwork, stained glass and charm.

● **The Moskovits Building★** (*Casa Moskovits*). *Str. Republicii, 15. Closed to the public.* On the corner of the road which leads to Traian park, this building was designed by **Kalman Rimanoczy Jr**, architect of the City Library and the Town Hall. Note the fluid lines of the undulating gable and a wealth of other ornamentation.

On the banks of the Criş Repede

> **A3** *From Str. Republicii, head towards the Criş Repede, past the theatre (Teatrul de Stat) and take a left down str. Iosif Vulcan. A passageway takes you on to the south bank.*

The café terraces lining the banks of the Criş Repede afford some great views of the town's lavish urban landscape.

On the south bank the str. Independenţei leads you back to the piaţa Unirii, passing in front of the **synagogue** (*Sinagoga*), built in 1890. Oradea's large Jewish community is vividly evoked in Albert Londres' *Le Juif errant est arrivé* (*The Arrival of the Wandering Jew*).

You are at a stone's throw from the piaţa 1 Decembrie (parking available).

●●● **To see in the area: Băile 1 Mai** and **Băile Felix** (*8 and 10km S-E of Oradea on the DN76; from Oradea, take the Beiuş and Deva road from bd Cantemir*). Enjoy the thermal pools at these two health spas in the heart of the Apuseni countryside. ●

From Beiuş to the Arieş Valley★★

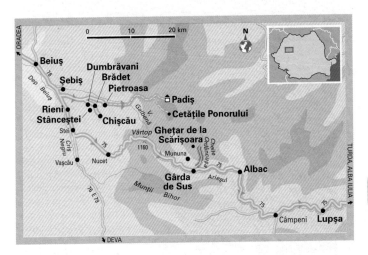

R ising above the fields of the Beiuş Valley are the steeples of countless wooden churches. Further into the hills, the wilderness of the Padiş plateau merges with the land of the Moţi, highlanders who live in little hamlets scattered around the Arieş hills.

Beiuş and its Valley★★

> *From Oradea, make for Beiuş and Deva (S-E) on the DN76.*

Dotted with peaceful villages, the Criş Negru Valley supports a richly fertile countryside. There is a local market at Beiuş on Thursdays.

Beiuş

> *63 km S-E of Oradea on the DN76.*

On the north bank of the Criş Negru, the wide avenues of this small town are lined with café terraces. There is a surprisingly good **History and Ethnographic Museum**★★ (*Muzeul Etnografic*; *piaţa S. Vulcan, 16* ☎ *32.22.47; open daily except Mon. 10am-3pm; admission charge*).

agenda

The **wooden churches** of the Beiuş Valley are rarely signposted: to find them you will need to get off the excellent main road (DN76) onto smaller, somewhat overgrown tracks that are nonetheless suitable for cars.

Accommodation is available in Gheţar, Gârda de Sus, Albac and Rimetea. It is highly advisable to stay for a few days in the Arieş Valley. You can spend a day **hiking** around Gârda de Sus (p. 130).

Address book p. 142. ●

The valley churches★★

> *From Beiuş, follow the DN76. About 7 km along the road take a small road on the left to Sebiş, then take the DN76 for 2 km and turn left towards Pietroasa.*

The grassy **Sebiş** cemetery surrounds a sublimely proportioned ♥ **wooden church**★★ which has the curious profile of a perched bird. The inside of

art

David Zugravul, painter-peasant

© Bernard Houliat

Perched above the village, the disturbing beauty of the 18th-century Brădet church is testament to the creative genius of local carpenters.

The painter David Zugravul was born in the middle of the 18th century in Curtea de Argeş, in Wallachia. There he became familiar with the post-Byzantine artistic tradition. Like others, he was a religious craftsman who, through his work, promoted Romanian culture in Transylvania and the surrounding area. At this time, the rise in standards of living meant that many churches were being built, repaired or redecorated, such as the churches in Maramureş *(p. 196)*, Crişana *(p. 127)* and the Salaj country *(p. 190)*. Icon workshops and travelling painters were therefore still very much in demand. He ventured as far as Crişana, where he was commissioned for frescoes and icons. It was here that he settled down to be a farmer. He used the same limited iconographic themes in all his church painting. He produced superb **iconostases** ↪, with the **Crucifixion** scene at the top and the procession of disciples surrounding the **Deisis** ↪ below.

On imperial doors, the **Annunciation** scene features, as seen in Zugravul's masterpieces at Brădet, Dumbrăveni and especially **Stânceşti** *(see below)* and Rieni *(see opposite)*. The side doors depict two Doctors of the Church: on the left Saint John Golden Mouth (Chrysostom) and on the right Saint Basil the Great. ●

this church, built in the 18th-century, still contains some of the magnificent decor painted by **David Zugravul** *(see above)*. To retrace the steps of this peasant artist, return to the DN 76 and take a left towards Pietroasa.

Amongst many other things, he painted the doors of the **iconostasis** ↪ in **Dumbrăvani Church**★ and the **Annunciation scene**★★ illuminating the **imperial doors** ↪ of the elegant **Stânceşti Church**★★ in the next village.

On the imperial doors of Stânceşti Church, the gentleness expressed on the faces of Mary and the archangel is particularly noticeable and is enhanced by their elongated bodies. When you reach **Brădet**, you must visit ♥ **the wooden church**★★, built in 1733. This majestic building combines perfect form and wonderfully intricate sculpture, as seen around **the entrance door**. Inside, the minimalist **Annunciation** scene on **the imperial doors** is also the work of David Zugravul.

Chişcău bear cave*

>*Peştera Urşilor. 87 km S-E of Oradea, 24 km S-E of Beiuş, 3 km S-E of Brădet. Open daily except Mon. 9am-5pm. Admission charge. Guided tour: 1 hr.*

In 1975, dozens of bear skeletons dating from the Palaeolithic period were found in caves near Chişcău.

●●● **In the area: Rieni** (*13 km S of Beiuş, 76 km S of Oradea on the DN76*) has a **wooden church**★★ dating from 1754 whose entrance door is edged with minutely carved decoration. The interior painting is also the work of David Zugravul.

Padiş plateau★★

> *117 km S-E of Oradea, 30 km N-E of Chişcău. From Chişcău, retrace your path until you reach Pietroasa. Take a right along the forest road for 22 km, which is in an appalling state (there is talk of repairing it). Address book p. 144.*

Isolated and without any permanent habitations, the Padiş plateau lies at the heart of a vast maze of chalky terrain, meadows and deep forests. The very bowels of the mountains are revealed here: canyons, massive sinkholes, and a multitude of caverns and pits (*see inset p. 130*).

The Ponor citadels★★★

> *Cetăţile Ponorului. S-W of the Padiş plateau.*

The most spectacular sight in this area is a naturally enclosed waterbasin drained by an underground stream which later comes to the surface in the **Galbena canyon**★ to the south-west. Three enormous sinkholes come together in the middle of this dense forest of fir trees: these are the Ponor citadels.

Exploring the citadels

From the forest road, following a path marked with blue signs, you can get down to the bottom of the first sinkhole. At the foot of a sheer cliff, 200 m high and crowned with fir trees, there is a 70 m tall archway.

© Cristian Ciubotarescu (Sfinx)

Through this colossal shadowy doorway are the Ponor citadels and a gushing torrent which disappears under a chaotic pile of rocks.

Alternatively, follow another path along the high ground, to admire the three sinkholes from a wooden walkway.

The Arieş Valley★★

> *From the Padiş plateau, take the DN76 then the DN75 to Gârda de Sus.*

The centre of the Apuseni is not ideal for motor vehicles, but some fantastic sights lie only an hour's walk away from the valley. At around 1,300 m above sea level and spread over dozens of kilometres you can find farms grouped in little hamlets or scattered between forests and prairies. The **Moţi** (pronounced " mots ") civilisation, an ancient Romanian mountain people, have made their natural habitat in this *crâng*, a sort of mountain grove. Their territory, the **Tara Moţilor** – Moţi country – stretches from the top of the Arieş valley, in the east of the Vârtop pass to just downstream from Câmpeni.

geography

The karstic Apuseni landscape

The sweet meadows and forests of the vast **Padiş plateau** hide some mysterious phenomena. Here and there, holes appear in the ground. Streams disappear in underground hollows without any apparent outlet (dolines). They then reappear suddenly above ground, sometimes in a canyon or at the bottom of a swallow-hole, in the form of massive springs. In the heart of the forest, huge pits open up and there are many caves where you can find fantastic stalagmites and stalactites, lakes and streams. This type of landscape, both above and below ground is known as "karstic" (after the Karst Mountains in Croatia, which contain good examples of the phenomenon). It only develops in limestone mountain ranges, as these can be worn away from the inside by streams rich in carbon dioxide which dissolves the calcium carbonate found in limestone. •

Hiking in the Moţi highlands★★

> *From Gârda de Sus (129 km S-E of Oradea, 97 km S-E of the Padiş plateau, 67 km S-E of Beiuş): 6 hrs easy walk on good paths; 400 m level change; feasible all year round.*

Once through the Vârtop pass, the mountains are immediately less austere and more luminous with hundreds of trails running off in all directions.

A hiking trail beginning in **Gârda de Sus** passes through the charming hamlet of **Mununa★** to the **Scărişoara cave★★** (*Gheţar de la Scărişoara*) where 60,000 m³ of ice has lain trapped for four thousand years. The trail follows the edge of the plateau, passing through frequently dense forest and into the wildly dramatic world of the **Ordâncuşa gorges★★**.

Lupşa

> *175 km S-E of Oradea, 113 km S-E of Beiuş, 62 km E of Gârda de Sus on the DN75.*

Follow the Arieş Valley via Câmpeni towards Turda. The river runs along a grassy valley dotted with charming villages and some beautiful views over the limestone massif.

Lupşa is well-known for its **monastery**, erected around a wooden church dating from 1429 and functioning again since 1992. A small **ethnographic museum** (*on the side of the road, in the centre of the village, open daily except Mon. 10am-5pm; admission charge*) contains thousands of traditional objects from the Moţi country: shackles made from silver birch bark and even equipment that would have been used for washing sand from the Arieş Valley, which contains gold. •

The eastern edge of the Apuseni Mountains★★

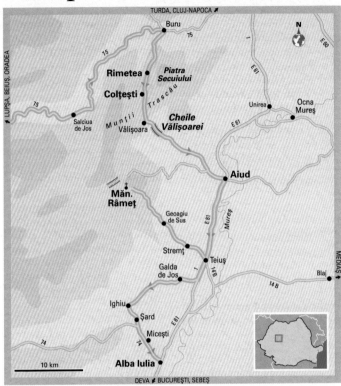

On the eastern slopes, the Apuseni mountains peter out beautifully, giving way to the lush hills of Transylvania.

Facing the rising sun, the long secondary range of the **Trascău Mountains** stretches forth with abrupt white, chalky cliffs and numerous gorges, such as **Râmeţ Gorges**, where a monastery has been established.

In the highlands, the scattered hamlets with their thathed roofs house exclusively Romanian communities.

Lower down in the foothills, the area becomes more typical of frontier country. Two historically and ethnically diverse cultures seem to live harmoniously side by side within two contrasting landscapes.

♥ Rimetea and around★★

> *From Lupşa, continue (E) to Buru on the DN 75 and take a road on the right which leads to Rimetea and Aiud.*

After the lush greenery of the banks of the Arieş river comes the beautiful **Rimetea Valley** (or Trascău hollow). Here the landscape is crowned with limestone peaks, with arid plateaux and sun-baked rocks which lend a Mediterranean feel.

The iron contained in the hills attracted first Roman, then Germanic settlers to the area in the 13th century. Hence the name Eisenburg ("Iron City") given to the valley's main village: Rimetea in Romanian and Torocko in Hungarian.

agenda

Journey through the Apuseni foothills. Take half a day to stroll around **Rimetea** *(see below)*, or stay the night and explore the surrounding valley. You can easily walk around the **Alba Iulia citadel** *(see opposite)* in half a day.

Accommodation is available in Rimetea, Aiud and there are basic hotels in Alba Iulia.

Address book p. 142. ●

♥ Rimetea★★

> *234 km S-E of Oradea, 59 km S of Lupşa on the DN 75, 57 km S of Cluj-Napoca on the DN 1 and the DN 75. Address book p. 144.*

White gables and green window frames line the wide streets of this village. On the far side of wooden gateways, long interior courtyards lie perpendicular to the road. The fascinating **Ethnographic Museum★** *(**Muzeul de Etnografie**; open daily except Mon. 10am-4pm; admission charge)* on the first floor of the town hall tells the story of the influence of the Magyar population who have inhabited the village since the 17th century.

Rimetea valley

> *From Rimetea head towards Aiud (S-E).*

From the main road you can see the **Piatra Secuiului★** mountain range rising on the left, which reaches an altitude of 1,128 m. Its sheer rock faces shelter the valley from the east wind and overlook a bucolic landscape full of sleepy villages.

From afar you can make out the intriguing profile of a ruined fortress. **Colţeşti Castle★** *(W from Colţeşti village, 1 hr easy walk on a cart road)* dates from at least the 13th century but was destroyed by Austrians in 1713.

A few kilometres on, the valley becomes narrower and the road passes through the **Vălişoara Gorges★** *(Cheile Vălişoarei)* before reaching the Apuseni foothills.

© Pierre Soissons

Thatched cottages are still a common sight throughout the eastern highlands of the Apuseni Mountains.

The Apuseni foothills★

> *From the Rimetea Valley, head to Aiud, and explore the roads around the DN 1 heading for Alba Iulia (S).*

The DN 1 Cluj-Napoca/Alba Iulia road which runs along the eastern edge of the Apuseni Mountains is uninteresting: you need to turn off this road to really get to know the Apuseni foothills.

Aiud★

> *257 km S-E of Oradea, 94 km S of Cluj-Napoca, 27 km N of Alba Iulia and 23 km S-E of Rimetea on the DN 1. **Address book** p. 142.*

You will easily find the central square of this Saxon town (Strassburg). Built between the 13th and 14th centuries on a Daco-Roman site within ramparts reinforced by eight towers, **Aiud citadel★** contains a **Gothic chapel★** built in 1333 and a church, used today by the Church, dating from the 15th-16th centuries with a huge bell-tower.

Râmeţ monastery★

> *Mănăstirea Râmeţ. 282 km S-E of Oradea, 25 km S-W of Aiud and 14 km N-W of Teiuş. From Aiud, head for Alba Iulia on the DN 1 to Teiuş, then turn right towards Stremţ.*

On the road leading to Stremţ, the valley narrows before coming up against a limestone cliff face cut through by the **Râmeţ Gorges★★**. An imposing monastic complex sits on the edge of this raging torrent. This isolated spot probably attracted hermits well before the construction of the modest **14th-century church★** which contains remains of the original frescoes inside. The monastery was demolished in 1762 by troops of the Austrian, General Bucow (p. 54). In 1982, a new church was built nearby. The **Monastery Museum** *(open by appointment, ask one of the nuns; admission charge)* has a collection of icons painted on glass and wood.

Alba Iulia★

> *284 km S-E of Oradea, 50 km S of Rimetea, 27 km S of Aiud and 16 km S of Teiuş on the DN 1. **Address book** p. 142.*

On the way back to **Teiuş**, keep on the DN 1 for 3 km before taking a right for **Galda de Jos,** then **Ighiu** and **Şard** where you will join the DN 74. The minor roads which lead to Alba Iulia give an insight into the bucolic lifestyle of these foothill villages given over to wine, maize, gardens and vegetable growing.

Alba Iulia occupies a site that has been inhabited since prehistoric times. During the Roman occupation it was the most important town in Dacia *(Apulum)*. From the 10th century, Alba Iulia belonged to Hungary *(see below)*. In 1541, it became the capital of the Principality of Transylvania, vassal of the Ottomans.

In 1600, **Michael the Brave** (Mihai Viteazul) arrived and made it the capital of the three Romanian countries when they were briefly united *(p. 45)*. In 1690, it became part of

The white town

When they invaded Transylvania in the 10th century, the Hungarians found a Romanian land held by voivode Gelu (or Gyula or Iulius). They named the main town Gyulafehervar, which means "the white town of Gyula". Latin clergymen and Romanians called it Alba Iulia; for Slavs, it was Belgrade and for Germans, Weissenburg. While they were ruling Transylvania, the Habsburgs tried to impose the name Alba Carolina (Karslburg) in homage to the emperor Charles VI. In 1918 it once again became Alba Iulia. ●

the Habsburg Empire and remained so for two centuries. On 1 December 1918, tens of thousands of Romanians gathered in Alba Iulia to witness the signing of the union between Transylvania and Romania (p. 50) conferring on the town a prestigious status in the history of the nation.

The citadel**

> *Cetate. Cross the town centre and take the str. Ardealului towards Sibiu to piaţa Naţiunii. Opposite the post office, take the first road to the right. Parking available close to the citadel. Tour by foot: allow about 1 hr.*

The citadel, designed by the Italian architect **Giovanni Visconti**, was erected between 1716 and 1735. It is a well-preserved example of a Vauban-style citadel with 12 km of brick ramparts forming a seven point star with seven bastion pierced by six monumental gates, three of which are decorated with Baroque sculpture.

● **B1 A triumphal entrance**. The entrance ramp leads up to the ornamental **first gate★** *(Poarta principala)*. Overhead, flanked by the Habsburg coat of arms are Venus and Mars.

Near the entrance ramp there is an **obelisk** *(Obeliscul)* commemorating the 1784 peasants' revolt *(see opposite)*. The ring leaders were imprisoned just a few feet away, above the citadel's **main entrance archway★** *(celula lui Horea)*. Through two openings in the roof above the central door, you can see the actual cell where they were kept. Enter the citadel through one of the three gateways, decorated with bas-reliefs and Atlantes .

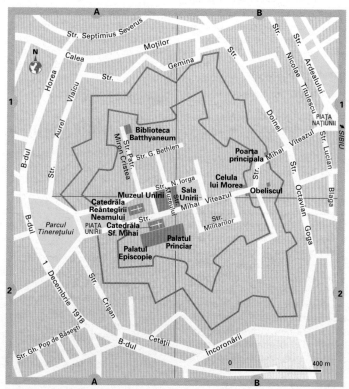

ALBA IULIA CITADEL

history

The Peasants' Revolt of 1784

In 1780, **Emperor Josef II** began a period of reforms, including one that intended to reduce the duties peasants were obliged to carry out for their nobles. Naturally, the nobles opposed these reforms.

Early in 1784, Josef II enticed peasants to join the army by rewarding them with an exemption of their feudal duties. However the nobles and local statesmen refused to stand by the promises made by the Emperor.

In October of this same year, the Apuseni peasants took up arms and within weeks, around 30,000 rebels had amassed. Concerned by the turn of events, authorities in Vienna sent in troops and the revolt was quashed by the beginning of December. The three ringleaders, **Horea** (Vasile Urs), **Cloşca** (Ion Oarga) and **Crişan** (Giurgiu Marcu) were given up by their own people, arrested and tortured. They were finally executed in February 1785 in Alba Iuliu, in the presence of representatives from the Romanian villages. Parts of their dismembered bodies were strung up throughout the entire province as an example. Serfdom was abolished later that same year. •

• **The heart of the citadel**. Beyond the esplanade on the left is the **Princely Palace** (*Palatul Princiar*) **A2/3**, built in the 16th century but subsequently modified several times. Opposite is **Unification Hall**★ (*Sala Unirii; open daily except Mon. 10am-5pm; admission charge*) **A1/2**, where, in 1918, representatives from every section of the Romanian population of Transylvania declared the unification of their province with the Kingdom of Romania (*see p.133*).

Next door, the **Museum of Unification**★ (*Muzeul Unirii* ☎ 81.33.00; *open daily except Mon. 10am-5pm; admission charge*) **AB1/2** contains a good collection of Roman relics (rooms 1 to 7), an interesting **ethnographic collection** and some beautiful icons on glass.

Outside the citadel on the north side, there is a disused Baroque church where, in 1794, the Catholic bishop Ignaz Batthyany founded one of the most famous libraries in Transylvania, the **Biblioteca Batthyaneum**★ (*open Mon.-Thur. 7am-3pm; free admission*), containing over 60,000 documents.

• **A2 The cathedrals**. The religious buildings are on the west side of the citadel and include the superb **St Michael's Cathedral**★★ (*Catedrăla Sf. Mihai; open daily 8am-7pm; free admission*). The original structure was Romanesque, built in the 13th century, then burnt down and demolished several times by Tatars, Turks and Saxons. Contrasting with the dimness of the interior, the Baroque altar is bathed in a soft light from the Gothic windows. **Iancu de Hunedoara's tomb** (*see inset p. 137*) is in the right-hand side aisle.

Built in the 16th century and restored in the 18th, the **Catholic Bishop's Palace** (*Palatul Episcopie*), is on the left as you leave the church.

The imposing **Orthodox Cathedral of National Unification** (*Catedrăla Reântegirii Neamului; open daily 8am-7pm, free admission*) was founded in 1922 for the coronation of King Ferdinand I and Queen Maria. A door with a tower above concludes your visit of the citadel and brings you out onto a large square. •

Dacian citadels★

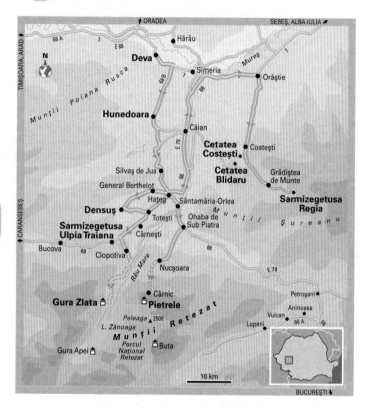

agenda

Whether you come from Alba Iulia, the Apuseni mountains or Hungary via Arad, this area is an excellent starting point for visiting Transylvania. Over 100 km, it will take you at least **a day** to explore the region and its Dacian citadels (some roads are not accessible for cars – you will have to walk). All round good **hiking** especially in the Retezat mountains.

Accommodation in Bucova, Deva, Hărău, Sântamăria-Orlea.

Address book p. 142. ●

Few places in Romania are filled with such a sense of history. Vestiges of Dacian civilisation, the epicentre of Romanian identity, are found in the mountain forests which for centuries offered refuge to this people from the invasions that swept the country.

Relics and remains abound in this small region where Transylvania meets the Banat and Oltenia: the capital of the Roman province of Dacia, as well as the legendary castles built by the princes who were instrumental in the making of Romanian and Hungarian history. The Mureş Valley, one of the major axes of European migration from Antiquity to the present day, winds through the varied mountain landscape: the

Apuseni, the alpine landscape of the Retezat mountains, the mysterious Şureanu mountains and the generous curves of the Poiana Ruscă region dotted with little villages.

Deva

> *Approx. 395 km N-W of Bucharest, about 150 km E of the western border, 80 km S-W of Alba Iulia. From Alba Iulia, take the DN 1 to Sebeş, then the DN 7. Parking available in str. Avram Iancu, bd 1 Decembrie 1918 or near the Decebel Hotel. Address book p.143.*

The capital of the Hunedoara area is a "modernised" town of 77,000 inhabitants. Although lacking in character, it is pleasant enough as a base for exploring the region. There are also two interesting sights in town.

The Museum of Dacian and Roman Civilisation*

> *Muzeul Civilizatiei Dacice si Romane Bd 1 Decembrie 1918, 39 ☎ 21.22.00. Open daily except Mon. 9am-5pm. Admission charge. Allow about 1 hr.*

The **Magna Curia** Palace was built in 1621 by Prince Bethlen. It is now a museum documenting Dacian and Roman history through a fascinating collection of artefacts. One highlight is a model of a Dacian citadel which will prepare you for visiting the real thing in nearby Costeşti (p. 141) or Sarmizegetusa (p. 141).

Deva citadel*

> *Cetatea Deva. From the park, take the left path: 180 m, approx 20 mins walk. Free admission.*

This eyrie acted as a bolt-hole for the inhabitants of the region. From the 16th century it became an almost unassailable military fortress. In 1849, during the conflict between Hungarian rebels and the Habsburgs, the fort was blown when munitions stored in the cellars exploded. A path leads you 180 m above the town for some great views of the Mureş Valley.

history

Iancu, the White Knight

Iancu de Hunedoara (1387-1456) came from an important Romanian family, part of the kingdom's elite, who were subsequently "magyarised": the family name changed from Hunedoara to Hunyadi. Iancu, voivode of Transylvania (1441-1456), was an indefatigable builder and a great warlord, famous for his resistance to the Ottoman conquest. His exploits made him famous throughout 15th-century Europe, earning him the nickname "The White Knight". He was governor of Hungary during the minority of the young of King Ladislav V (1446-1453) and after his death. His son Matei Corvin was elected King of Hungary in 1458 (see inset p. 190). ●

Hunedoara: the Corvin Family Castle**

> *Castelul Corvineştilor. 20 km S of Deva. From Deva take the DN 68 B to Hunedoara ☎ 71.14.23. Open daily except Mon. 9am-5pm. Admission charge. Allow approx. 1 hr. Parking available.*

Romania's largest castle occupies an incongruous position, surrounded by the blast furnaces of the steel-producing city of Hunedoara. In 1409, King Sigismond gave the stronghold of Hunedoara, already well-known in the 13th century, to Voicu Corvin. His son, **Iancu** (see above), rebuilt the fortress between 1440 and 1453. The west wing, where the **Knight's Hall*** is found, dates from this period. Iancu's son, Mathias Corvin (see p. 190), extended the castle on the north side, it its present aspect: a collection of spectacular, severe-looking towers, pepper-pot turrets, pointed keeps, battlements and machicolations. The entrance is no less theatrical: a narrow bridge leads to a darkly menacing door with a spooky looking tower rising above. The castle vaults house a **museum** where you can find, amongst other local ethnography, a collection of ancient weapons.

●●● **In the area**: the road leading to Densuş passes through a village with a rather surprising name: **General Berthelot** *(23 km S of Hunedoara, 5 km S-W of Haţeg; from Hunedoara head for Haţeg on the DN 68 B, then take a right turning towards Densuş)*. Here is the estate given by a grateful Romania to the famous French general *(see below)*.

♥ Densuş Church★

> *Biserica Densuş. 45 km S of Deva, 25 km S of Hunedoara. From Hunedoara take the DN 68 B towards Haţeg, then turn right towards Densuş. For a tour ask at the nearest house or at n° 15 on the main street. Free admission.*

Stones from the ruins of the Roman city of Sarmizegetusa (cap-itals, gravestones) were used in the construction of this church, probably built in the 12th century. It was extended on several occasions and now has an unusual silhouette. What remains of the **frescoes** (1443) shows the stylistic influence of Wallachian wall-painting, in particular that in the Church of Saint Nicholas in Curtea de Argeş *(p. 97)*.

The Roman ruins of Sarmizegetusa★

> *Sarmizegetusa Ulpia Traiana. 59 km S of Deva, 14 km S of Densuş. From Densuş get back on the DN 68 via Toteşti then take a right turn towards Caransebeş. Open daily 8am-5pm. Admission charge. Allow approx. 30 mins.*

The *Colonia Ulpia Traiana Augusta Dacica* was established under the Emperor Trajan, between 108 AD and 110 AD, not far from Sarmizegetusa, recently conquered capital of Dacia *(p. 141)*. The colony later took on the name of the nearby town and became the capital of the Roman province of Dacia until 271 AD.

---

portrait

Brave General Berthelot (1861-1931)

In 1916, a large French military force was sent to Iaşi *(p. 251)* to reorganise the 15 Romanian army divisions held up in Moldavia, to where the Romanian Court and government had fled from Bucharest. Chosen by Joffre for "his experience and military expertise, […] and optimism", General Berthelot commanded this force (1916-1918). Under his orders, 350 French officers brought their experience to bear on the Romanian troops, who, thus rallied, defeated the Austro-German troops at Maraşeşti (Moldavia). The General became inflamed by the Romanian cause and contributed to the creation of Greater Romania *(p. 50)*.

In recognition, he was made a citizen of Romania, where he is still a hero, and was given, a 60-hectare estate in Transylvania, near **Haţeg**. A lover of life's simple pleasures, the old military man liked to be among the people who loved him as much as he cared for them. You will find more roads named after General Berthelot in Romania than you will in France. ●

hiking

© Victor Bortas

The Haţeg Mountains, furrowed by centuries of agricultural labour are undergoing a gradual exodus as the local people move to towns and neighbouring valleys, bringing an end to this ancient way of life.

The massif is full of marked hiking trails. The rules of the national park forbid you to leave these paths. You have to pay an **entry tax**, either in the refuges or on the access roads. You will receive a ticket *(bilet de vizitare)* and a map of the massif with accommodation points indicated (often only basic conveniences) and the trails to follow. Do not hesitate to ask for advice from refuge workers or the Salvamont volunteers (mountain rescue).

Info: the Retezat National Park office, bd 22 Decembrie, bloc 4, parter, Deva ☎ (0254) 21.88.29, < www.retezat.ro >. ●

This was an important town if the remains that have been found on the site are anything to go by. The city ramparts covered some 600 m by 500 m at the centre of which were **sanctuaries** and a **forum**. To the north there was an amphitheatre with a capacity of up to 5,000 spectators.

Just nearby, the **museum** *(☎ 77.64.18; open daily except Mon. 10am-5pm; admission charge)* displays artifacts from the site. For centuries, the wreckage of the city has supplied the region with building material.

The Retezat Mountains**★★**

> *Munţii Retezat*. *Haţeg: 16 km N-E of Sarmizegetusa, 34 km S of Deva via Haţeg.*

One mountain range in this wild, isolated region, where the Banat, Oltenia and Transylvania meet, distinguishes itself from the rest of the Romanian Carpathians: the Retezat range which are gentler and full of lakes. In the shadow of **Mount Peleaga**, at 2,509 m, a classic granite landscape spreads forth. In the high-

Retezat: nature's riches

From low in the neighbouring valleys to around 1,700 m above sea level, the landscape is covered with deep **forests** ofbeech, fir and spruce. Above this and up to about 1,900 m, the only large tree that can survive is the **stone pine**: in exposed situations, there are only individual trees which have become wonderfully twisted by the inclement weather. In more sheltered areas, this pine forms natural groves providing nesting and food for birds, and is of great ecological interest. At this altitude, expanses of juniper bushes (on sunny slopes) and rhododendrons (in the shade) grow on the scree. Above 2,000 m, the Retezat Mountains bloom with a remarkable variety of alpine flora.

In the forests there are bears, lynx, wild cats, several varieties of deer, and the mountain cockerel. Wolves, foxes and wild boar roam between valleys, forests and meadows whereas up in the heights of the mountain chamois, marmot, ermine, and the golden eagle make their home. ●

lands, glacial erosion has hollowed out a string of cavities or sinkholes that have filled up and formed about 80 lakes. The slopes are covered with scree and ancient glacial deposits.

The National Park...

> *Parcul Naţional Retezat. From Sarmizegetusa, turn right 2 km after Haţeg.*

Thanks to the biological richness and the uniqueness of the massif (*see above*) this area became Romania's first national park in 1935 and has since acquired the status of Biosphere Reserve.

... and its access points

The **Haţeg region** offers the most interesting paths into the Retezat national park, many of them marked (*see p. 139*).

● **Via the Râu Mare Valley**. Take the DN 68 towards Caransebeş, continue for 11 km, then take a left towards Clopotiva. The tarmac road follows the Râu Mare Valley to the Guru Apei dam *(approx. 28 km)*. After 18 km you will reach the **Gura Zlata** Refuge (*Cabana Guru Zlata* ☎ 0254.77.72.80; *restaurant; 775 m altitude*). From here, trails (red trian-

gles) will lead you to the high-altitude lakes, including Zănoaga.

● *Via* **the Pietrele Refuge**. Follow the DN 66 to Ohaba de Sub Piatra *(10 km S of Haţeg)*, then turn right towards Nucşoara *(14 km S)*. Continue for 6 km along a track suitable for vehicles, until you reach the Cârnic forest house *(safe parking)*. From here, you have to walk for an hour and a half to reach the **Pietrele refuge** (*Cabana Pietrele* ☎ 0721. 29.17.79 [mobile]; 150 beds; basic; food available; 1,480 m altitude) from where, you can access the most spectacular trails in the Retezat range, but it can be very popular, especially in summer.

The heart of the Dacian kingdom★★

> *From Haţeg, head towards Simeria and Orăştie on the DN 66 and the DN 68. Head S at Orăştie and continue to Costeşti.*

The visitor who lingers in these wooded and not easily accessible hills sense the force and sophistication of the Dacian civilisation in the strange remains scattered around and about. Apart from the Greeks

From mud to stone walls

Between the 1st century BC and the end of the 1st century AD, the Dacians developed a sophisticated system to defend their kingdom. This was particularly well-developed in the south-west of Transylvania and south of Mureş. A chain of citadels controlled all the main access points leading to the capital, **Sarmizegetusa** *(see below)*, itself protected by its remoteness and difficulty of access. The most primitive fortifications would have had earth embankments and wooden fencing. However, numerous exchanges with **Black Sea Greek colonies** *(p. 288)* made the Dacians aware of more elaborate building techniques. Greek inscriptions have been discovered on carved stone in the Dacian area that indicate that when King **Burebista** seized these Greek colonies in around 55 BC, he undoubtedly recruited the talents of their builders and stone-cutters. The citadels have thick walls and bastions, whereas the civil and religious buildings became increasingly refined under these Hellenic influences. ●

and Romans, no other ancient European civilisation has left behind such an impressive amount of evidence *(see above)*.

From Costeşti to Sarmizegetusca Regia★

> *Costeşti: 43 km S-E of Deva, 16 km S of Orăştie. From the Costeşti refuge, a sign indicates the path leading to the citadel; 561 m, 20 mins walk.*

It seems that **Costeşti Citadel** (*Cetatea Costeşti*) was the main residence of the Dacian King **Burebista** as well as a stronghold.

Stronger still was **Blidaru Citadel★** (*Cetatea Blidaru*; *3 km S of the Costeşti Citadel*), occupying a key position, protecting Sarmizegetusa Regia, the Dacian capital, by blocking off the valley from attack.

♥ Sarmizegetusa Regia★★

> *68 km S-E of Deva, 42 km S-E of Orăştie, approx 25 km S-E of Costeşti. From Costeşti, take the non-tarmac road towards Grădiştea de Munte, then continue on foot for about 5 km as the forestry road is not really suitable for cars.*

Hidden in the depths of the mountains at an altitude (1,200 m) where living conditions are harsh, the site of Sarmizegetusa reveals archeological remains that tell a lot about the organisation of this region during the Dacian era *(see above)*. This was the military, political and religious capital of the State of **Decebal** *(p. 39)*. The complex was made up of two residential zones with a 3.5 hectare citadel and a sacred area in between, where excavations have unearthed rectangular sanctuaries lined with double rows of columns.

There are also two **circular sanctuaries**: blocks of andesite (volcanic rock) form a mysterious circle. The site had paved streets, and a water conveyance and sewerage system.

The Dacians must have had a colossal workforce at their disposal to transport such quantities of stone as there is no natural supply nearby. A similar force would have been used by the Romans to destroy these citadels and decimate this fascinating civilisation. ●

Address book

Forestry provides a living for the Moți people in the Apuseni Mountains.

Aiud

> Dialling code ☎ 058. See p. 133.

Accommodation

▲▲ **Pensiune Varga**, str. Transilvaniei, 120 ☎ 86.27.72. *4 rooms*. Outskirts of town, towards Alba Iulia. This is a pleasant private guest house which has plans to expand. *Restaurant.*

Albac

> Dialling code ☎ 058. See p. 130.

Accommodation

▲▲ **Pensiune Aurora** ☎ 77.70.57. *9 rooms and meals provided.* Left of the main road. From Gârda de Sus, after the town hall. A welcoming family and excellent food. Ask for the bedroom with a private bathroom.

▲▲ **Pensiune Tibiana**, Cionești hamlet, 10 ☎ 77.70.48. *5 rooms and meals provided.* Centre of Albac, turn left on the DJ 68 (to Horea and Huedin). On the right after approx. 2 km. Near the forest.

Alba Iulia

> Dialling code ☎ 058. See p. 133.

Getting there

● **By train**. Daily connections with Bucharest, Budapest, Timişoara, Cluj, Iaşi. **Station** *(Gara)*, approx. 2 km to the S-E of the citadel, near the main road (towards Sibiu). The **Railways Agency** *(Agenţia CFR)*, str. Motilor, 1 ☎ 81.36.89 or 81.66.78.

● **By bus**. Daily connections with Bucharest, Arad, Sibiu, Cluj and other villages in the region. **Bus station** *(Autogara)*, str. Iaşilor, 94 ☎ 81.29.67. Near the railway station.

Accommodation

▲▲ **Hotel Cetate**, str. Unirii, 3 ☎ 81. 17.80, fax 83.15.01. *110 rooms.* Just a stone's throw from the citadel.

▲▲ **Hotel Transilvania,** piaţa Iuliu Maniu, 22 ☎ 81.20.25, fax 81.11.95. *83 rooms.* Pretty basic hotel in the town centre. Ordinary *restaurant.*

Market

Piaţa Cetate, bd Revoluţiei 1989. Right on the S-W (bd Transilvaniei) corner of the citadel. Food market and likeable bazaar. There are eat-in and take away restaurants all around.

Bucova

> Dialling code ☎ 055. Map p. 136.

Accommodation

▲▲ **Casa Irina** ☎ 52.49.21. This peaceful village lies on the DN 68 between Caransebeş and Haţeg. *3 comfortable and pleasant guest rooms.* A rural setting, outside the village, at approx. 700 m altitude with a view of the Târcau mountains. *Meals provided.*

Costești

> *Dialling code* ☎ *0254. See p. 141.*

Accommodation

Mountain refuge (*Cabana Costești*)
☎ 21.19.76. *23 beds and 132-bed chalets.* You can stay at least two days on site. Running water. Basic conveniences. Car park.

Deva

> *Dialling code* ☎ *054. See p. 137.*

Accommodation

▲▲▲ **Hotel Decebal**, str. 1 Decembrie 1918, 37 A ☎ 21.24.13. *36 rooms.* Ideally situated in a quiet, grassy spot near a citadel. *Restaurant.*

Gârda de Sus

> *Dialling code* ☎ *058. See p. 130.*

Accommodation

▲▲ **Familia Danciu** ☎ 77.80.06. *7 rooms and meals provided.* In the heart of the village, heading down river, turn left just before the bridge: the large house belonging to the Danciu family is on the river bank. There is a footpath opposite leading to the Scărișoara cave. This guesthouse is famous for its food.

Sport

The **Sphinx** Speleology Association (*Asociatia Speologica Sfinx*) ☎ 0744. 33.16.72 (mobile), < cristigarda@ yahoo.com >. Info. on caving in the Apuseni mountains. Ask for Cristian Ciubotarescu, who speaks English.

Ghețar (Scărișoara cave)

> *Dialling code* ☎ *058. See p. 130.*

❶ Near the Ghețar crossroads, an old barn with a fir branch roof has been converted into an information centre and craft shop.

Accommodation

▲▲ **Familia Lucian Dobra**, house n° 233 ☎ 0740.89.49.96 (mobile). *2 rooms and hiking refuge.* At the Ghețar crossroads 15 mins from the Scărișoara ice cave. The guide lives here. No bathroom: there is a basin for washing.

▲▲ **Familia Marin Lazea**, house n° 230 ☎ 0745.27.54.99 (mobile). *3 rooms.* A traditional Apuseni house. Not far from the Famila Lucian Dobra. No bathroom.

Hărău

> *Dialling code* ☎ *054. Map p. 136.*

Accommodation

▲▲ **Angelica Lenuța**, house n° 197 ☎ 0744.52.14.02 (mobile). *2 rooms and meals provided.* A peaceful house, just a few kms from Deva.

Oradea

> *Dialling code* ☎ *059. See p. 122.*

Getting there

● **By plane**. Several connections a week with Bucharest on **Tarom** flights (days and times change regularly). **Airport** is on the Arad road, 8 km from the centre **Off map by A3**. **Tarom agency** (*Agenția Tarom*), piața Regele Ferdinand, 2 **A3** ☎ 44.40.55 or 13.19.18.

● **By train**. Several connections a day with Arad, Cluj and Budapest. **Station** (*Gara*), piața București. From Str. Republicii, continue to the north of town, near the Baroque Palace **A1**. Take trams 1 or 4 to the centre of town (piața Unirii). **Railways Agency** (*Agenția CFR*), str. Republicii, 2 **B1** ☎ 13.05.78 or 41. 49.70.

Accommodation

▲▲▲ **Pensuine Atlantic** ♥ **A3**, str. Iosif Vulcan, 9 ☎ 42.69.11, < www.wpg. ro >. *8 rooms.* Try the honeymoon suite, which has an enormous bed and a nice sweet-wrapper blue décor. Well-situated near the banks of the Criş. *Restaurant.*

▲▲▲ **Pension Gobe ♥**, str. Avântului, 4/A **Off map by B3** ☎41.35.13. *23 beds.* Just to the E of the citadel, near the Cluj-Napoca road. This restaurant has a great rustic atmosphere, the cuisine specialises in Hungarian-style dished and from time to time, musicians from Bihor accompany your dining.

Restaurants

♦♦ **Capitolium**, str. Avram Iancu, 8 **A3** ☎ 13.05.51. Good for Hungarian specialities.

♦ **Criş**, str. George Enescu, 30 **B2** ☎41.72.06. *Vegetarian and non-smoking restaurant.*

♦ **Oradea**, str. Losif Vulcan, 1 **A3** ☎13.43.39. Ordinary food but a pleasant garden terrace. Ideally situated, overlooking the piaţa Regele Ferdinand in the centre of town.

♦ **Patiseria Trei Zorele**, piaţa Regele Ferdinand, 5 **A3**. On the ground floor of the Casa Poynar, next door to the Eminescu library, this is a great place to grab a take-away snack. The small shop serves piping hot food fresh from the oven including cheese, nut and apple strudels and potato and cabbage pasties.

Bars

Café Mirage, str. Vasile Alexandri, 2-4 **A3**. Within the Black Eagle Palace.

Kelly's Irish Pub, str. Republicii, 2 **B1/2**. In the old bazaar building.

Useful addresses

• **24 hr Chemist**. *Farmacia Concordia*, piaţa Bucureşti, 2 **A1** ☎44.93.18. Opposite the station.

• **Post office**. *Poşta*, str. Roman Ciorogariu, 12 **A2**. Open Mon.-Sat. 8am-6pm.

Padiş plateau

> *Dialling code* ☎ *059. See p. 129.*

Accommodation

▲▲ **Cabana Padiş** ☎ 0748.59.18.90 (mobile). *30 beds.* Hiking refuge at 1,300 m altitude in the heart of the massif. Basic comforts. *Open May-Sept.*

Useful address.

• **Mountain rescue**. Salvamont Bihor ☎ (059) 33.03.98.

Rimetea

> *Dialling code* ☎ *058. See p. 132.*

Accommodation

▲▲ **Deák Tulit Zsuzsa**, house n° 285 ☎76.80.62 or 0745.50.64.47 (mobile). *4 rooms.* A real family atmosphere and traditional Magyar décor. Fabulous cooking by Zsuzsi (pronounced "Suzy").

▲▲ **Fodor Sára**, house n°213 ☎76.80.14. *6 rooms.* Comfortable and quiet. Good food.

Bar

Forras ♥. Don't miss this bar belonging to the very friendly Janos. 100 m from the town hall.

Sântamăria-Orlea

> *Dialling code* ☎ *054. See p. 136.*

Accommodation

▲▲ **Castel Orlea** ☎77.77.68, fax 77.22.00. *14 rooms.* Originally this was a castle built in the 13th century. Rebuilt in 1782 and further renovated after 1945. It is now a reasonably-priced mid-range hotel . Restaurant (superb dining room). In the local area, there is a 13th-century church with interior frescoes. •

Southern Transylvania

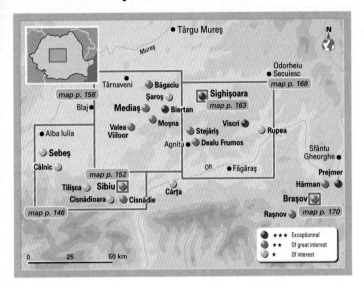

For many people, the name Transylvania evokes a mythical country. But this land "beyond the forests" (*trans silvania* in latin) is a real European region which has suffered a turbulent history. At one time it was centre of the Dacian realm; then, following occupation by the Roman Empire, the territory was subjected to countless invasions and different rulers before finally becoming part of Romania in 1918. Lying in the shelter of the Carpathian mountains, this area has great symbolic significance for the history and identity of Romania and the German and Magyar civilisations here. The "Saxons" also civilised the southern part of the region for nine centuries, leaving behind them some marvellous towns and villages. By the end of the Middle Ages, the territory was very much part of Central Europe welcoming artists from Vienna, Prague and Nuremberg. It was the most easterly sphere of Catholic influence in Europe in contact with the Orthodox tradition. As well as this outstanding cultural heritage, Southern Transylvania has vast tracts of wilderness dominated by the Carpathian Mountains and their highest peak, Moldoveanu (2,544 m).

© Pierre Soissons

The Carpathians to Sibiu★

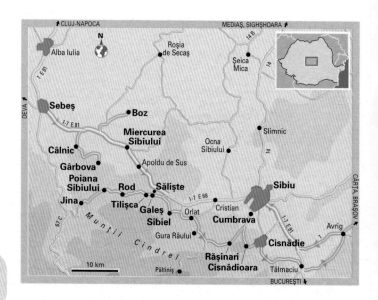

Sheltered by the flanks of the Carpathians, the descendants of the Dacian people witnessed the arrival of the original German settlers in south-west Transylvania. **Sebeş** was the first in a series of Germanic market towns which stretch all the way to Sibiu. At the same time, Cistercian monks founded **Cârţa Abbey**, bringing their building skills to Transylvania. In the superb valley of **Marginimea Sibiului**, Romanian shepherds proudly maintain a unique culture.

agenda

Around 100 km from Sebeş to Sibiu exploring the little roads which lead to shepherds villages and saxon settlements. There is plenty of **accommodation** at Cristian, Gura Râului, Răşinari, Sălişte, Sibiel, Sibiu and Tilişca.
Address book p. 174. ●

Sebeş and around★

> **Mülhbach** in German. 65 km E of Deva on the DN 7, 55 km W of Sibiu on the DN 1-7, 19 km S-E of Alba Iulia on the DN 1.

Remains of town ramparts are evidence that Sebeş, a town of 30,000 inhabitants, was an important Saxon town in the 13th century.

● **The Evangelical Church**★★ (*Biserica Evanghelică*). *Open daily 9am-5pm. Admission charge.* Only the nave remains of the 13th-century Romanesque edifice. At the centre of the Gothic choir there is a ♥ **polychrome wooden altarpiece**★★★ (*p. 164*), 13 m tall dating from 1524. This stunning work expressively depicts scenes from Christ's life, a **Virgin and Child** and a **Tree of Jesse** ↪. Above it, hover three angels and a garland of gilded carved wooden foliage.

On the buttresses of the choir outside is the finest collection of **Gothic statues** in Transylvania.

● **Citadels between Sebeş and Sălişte★**. *Take the DN 1-7 towards Sibiu, minor roads lead to the region's villages.* All along the Sibiu road, or just set back from it, you can see charming Saxon villages such as **Câlnic★**, **Gârbova★**, **Boz★** and **Miercurea Sibiului★**, with beautifully decorated houses and their own citadels.

Beyond Apoldu du Sus, the DN 1-7 traverses a small pass with a great views of the Carpathians, before dropping back down to Sălişte.

Marginimea Sibiului, sheep raising country

> *From Sebeş, take the DN 1-7 towards Sibiu.*

In the foothills of the **Cindrel Mountains**, a string of 18 villages exclusively populated by Romanians still maintain a strong **pastoral tradition** *(see inset p. 148 and p. 198).* Inevitably, the traditional Saxon-influenced buildings are slowly being replaced by more modern constructions. Villagers still dress up in traditional costume on festival days, men wearing the black bell-shaped hat and women elegantly attired in the traditional black and white costume.

♥ **Shepherding villages★★**

> *Get off the DN 1-7 to get to Sălişte. In the centre, turn right and follow the road along the river upstream.*

The villagers *(the Margineni)* have adapted to this narrow and impractical valley by tiering: at the bottom, the house; further up, the garden; halfway up the mountain, the hay fields; further up or further afield, the pastures.

In **Galeş**, you can visit the workshop of the last remaining hatter making the **traditional bell-shaped hats★** *(Virgil Ilieş, house n° 43 ☎ 55.34.31 or 55.33.08).*

The pass narrows at **Tilişca★**, a good base for some great hiking. The road continues climbing to the highest villages, spread out on the upper reaches of the Cindrel Mountains: **Rod★**, **Poiana Sibiului★** with its famous **Shepherds' Fair★** *(19 Sept.),* and **Jina★** are three of the highest settlements in Romania, all above 1,000 m.

Romanian villages and Saxon churches

> *Return to Sălişte and take the road on the right, continue for 6 km (rough driving conditions).*

While sticking close to the Carpathian foothills, the other villages around Marginimea Sibiului are less huddled, and Romanian communities co-exist with Saxon citadels.

● **From Sibiel to Emil Cioran's village**. A small stream trickles through the bucolic village of **Sibiel★**. Near the Church of Saint Trinity (Sfânta Treime), there is a

history

Why are they called Saxons?

It remains a mystery why Transylvanian Germans came to be known as Saxons — they are identified as such in documents dating from the early 13th century. These immigrant populations originated mostly from the Rhine and Moselle regions and seemingly had nothing to do with Saxony, a region in the far north-west. It is possible that a few of these immigrants were miners from Harz, a Saxon region, and that by association the rest of the settlers became known as "Saxons". Another explanation is that one of the immigrants stopped off in Saxony *en route.* ●

tradition

A pastoral civilisation

© Pierre Soissons

Wool remains an important economic resource for the shepherds in the region.

Sheep rearing is a major pillar of Romanian identity. Descendants of the Dacian and Roman communities used to escape invasions by hiding in the forests or on the flanks of the Carpathian mountains. Knowing that every crop and fixed settlement would be destroyed, another way to survive was to keep on the move with herds of animals. These two strategies, mobility and refuge, are combined in the lifestyle of the Marginimea Sibiului communities and, even now, long after the threat of invasion has disappeared, a semi-nomadic way of life remains ingrained in the mentality **Margineni** people and their relationship with the world. Until the beginning of the 20th century, shepherds and their flocks would set off on travels that could last for years, venturing as far as the Caucasus. Today, they do not venture much further afield than **Dobrogea** or the **Banat**. So, do not be surprised to see a flock driven by a shepherd wearing the famous bell-shaped hat! ●

museum of icons on glass★ (*Muzeul de Icoane pe Sticlă*; by appointment only ☎ 55.38.18; admission charge) which has around 700 works of art.

Take a right 3 km down the road for **Orlat** then **Gura Râului** (*tarmac road*). At the entrance to this handsome village, a road turns to the left to **Răşinari★** (*approx. 16 km from*

Sibiel, 12 km from Sibiu; connection by tram; inset p. 157), where the philosopher **Emil Cioran** (1911-1995; p. 323 and p. 325) grew up.

●●● **Around Răşinari**: the road climbs towards **Păltiniş** (*1,450 m; 35 km from Sibiu*), the country's first ski resort, surrounded by pine forests. It normally has plentiful snowfall.

- **Cisnădioara*** *(Michelsberg in German)*. *12 km E of Rășinari, 12 km W of Sibiu; on the road to Sibiu, turn right after 6 km.* Isolated on a promontory, this Romanesque village church was protected by walls made from shingle and shale: it used to be traditional for every Saxon male to lay a large stone before the citadel if he wished to re-marry. Today, this inspiring location fosters events such as the Sibiu **Theatre Festival**.

- **Cisnădie and the Braller Madonna**** *(Heltau in German)*. *5 km E of Cisnădioara, 7 km S of Sibiu.* This **citadel*** displays a successful combination of spaces: 15th century fortifications protect a 13th century Romanesque church onto which defensive towers have beed grafted. The altar of the Saxon church at Bruiu *(Braller, between Agnita and Făgăraș)* has recently been moved to this church for safe-keeping. In the centre, there is a poignant statue of the Virgin and Child, better known as the ***Braller Madonna**** (1520).

- **Cârța Abbey***. *From Cisnădie, make for Tălmaciu, then Avrig, where you will rejoin the DN1. Turn left after 18 km. Free admission. By appointment only.* In 1190, thirteen monks left the Cistercian Abbey of Pontigny in Bourgogne, France. After months of travelling, they settled in this inhospitable valley and founded a powerful monastic settlement, introducing the Cistercian architectural model to Transylva-

© Hermann Fabini

The Braller Madonna is now housed in the church of Cisnădie.

nia. The abbey was abandoned in 1474 and today only the church remains in good order, with proportions and openings characteristic of Cistercian architecture. It is still in use as an Evangelical church for the local Saxon community.

●●● **In the area:** On your way to Sibiu, the DN7C, or ***Trans-făgărașan***, leads off on your left. At 2,034 m, this is the highest road in the country. ●

The Saxons and their citadels

The arrival of German settlers in Transylvania sparked off one of the greatest periods of development ever seen in Europe and, in a climate of insecurity, villages turned their churches into citadels.

The territorial policy of King Geza

At the request of **Geza II**, King of Hungary (1141-1162), around 500 families of freed peasants and minor nobility from Luxembourg, the Rhine, Lorraine and Wallonia crossed Europe to settle in the **Sibiu region**. Here they received royal land and considerable privileges. In so doing, the king hoped to exploit the land in his realm and to establish a power to counter that of the Hungarian nobility of Transylvania. Furthermore, **Teutonic knights** were stationed around **Bârsa** (Braşov) in the east to protect this particularly vulnerable region.

A privileged status

Subordinated only to the king, the Saxons administered their own artistic and commercial activities, and common law, a set of privileges decreed by **Andrew II of Hungary** in 1224 in a document called the ***Andreanum.*** Powerful commercial towns thus began to develop. At the end of the 15th century, the **Universitas saxonum** (Saxon University) was established. This Saxon "government" was responsible for controlling internal affairs and representing them to the Diet (parliament) of Transylvania. The Universitas saxonum and the special privileges were, however, withdrawn in 1876.

A highly organised urban system

The first groups of settlers received equal-sized plots of land: long narrow strips lining a wide main street, often dominated by a church. Their houses were all built to the same size with no exuberant decoration, lending a certain uniformity to the settlements. Each facade

Even today, most of the villages retain the structure of the original site, with land divided into long and narrow plots.

© Pierre Soissons

was made up of a gable and a doorway within a large wall which concealed a long interior courtyard with rows of farm buildings. On the other side, a large barn closed off the courtyard with orchards beyond. Unfortunately, although well-organised, this system was still vulnerable to attack.

The citadels

After the devastating **Tatar** invasions of 1241, the Saxon settlements surrounded their churches with ramparts, within which everything was organised to withold a siege: reserves of wine and food managed by neighbourhood associations (Nachbarschaft), with the space between the wall and the church being used keep the livestock. The church itself was often fortified, sometimes giving it the look of some kind of fantastical spacecraft. Every village had its own architectural solution adapted to its means, the space available and the shape of the original church. ●

The citadel at Cincşor.

Sibiu★★

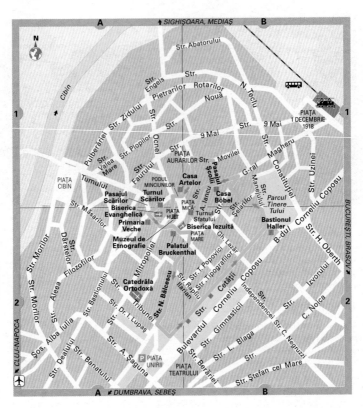

Of all Romania's towns, Sibiu (population 170,000) has the best preserved historic centre. It was the birthplace of Saxon civilisation and, wandering around it, you could almost be in an old German town in Franconia. The old part of the town covers 70 hectares: a maze of ancient cobbled streets, passageways, staircases, secret gardens, little squares, and houses with green shutters and faded paintwork. Elongated dormer windows blink like half open eyelids among the jumbled rooftops, giving the impression the town is dozing or spying on passers-by.

A SAXON SETTLEMENT

Around 1150, the first German settlers arrived in the Cibin valley (this is where the Romanian name for the town originated). Inhabited since pre-history, the site lies at a crossroads of trade routes once used by Romans. These routes link Alba Iulia to the Bârsa region (Braşov) and the Balkans with Central Europe.

Named *Villa Hermanni* in Latin, *Hermannstadt* in German, a small town grew up from just one row of houses – on the site of today's str. 9 Mai *(p. 154)* – which was sadly obliterated by the Tatars in 1241.

SIBIU, A FREE TOWN

To stimulate its reconstruction, the King of Hungary granted the town the status of "free town", administrated by its guilds. Ramparts were built to protect the wealth of the town and were extended in concentric circles until, by the 15th century, Hermannstadt was the military and economic capital of Transylvania. From the 18th century, the Saxons shared the town with Romanians, Jews and Hungarians. A movement campaigning for the interests and rights of Transylvanian Romanians created an association, ASTRA (*Asociaţia Transilvene de Artă şi Literatură)*, here in 1861, still known for its remarkble museum collections.

The upper town fortifications

> **A/B2** *From the piaţa Unirii, take the str. Cetăţii.*

Well-preserved sections of the fortifications are found south-east of the piaţa Unirii. **Str. Cetăţii** runs along the inside of the city wall interspersed with three 15th-century towers, an old 16th-century artillery bastion and the Haller Bastion (1552).

From Avram Iancu to the low town★

> **B1/2** *From the Haller Bastion, take the str. Manejului which follows the town wall (N-E), then the str. Funarilor which takes you down to str. Constituţiei. Take two left turns to get to str. Magheru then turn right down str. Avram Iancu.*

This street is typical of the upper town lived in by Saxon merchants. The houses have interior courtyards, originally used for storing goods and merchandise, which, with a few exceptions, you can discretely visit, taking care not to disturb the inhabitants.

Str. Avram Iancu and the interior courtyards★

Head towards piaţa Mare and take a peek inside the courtyards. You will discover a world that is beautiful and poetic, sometimes very modest, a junk yard or a kitchen garden.

At n°7, for example, at the back of the courtyard, some steps lead up to a terrace bordered by a brick wall: remains of the city ramparts. At n° 16, you can see the triangular facade of the 15th-century **Casa Böbel★**.

---

essentials

- **Position**. 275 km N-W of Bucharest, 273 km E of the border (Arad), 55 km E of Sebeş on the DN 1-7, 47 km W of Cârţa on the DN 1.
- **Getting your bearings**. The main roads converge on str. Andrei Şaguna, which crosses Sibiu along the south-west side of the historic centre, and then **piaţa Unirii A2**, in the middle of the new town. **Str. Nicolae Bălcescu A2** leads off this square to the historic old town and **piaţa Mare A-B2**. The **station B1** lies to the N-E of the old town. The **airport, off map** *via* **A2**, is out of town, W on the DN 1 to Alba Iulia
- **Getting around**. The best way to discover the town is on foot. Take some binoculars and good walking shoes (loose cobblestones). You can leave your car in the car park on **piaţa Unirii**.
- **Exploring the area**. If you only have a couple of hours, visit the upper town. Given a whole day you should also wander the tiny streets and squares of the low town. In summer, there are organ recitals on Wednesday evenings in the Evangelical Church.
- ***Address book** p. 176.* •

architecture

Successive fortifications

A few years after the Tatar invasion (1241), the town built its first set of city ramparts, enclosing the area around today's piaţa Huet *(see opposite)* and the Church of Saint Mary. The main residential area lay outside the city walls so that every time there was warning of attack, crowds would quickly make their way into the *Burg*. As the city expanded so did its fortifications. At the beginning of the 14th century, they enclosed today's piaţa Mică *(see opposite)*; by the beginning of the 15th century, they surrounded the whole of the upper town including the municipal buildings and the residences of the town's worthies. A few decades later, the walls encircled the entire low town as far as the Cibin river *(p. 152)*. With ramparts reinforced with 39 defensive towers and four bastions, Hermannstadt became the most powerful town in Transylvania with a fortified surface area equal to that of Vienna at that time. In the 19th century, some of the walls, towers and gateways were destroyed to remodel the town. ●

♥ The town's oldest streets*

Opposite Casa Böbel (n° 16) in str. Avram Iancu, the **School children's Passageway*** *(Pasajul Şcolii)* runs between the houses right up to the picturesque **str. Movilei*** where the gutter runs in the middle of the uneven cobbled street. This and the parallel streets (str. 9 Mai, str. Nouă) are the oldest streets in the city dating from the mid-12th century.

♥ Piaţa Aurarilor**

> **B1** *From str. Movilei, take a left down the hill.*

This peaceful, intimate square, surrounded by delightful 16th-century houses was, for a long time, the main point of passage between the low town and piaţa Mică. Carts clattered by, sometimes bashing the walls, hence the enormous protective cornerstones on the houses. At

© Victor Bortas

The Council Tower dominates the roofs of the old town.

n° 5, a long, narrow interior courtyard leads to a little garden and one of the defensive towers crowed by an 18th-century garret.

Before leaving the square, on the left, at n° 10, a gateway leads into a courtyard enclosed to the south by a bit of the 14th-century ramparts.

Under an archway dating from 1567, climb the stairway back to piaţa Mică.

The little squares of the upper town

Although most of the craftsmen were confined to the low town, the institutions and affluent classes resided in the upper town, easier to defend and more spacious.

Piaţa Mică★★

> **B2** *From piaţa Aurarilor, take the steps which lead to piaţa Mică (S-W).*

The town's most prestigious master craftsmen lived on the north and east sides of this square, in rows of arcaded houses.

The **House of Arts★** (*Casa Artelor*) dating from 1370, was once the covered vegetable market, then the meat market. Today it is an exhibition space.

Piaţa Huet and the surrounding area

> **A2** *From piaţa Mică (S-W), take the Liar's Bridge.*

Over **Liar's Bridge** (*Podul Minciunilor*), a cast-iron bridge inaugurated in 1860, you reach piaţa Huet. The ring of houses encircling the Evangelical Church corresponds to the position of the original ring of fortifications (*see inset opposite*).

● **A2 The Emil Sigerus Museum of Saxon Ethnography★★** (*Muzeul de Etnografie Săsească Emil Sigerus*). *Piaţa Huet, 12* ☎ *21.81.95. Open daily except Mon. 9am-5pm. Admission charge. Allow 1 hr.* Founded in 1997, the museum pro-

The Evangelical Church in Sibiu.

© Pierre Soissons

vides a fascinating insight into the German civilisation in Transylvania through collections of furniture, textiles and ceramic artefacts including a number of faïence stoves.

● **The Evangelical Church★** (*Biserica Evanghelică*). *Open daily 6am-8pm. Free admission except to the crypt and during services (open daily 10am-6pm in summer, 11am-4pm in winter; admission charge). Allow about 30 mins.* Walking around the town, the imposing belfry serves as a central landmark. Building of the church began in 1321 on the foundations of a Romanesque basilica, and was completed in 1520. It was originally dedicated to the Virgin Mary before becoming a Lutheran church.

Through the southern door on the left, there is a chapel separated from the rest of the church. Inside are 67 carved tombstones of Sibiu's his-

history

Saxon memories

In the 1930s, a part of the Saxon minority in Romanian was seduced by Nazi propaganda and joined Hitler's SS. Following the war, the Soviet occupiers and their allies, in an act of revenge, deported thousands of Saxons to Siberia. Those who remained integrated into Romanian society; however, with the fall of Communism in Romania, some chose to move back to Germany.

Today, Germany and Romania have initiated a number of international projects to safeguard the Saxon heritage and way of life in Romania. ●

Piaţa Mare: the heart of the upper town ★★

> **A/B2** *From the Town Hall, continue to piaţa Mare (E).*

Nothing seems out of place in this large, partly pedestrianised square: a perfect harmony of varying proportions, styles and colours.

● **A2 Brukenthal Palace*** *(Palatul Brukenthal). Piaţa Mare, 3-5* ☎ *41.76.91 and 41.15.45. Open daily except Mon. 9am-5pm. Admission charge. Allow about 1 hr).* This three-storey Baroque palace, completed in 1787, was commissioned by Baron Samuel von Brukenthal (1721-1803). Minister for the Saxons and governor of Transylvania, the baron was also counsellor to the Empress Maria-Theresa. He was an amateur artist who collected paintings, antiques, coins and books. In 1817, a museum was opened displaying his private collections on the second floor. There are also paintings by Flemish, Dutch (Van Dyck and Brueghel the Elder), German and Italian artists.

● **A/B2 The Baroque Jesuit Church** *(Biserica Iezuită). Piaţa Mare, 3.* The Reformation had a great impact on this town. The building of this church, between 1726 and 1733, symbolised the enforced return of the Catholic Church by the Habsburg Empire.

● **B2 The Council Tower**** *(Turnul Sfâtului). Open daily except Mon. 10am-6pm. Admission charge.* Mentioned in documents dating from 1370, this tower overlooked the entrance to the second ring of city walls. It takes its name from the Town Council building which abuts it.

It collapsed during the 1568 earthquake crushing to death the painter Johannis David who was in the process of decorating it. Rebuilt in 1588, its present aspect dates from 1826. Climb to the seventh floor for a

toric figures. One of the oldest belongs to the son of the famous **Vlad Tepes** *(see inset p. 43),* **Mihnea cel Rău** (Mihnea the Bad), who was murdered just outside the church. A cross and an inverted moon are engraved on his sepulchre. The large **fresco of the Crucifixion*** on the north wall of the choir was painted in 1445 by Johannes de Rosenau and later badly restored in 1650. The Baroque organ (renovated in 1997) dates from 1672.

Leave by the north door and pass under the **Staircase Tower*** *(Turnul Scărilor),* which was one of the gates of the first city wall *(see inset p. 154).* A hundred or so steps down, take the Passage of Stairs on the left which leads back to the upper town.

● **A2 The Old City Hall** *(Primaria Veche). Open daily except Mon. 9am-5pm. Admission charge.* The building (1470) is typical of Transylvanian Gothic civil architecture, and houses the **History Museum** *(Muzeul de Istorie).* Here, you are just a few steps from the town centre.

© Pierre Soissons

The squares of the historic centre have the old-fashioned charm of old German towns.

superb **panoramic view of the town**★★. You can get back to the car park on piața Unirii by taking **str. Nicolae Bălcescu**, a pedestrianised shopping street.

♥The Dumbrava Sibiului open-air museum★★

> **Off map by A2** *Muzeul în aer liber din Dumbrava Sibiului. Calea Rășinari* ☎ *24.24.19. Open daily Tue.-Sun. 9am-5pm in winter; Wed.-Fri. 10am-6pm and Sat.-Sun. 10am-8pm in summer. Admission charge. Map and explanatory leaflet on sale at entrance. Allow 2-5 hrs.*

Over some 96 hectares in the Dumbrava Sibiului woods, the technological legacy of the Romanian peoples is displayed in this eco-museum along 10 km of alleys in over 300 buildings including mills, sawmills, hydraulic forges, presses, sheepfolds and much more. Two old inns *(information and*

reservations ☎ *24.21.77 or 24.22.67)* have been reconstructed, one in the centre of the complex *(Cârciuma din Bătrâni)* and one at the entrance *(Han de Tulgheș)*. Festivals and crafts fairs regularly take place here. ●

directions

Dumbrava open-air museum

The museum is 2 km S of the centre of Sibiu, on the **Rășinari** road *(p. 148)*. From the station or from piața Unirii take trolleybus n° 1 or 5 to the cemetery, then the only tram (which goes all the way to **Rășinari**). At peak times (7am-9pm and 1pm-3pm), it runs every 30 mins and every hour for the rest of the day. ●

Mediaş and the Târnava citadels★★★

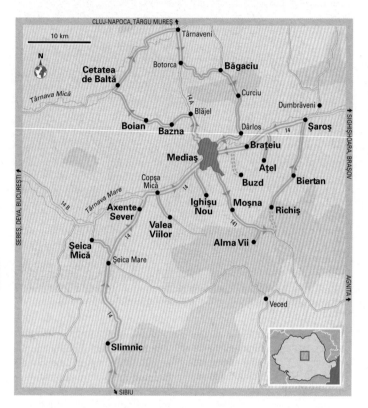

The church towers and steeples emerging from the roofs are a reminder that **Mediaş** was once a rival of Sighişoara and Biertan. Within a 25 km radius, the little tributary valleys of the Târnava harbour some of the most beautiful Saxon villages. Several of their churches still contain sublime **altarpieces** (*p.164*), masterpieces of Gothic art.

Sibiu to Mediaş★★

> *From Sibiu take the DN14 for Mediaş.*

When driving through the hilly countryside, watch out for the romantic silhouette of the partially ruined **Slimnic**★ Fortress (*Stolzen-*

agenda

The trip from Sibiu to Mediaş is 92 km, and you will take at least two days. Allow more if you want to visit the Saxon villages, often a few kilometres off the main road. Take care driving on the rougher country lanes. In early May, the orchards are weighed down with blossom. In October a beautiful autumnal light bathes the villages.

Accommodation at Sibiu, Mediaş, Băgaciu, Biertan.

Address book *p. 174.* ●

burg in German). With **Şeica Mică★** *(Kleinschelden in German)* citadel on your left, you pass through **Axente Sever★** *(Frauendorf in German)* a small village with a sleepy citadel at its centre.

In **Copşa Mică** *(Kleinkopschen in German)*, take a right towards **Valea Viilor** *(Würmloch in German)*, which has the most impressive **citadel★★** in the region. Encircled by strong ramparts, the hall church is heavily fortified with a massive tower on the west side and the raised choir pierced with loopholes.

Back on the DN 14, take a right turn 3 km before Mediaş towards **Ighişu Nou citadel★** *(Eibesdorf in German)*. This strangely proportioned complex is dominated by a tower (14th-15th-centuries) as big as the church itself.

Mediaş★★

> *59 km N-E of Sibiu on the DN 14.*

This town of 65,000 inhabitants had its hour of glory during the Middle Ages, when its geographical position at the heart of Transylvania gave it a certain political and economical advantage. For a long time it was one of the cultural centres for the Saxons, who held an assembly here in 1919, declaring their union with the new Romania. Mediaş is now an industrial centre.

Piaţa Regele Ferdinand I★

Str. L. Roth and Petöfi Sandor open out onto this vast pedestrianised area complete with lawns and benches. A multitude of different coloured facades dating from all eras surround the square.

On the north-east corner of the square the large white building, the **Schuller House★** *(Casa Schuller; 15th century)*, was once the residence of the Transylvanian princes, and headquarters of the town's Saxon establishment.

● **Getting around**. The main road from Sibiu to Sighişoara passes over the railway line. Opposite the Forkesch Tower, turn left down str. Unirii, which bears right (str. Pompierilor) about 100 m from the railway station. Str. L. Roth and str. Petöfi Sandor (car park) both lead to the central town square, piaţa Regele Ferdinand I. Otherwise continue along the main avenue and take a right down str. Turnului (paying car park).

● **Getting your bearings**. The most interesting streets in town lead off piaţa Regele Ferdinand I.

● **Exploring the area**. Allow at least two hours to explore the town on foot. An overnight stay will give you time to visit the citadels in the region and attend an organ recital or church service (in German) in the Gothic church. ●

A town within a town: the Kastell★★

> *From piaţa Regele Ferdinand I, take the little path (closed between 5pm and 8am); the main entrance is in piaţa Enescu.*

This Saxon citadel, or *Kastell*, has a double surrounding wall and four fortified towers. The majority of it has been built over by later constructions but some of the original ramparts are still visible.

The **Gothic church** stands in the middle of the citadel. Leaning slightly, and topped with glazed tiles, the tower (68 m) provided an excellent lookout post. An alarm would be sounded by trumpet from here to announce a fire or enemy attack, hence the name: the **Trumpet Tower★**.

The Gothic church and its altarpieces★★

> *Open daily 8am-7pm. Admission charge.*

Originally a Romanesque basilica, this church was eventually completed in the 15th century, and was dedicated to Saint Margaret until the Reformation. There are some real treasures to be found in the expansive interior: on the north wall there are the remains of some **early 15th-century frescoes★**, including a fragment depicting the **Tree of Jesse** ↪. In the 16th century this scene was used a lot in Moldavian churches but this is the first use in Romania, and is the only example of its use in a fresco in Transylvania. A magnificent ♥ **altarpiece★★** (late 15th century; *p.164*) sits at the centre of the choir, the work of an unknown artist, perhaps Viennese. During the week, when the shutters of the altarpiece are closed, a superb depiction of the cycle of the **Passion Narratives** is revealed in all its subtle refinement. The church also has three altarpieces from other churches in the region: the sumptuous ♥ **Dupuş altarpiece★★** *(Tobsdorf in German)* contains some lively, colourful scenes. The altarpiece from **Şoroştin★** *(Schorsten in German)* has a particularly impressive image of the face of Christ at its centre.

Citadels north of Mediaş★★

> *From Mediaş, take the DN 14A towards Târnaveni.*

Around Târnava Mare and Târnava Mică, you can find some particularly robust citadels even though this hilly region can hardly have been the most susceptible to attack.

Bazna citadel★

> *Baasen (in German). 18 km N-W of Mediaş, 5 km W of Blăjel. Take the DN 14A towards Târgu Mureş. In Blăjel, take a left. To visit the citadel, contact the Binder family ☎ 85.01.01.*

The severe looking entrance tower of the Bazna citadel looks down on the crossroads of the two main roads of the village. The strange shape of the 13th century-church is due to the elevated choir, built in the 15th century at the same time as the ramparts.

♥ Boian citadel and the hills of Târnava Mică★

> *Boian (Bonnesdorf in German): 23 km N of Mediaş, 5 km N-W of Bazna. From Bazna, get back on the road heading west.*

The citadel in Boian has circular ramparts. The entrance tower and

The citadel's church looks over Mediaş and the piaţa Regele Ferdinand I.

© Pierre Soissons

© Hermann Fabini

The astonishing citadel at Băgaciu has one of the most beautiful altarpieces in Transylvania.

the north side of the church display the Moldavian emblem (the head of an aurochs with a star on its forehead) as this village was once dependent on the estate of Cetatea de Baltă which, for a time, belonged to the Moldavian voivodes ↪. Continue down the Târnava Mică valley to the heart of the **Jidvei vineyard**. Turn right towards Târgu Mureș and pass through **Cetatea de Baltă★** which, after the Moldavian princes, passed into the hands of the Bethlen family, who built a **castle★** here in the 17th century.

Băgaciu citadel★★

> *Bogesdorf (in German). 25 km W of Cetatea de Baltă, 19 km N of Mediaș. Before Târnaveni, take the DN 14 A towards Mediaș. After 7 km in Botorca, take a left. To visit, contact Suzana Sălccianu, house n° 62 ☎ 42.56.93.*

Enter the 15th-century church through the ornately decorated Gothic doorway. At the centre of the **altarpiece★★** (1518; *p. 164*), the sculpted group represents the Virgin and Child, flanked by Saint Catherine and Saint Mary-Magdalene. Return to Mediaș via Curciu and Dârlos.

Târnava Mare valley citadels★★★

> *Between Mediaș and Sighișoara.*

Târnava Valley (*Kokeltal in German*) and its tributary valleys contain more Saxon citadels than any other region.

Moșna citadel★★

> *Meschen (in German). 10 km S of Mediaș. From Mediaș, take the DJ 141 towards Agnita. To visit the citadel, contact Ilse Diplas ☎ 86.21.54.*

With its huge dimensions and complex set of tall ramparts and towers, this citadel sets itself apart from others in the region (except those in

Mediaş and Biertan). In the choir of the Gothic church, built in 1486, there is a finely carved **stone tabernacle★**.

Alma Vii citadel★

> **Almen** *(in German). 7 km S of Moşna on the DJ 141. Follow a dirt road on your right for 2 km.*

This charming village, lost in its solitude, is dominated by a seemingly abandoned citadel. The hall church slumbers amid wild grass while the ramparts slowly shed their rendering, revealing the brick wall underneath, like a pink wound.

Richiş citadel★

> **Reichesdorf** *(in German). 5 km N-E of Alma Vii. Get back onto the DJ 141. Turn right, then, after 2 km, turn left onto a dirt road for 3 km.*

Nestling in one of the Tâvarna tributary valleys, **Richiş Church** provides two good reasons for a diversion. Firstly, the tympanum above the west door with its beautifully sculpted Crucifixion – a lively composition of free-standing figures.

Secondly, the Baroque altar inside, one of the finest in Transylvania: the angels invite the congregation to gaze upon the crucified Christ.

Biertan★★★

> **Birthälm** *(in German). 26 km S-E of Mediaş, 8 km N-W of Richiş by the only valley road. **The citadel:** the entrance is on the village square (S-E); open daily 9am-4pm except during Sun. morning service; admission charge. Allow 30 mins.*

Biertan was the Episcopal seat of the Saxon evangelical community between 1572 and 1867. The church was built between 1492 and 1516 on a hill plateau and fortified by eight towers and triple-layered ramparts which reach right down to the foot of the hill. A covered staircase leads to the church, which from a distance looks like an arched back. The choir is considerably lower and narrower than the rest of the church, which is surprisingly large. The length of the three naves is shorter than usual due to the limited space on the hill top.

The **stone pulpit** is sculpted in bas-relief depicting scenes from the Passion. The **altarpiece★★** (1524) is a masterpiece of its genre *(p. 146)*, representing scenes from the Life of Mary. In the centre is a wooden Crucifixion, sculpted and gilded.

Between Şaroş and Mediaş★

> *Şaroş: 35 km from Mediaş via Biertan on the DN 14, 9 km N of Biertan.*

Follow the river to the Târnava Mare Valley near the **Şaroş citadel★** *(Scharosch in German)*.

●●● **If you pass back through Mediaş**, take time to visit the **citadels** in Braţeiu★ *(Pretai in German)* and, in nearby valleys, Aţel★ *(Hetzeldorf in German)* which has a superb Baroque altar, and the incredible **Buzd Church★★** *(Bussd in German)*, with its 15th-century raised fortified choir.

From **Şaroş★**, take the DN 14 eastwards to Sighişoara. ●

Sighişoara★★★

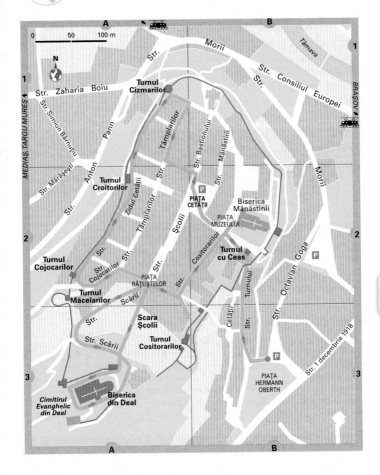

The historic quarter overlooks a narrow passage of the river Târnava and two other tributary valleys, where the low town and the more recent suburbs lie. To this day, Sighişoara, with a population of 37,000 inhabitants, has managed to retain the specific character of an old German town. Architecturally of a piece, the town still exudes simple charm at every turn. For those who really like to explore a town's secrets, there are little gardens, streets with wobbly cobblestones and rows of houses painted sky-blue, yellow, green and pink, not to mention the passageways, paths and steps leading from the low town to the upper town.

THE BIRTH OF A CITY

German settlers supposedly founded a first village around 1191 on the upper plateau of the hill (inhabited in prehistoric times, and then again by Daco-Romans). Destroyed by the Tatars in 1241, it was subsequently rebuilt, becoming the market town of Schaessburg in German, Sighişoara in Romanian and Segesvar in Hungarian. The settlement expanded greatly in the 14th century when it obtained

Saxon altarpieces

Around the middle of the 15th century, Transylvanian Saxons started embellishing their churches with sophisticated altarpieces illustrated with colourful biblical scenes. This practice was all the rage throughout Germanic Central Europe, from Alsace to Vienna and the Carpathians.

© Hermann Fabini

The polychrome wooden altarpiece at **Sebeş** (1524) shows the Virgin and Child in the centre and, in the side panels, a Tree of Jesse along with scenes from the Life of Christ and from the Life of the Virgin Mary.

Shuttered altarpieces

An altarpiece is a carved and painted wooden construction which sits above the altar. The most widely used model was the **shuttered altarpiece** (*Flügelaltar* in German) known as a polyptych. This is normally made up of four panels (two moving and two fixed) which are attached to a central niche. Each panel is decorated with two scenes, one above the other. The two fixed panels are only visible when the moveable panels are open.

Detail of the polychrome wooden altarpiece at **Dupuş**. The left panel depicts the Way of the Cross and the right one the Crucifixion with the Virgin Mary and Saint John.

© Hermann Fabini

© Hermann Fabini

Feast days and ordinary days

Altogether the panels display a series of eight scenes. The altarpiece remains closed on weekdays, and during Lent and Advent; this is called the "ordinary days" position *(Alltagsseite* or *Werkstagseite).* The two moveable panels are only opened on feast days *(Feiertagsseite).* Then, like a chest revealing its treasure, the central recess is revealed to the congregation. It gives significance to the whole work: a suptuously decorated frame for the Crucifixion, the Virgin and Child or other figures, sculpted or painted, or more rarely for another iconography.

Between Gothic and Renaissance

The Passion Cycle is the most common theme for the eight scenes of the *Werkstagseite.* Their style reveals a crossing-over: some Gothic notes are still present, but the spirit of the Renaissance has clearly crept into artists' inspiration. For example, the natural world is no longer a decorative backdrop, the countryside is alive. A better understanding and mastery of perspective enabled a clearer distinction between the foreground, background and everything in-between. As for the figures, they became more and more refined, and less and less static.

This golden era of altarpieces was short-lived. After 1545, the Reformation forbade such depictions or had them painted over. A hundred or so of these masterpieces disappeared in Transylvania, leaving only 27 intact. Some are in museums in Sibiu, Cluj, Bucharest and Budapest; others are in their original churches. A few have been from isolated locations to safer churches: the magnificent **Braller Madona** (p. 149) is in **Cisnădie** (**Heltau**); the famous altarpieces from **Dupuş** (Tobsdorf, p. 160) and **Şoroştin★** (**Schorsten**, p. 160) now enchant **Mediaş** Church (p. 160). Other beautiful Transylvanian altarpieces can be found in Sebeş (p. 146), Băgaciu (p. 161), Biertan (p. 162), Malâncrav, Sighişoara (p. 163), Cincu (p. 168), Hălchiu and in the Brukenthal Museum in Sibiu (p. 156). ●

The polychrome wooden altarpiece of **Băgaciu** depicts the Virgin and her Child with Saints Catherine and Mary-Magdalene. The side panels illustrate scenes from the Life of the Virgin Mary.

getting around

● **Position.** 280 km N of Bucharest, 96 km N-E of Sibiu, 55 km S of Târgu Mureş, 37 km E of Mediaş.

● **Getting there.** The main road from Mediaş to Braşov or Târgu Mureş to Braşov follows the valley, passing through the low town and the new suburbs. There is **paying car park by the citadel** on str. Morii **B2** and 200 m further on in piaţa Hermann Oberth **B3**. There is another **paying car park inside the citadel** on piaţa Cetăţii **B2**. The **railway station** is 1 km outside the town **off map by A1**.

● **Exploring the area.** You will need at least half a day to explore the town. The terrace of **Casa Wagner**, on piaţa Cetăţii, is a pleasant place to have lunch. Autumn is the best time to visit: the citadel slips back into its sleepy rhythm and cats bask on the warm cobblestones.

● *Address book p. 174.* ●

the status of a free town, giving it certain privileges including jurisdictional autonomy. This period of prosperity also saw the construction of strong city defences. The low town grew up outside the city walls, inhabited over the centuries by Romanians, Hungarians, Jews and others.

EARLY GERMAN TOWN PLANNING

The town plan is typical of the German model from the late Middle Ages. It follows the "two street system" (*Zweistrassensystem*) whereby the town develops around two main parallel streets: here, str. Tâmplarilor (W) and the larger str. Şcolii (E) which becomes str. Bastionului. A longitudinal axis cuts across these two streets. The liveliest part of town is **piaţa Cetăţii** where it meets str. Şcolii.

As with German towns, craft guilds constructed and maintained the defence system which here comprised 930 m of fortifications. Today, there are only nine towers, two bastions and one section of the ramparts remaining. Gradually, different architectural styles were added (notably after the fire of 1676), but the mix of Gothic, Renaissance, Baroque and other 19th-century eclectic styles meld together subtly in an urban symphony.

The Clock Tower★★

> **A2** *Turnul cu Ceas. West of the piaţa Oberth (car park), a street leads to the citadel's main entrance and the piaţa Muzeului. Open Tue.-Sun. 9am-4pm. Admission charge. Allow 1 hr.*

Symbol of the institutions it once housed, the Clock Tower was the only tower that did not belong to a craft guild. In the 17th century, a local craftsman, installed a **double faced clock**★: one face looks over the low town and the other looks towards the citadel (*cetate* in Romanian, *burg* in German). Every night, on the sixth stroke of midnight, wooden figures, 80 cm-high, emerge on the clock faces: on the low town side, a statuette representing a day of the week replaces its predecessor. On the citadel side, figures symbolizing Law, Justice and Peace come out accompanied by a tambourine beating the hours. The Angel of Day emerges at 6am and is replaced at 4pm by the Angel of Night, bearing candles hereby announcing the opening hours of the workshops to the town.

Until 1556, the town council met in the tower which now houses the **History Museum**★ (*Muzeul de Istorie*).

On the first floor there is a scale model of the citadel as it was in

1735. The other floors are dedicated to the guilds, an old pharmacy and a collection of furniture. On the fifth floor, you can view the clock mechanism and from the roof walkway there is a great panoramic view of the city.

The Church on the Hill★

> **A3** *Biserica din Deal. From piaţa Muzeului, take str. Cositorarilor and turn right in piaţa Răţuştelor. Open daily. Admission charge.*

The 175 steps of the **Scholars' Steps★** (*Scara Şcolii*), a covered wooden staircase built in 1642, take you to the summit of the hill where you will find the **Church on the Hill**. Dedicated to Saint Nicholas, construction began in 1345 on the site of a 13th-century Romanesque church. It was designed according to the German Gothic model of a hall church (*Hallenkirche*). The luminous interior has the remains of some frescoes that were painted over during the time of the Reformation. In the north aisle, there is a superb **shuttered altarpiece★★** (*p. 164*).

Towards piaţa Cetăţii

> **A3/2/1** *From the Church on the Hill, take the street past the cemetery and ramparts (W), then head along str. Tâmplarilor and turn left to the piaţa Cetăţii.*

Passing the remains of the city ramparts, the road veers to the right, bringing you to a covered staircase. Head left down str. Cojocarilor, to one of the most delightful spots in town. The **Butchers' Tower** (*Turnul Măcelarilor*) stands next to the **Furriers' Tower** (*Turnul Cojocarilor*). Follow the ramparts to the 14th-century **Tailors' Tower** (*Turnul Croitorilor*), which is also the main city entrance. A bit further along the ramparts is the **Cobblers' Tower** (*Turnul Cizmarilor*).

Take str. Tâmplarilor back uphill. At n° 9, turn left down a little alleyway which leads to **piaţa Cetăţii**. This square exudes an atmosphere of peace and tranquility, undoubtedly due to its architectural harmony: no one building dominates. There are benches, plenty of shade, café terraces and restaurants. ●

© Pierre Soissons

The 64-m tall Clock Tower presides over the lower part of the town.

Sighişoara to Rupea★★

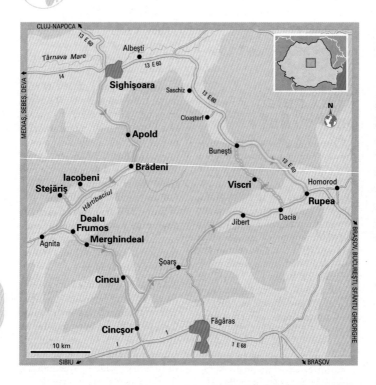

The Transylvanian hills become increasingly wild and abandoned in this area, striking in its austerity, especially when, at a turn in a road, you encounter the daunting profile of a massive citadel.

agenda

About 230 km from Sighişoara to Braşov. Allow at least 2 days. The best times to go are May, June or October. **Accommodation** at Sighişoara, Şoarş and Viscri.

Address book p. 174. ●

Hârtibaciu Valley★★

> **Harbachtal** (in German). 65 km S from Sighişoara to Cincşor. Leave Sighişoara and head for Agnita (S).

There are many citadels in this peaceful valley, including **Apold**★ (**Kleinpold** in German) and **Brădeni**★ (**Henndorf** in German). Take a right about 9 km into the valley, continue for 2 km and you will find the **Iacobeni citadel**★ (**Jakobsdorf** in German). Back to the Agnita road, after 4 km, take a right onto a non-tarmacked road to **Stejăriş**★★ (**Probstdorf** in German), a village with its **citadel** ★★ right at the centre. At the entrance to Agnita, turn left to find: **Dealu Frumos**★★ (**Schönberg** in German), a village with quadrilateral city walls with towers at each corner; **Merghindeal citadel**★ (**Mergeln** in German); the superb altar of **Cincu**★ **Church** (**Grosschenk** in German); and **Cincşor citadel**★ (**Kleinschenk** in German).

Viscri and the area around Rupea★★★

> *48 km from Cincşor to Rupea. From Cincşor, return towards Agnita and, after 3 km, turn right for Rupea.*

Saxon Transylvania was divided into jurisdictions or seats *(Stuhle)*. The **Rupea** jurisdiction is the eastern-most limit of the region, bordering Szekely Land *(p. 180)*.

● **Viscri** *(Deutsch-Weisskirch in German). On leaving Dacia, 7 km before Rupea coming from Cincşor, turn left onto a non-tarmacked road (8 km).* This village, situated in one of the most solitary parts of South-ern Transylvania, has remained miraculously intact. A long street climbs past the pastel-coloured facades of the village houses, tra-versed by a stream and regiments of poultry.

The **citadel★★★** *(to visit contact Car-oline Fernolend, house n° 13)* is visi-ble over the rooftops. A shaded alleyway brings you to the white entrance tower. The city walls (14th century and later) include three defensive towers and two bastions, crowned by a wooden walkway and a pyramidal roof.

From the top of the tower on the west side of the church (built 14th-century), you can see a typical example of the model plan of a Saxon village, including the way the plots of land are organised and the uniformity of its buildings *(p. 150)*.

●●● **In the area**: the citadels of **Cloaşterf★** and **Saschiz★** are on or near the DN 13, heading (N-W) for Sighişoara.

● **Rupea★**. *From Viscri, continue along the non-tarmacked road to Buneşti (9 km). Turn right onto the DN 13.* Overlooked by the ruins of a 13th-century citadel, the main street lined with old, faded house fronts is a reminder of the past importance of the town.

●●● **In the area**: Homorod citadel★, 3 km N-E of Rupea.

Get back onto the DN 13 which takes you to Braşov. ●

The citadel of Viscri.

© Pierre Soissons

Braşov and around★★

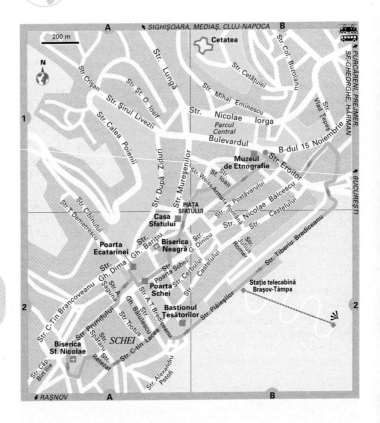

SIGHIŞOARA, MEDIAŞ, CLUJ-NAPOCA

The **Bârsa country** (*Ţara Bârsei*) extends across a plateau wedged in the mountains, within easy reach of major trade routes such as the Prahova Valley and the Rucar-Bran corridor. If the Germanic heritage of the area is still perceptible in street layouts, the native Romanian character of the mountain villages has also survived the centuries. Braşov and some of the surrounding villages in the Bârsa country also have a small Hungarian population. In addition to this multi-cultural richness, the region has another trump card: its proximity to the mountains offering endless possibilities for hiking and superb skiing in winter around Poiana Braşov.

As early as 1235, Braşov was known as Corona, which became Kronstadt in German. Its name in Romanian (Braşov) and Hungarian (Brasso) come from the river Bârsa. Protected by ramparts and the naturally difficult terrain, Kronstadt quickly became a prosperous city of powerful merchants and craftsmen. It was a key commercial town for the Romanian regions beyond the Carpathians, for Asia Minor, the Adriatic, and Central and Baltic Europe. Convoys of Romanian carts would set off from the Schei quarter of town to travel all over the continent. In the 16th century, the humanist **Johannes Honterus** (1498-1549) brought his philosophy to bear on the region. He was a propagator of the Reformation in Transylvania and organiser of the Saxon Evangelical Church. Braşov became one of the main Romanian industrial towns and it was here, in 1987, that the uprising began which brought about the downfall of the Ceauşescu regime. Today, there are 320,000 people living in Braşov.

Council Square★★

> *Piaţa Sfatului (Marktplatz in German). From bd Eroilor (car park), take str. Republicii, then turn right down str. Michail Weiss to piaţa Enescu.*

At one end of piaţa Enescu, an alley runs between the houses, leading to the main square, near the Orthodox church.

Houses from all eras, none more tha four floors high, form a homogenous picture around this vast square, where important fairs were held for many years.

The Council House★★

> **A2** *Casa Sfatului. Open daily except Mon. 10am-5pm. Admission charge.*

Gothic, Renaissance and Baroque styles are all found in this building situated in the middle of the square.

After centuries housing the municipal offices, the 14th-century Council House is now the **Departmental History Museum** (*Muzeul Judeţean de Istorie*), with good collections of archaeological finds and antique furniture as well as plentiful evidence of the prosperity of the Saxon guilds.

Little intimate streets such as str A. Hirscher are found to the south of the square; the west side is dominated by the imposing form of the Black Church.

The Black Church★★

> **A2** *Biserica Neagră (Schwarzkirch in German). Open daily except Sun. (for worship only) 7am-7pm. Admission charge, unless attending a service. About 30 mins.*

Built during a period of constant threat, construction of the church (1383-1477) was interrupted several times. The choir was finished early in the 15th century, at the height of the Gothic period. At the same time, statues were added to the buttresses, posed on plinths and sheltered by a canopy. Today, copies have replaced the original statues, which are mostly found in the **lapidarium★** in the western part of the church.

---

essentials

● **Position**. 145 km E of Sibiu on the DN 1, about 168 km N of Bucharest, 60 km from Rupea by the DN 13.

● **Getting around**. The historic centre is situated to the S-W of town and the train station to the N. The main road from Sighişoara to Bucharest runs right through the centre of town along str. Lungă, bd Eroilor, bd 15 Noiembrie and calea Bucureşti. There is a handy car park near the post office between bd Eroilor and str. Nicolae Iorga **B1**.

● **Transport**. The centre of town is pedestrian only. Bus, tram and trolley tickets are on sale in RATBV kiosks. Bus 20 serves Poiana Braşov.

● **Exploring the area**. You can see most of the town in half a day. Do not hesitate to have a look around the residential courtyards, remembering to look up to see the many pediments, caryatids and balconies. Piaţa Enescu is a nice spot to have lunch. A round trip by cable car up Mount Tâmpa and the Prejmer citadel will nicely complete your visit.

Accommodation available in Purcăreni p. 176. ***Address book*** p. 174. ●

Aerial view of the historic centre of Braşov dominated by the Black Church.

The **west door★** is a fine example of Central European Flamboyant Gothic, crowned with polyfoil arches surmounted by rows of intricately sculpted vine leaves.

In October 1542, the first Lutheran church service was taken in German by the great humanist **Johannes Honterus** (1498-1549), who brought the Reformation to Saxon Transylvania. During a fire, started by Austrian troops in 1689, the vaults of the nave collapsed and three quarters of the building was reduced to a blackened carcass. Hence the name.

The **collection of oriental carpets★** inside was built up over the 17th and 18th centuries, gifts from the town's travelling merchants.

The Schei quarter★

> **A2** *Schei. From the Black Church, take str. Benker, and then str. Poarta Schei on the right which leads to str. Prundului.*

As in their other towns, for a long time the Saxons would not allow other nationalities the right to live inside the citadel. A large Romanian community, established here long before the Saxons arrived, were forced to live outside the city walls, in the Schei quarter. The **Schei Door** (***Poarta Schei***), built in 1827, is its symbolic entrance.

●●● **In the area**. Leave the city through the **Poarta Schei**. On the right, **Catherine's Gate★** (***Poarta Ecatarinei***) dates from 1559 and is embellished with four watchtowers. The district grew up around the **Orthodox Church of Saint Nicholas★** (***Biserica Sf. Nicolae***) which, built in the 16th century and renovated in the 18th century, contains a bizarre mix of styles.

From the Church of Saint Nicholas, From thhead south-east along str. Retezat then str. Lacea. On your right before entering the old town, you will see the 15th-century Weavers Bastion (***Bastionul Ţesătorilor***); this is the best preserved of the seven bastions which reinforced the city walls.

Mount Tâmpa

> **B2** *From the Weaver's Bastion, take aleea Tiberiu Brediceanu.*

Walk along the ramparts for 1 km, the town on one side, and woods and Mount Tâmpa on the other.

●●● **Panorama★★**: there is a cable car (*open daily in summer 9am-7pm;*

winter 9.30am-4.45pm) and a path through woods (a 1 hr walk) to the top of Mount Tâmpa (*restaurant p. 175*): the town is at your feet.

Continue along alley Tiberiu Brediceanu, which brings you back to town near the post office car park. On your way down, take a break in **Titulescu Park**, where chess players sit among the trees.

●●● **Before you leave Braşov**: the **Ethnographic Museum★ B2** (*Muzeul de Etnografie*; bd Eroilor, 21 A, near the post office car park; ☎/fax 47. 55.62; open Tue.-Sun. 10am-5pm) tells the story of the region's textile heritage.

Prejmer★★★

> *Leave Braşov by the DN 11 towards Bacău. Continue for 11 km then turn right onto the DN 10 (towards Buzău). Open Tue.-Fri. 9am-5pm, Sat. 9am-2pm, Sun. noon-5pm. Free admission but donations are welcome. Allow 1 hr.*

Under the protection of Teutonic Knights, Saxon settlers took over the fertile land of the Bârsa plain. This large, open landscape is, however, vulnerable to attack. Peasants from Prejmer and Hărman therefore built massive citadels which, in case of a sustained siege, could house their entire communities.

The powerful Prejmer citadel (*Tartlau in German*) is far removed from the rustic citadels of the tiny Târnava villages (*p. 161*). A long, 18th-century vaulted passageway leads from the first row of fortifications to a **first interior courtyard** (*private; closed to the public*). A second galleried walkway gives access to the heart of the site protected by 12 m-high, 3/4 m-thick walls reinforced with bastions. Inside, lining the ramparts, are 272 storerooms, used by families of the community to store provisions. Livestock were kept in the courtyard around the church, which dates from 1250 and has the oldest altarpiece in Transylvania.

© Pierre Soissons

The Prejmer Church is typical of the work of Cistercian builders from Cârţa. (p. 149).

A little **museum★** completes the visit: furniture, clothing and other objects tell the visitor about the daily lives of Saxon peasants.

●●● **In the area**: the **Hărman citadel★★** (*Hönigberg in German; head back towards Braşov, after about 1 km on the DN11, take a right turn; open Tue.-Sun. 9am-noon, 1-5pm; admission charge; allow 30 mins*) is another similar, if more modestly-sized citadel.

Raşnov★★

> *About 10 km S-W of Braşov on the DN 73 towards Campulung.*

Perched on a rocky spur overlooking the town of Raşnov is a beautiful 14th-century peasant citadel. Behind the ramparts, a group of small houses has been restored to lodge tourists. The 140 m-deep well is said to have been dug by Turkish prisoners in exchange for their freedom. There is a small museum.

●●● **Suggested route**: south of Raşnov, on the DN 73, head for **Bran Castle** (12 km, *p. 96*). ●

Address book

Manfred Werner, one of the last Meşendorf (Viscri) Saxons.

© Bernard Houliat

Băgaciu

> Dialling code ☎ 265. See p. 161.

Accommodation

▲▲ **Suzana Sălcianu**, n° 62 ☎ 42. 56.93. Private guesthouse. *About 40 beds* available in several restored Saxon houses. *Meals provided* on request. Suzana will also show you around the citadel.

Biertan

>Dialling code ☎ 269. See p. 162.

❶ **Natura International**, str. 1 Decembrie, 1 ☎ 80.66.99, < www. biertan.ro >. Providing info. and hotel reservation in the village.

Accommodation

▲▲ **Pensiunea Omi**, str. Aurel Vlaicu, 1 ☎ 86.81.19. *3 rooms and meals provided*. This house dates from 1517; the pharmacy has been here since 1821.

Restaurant

◆◆◆ **Unglerus**. This is a rustic "medieval" style *restaurant* managed by Natura International. Good wine list. Art gallery.

Brașov

> Dialling code ☎ 268. Map p. 170.

Getting there

● **By train**. Many connections with Bucharest (over 3 hrs for 166 km) and other large towns in Transylvania. **Station**: 1 km N-E of the old town **Off map by B2**. **Railways agency** *(Agenția CFR)*, str. Republicii, 53 ☎ 47.06.96. *Open Mon.-Fri. 7am-7pm.*

● **By bus**. Brașov has bus routes to all the towns in the country. You can also catch coaches to Germany, Hun-

---

transport

Visiting Saxon towns by train

There is a good rail service between the various Saxon towns and with **Bucharest** and **Budapest**. There are several daily trains from Bucharest to Brașov, Sighișoara and Mediaș. The Dacia train (cheap sleepers) is useful as it journeys around the old Dacian region. It departs from Vienna, passes through Budapest, Mediaș, Sighișoara and Brașov before reaching Bucharest. Several daily trains also run between Sibiu and Mediaș. For information contact the railway agency of any town *(Agenția CFR)* or < www.cfr.ro >. ●

gary and France. **Atlassib** Reisen: str. Lungă, 1 **A1** ☎/fax 15.27.74. **Bus station** *(Autogara)*: near the railway station ☎ 42.68.82. **Minibus and maxitaxis**: on the station car park; departures for Bucharest and other big towns.

Useful addresses

● **Post office**. Str. Nicolae Iorga, 1 **B1**. *Open Mon.-Fri. 8am-8.30pm, Sat. 8am-1pm.*

Accommodation

▲▲▲ **Montana**, str. Stejerişului, 2A **off map by A2** ☎/fax 47.27.31. *7 large rooms.* Superbly situated on the Poiana Braşov road. Lovely view over the town. Supervised car park. *Restaurant.*

▲▲▲ **Pensiunea Stejeriş**, str. Stejerişului, 15 **Off map by A2** ☎ 15.23.85, fax 15.20.78. *5 rooms.* On the Poiana Braşov road. A terrace with a great view and a *restaurant.*

▲▲ **Hotel Coroana**, str. Republicii, 62 **B1** ☎ 14.43.30, fax 14.15.05. *75 rooms.* Superbly situated in the town centre.

▲▲ **Hotel Helis** ♥, str. Memorandului, 29 **off map by A1** ☎41.02.23, fax 41.50.19. *18 rooms* including 2 single, 10 double, 6 triples. Down an ordinary quiet street, parallel to str. Lungă (on the right from Sighişoara and Sibiu). Simple, clean and bright. *Restaurant.* Very reasonably priced. French, English and German speaking.

Restaurants

♦♦♦ **Bistro de l'Arte** ♥, piaţa Enescu, 11 bis **A1** ☎47.39.94. Intimately decorated with paintings and sculpture. Attentive service and good music.

♦♦ **Blue Corner** ♥, piaţa Enescu, 13 ☎ 0744.57.33.38 (mobile). A good choice of restaurant serving Romanian and French dishes.

♦♦ **Panoramic B2** ☎ 47.53.49. At the top of the Tâmpa cable car. Go for the superb view over the town. *Open 10am-4pm.*

♦♦ **Taverna**, str. Politehnicii, 6 ☎ 47.46.18. On a street off the str. Republicii. A large choice, good cooking and decent service.

Festivals

● **October**. Beer festival *(Festivalul Berii).* A great atmosphere.

Cristian

> Dialling code ☎ 269. Map p. 146.

Accommodation

▲▲ **Gasthaus Kasper** ☎ 57.92.96. *8 rooms.* One of the two inns in this handsome Saxon village, 9 km from Sibiu (4 km from the airport). *Restaurant.*

▲▲ **Gasthaus Spack** ♥ ☎ 57.92.62. *5 rooms.* A comfortable and welcoming little Saxon inn.

Gura Râului

> Dialling code ☎ 268. See p. 148.

Accommodation

▲▲ **Ţepeş Nicolae** ♥, n° 958 ☎ 57.23.24. *3 private guest rooms.* A traditional but recently renovated home built around a large interior courtyard. *Meals provided* from their local farm produce.

Mediaş

> Dialling code ☎ 269. See p. 159.

Getting there

● **By train**. Rail links to Cluj-Napoca, Sibiu, Sighişoara and Braşov *(see opposite).* **Station**: piaţa Unirii, 1. S-W from the centre of town. **The railways agency** *(Agenţia CFR)*: piaţa Regele Ferdinand, 5 ☎ 84.13. 51. *Open Mon.-Fri. 7.30am-7.30pm.*

● **By bus**. Daily links with the main Romanian towns. **Bus station** *(Autogara)*, piaţa Unirii, 8 ☎ 84.43.26. Near the railway station.

Useful address

Post office. Piaţa Unirii, 3. S-W of the old town.

Accommodation

▲▲▲ **Vila Flora ♥**, str. Hermann Oberth, 43 ☎ 83.56.65. *14 rooms*. Comfortable, on the main highway, near the exit to Sibiu.

▲▲ **Hotel Select**, str. Peföfi Sandor, 3 ☎ 83.48.74. *15 rooms*. In a road just off the main square. *Restaurant*.

▲ **Hotel Central**, str. Eminescu, 4-7 ☎ 84.17.87, fax 84.17.22. *128 rooms*. An ugly building but the bedrooms are respectable and reasonably priced.

Restaurant

♦♦ **Traube**, piaţa Regele Ferdinand I, 16 ☎ 84.48.98. There is a great terrace over-looking the main square.

Purcăreni

> *Dialling code* ☎ *268. Map p. 170.*

Accommodation

▲▲ **Lajos et Vilmi Matyas**, str. Principala, 509 ☎ 36.55.50 and 0745.81.86.83 (mobile), < arbredejoie@online.fr >. *4 private guest rooms*, 2 shared bathrooms. Hungarian and Romanian *cooking*. Well-situated, 20 km from Braşov.

▲▲ **Sandor et Erika Petö**, str. Zizin, 344 ☎ 0744.48.22.60 (mobile). *1 private guest room with 2 beds* and a bathroom. Generous *meals provided*.

Răşinari

> *Dialling code* ☎ *269. See p. 148.*

Accommodation

▲▲ **Petru Cioran**, str. Protopop Emil Cioran, 1503 ☎ 55.71.70. *6 rooms*. The famous philosopher's family is known for its friendliness and generosity: they will introduce you to their wine cellar and plum brandy. Safe parking.

Salişte

> *Dialling code* ☎ *269. Map p. 147.*

Accommodation

▲▲ **Casa Ittu**, str. Nicolae Iorga, 1271 ☎ 1271 55.39.03, < www.casa-ittu.ro >. *4 comfortable rooms*. A grand old building in the centre of the village. *Meals provided*.

Sibiel

> *Dialling code* ☎ *269. See p. 147.*

Accommodation

▲▲ **Casa Bunica Eugenia ♥** ☎ 55.25.09. *5 rooms and excellent meals provided*. Staying with the Grandma (*bunica* in Romanian) Eugenia Pau. A delightfully welcoming house in a rustic village; you will be made to feel a part of the family.

▲▲ **Cândea Maria** ☎ 55.25.32. *3 rooms* and *meals provided*. Another good address among around 30 host families in the village.

Sibiu

> *Dialling code* ☎ *269. Map p. 152.*

❶ **Tourist information centre** (*Centrul de Informare a Turiştilor*), piaţa Mare, 7 ☎ 21.11.10, fax 21.60.33, < www.sibiu.ro >. *Open Mon.-Fri. 9am-5pm, Sat. 9am-1pm*.

Getting there

● **By plane**. Sibiu international airport **Off map by A2** ☎ 21.11.39. 6 km along the Alba Iuliu road. **Tarom** flights from Bucharest to Munich stop over at Sibiu (5 flights per week). Daily **Carpatair** flights to Timişoara (219 km), from here there are international connections to Germany and Italy. **Tarom agency**: str. Nicolae Bălcescu, 10 **A2** ☎ 21.11.57. *Open Mon.-Fri. 8am-7pm, Sat. 8am-1pm*.

● **By train**. Daily links with Bucharest, Braşov and Mediaş. **Station**: piaţa 1 Decembrie 1918 **B1**,

N-E of the old town. **Railways agency** *(Agentia CFR)*: str. Nicolae Bălcescu, 6 **A2** ☎ 21.20.85. *Open Mon.-Fri. 7.30am-7.30pm.*

● **By bus**. Regular links with Germany, Italy and France. **Atlassib Reisen:** ☎ 22.92.24, < www.atlassib. ro >. **Bus station:** next to the railway station **B1** ☎ 21.77.57. Several buses a day to Bucharest and other large Romanian towns.

Useful addresses

● **Pharmacy**. **Farmasib**, str. Nicolae Bălcescu, 53 **A2** ☎ 21.78.97. *Open 24 hours a day.*

● **Post office**. Str. Mitropoliei, 14. **A2** *Open Mon.-Fri. 7am-8pm, Sat. 8am-1pm.*

Accommodation

▲▲▲▲ **Impăratul Romanilor** ♥, str. Nicolae Bălcescu, 4 **A2** ☎ 21.56.00. *96 rooms.* There has been an inn on this site since 1555, and it has received such notable guests as Emperor Joseph II, Franz Liszt, Johannes Brahms and Mihai Eminescu. The present building dates from 1895. *Restaurant.*

▲▲▲ **Bulevard**, piaţa Unirii, 10 **A2** ☎ 21.60.60. *122 rooms.* Ideally situated in the centre of town, comfortable and well-priced.

▲▲▲ **Ela**, str. Nouă, 43 **B1** ☎/fax 21. 51.97. *7 rooms.* An ancient house in the lower town.

▲▲▲ **Gasthof Clara**, str. Râului, 24 **A1** ☎ 22.29.14. A traditional Transylvanian atmosphere, for a reasonable price. On the edge of Cibin (there is a lot of traffic). *Good restaurant.*

Restaurants

♦♦♦ **Butoiul de Aur** ♥, pasajul Scărilor **A2** ☎ 21.45.75. Transylvania food in a pleasant decor, one of the town's oldest houses.

♦♦♦ **La Turn**, piaţa Mare, 1 **B2** ☎ 21.39.85. Next to the Council's Tower. A nice place even if the cook-ing is fairly ordinary. In summer, there is a terrace on the square.

♦♦ **Crama Ileana**, piaţa Teatrului, 2 **A/B2** ☎ 43.43.43. Relaxed atmosphere and good food.

♦♦ **Hermannstadt**, piaţa Mare, 8 **B2** ☎ 21.56.37. Good traditional Transylvanian cooking.

Bar

Art Cafe, str. Filarmonicii **B2**. In the basement of the concert hall. Art gallery and jazz music.

Shopping

● **Antiques**. **Antic**, str. Nicolae Bălcescu, 23 **A2** ☎ 21.16.04. Art Antic, piaţa Huet, 1 ☎ 21.11.15.

● **Crafts**. **Galeriile de Arta Populara**, str. Avram Iancu, 4 **B1**.

● **Market**. Piaţa agro-alimentară Cibin **A1**.

Festivals

● **June**. Romanian craft fair ♥, Dumbrava open-air museum.

● **August**. Sibiu festival and beer festival.

● **September**. Pottery festival, Dumbrava open-air museum.

● **October**. International jazz festival.

Sighişoara

> *Dialing code* ☎ 269. *Map p. 163.*

Getting there

● **By train** *(see inset p. 174)*. **Station:** piaţa Libertăţii, 51 **Off map by A1/B1** (N of the city). **Railways agency** *(Agentia CFR)*: str. 1 Decembrie 1918, 2 ☎ 77.18.20. *Open Mon.-Fri. 7.30am-7.30pm.*

● **By bus**. Daily links with Germany. Several links a day to Bucharest and other big towns in Romania. **Autogara Off map by A1/B1** ☎ 77.12. 60. Next to the station.

Accommodation

▲▲▲▲ **Casa cu Cerb** str. Şcolii, 1 **A2** ☎ 77.46.25, fax 77.73.49, *9 rooms.*

Very comfortable. One of the oldest houses in the heart of the citadel. It gets its name from the stag's head fixed on the corner of the building.

▲▲▲▲ **Casa Wagner ♥**, piaţa Cetăţii, 6 **B2** ☎ 50.60.14 fax 50.60.15, < www. casa-wagner.com >. *3 large rooms* with Gothic arches, fine decor and antique furniture. *Excellent restaurant* (Romanian, Saxon and Hungarian cooking). Terrace on the square, under a walnut tree.

▲▲▲ **Hotel Sighişoara**, str. Şcolii, 4-6 **A2** ☎ 77.10.00. *29 rooms.* Right at the heart of the citadel, just a stone's throw from piaţa Cetăţii. Comfortable, simple. *Restaurant, wine cellar.* Conference room.

▲▲ **Hotel-restaurant Claudiu**, str. Ilarie Chendi, 28 **Off map by A3** ☎/fax 77.98.82. *16 rooms.* Simple, comfortable, in a street along the south side of the citadel (towards Agnita). *Restaurant.*

▲ **Hotel Steaua ♥**, str. 1 Decembrie 1918, 12 **B3** ☎ 77.15.94. *50 rooms.* At the beginning of the 20th century, this hotel was the pride of the town. Today it is a bit run-down but still has a quaint charm and beautiful façade. Welcoming staff. *Restaurant.*

Şoarş

> *Dialling code* ☎ *268. See p. 168.*

Accommodation

▲▲ **Mihai Patrichi**, str. Principala, 155 ☎ 40.48.48. *3 private guest rooms and meals provided.* A welcoming family, with a contagious sense of humour. Some of the best *cooking* in Transylvania, served in the garden.

▲ **Maria et Viorel Giurgu**, str. Principala, 145. *2 private guest rooms and meals provided.* No telephone but a

fantastic welcome. *Excellent cooking.* The rooms are in an independent little house.

Tilişca

> *Dialling code* ☎ *269. See p. 147.*

Accommodation

▲▲ **Irina et Nicuşor Balea**, str. Şcolii, 535 ☎ 55.40.09 and 0744.31.31.02 (mobile). *5 rooms.* A modern and comfortable house. Superb cooking.

▲▲ **Mihai Rodean**, str. Principala, 84 ☎ 55.41.73. *4 rooms.* A genuine shepherding family. Excellent cooking served with the owner's home made white wine. This old shepherd has the mean look of someone who has spent years in the outdoors, following his flock.

▲ **Elena Luga**, str. Principala, 561 ☎ 55.40.12. *2 rooms.* The delightful and French-speaking Elena will tell you the epic story of her family of shepherds and will show you around the little village Ethnographic museum.

Viscri

> *Dialling code* ☎ *268. See p. 169.*

Accommodation

▲ **Fundaţia Alba Fglesia**, house n° 13 ☎ 0724.57.09.92 (mobile). *About 20 private guest rooms* around the village. An association promoting the interests of Viscri, Caroline and Walter Fernolend will find you accommodation with a family in the village. A warm welcome and good cooking. The homes are all old Saxon cottages. They have wash basins but for the most part the lavatory is outside (shed in the garden). ●

The heart of Transylvania

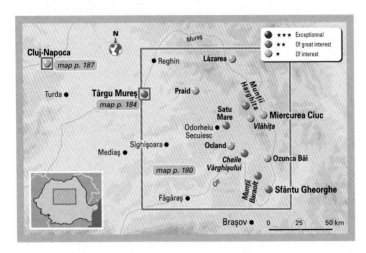

● ★★★	Exceptionnal
● ★★	Of great interest
● ★	Of interest

Cluj-Napoca
map p. 187

Mureş

Reghin ● Lăzarea ●

Turda ● **Târgu Mureş** ● Praid ●
map p. 184

Munţii Harghita

Satu Mare ● ● Miercurea Ciuc
Odorheiu ● Vlăhiţa
Secuiesc

Sighişoara ● Ocland ●

Mediaş ● Cheile ● Ozunca Băi
map p. 180 Vârghişului

Olt

Munţii Baraolt ● Sfântu Gheorghe

Făgăraş ●

Braşov ● 0 25 50 km

The Transylvania of myth lies to the east, bordering the Carpathians. The landscape takes on an disturbingly savage beauty. Mist swirls around the **Harghita Mountains**, where wild bears and wolves take refuge, and sulphurous springs bubble up. To the south, you can almost picture a procession of children skipping out of one of the caves, following the Pied Piper *(see inset p. 182)*. It is difficult to know how to describe the **Szeklers**, a fascinating people similar to the Magyars, inhabiting the forests and bitter cold high plateaux, a people proud of their epic history.

To the west, a different, gentler Transylvania stretches out, that of the Enlightenment and of opening up to the world. A kaleidoscope of different identities manifests, collectively and individually, the uniqueness of Transylvanian culture: Cluj-Napoca and its universities; Târgu Mureş and the cultural frenzy of the 1900s; the robust Saxon civilisation *(p. 150)*; and the faded memory of the Hungarian aristocracy with its ruined castles.

© Pierre Soissons

Szekely Land★★

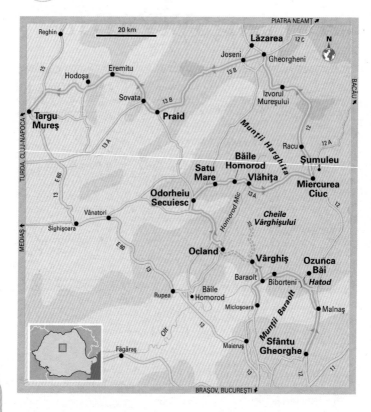

In the west, the land of the Szeklers (*Székelyföld in Hungarian*) is sheltered by the Harghita Mountains and their of foothills, and in the east, by the Carpathians. In the middle, large areas of low-lying lands, the coldest in Romania, are drained by the **Olt** and **Mureş** rivers. Almost 700,000 Szeklers – out of an estimated 1,700,000 citizens constituting Romania's Hungarian minority – live here, concentrated in the districts of Harghita, where they represent roughly 85% of the population, Covasna (74%) and Mureş (less than half). The majority are Lutheran, Unitarian, or Catholic *(see inset p.186)*. That Hungarians have Asian roots is well known; where Szeklers come from is uncertain.

Migration took place in two phases: **Attila** and his **Huns** crossed the Carpathians in the 5th century and the seven Hungarian tribes, led by **Arpad,** swept into the area at the end of the 9th century.

The Szeklers like to say they are descendants of the Huns, some of whom settled here. Isolated in the middle of the Carpathians, they have perpetuated their traditions and a language full of archaisms. For a long time, they used a strange form of cuneiform writing.

Those who love love hiking will feel the primal call of Nature: moist peat moss, sulphurous or salty springs, pine trees veiled with lichen and even bears' footprints on the humid forest floors.

Sfântu Gheorghe to the Harghita Mountains★★

> *From Sfântu Gheorghe take the DN 12 towards Odorheiu Secuiesc.*

This bushy route merely gives a glimpse of a little known region of spectacular landscapes, traditional villages and rich cultural heritage, where the slightest town has either a castles or a fortified church.

The Sfântu Gheorghe Museum★★

> *Muzeul Naţional Secuiesc or Székely Múzeum. Sfântu Gheorghe (Sepsiszentgyörgy in Hungarian): about 188 km N of Bucharest on the DN 1, DN 11, DN 12, 32 km N of Braşov on the DN 11 and DN 12. Str. Kos Karoly, 10 ☎ 31.24.42. Open Tue.-Fri. 9am-4pm, Sat.-Sun. 9am-1pm, closed on Mon. Admission charge. Tour: approx. 1 hr. Address book p. 193.*

Apart from its fascinating ethnographical collections, the **Szekler Museum★★** has a vast amount of documentation on the history and culture of this people. A collection of traditional doors is exhibited in the grounds, along with a reconstruction of a Szekler home.

The Baraolt Mountains and the Vârghiş Gorges★★

> *Vârghiş: 55 km N-W of Sfântu Gheorghe. From Sfântu Gheorghe take the DN 12 towards Miercurea Ciuc. At Malnaş, take a left to Baraolt.*

The **Hatod Pass★** (710 m) reveals a grassy landscape dotted with beech trees.

Beyond the pass, to the right, a road leads off near the **Hatod Inn** to **Ozunca Băi★** ("Ozunca" springs), a thermal hamlet lying in the bottom of a little grassy valley.

Back on the main road, your next stop will be **Biborteni**, a village renown for its mineral spring water. Then, in Baraolt, turn right to Odorheiu Secuiesc.

exploring

Approx. 250 km from Sfântu Gheorghe to Târgu Mureş.

Roads are good except from Vârghiş to Odorheiu Secuiesc and Gheorgheni to Praid. Allow at least two days.

In May, the meadows bloom with daffodils and in September, woods are ablaze with colour.

Accommodation in Băile Homorod, Ozunca Băi, Odorheiu Secuiesc, Micloşoara.

Address book p. 191. ●

In **Vârghiş★**, the village's municipal offices are in the 17th-century **Daniel Castle★** once owned by an important Szekler family.

On leaving the town towards Odorheiu Secuiesc, take a right down an unpaved road. The ♥ **Vârghiş Gorges★★** *(Cheile Vârghişului)* is 13 km down this track. The torrent has created a narrow, 4 km-long passage through the limestone.

♥ From Vârghiş to the Vlăhiţa Pass★★

> *Vlăhiţa: about 110 km N of Sf. Gheorghe, 67 km N of Vârghiş, 25 km N of Odorheiu Secuiesc. From Vârghiş, take a right towards Odorheiu Secuiesc.*

Here, the road takes you through one of the most magical landscapes in Transylvania. Turn right when you reach the **Homorod Mic Valley★**.

Surrounded by small ramparts, the **Ocland Church★**, built in the 13th-century, belongs, like many others in this valley, to the Unitarian Church *(see inset p. 186).*

You drive through an isolated yet beautiful landscape, dotted with church steeples, before finally reaching **Odorheiu Secuiesc** *(Székelyudvarhely in Hungarian)*, a former Roman encampment. A little legend

The Pied Piper of Hameln

In 1284, the market village of Hameln (N. Germany) was overrun by rats. One day, a stranger came to town and offered a solution to the problem, for a small fee. As soon as the deal was done, the man took out a flute and started playing. A haunting melody filled the air bringing rats pouring out from all around; they followed the man all the way to the river Weser where they drowned. When he returned to claim his fee, however, the authorities refused to honour their promise. So, some days later, on the 26th June, the Feast of Saints Peter and Paul, the man returned. Taking out a golden flute, he started playing such a sweet melody that all 130 children from Hameln followed him. Heading west they disappeared into a cave, never to be seen again. This tale exists in many versions; some say the children ended up much further east, in Transylvania, and were the origin of its German population. The Piper and his followers were supposed to have emerged from none other than the **Almaş** (or Mereşti) **Cave** , in the **Vârghiş Gorges** (p. 181). ●

further on, in **Satu Mare,** ♥ **traditional gateways**★★ (p. 204) line both sides of the road, some of which date from the 19th century.

The road rises and passes the thermal pools in **Băile Homorod**★. Here, the forest hides countless springs and wooden cabins. At the heart of the ♥ **Harghita Mountains**★★ (*Munţii Harghita*), amid the dense forest stretching for miles, are hints of ancient craters. Patches of light come from a rare meadow, an inhospitable ridge top or vast peat bogs where, narcissi, dwarf birches and conifers struggle against the cold and the wind.

Drive on from the **Vlăhiţa Pass**★ to Ciuc country (*Csík in Hungarian*).

Olt, Mureş and the salt marshes

The **Olt**, one of the biggest rivers in Romania, starts its journey above the low, flat **Ciuc country** separated by a small pass from a high valley, **Giurgeu country** (*Gyergyó in Hungarian*), from where another large river begins, the **Mureş**. This is the spriritual home of the Szeklers: the plateaux between these two rivers, scene of many tragic episodes in their history.

Miercurea Ciuc★ and around

> *Csíkszereda in Hungarian. 270 km N of Bucharest, 133 km N of Sf. Gheorghe, 48 km E of Odorheiu Secuiesc. From Odorheiu Secuiesc or Vlăhiţa Pass, take the DN 13 A.* **Address Book** *p. 192.*

The capital of both Harghita and Ciuc regions, has been partially modernised: some interesting relics remain, however, in the pedestrian street **Petőfi Sandor**★, among rows of elegant facades and restaurants.

In the upper town, west of the town hall, there is a citadel fortified with bastions.

● **Ciuc Szekler Museum**★ (*Muzeul Secuiesc al Ciucului*). *Piaţa Cetăţii, 2* ☎ *11.17.27. Open Tue.-Fri. 9am-4pm, Sat.-Sun. 9am-1pm, closed Mon. Admission charge. Tour: approx. 30 mins.* The Ciuc region's Szekler Museum is housed in **Count Miko Castle**. Construction finished in the 17th century and the Austrians fortified it later in 1714. The museum has an interesting ethnographic section as well as some traditional Szekler doorways and houses.

● **The Franciscan Monastery in Şumuleu★** *(Csíksomlyó in Hungarian). From Miercurea Ciuc, take the Gheorgheni road (N) and turn right towards Şumuleu. Cathedral open every day 8am-6pm; free admission.* A Franciscan monastery and school were founded on this site in 1442 by **Iancu de Hunedoara** *(see inset p. 137).* It was devastated, however, by General Basta in 1600 and then obliterated by the Tatars in 1661.

Work on the present Franciscan **cathedral** begun in 1802, was only completed 70 years later. It stands in the middle of a monastic settlement, the spiritual centre of the Szeklers, whose destiny the Franciscans have always shared.

Miercurea Ciuc to Lăzarea★

> *Lăzarea: 196 km W of Sf. Gheorghe, 63 km N of Miercurea Ciuc, 6 km N of Gheorgheni. From Miercurea Ciuc, take the DN 12 to Gheorgheni and Lăzarea.*

Winding through an ever-greener countryside, the road climbs over the **Izvorul Mureşului Pass,** source of the River Mureş, and into **Giurgeu country** *(Gyergyó in Hungarian).*

The small village of **Lăzarea★** *(Gyergyószárhegy in Hungarian)* follows **Gheorgheni**. It is overshadowed by a Franciscan monastery and **Lăzar Castle★** with its original ramparts and turrets, built in the 16th century by a noble Szekler family.

From **Lăzarea** or **Gheorgheni**, an overgrown country road leads to **Praid** *(Parajd in Hungarian).*

●●● **Suggested route:** The DN 12 C passes right through **Gheorgheni**. This road meanders through Moldavia, around **Lake Roşu** and the **Bicaz Gorges** *(p. 267).*

The Praid salt mine★

> *Salina Praid. 276 km N-W of Sf. Gheorghe, 85 km W of Lăzarea. From Lăzarea, take a right towards Joseni then take the DN 13 B (bad condition) as far as Praid. In the town center, take the DN 13 A on the right, then turn left onto a road just before the end of town. The mine is open every day 9am-7pm ; tickets can be bought from the bus driver. Tour: 70 min. **Address book** p. 193.*

This thermal town is famous for its salt mines. The entrance lies about 50 m from the main road: not only does the mine still manage to extract 500 tonnes of salt per month, it also has a therapeutic centre for **asthma** sufferers and those with **delicate lungs.**

An incredible chamber has been cut out of the salt face at a depth of 180 m, 15 m high and covering two hectares. People come here to spend a few hours breathing in the fine salt particles that float in the air.

●●● **In the area:** back in **Târgu Mureş**, turn right at Sovata, a famous spa, and continue through beautiful countryside to the villages of **Eremitu** and **Hodoşa.**

Târgu Mureş★★

> **Marosvasarhely** in Hungarian.
336 km N of Bucharest, 57 km W of Praid.
From Praid take the DN 13 to Sovata then
a right. Back on the DN 13, turn right.
Address book p. 193.

As the name suggests ("Mureş market"), Târgu Mureş has long been the commercial and economic hub of Central Transylvania. In the 16th century, each of the seven citadel towers was owned by a different guild. This market town not only played a part in the 1848 Revolution, it was also a hotbed of cultural activity – mainly in the fields of theatre and music. In the early 20th century, a young mayor, **Bernady György**, reinvented the town centre with the help of the cream of Hungary's avant-garde creative talent. Today, this bilingual town has an dynamic atmosphere.

The Prefecture★

> **A1 Prefectura**. S-E of the piaţa
Trandafirilor. Piaţa Victoriei. Open Mon.-
Fri. 9am-6pm. Free admission (main hall).

The building is easily recognisable thanks to its distinctive glazed roof-

essentials

● **Târgu Mureş**: capital of the Mureş.district. Population of approx 170,000.

● **Finding your way**. The most interesting part of town is around piaţa Trandafirilor **A-B1**. "Roses Square" is effectively a stretch of avenue with a raised bed of roses running along the centre. The train station **off map by A2** is on the outskirts of town to the west. The airport **off map by A2** is on the Cluj-Napoca road (12 km W). **Parking** in piaţa Trandafirilor and adjacent streets.

● **Sightseeing**. 2 hrs should suffice to see the town unless 1900s art is a particular passion. The piaţa Trandafirilor is closed to traffic on Sundays and holidays: the perfect opportunity to appreciate the Secession façades before settling down in one of the café terraces.

Address book p. 193. ●

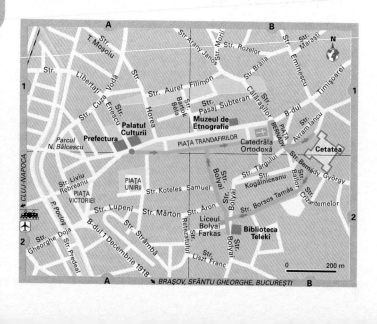

Severe on the outside, the interior of the Târgu Mureş' Palace of Culture is sensual and poetic.

tiles and the 60m-high bell-tower. Built in 1907 by the famous architects **Jakab and Komor** *(p. 125)*, it was the first in a series of Secessionist buildings that marked the town centre's renovation in the early 20th century *(see inset p. 125)*. The **entrance hall** has a strangely poetic feel. The ribs of the vault form a star pattern with large flowers at their centre. A winged stone bench rests upon the paws of some kind of beast and the parapet of the main staircase is carved to resemble folds of negligently undulating cloth.

♥ The Palace of Culture**

> **A2** *Palatul Culturii*. *Piaţa Trandafirilor. Open Tue.-Fri. 9am-4pm, Sat.-Sun. 9am-1pm. Visit: about 1 hr.*

Bernady György's urban renewal plan culminated in 1913 with the inauguration of this building, the most typical example of the **Transylvanian Secession** style *(see inset p. 125)*. The architects **Jakab and Komor** yielded to the Viennese style, a style they tried to break free from in their work in Oradea *(p. 125)*. They have relinquished their typically sinuous forms for a more geometric vocabulary. The main feature of this palace is its decor, which called for the talents of the greatest artists of the day in ceramics, stained glass, painting, cabinet making, etc.

● **The Hall of Honour**. *Free admission*. This 45m-long domed hall is decorated with plant motifs and frescoes depicting epic tales from Szekler mythology. This "idealised" people is a recurrent theme in the interior design of the palace; even their traditional embroidery patterns have influenced the ornamentation.

● **The Hall of Mirrors**** *(Sala Oglinzi)*. The finest example of this decorative style is found in the breathtaking hall on the first floor. With mirrors lining both sides of the room, an illusion of infinite

religion

The Unitarian Church

What do President Jefferson, Newton, Darwin and Dickens have in common? They were all members of a cult born in the 16th century in Transylvania after the Reformation. Its founder, **David Ferencs**, was a brilliant theologian, who was, in turn, a Catholic, Lutheran, and Calvinist priest. He took up the theories of Michael Servet (1511-1553) who questioned the dogmas set down in the 4th and 5th centuries, including those of the Trinity, the Incarnation and Original Sin. For these reformers, God was One (hence "Unitarian") and Jesus was man and prophet. The Prince of Transylvania, **John Sigismund**, was a convert. Ferencs founded the first **Unitarian Church** in Cluj in 1568. In the same year, the Prince proclaimed the **Edict for Religious Toleration**, to install some freedom of thought at a time when Europe was ravaged by religious wars. Later, Transylvanian Unitarianism spread to England and America. Today, there are 160 churches and 60,000 worshipers in Transylvania. ●

depth is created. However, it is the huge stained glass windows which really catch the eye.

Some of these were created by the Hungarian painter **Nagy Sandor**, who has depicted the tragic episodes of Szekler history. But, instead of glorifying the proverbial coarseness of his warrior-people, the artist has depicted unconstrained figures, faces with expressions of doubt, ambiguous stares. As if this long room lacked sensuality, the designers have dreamt up the most exquisite furniture in the shape of tulips.

Before leaving the Hall of Mirrors, ask if you can slip into the circle of the **concert hall** to check out superb decor and renowned acoustics. The excellent **philharmonic orchestra** gives concerts here (p. 194). Organ recitals are also given on the huge 1914 organ.

The Ethnographic Museum*

> **B1** *Muzeul de Etnografie şi Artă Populară. Piaţa Trandafirilor, 11* ☎ *21.58.07. Open Tue.-Fri. 9am-4pm, Sat.-Sun. 9am-1pm. Admission charge.*

Tholdologi Palace, built in 1762 in a Baroque style, houses the town's ethnographic museum, an excellent introduction to Central Transylvanian folk art.

●●● **In the area: on the north side** of **piaţa Trandafirilor** there is a fine row of Secession facades; on the **east** side is the **Orthodox Cathedral** (*Catedrăla Ortodoxă*, 1934).

Teleki Library*

> **B2** *Biblioteca Teleki. S side of the piaţa Trandafirilor. Str. Bolyai, 17. Open Tue.-Fri. 9am-4pm; Sat.-Sun. 9am-1pm. Admission charge.*

In this palace, completed in 1802, the Chancellor of Transylvania, Count **Samuel Teleki,** founded a library, donating 40,000 books from his personal collection. Later, 90,000 other works from the reformed college were added to the collection.

The palace also pays hommage to the mathematicians **Farkas** and **János Bolyai** who developed non-Euclidean geometry.

From Târgu Mureş, you are a 105 km drive away from Cluj-Napoca, *via* **Turda.** ●

Cluj-Napoca ★

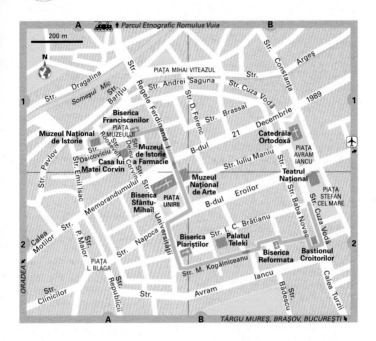

Since prehistoric times, people have been drawn to this area and its hills huddling close to the River Someș forming a transverse valley or cluse (*clusius* in Latin, hence the name of the town). The Dacians (*see p. 39*) founded a base here which played a strategic role in the Roman invasion of Dacia, but its precise location is unknown. **Napoca** on the other hand is known to have been Roman as early as 108 AD. At the end of the 11th century, the whole region was annexed by the Hungarian Kingdom.

A MAJOR CROSSROADS

Cluj-Napoca lies at the crossroads of two major axes: the east-west route from Transylvania to the plains of Central Europe via Oradea (*p. 122*) and the north-south route that links Moldavia to Galicia and on to the eastern foothills of the Apuseni Mountains (*p. 131*). This strategic position attracted the Saxons as early as the late 12th century. In 1316, Charles-Robert, King of Hungary granted the town the privileged status of a free town. From then on Cluj flourished: it rebuilt its ramparts and designed a town plan much like a chessboard, still visible today.

THE CULTURAL CENTRE OF TRANSYLVANIA

When **Matei Corvin** (*see inset p. 190*), born in Cluj, became King of Hungary, his native town benefitted. In 1568, Prince **John Sigismund** proclaimed the **Edict for Religious Tolerance** (*see opposite*). Slowly taking over from Alba Iulia as the cultural centre of Transylvania, Cluj theen became the region's administrative capital from 1790 to 1867. From then on, under Habsburg rule, architects and sculptors were drawn to Transylvania, bringing Baroque currents to the town and region.

● **Position**. About 440 km N-W of Bucharest, 152 km E of the border *via* Oradea on the DN 1, 105 km N-W of Târgu Mureş on the DN 15 and DN 1. Capital of the Cluj district. Population 450,000.

● **Finding your way**. The two main roads cross the sprawling modern part of town, and converge towards the historic centre between piaţa Unirii **A2**, piaţa Muzeului **A1**, and piaţa Ştefan cel Mare **B1** and piaţa Avram Iancu **B2**. Parking available. The train station (N **off map by A1**) is linked to the centre by tram 101 or taxis. The airport is 6 km N-E of town **off map by B1**.

● **Sightseeing**. At least half a day is necessary to explore piaţa Unirii and the neighbouring area and an evening enjoying the student atmosphere in the city's bars.

Address book p. 191. ●

True to its past, Cluj-Napoca is still a bustling hive of cultural activity today: next to the trilingual university (Romanian, Hungarian and German) that can take up to 40,000 students, there is a Romanian theatre and a Hungarian theatre, as well as British, German and French cultural centres.

Piaţa Unirii★

The square is surrounded with facades of contrasting styles, sometimes one on top of the other, with Baroque features juxtaposing remains of Gothic, Renaissance and Neoclassical buildings. The space is dominated by St Michael's Church and the Banffy Palace.

St Michael's Church★

> **A2** *Biserica Sfântu Mihail. Piaţa Unirii. Open daily 6am-8pm. Free admission. (not during services). Visit: about 30 mins.*

This church dates from the mid-14th century but has been modified several times. On the western facade, there is a doorway from 1444, where St Michael stands under a trilobate arch, early evidence of the Renaissance. Inside, slender ribbed vaults enhance the space. Note the **sacristy door★**: the surround (1528) is abundantly carved with motifs taken from the Italian Renaissance.

♥ The National Art Museum★

> **A2** *Muzeul Naţional de Arte. Piaţa Unirii, 30 ☎ 19.69.52. Open Wed.-Sun. 12pm-7pm. Admission charge. Visit: 1 hr.*

Between 1774 and 1785, the Saxon architect Johann Eberhardt Blaumann (creator of Brukenthal Palace in Sibiu) undertook the construction of **Banffy Palace** for the family of the Governor of Transylvania, Banffy György. On top of the balustrade crowning the Baroque facade are statues of ancient divinities, surmounted by the family coat of arms. The palace houses the **National Art Museum's★** bountiful collection of works from the 16th century to the present day. Among the oldest pieces are the **Jimbor Polyptych★** (16th century), a fine example of Saxon art, and a **collection of icons**.

North of the square

> **A2** *Cross the square towards **str. Regele Ferdinand I**. Then towards piaţa Muzeului.*

On the site of the town's first pharmacy (1573), **Hintz House** now contains the **Museum of Pharmacy History★** (*Muzeul de Istorie a Farmacie; piaţa Unirii, 28 ☎ 59.75.67; open Mon.-Sat. 10am-4pm; admission charge*), with over 2,300 exhibits.

The house where Matei Corvin was born in Cluj-Napoca.

© Bernard Houliat

Continue around the square and take str. Vasile Goldiș on the right; at the end of which is **Mathias Corvin's house** (*Casa lui Matei Corvin*; *str. Matei Corvin, 6; closed to the public*), partly 15th-century, the birthplace of the future King of Hungary (*see inset p. 190*).

The road on the right of the house leads to piața Muzeului. On the right, stands the **Franciscan Church** (*Biserica Franciscanilor*; *str. Victor Deleu, 4; open daily 7am-7pm; free admission except during services*), built on the site of a Romanesque edifice, destroyed by the Tatars in 1241. It was renovated during the Baroque period.

The History Museum is on the other side of this small square.

The History Museum★ (*Muzeul Național de Istorie a Transilvaniei*; *str. Daicoviciu, 2* ☎ *19.17. 18; open daily except Mon. 10am-4pm; admission charge*) displays a variety of Gothic and Renaissance doorframes and ornamental sculptures on the ground floor. The first floor is dedicated to prehistory and the Dacian period.

The university district★

> **A/B2** *From piața Unirii, head S passing the Hotel* Continental *on the corner of str. Universității.*

Follow this road and you pass the elegant Baroque **Piarist Church** (*Biserica Piariștilor*; *str. Universității, 5; open daily 7.30am-6.30pm; free admission except services*), constructed between 1718 and 1724.

Next, you come to **Teleki Palace** (*Palatul Teleki*), finished in 1795, which now houses the library (*Biblioteca Judeteana*; *str. M. Kogălniceanu, 7. Open Mon.-Fri. 9am-7.45pm, Sat. 9am-12.45pm; free admission*).

Towards the end of the street is the **Hungarian Reformed Church★** (*Biserica Reformata*; *str. Kogălniceanu, 21; open daily 8.30am-6pm except in winter; free admission except during services*). Its stark, robust form is punctuated by massive buttresses. It was built in late Gothic-style, commenced under Mathias Corvin (*inset p. 190*) in 1486 and completed in 1516.

portrait

Matei Corvin

Cluj provided Hungary with one of its greatest rulers: Matei (Mathias I) Corvin (1443-1490). In 1458, this young son of **Iancu de Hunedoara** (John Hunyadi; *see inset p. 137*) was elected King of Hungary despite the formidable opposition put forward by supporters of the Austrian Emperor Frederick III of Habsburg. While reforming and centralising his power, he proved himself in battle by containing the advancing Turks and the pretentions of his aspiring neighbour, Austria. Having momentarily pushed back the Habsburg Empire in 1480, he set up residence in Vienna, where he died in 1490.

His rule was also characterised by his versatile and often ambiguous relationships with two great Romanian princes, his cousin Vlad Tepeş, alias Dracula *(see inset p. 43)*, and **Stefan the Great** *(p. 43)*, Voivode of Moldavia: he did not hesitate to betray their trust and often claimed the glory for battles they won against the Turks.

He is remembered for his humanism and for his passion for art. His third marriage, to **Beatrice**, **daughter to the King of Naples**, brought many Italian artists to Central Europe. The spirit of the Renaissance was thus brought to Cluj and subsequently spread through Transylvania over the following decades. ●

The road continues on to a vestige of the Medieval city ramparts: a massive tower, the **Tailors' Bastion★** *(Bastionul Croitorilor; closed to the public)*.

Further east you emerge onto piaţa Ştefan cel Mare to the south, and piaţa Avram Iancu to the north. Between the two is the **National Theatre★** *(Teatrul Naţional)*, a flamboyant building, whose towers are topped by chariots being pulled by lions.

On piaţa Avram Iancu stands the imposing **Orthodox Cathedral** *(Catedrăla Ortodoxă)* completed in 1933.

●●● **Suggested route**: on your way back to Maramureş *(p. 195)* you can visit the village of **Bistriţa** *(124 km N-E of Cluj-Napoca on the DN 17)*, which was once a large Saxon settlement, and experience the grandiose scenery of the **Bârgau Mountains** *(Munţii Bârgău)*.

Romulus Vuia Ethnographic Park★

> **Off map by A1** *Parcul Etnografic. 5 km N-W of piaţa Unirii, by n° 30 bus. Str. Tăietura Turcului ☎ 18.67.76 or 58.67. 76. Open daily May-Sept. 10am-5pm, Oct.-April 9am-4pm. Admission charge.*

The Transylvanian **Tower of Babel** is well represented by some 200 Romanian, Saxon, Hungarian and Szekler constructions. One part of the park is dedicated to traditional housing, another to outbuildings: for grinding gold-bearing ores, sheep rearing, forges and tanneries. The park also contains three 18th-century wooden churches, originally from Transylvanian villages, including the Cizer Church, the work of Horea *(p. 135)*, a Moţi artisan. This church is from the **Salaj** region (between Cluj and Oradea), renowned for its wooden churches, the most famous of which is **Fildu du Sus Church★** (18th century). ●

Address book

Cluj-Napoca national theatre.

© Pierre Soissons

Băile Homorod (Homoródfürdo)

> *Dialling code* ☎ *266. See p. 182.*

Accommodation

▲▲ Pensiunea Lobogó ☎ 24.75.45. *11 rooms.* A nice stop-over, even though it is on the side of the road. Restaurant (a goulash will warm you up in cold weather). Thermal spring and forest walks nearby.

Cluj-Napoca (Kolozsvar)

> *Dialling code* ☎ *264. See p. 187.*

❶ **Pan Travel**, str. Traian Grozavescu ☎/fax 42.05.16, **Off map by A1** < www.pantravel.ro >. *Open Mon.-Fri. 9am-5pm.* A helpful little travel agency. Information and hotel reser-

vations. **Car rental** available at good prices.

Getting there

● **By plane**. Daily connections with Bucharest (Tarom) and Budapest (Carpatair). Weekly flights to Frankfurt (Tarom) and Vienna (Austrian Airlines). **International airport**: str. Traian Vuia, 149 **Off map by B1** (Dej road), 8 km from Cluj-Napoca town centre. **Tarom agency** piața Mihai Viteazu, 11 **A1/B1** ☎ 53.01.16, fax 43.25.24. *Open Mon.-Fri. 8am-1pm, 2pm-7pm; Sat. 9am-1pm.* **Carpatair agency**: airport ☎ 41.60.16, fax 41.68.53, < www.carpatair.ro >. *Open Mon.-Fri. 9am-6pm; Sat. 9am-12pm.*

● **By train**. Daily connections with Bucharest and other big towns in W. Romania. Two departures per day to Oradea and Budapest. **Railway station Off map by A1**: N of Cluj

Napoca. Railway company *(Agenţia CFR)*: piaţa Mihai Viteazu, 10 **A1/B1**, ☎ 43.20.01. *Open Mon.-Fri. 7am-7pm.*

• **By bus**. Many daily departures to Bucharest and other big towns in Romania. Connections with western Europe. **Bus station** *(Autogara)*: str. Giordano Bruno, 3-5, (near the railway station) **Off map by A1** ☎ 43.52.78. **Eurolines**: bd 21 Decembrie, 54-56 (Hotel *Victoria*) ☎/fax 43. 19.61. *Open Mon.-Fri. 9am-7pm.*

Accommodation

▲▲▲▲ Vila Casa Alba ♥, str. Emil Racovita, 22 **Off map by A1** ☎/fax 43.22.77. *18 rooms*. Near the town centre, in a quiet district, a big white house with garden. Luxury comfort. Restaurant and terrace. Secure parking.

▲▲▲ Hotel Topaz, str. Septimiu Albini, 10 **Off map by B2** ☎ 41.40.21. *51 rooms. Restaurant.*

▲▲ Hotel Meteor, str. Eroilor, 29 **B2** ☎/fax 59.10.60,< www.hotelmeteor. ro>. *25 rooms. Restaurant.*

▲▲ Hotel Vladeasa, str. Regele Ferdinand, 20 **A1** ☎/fax 59.44.29. *20 rooms*. In the centre of town, reasonable. *Restaurant.*

Restaurants

♦♦♦ Escorial ♥, piaţa Unirii, 23 **A2** ☎ 19.69.09. Converted basement, in the same building as the Hungarian Consulat. Musty atmosphere, Hungarian cuisine.

♦♦♦ Red House, bd Brâncuşi, 14 **Off map by B2** ☎ 44.21.86. Transylvainian cuisine.

♦♦ Ciuleandra, str. Septimiu Albini, 10 ☎ 41.40.21. Traditional romanian cuisine.

♦ Mary, str. Pavlov, 27 **A1/2**. Restaurant with a pleasant terrace, very quiet and inexpensive.

♦ Roata, str. Alexandru Ciulea, 6A ☎ 59.20.22. Romanian cuisine.

Cafés

Amadeus Mozart Cafe, str. Pavlov, 7 **A1/2**. Coffee and cake shop.

Cafe Bulgakov, str. I.M. Klein, 17 **A2**. Near piaţa L. Blaga. A curious café: a sort of library where you can sip coffee while listening to music.

Useful Addresses

• **French Cultural centre**, str. I.C. Bratianu, 22 ☎ 19.85.51 or 19.75. 95, < www.ccfc.ro >. Opened in 1991, this centre is situated in the longstanding Béldi palace (18th century). Exhibitions, concerts, information about local cultures.

• **Pharmacy**. *Farmacia* 24 hr, str. Calea Floreşti, 75 **Off map by A2** ☎ 42.62.72.

Lăzarea (Gyergyószarhegy)

> *Dialling code* ☎ *266. See p.183.*

Accommodation

▲▲ Pap Emma ♥, srt. Szini, 1285 ☎ 16.46.95. *3 private guest rooms*. An impeccable home and a perfectly discreet service.

Micloşoara (Miklosvar)

>*Dialling code* ☎ *267. See p.180.*

Accommodation

▲▲▲▲ Count Kalnoky's Guest House ♥ ☎ 37.46.02, < www.tran sylvaniancastle.com >. *8 rooms in old restored houses. Meals provided*. Marvellous atmosphere: Antique Transylvanian furniture, earthenware, feather bed spreads, sauna. Tibor Kalnoky likes to tell you the history of his family (which

Cluj-Napoca: Map p. 187

is also that of Transylvania). Excellent base for walking and horse riding.

Miercurea Ciuc (Csíkszereda)

> *Dialling code* ☎ *266. See p. 182.*

Accommodation

▲▲▲▲ **Hotel Fenyö ♥**, str. N. Balcescu, 11 ☎ 31.14.93, fax 17.21.81, < www.hunguest-fenyo.ro >, *104 rooms.* The best hotel in the region. Impeccable service. *Restaurant.*

▲▲▲ **Hotel Park**, str. Szenk, 58/A ☎ 11.38.33, fax 11.40.95. *19 rooms.* Unusual decor, but very comfortable. *Restaurant.*

▲▲ **Betty Panzió**, str. Jigodin, 5 ☎ 31. 13.50 or 0723.97.28.01 (mobile), *4 rooms.* (18 beds). Near the exit to Braşov. *Restaurant.*

Restaurants

There are restaurants and pizzerias in the pedestrianised area (Petöfi Sandor str.).

Odorheiu Secuiesc (Székelyudvarhely)

> *Dialling code* ☎ *266. See p. 181.*

❶ **Turisztikai Informacios Iroda**, piaţa Primăriei, 1 ☎/fax 21.74.27.

Accommodation

▲▲ **Korona Panzió ♥**, piaţa Primăriei (Városháza), 12 ☎/fax 21.80.61, < www.koronapanzio.ro >. *6 rooms.* An old building. Clean and simple rooms overlooking the courtyard, where there is the best bar in town; with wooden tables and cosy corners. In summer the bar never closes before midnight.

▲▲ **Maestro Panzió**, piaţa Primăriei (Városháza), 3 ☎ 21.56.00, fax 21.82. 34, < www.maestro-panzio.ro >. *7 rooms.* Good quality.

Ozunca Băi (Uzonkafürdo)

> *Dialling code* ☎ *267. See p. 181.*

Accommodation

▲ **Hatod Fogadó ♥** ☎ 34.43.10. *3 rooms.* Communal bathroom. Friendly, rural setting with dining in the garden. *Good restaurant.* On Saturday nights the place fills with local and out of town people so if you can not sleep shy not join the party...

Praid (Parajd)

> *Dialling code* ☎ *266. See p. 183.*

Accommodation

▲▲ **Pensiunea Szekeres**, n° 1007 ☎ 0740.18.25.96 (mobile). *4 guest rooms and meals provided.* Anna and Imre Szekeres serve home-made dairy produce, excellent ewe's milk cheese and garden vegetables.

Racu (Csíkrákos)

> *Dialling code* ☎ *266. See p. 180.*

Restaurant

▲▲ **Cserekert Fogadó ♥**, n° 185 ☎ 37.91.11. A picturesque little hostel, decorated in the "Szekler" style.

Sfântu Gheorghe (Sepsiszentgyörgy)

> *Dialling code* ☎ *267. See p. 181.*

Accommodation

▲▲▲ **Hotel Castel**, str. Izvorului, 1 ☎/fax 31.87.00. *22 rooms.* At the end of town, take towards Miercurea Ciuc. Not a pretty building but the rooms are very comfortable. *Decent restaurant.*

Târgu Mureş (Marosvasarhely)

> *Dialling code* ☎ *265. See p. 184.*

Getting there

● **By plane**. To Bucharest, 3 flights/week. (Tarom). **Airport:** 12 km from town, on the Cluj road **Off map by A2**. **Tarom agency:** piaţa Trandafirilor, 6-8 **A1/B1** ☎ 13.62. 00.

● **By train**. Târgu Mureş is not well connected. Two daily departures to Bucarest; several connections with Cluj et Braşov (train liaisons to catch); 1 daily connection to Budapest. **Railway station:** piaţa Garii **Off map A2** (W. of town). **Railway company** *(Agenţia CFR)*: piaţa Teatrului, 1 **A2** ☎ 16.62.03, < www.cfr.ro >. *Open Mon.-Fri. 7am-6pm.*

● **By bus**. Numerous daily departures for Bucharest and other big towns in Romania. Connections to Hungary and W. Europe. **Bus station** *(Autogara)*: str. Gh. Doja, 10 **Off map by A2**.

Accommodation

▲▲▲ **Hotel Helvetia**, str. Borsos Tamas, 13 **B2** ☎ 21.69.54, fax 21.

Târgu Mureş: Map p. 184

50.99. *11 rooms*. Lies between the library and the citadel, very peaceful. *Restaurant.*

▲▲▲ **Pensiunea Doïna & Jeno**, str. Eroilor Martiri, 25/C **Off map by B2** ☎ 25.59.26. *70 rooms. Restaurant.*

▲▲▲ **Pensiunea Tip Top**, str. Plopilor, 7 **Off map by A1** ☎ 21.92.34. *14 rooms. Restaurant.*

▲▲ **Hotel Transilvania**, piaţa Trandafirilor, 46 **A1/B1** ☎ 16.56.16, fax 16.60.28. *105 rooms*. Reasonable and well situated in the town centre.

Restaurant

◆◆ **Restaurant Tempo**, str Morii, 27 **B1** ☎21.35.52. Good Transylvanian cuisine.

Concerts

The Palace of Culture. The philharmonic orchestra plays here *Sept.-June, Thur. 7pm*. Info and reservations: **Casa de bilete**, on the corner of the building, piaţa Trandafirilor side **A1/B1** ☎26.14.20. *Open every day Mon.-Fri. 10am-1pm, on concert days also 5pm-7pm.*

Shopping

Liliput Antique, str Horia, 7 **A1** ☎ 26.72.20. An Ali Baba's cavern but prices are skyhigh. *Open every day 9am-6pm.* ●

Maramureş

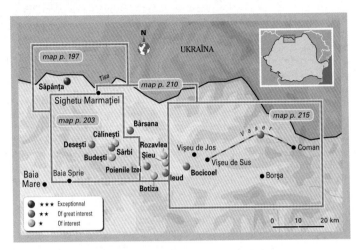

T he ancient territory of Maramureş (pronounced "maramuresh") lies in the north-west of Romania. To the west and south, dormant volcanic mountains form a natural border with Transylvania. To the east, the **Rodna Mountains** (Pietrosul, 2,302 m) stretch to the horizon, one of the most beautiful massifs in the Carpathians. This landscape continues northwards, before petering out in the **Tisa Plain**, which today borders the Ukraine.

Naturally cut off from the rest of the country, Maramureş has managed to maintain its unique identity and folk traditions, which date back centuries, like an oasis of Romanian culture in the middle of a harsh, mountainous terrain. Since 1918, most of the Maramureş territory (north of the Tisa River) lies outside the Romania (p. 50), in the Carpathian region of the Ukraine.

An abundant landscape

The landscape breathes quiet abundance. The highlands are covered with conifer and broad-leaved forests inhabited by bears. Further south, long, flat terraces, moulded by centuries-old farming methods are covered with meadows and fields of maize, potatoes and beans. During the summer months, the country is ablaze with colour and teeming

© Bernard Houliat

with people. Hazelnut groves, vast orchards and the occasional ash tree offer shade to the worn out hay-maker. Gentle rivers (the Vişeu, Mara, Cosău and Iza) meander along valley bottoms feeding into the River Tisa which flows on to Hungary via the Ukraine before joining the Danube.

AN INVIGORATING COUNTRY

An invigorating, carefree atmosphere floats in the air. The local people have great strength of character and, although naturally vivacious, have a profound respect for their religion. This undoubtedly helped them resist oppression and foreign influences and preserve, to this day, traces of a strong rural society which has known a rich and colourful past.

String of ancient villages lie along the valleys, their little roads invari-ably leading to an ancient wooden church which fills every Sunday and feast day with the villagers dressed in their traditional costumes. Sadly, the architectural unity of these villages is beginning to be disrupted by the huge villas of people who have made their fortune in Western Europe.

THE CULTURE OF WOOD

Maramureş is synonymous with the culture of wood in all its forms and uses. From religious art to the small-est details of everyday life, the natu-ral building instinct of these peas-ants combines spirituality, delicacy and technical mastery of the wood. You see countless wooden houses 'thatched' with pine bark, often sep-arated from the road by a large wooden gateway carved with sym-bols depicting the primal forces of life *(p. 204)*. However, it is in their churches that these master crafts-men truly express their talent. Today, they continue to cut, join and carve as before.

RELIGIOUS ART IN DIFFICULT TIMES

Only a few pre-1717 religious build-ings still exist in Maramureş. This was the date of the last Tatar inva-sion, which destroyed most of the churches in this Orthodox region. At the time, Central Europe was undergoing a geopolitical and cul-tural upheaval, a result of which was the integration of the Principality of Transylvania (including Mara-mureş) into Hungary. Orthodox Romanians were forced to become part of the Greco-Catholic (Uniate) Church, promoted by the imperial authorities. Reform and Counter-Reform clashed across Europe. Rele-gated to the villages, Romanian Orthodox culture cocooned itself around its **wooden churches**, sym-bols of community's identity.

The **frescoes** which illuminate the musky half-light of the wooden churches of Maramureş bear wit-ness to the touching communion between these rural communities and their church. They were exe-cuted for the most part by artists from the region's villages between the 18th and early 19th centuries, under the vigilance of Greco-Catholic priests, when the churches were repaired or rebuilt after the Tatar invasions. Travelling through-out Transylvania and Maramureş, these artists decorated churches and painted icons, thus spreading differ-ent themes and expressive styles.

In and around Sighet★

Maramureş' principal town, Sighetu Marmaţiei, known locally as **Sighet**, and its cosmopolitan personality, makes for a great introduction to the region. Through its markets and museums, you will learn about village life in the surrounding valleys. The Săpânţa cemetery gives an insight into the poetic verve of the local people.

The heart of the Maramureş region, the Tisa Valley, is scarcely two hours' drive from Satu Mare (cross the Hungarian boarder at Petea or Valea lui Mihai). All along the banks of the River Tisa to the town of Sighet there are frontier villages that are alternately inhabited by Romanians, Hungarians and Ukrainians (Ruthenians).

Săpânţa★

> 86 km E of Satu Mare on the DN1C and DN 19. **Address book** p. 218.

An ancient centre of Romanian culture, Săpânţa is famous for its cemetery and the wooden crosses adorning the graves, colourfully decorated by a local peasant-painter.

agenda

If you arrive in Romania by car, **Săpânţa** is a great first stop. You can explore the village in an afternoon (and spend the night in a guesthouse).

In **Sighetu Marmaţiei,** you will find everything you need: cash points and a service station accepting credit cards. You will need at least half a day to explore the museums, the shops and the market.

Accommodation in Săpânţa and Sighet.

Address book p. 216. ●

♥ The cemetery★★★

> **Cimitirul Vesel**. In the centre of the village. Open daily 7am-7pm. Admission charge. Allow at least 1 hr.

From the entrance of the cemetery (strangely known as the "Merry Cemetery"), you are immediately surrounded by a profusion of dark blue crosses outlined in bright

At the "stâna"

Village communities maintain a lively pastoral tradition based around the sheepfold or stâna. This mythical word evokes a meticulous organisation and a mysterious universe at the boundary between wild and domestic, between man and beast, and between the natural and supernatural worlds.

A ritual calendar

A *stâna* is made up of five or six herds (or *botei*) of sheep. They are penned close to the village until the end of May, when they get moved to mountain pastures (2 to 6 days' walk from the village) by shepherds who shelter in wooden cabins en route. The *stâna* is run by a head shepherd (*gazda de stâna*), a farmer from the village, usually a position taken by the owner of the most sheep. He regularly visits the sheepfold to watch over the whole functioning of the group and ensures rituals are respected. He provides the necessary tools: copper cauldrons, ladles, and wooden containers. An older shepherd, the baciu, directs the team of shepherds and organises cheese-making. Each *botei* of 200 sheep has three men to take care of them: the shepherd, his assistant and a young apprentice. In this region, the word for "shepherd" is *păcurar*, from the Latin *pecuarius*, whereas in the rest of Romania, the Turkish term *cioban* is used. In winter, each family takes care of its own animals (2 to 12 per family). In April, they are entrusted back to the shepherds, who put them to graze around the village until they leave for the mountains. In May, the much awaited ritual of the measurement of the milk (**mulsul măsurii**) takes place.

Large dogs protect the herd from bear and wolf attacks.

© Diane Dufresne

© Pierre Soissons

Mulsul măsurii

First, the division of the sheep *(ruptul sterpelor)* takes place, separating out the flock into the sheep which give milk from those that do not. This is followed by the measurement of the milk. The quantity of milk that each of the animals provide on this one day is used to determine the amount of cheese their owner will receive during the summer. Towards noon, to the lugubrious sound of metal horns, the families gather around the *stâna*, in the middle of which stands a fir tree, decorated with crowns of bread and flowers. The buckets *(budac)* are turned upside down to prove that they are empty and the sheep are paraded in front of each of the milkers. A priest blesses the animals, the shepherds, the sheepfold and the milking tools. The head of the sheepfold recites an *Our Father* and the measurement begins. Afterwards the real celebrations begin, a great feast accompanied by plenty of plum brandy and violin playing, interspersed with rituals approaching the realms of the magical: the head of the sheepfold sprinkles the sheep with the water which was used to clean out the buckets. The sound of the shepherds' horns lend the occasion a certain mystery.

In Botiza, Ieud and Poienile Izei, guest house families will take you to visit a *stâna (Address book p. 216)*. ●

Twice a day, the sheep are gathered in a pen for milking.

Fresh from the cauldron the cheese is wrapped in cloths and hung out to drain.

© Antoine Schneck

© Pierre Soissons

Nearly half a century of life in Săpânţa is chronicled before your eyes in these colourfully naïve tombstones in the village cemetery.

colours. For 40 years, a sculptor from the village, **Ion Stan Patras** (1909-1977), dedicated his life to the dead, keeping their memory alive in his own special way. On oak boards, he chiselled out crosses bearing personalised homages in the form of small, embossed scenes in lively colours. These images depict the main feature of the deceased person's life or, sometimes, the circumstances of their death. Below, a short epitaph completes the tableau. In this way, the dead person humbly presents himself, often humorously, always tenderly, to the person standing in front of their grave.

The verve and humour of the Maramureş people is represented in the epitaphs and their pictorial language. There is an image of a drunkard with a bottle in his hand (an oft repeated scene!); a womaniser surrounded by girls; the model peasant-girl milking her cow; a shepherd and his sheep; a musician with his instrument. The graveyard is not, however, quite as cheerful as some guide books make out: the story of the shepherd decapitated by a Hungarian soldier is not a funny one; neither is that of Mihai Stan Patras, a First World War soldier, who never returned from the Italian front, leaving a widow and three children, including Ion Stan. The scenes on the graves of children are especially disturbing: the image of a little girl hit by a car (you can even read the number plate); another infant, not even a year old, is pictured with angel's wings. Each time, a short poem expresses the parents' grief, also that of the community, including the sculptor himself, collector and interpreter of the village's grief.

Ion Stan carved his own cross, before he died. You can find it opposite the entrance to the church. A former apprentice carries on the work in Ion Stan's old workshop.

A working museum*

> *From the cemetery take two left turnings. Continue down a track for 300 m and turn left again. Open daily. Admission charge.*

Dumitru Pop modestly continues the work of his master. As well as carving out his village's memorial, he restores the wooden headstones which have become worn away over time. He also carves and paints religious objects and furniture. His house has been turned into a museum but, sadly, due to lack of financial support, the entire collection is not on display. Ion Stan also made furniture and executed commissioned pictures like the extraordinary homage to a member of the Executive Committee of the Communist Party or the portraits of Nicolae and Elena Ceauşescu.

Peri Monastery*

> *Mănăstirea Peri. From the cemetery road, get back onto the main street and take a right turning towards Sighetu Marmaţiei. Continue for 300 m, then turn left. Just after a small bridge, take the path along the stream. Continue for 1 km, you will come across the site in an oak forest.*

There used to be a monastery of the same name on the opposite bank of the River Tisa, today in the Ukraine. This was particularly significant for the locals since, in 1394, the Patriarch of Constantinople granted autonomy to the monastery, a sign of a well-established Orthodoxy. The reconstruction of Peri Monastery started at Săpânţa, on this side of the Tisa, in the early 1990s. The building site is in the middle of the forest. The builders use the surrounding oak trees as and when they need them, perpetuating the traditional methods used by the modest church builders of Maramureş.

---

photography

It is forbidden to take photographs inside the churches. •

Sighetu Marmaţiei

> *Approx. 600 km N-W of Bucharest, 105 km E of Satu Mare and 19 km E of Săpânţa on the DN 1 C and DN 19.* **Address book** *p. 218.*

Sighetu Marmaţiei, (or **Sighet**), has kept the character of the trading town it once was during the Austro-Hungarian Empire. Despite some unfortunate recent constructions, there is a lot to learn here about the complex history of the region.

The heart of the town spreads out around the long **central avenue** – or **square** – (**piaţa Libertăţii**). Nearby is the Ethnographic Museum, the Memorial to the Victims of Communism, the house of Elie Wiesel which has been turned into a museum, the food market and all the usual shops and services. The Ukrainian bazaar, the showground and the open-air Village Museum are found on the outskirts of town, towards Baia Mare and Vadu Izei.

Ethnographic Museum**

> *Muzeul de Etnografie. Str. Libertăţii, 15* ☎ *31.15.21. Open Tue.-Sun. 10am-6pm. Admission charge. Allow about 1 hr.*

The museum is a perfect introduction to the Maramureş region. A lot of space is dedicated to the culture of wood including carved doorways, furniture and other domestic objects. There is also a superb range of textiles on display, including woollen bed covers and carpets and traditional costumes. Do not miss the good collection of icons on glass and wood. There is an interesting open-air annex to the museum outside town *(p. 202)*.

Memorial to the Victims of Communism and the Anti-Communist Resistance**

> *Memorialul Victimelor Comunismului şi al Rezistenţei. Cross the square (piaţa Libertăţii) and take the first right after the town hall. Str. Corneliu Coposu, 4* ☎ *31. 94.24. Open Tue.-Sun. 10am-6pm. Admission charge.*

Set out in the former prison, this memorial soberly presents one of the least known faces of communist brutality. You can visit the cells, the yard where they took excercise. Also on display of the prisoners' writings which bitterly recount the suffering they endured.

Within these walls, the entire pre-1940 Romanian political elite were slowly liquidated alongside priests and bishops of the Uniate Church *(see inset p. 186)* – banned in Maramureş after 1948 – and even simple village folk who had been members of the anti-Communist resistance which was active in the forests of the region.

The Jewish Town*

> *Return to the main square (piaţa Libertăţii) and cross over to a small park.*

Sighet was one of the beacons of Jewish culture in Central Europe. In 1930, 34,000 Jews were living in Maramureş including farmers. This meant there were always kosher sheepfolds in the Rodna and Maramureş Mountains. This community is remembered in *All Rivers Run to the Sea* by the most famous of the town's children, **Elie Wiesel** *(p. 326)*, who was born here in 1928, and deported in 1944. The Nobel Prize winner's birthplace *(**Casa Memorială Elie Wiesel, Muzeul Culturii Evreiesti din Maramureş**; str Tudor Vladimirescu, 1 ☎ 31.15.21; open Mon.-Fri. 9am-3pm; admission charge)* has been turned into the **Maramureş Museum of Jewish Culture***. Nearby is the **Wijnitzer Klaus Synagogue** *(str. Basarabia, 10)*. The house next door *(str. Basarabia, 8 ☎ 31.16.52)* accommodates the headquarters of the Jewish Community in Sighet. Enquire here to visit the synagogue or the **Jewish Cemetery** *(**Cimitirul Evreiesc**; south of the town centre)*.

In most of the region's villages, the houses belonging to Jewish families are recognisable for the double edg-

A Maramureş carved door frame

© Pierre Soissons

ing at the corners of the window frames. Such is the case at the ancient **Drimer Inn** in Bârsana *(p. 210)*, rebuilt today in the open-air annex to the Ethnographic Museum.

The Maramureş Village Museum**

> *Muzeul Satului Maramureşan. On the outskirts of Sighet making towards Baia Mare there is a small road on the left, 400 m after the Petrom service station. Str. Muzeului, 1 ☎ 31.42.29. Open daily except Mon. 10am-6pm. Admission charge.*

Reassembled on top of a hill dominating the Tisa plain is this wide-ranging collection of houses and farm buildings surrounding a beautiful church. Providing a great introduction to the traditional woodwork of the area, this open-air museum is the perfect complement to the Ethnographic Museum in town *(p. 201)*. At the reception area, you can pick up detailed information on the museum and the whole region. ●

Mara and Cosău Valleys★★★

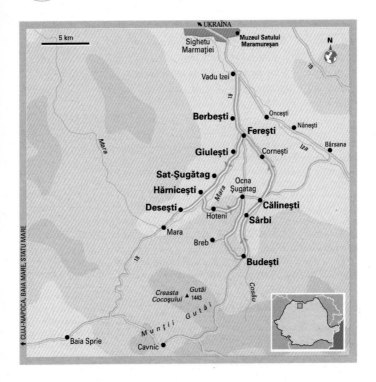

This dense and bushy land-scape, teeming with life, lies in the shadow of the imposing blueberry-covered **Gutâi massif** (1,443 m) and "Cock's Crest" (*Creasta Cocoşului*; 1,428 m) ranges of volcanic mountains.The Mara and Cosău Valleys are the most traditional areas in Maramureş. There are about a dozen wooden churches to visit and some lovely, peaceful villages.

Each home has a small plot of land with an orchard, a garden and various outbuildings, barns for cattle and for storing hay, and a well. The children share the yard with cats, poultry and perhaps their grandmother spinning wool. Saucepans hang from walls and trees in the

agenda

A trip of 70km around **Vadu Izei**. The DN 18 Sighetu Marmaţiei-Baia Mare follows **Mara Valley**, where a minor road branches off to **Cosău Valley** and to **Budeşti**, the village the furthest upstream. From here, the road follows the valley back to Vadu Izei. **Accommodation** in Vadu Izei.

Address book p. 216. ●

garden. Sheets edged with lace, embroidered materials, floral skirts and white shirts are put out to dry above the cabbage patch.

Sculpted gateways

The traditional wooden gateways are still a common feature of villages throughout Maramureş. Evidence of skills and techniques that have been passed down over the centuries, the ornately carved symbols perpetuate an very ancient vision of the universe.

Technical and artistic know-how

The artists who created these masterpieces were modest village craftsmen. **Technical know-how** is coupled with an artistic sense that has been thoroughly trained in the rules of ornamentation which have been followed for centuries. These rules imply the **use of symbols** whose importance the artist does not necessarily understand. At the very most, the sculptor may introduce some personal touches to the friezes and edging. The gateway is held by three oak pillars, decorated with embossed sculpture, which frame a small door for people and a larger one for carts to pass through. This is all crowned by a shingle roof *(draniţa)*. The gateways, however, are not merely functional.

The threshold between two worlds

These monumental gateways mark, in a theatrical way, the boundary between the safe domestic world and the dangerous outside one. Endowed with **magical powers,** the gateways are a sort of obstacle to evil. Money, basil and holy water used to be placed on the doorstep to ward off disease.

The symbol of the snake has a complex role. Before being known as the evil that tempted Eve, the snake had been, for a long time, seen as a protector of the home and as a healer (the symbol, in fact, for medicine).

© Diane Dufresne

© Bernard Houliat

© Pierre Soissons

The gateway is carved with universally **recognisable symbols**, such as the circle, metaphor for the sun, or the rope with 45-degree " branches ", representing the tree of life. This is a local variant of the universal cult of the tree, which is found on the calvaries of Oltenia, in the carved bouquet that is added by the carpenter as the finishing touch to the frame of a house or on crosses traditionally placed on graves.

The gateways made today are often over-elaborate and are losing their magical aspect. ●

The twisted rope represents infinity and is often found on the external walls of churches.

Circles and rosettes represent the sun, symbol of life and object of universal worship.

© Bernard Houliat

© Bernard Houliat

Vadu Izei

> 6 km S of Sighetu Marmatiei on the DN 18. **Address book** p. 219.

Vadu Izei sits at the confluence of the Mara and Iza Valleys and is renowned for its craftsmen: wood carvers (some of the region's most interesting carved gateways are found here), weavers and even a painter of icons on glass, Ion Borlean, who also offers bed and breakfast (p. 219). This village is an excellent base for exploring the Mara and Coşău Valleys.

Mara Valley

> From Vadu Izei, towards Baia Mare (S) on the DN 18.

About 2 km from Vadu Izei, on the right as you enter **Berbeşti**, is the 18th-century **Rednic★ wooden Calvary** (**Troiţă Rednicenilor**). A shingle-covered shelter protects the figure of Christ and the other figures,

The figures in the Rednic Calvary seem to be lost in profound meditation.

© Diane Dufresne

nevertheless weathered with time. There are still plenty of old houses, some magnificent gateways and a bustle of activity in the villages of **Berbeşti★**, **Fereşti★** and **Giuleşti★**.

In **Sat-Şugatag★**, there is a fine example of a **wooden church★** (in the cemetery; to visit contact the priest Vasile Danci, at n° 87 ☎ 37. 49.78).

A further 3 km brings you to the village of **Hărniceşti★**. A discreet **wooden church★** sits enthroned in an overgrown graveyard (in the centre of the village, take a right; to visit contact the priest Stefan Peter ☎ 37.26.79). There are some valuable **icons** inside.

♥ Deseşti Church★★

> 20 km S of Vadu Izei, approx. 3 km S of Hărniceşti, 150 m from the DN 18. In the centre of the village, take the path uphill on the right opposite the school. To visit, contact priest Ion Sigartău, near the church ☎ 37.26.14. Admission charge.

This church (1770) is dedicated to Saint Paraschiva. Executed in 1780 and restored in the 1990s, the wall paintings inside are the the masterpiece of **Radu Munteanu** (see inset p. 208), who came originally from Ungureni, in the region of Lăpuş (on the other side of the mountain), and Gheorghe Zugravul.

From the moment you step inside, you are caught up in an enchanted, fairytale world. Painted on brightly-coloured and pastel backgrounds, each section is outlined with foliage-motif friezes.

On the vault of the naos↬, on the south side, the **Genesis** is depicted: the creation of **Adam** and then **Eve** by a paternal looking God, severe and benevolent, against a pink background scattered with stars and angels. The paintings have a rustic simplicity: note the clumsiness of Adam who seems to have trouble standing upright. On the opposite wall is the scene of the murder of **Abel** by **Cain**, sons of Adam and

Eve, the first in a series representing the sins of mankind. At the base of the vault on the north wall of the naos, an angel is inflicting blows with a trident on the towns of **Sodom** and **Gomorrah**. Painted upside down, heaven is found at the bottom of the painting. There are also references to the Old Testament higher up and to the more serious sins which are set out as a warning.

Just below, at window level, is a depiction of scenes from the New Testament including the Redemption of Sins. **The Passion narrative** is set out in 16 scenes around the naos, illustrating the last days of Christ's life, from his arrest to his crucifixion and entombment. The **Last Judgment** scene dominates the **pronaos**↪, above the door into the **naos**. Surrounded by disciples, Christ sits deliberating upon the fate of man. Below, one on each side, are the kneeling figures of Adam and Eve. On the north wall are the righteous; opposite, the sinners in picturesque costumes: Jews, Turks, Tatars, Germans and, in the corner, on the west wall, some enigmatic "Francs" (*frânci*).

Radu Munteanu's fresco technique is similar to the rustic style of icons on glass: flat areas of colour or lightly drawn lines with definite outlines. This peasant-artist seems to have been pre-occupied with decorative effect and has taken some liberties with post-Byzantine iconography, notably in the sequencing of the scenes.

Deseşti Church also has some 18th-century icons on wood and some 19th-century icons on glass.

Between Mara and Cosău★★

> *From Hărnicești, take the small road on the right to Ocna Sugatag (W).*

The road passes through **Hoteni** where, on the second Sunday in May, the spectacular **Tânjeaua de pe Mara★** Spring festival is held.

© Pierre Soissons

In the Mara Valley, this clever and hygienic method of drying saucepans also indicates there is a girl of marrying age in the house.

The road leading to Budeşti (*2 km after Hoteni, leaving Ocna Şugatag on the left, take a right*) follows the mountain ridge with **Sârbi's** uninterrupted string of houses below on the left. The **Breb highlands★** offer one of the most beautiful farming landscapes in Maramureş, a mosaic of different crops (maize, beans, potatoes and domestic gardens) and hay fields dotted with trees (birch, ash, aspen, oak and fruit trees).

Cosău Valley★★★

The soul of old Maramureş still beats here: traditional houses, mills, fullers, washhouses and alembic stills are dotted along the river. Unlike some others, the communities in this valley continue to live harmoniously, leading a way of life that, sadly, cannot last. This is why you must visit the area now!

Church iconography

Like neighbouring Moldavia, the artistic tradition in Maramureş is post-Byzantine. Church iconography generally contains a moral which varies little from one tiny church to another.

As a rule, you will find Old Testament scenes in the **naos** ↪, in particular the **Creation of Adam and Eve** and **Original Sin**. Parallel to these are scenes from the New Testament, mainly the **Passion Cycle** – Christ's last days, from his arrest to the Crucifixion and the Entombment – which leads to the **Redemption of Sins**.

Gradually, Maramureş painters started distancing themselves from the Byzantine norms, favouring more elaborate decorative effects, and even integrating here and there a Western Baroque influence (Bârsana Church p. 210).

The allure of Maramureş wall paintings comes from their freshness. The pictorial language recalls the vivacious personality of the people of the region and the rural communities with which these church painters shared their daily lives. This gaity of spirit is palpable; it is demonstrated in the carved eulogies in Săpânta Cemetery (p. 197) and is still seen in the liveliness of Maramureş villages today.

Three masters and three very different styles: **Alexandru Ponehalski** in Budeşti-Susani (see below), Calineşti-Câieni (p. 209) and Ieud (p. 213); **Radu Munteanu** in Deseşti (p. 206); and **Toader Hodor** in Bârsana (p. 210). ●

Budeşti*

> 20 km S of Vadu Izei, 7 km S of Ocna Şugatag. From the upper part of Budeşti, take a right towards the valley.

Lying in the foothills around the Cosău Valley this village is criss-crossed with earth and gravel lanes.

● **The Upper Church★★** (*Biserica din Budeşti-Susani*). *From the centre of the village, take the path opposite the lower church; follow it upriver for 1 km.* The church was built in 1760, on the site of an older church of which only the imperial doors remain (1628). Some of the wall paintings by **Alexandru Ponehalski** (*see above*) have survived, namely on the walls of the naos ↪, the iconostasis ↪ and in the sanctuary ↪. The use of bright reds, blues, greens and yellows give these frescoes the look of miniatures.

On the north wall of the naos, there are scenes from the Old Testament. The gentle hills of Paradise resemble those of Maramureş and are populated with animals both real and imaginary, drawn with a gauche yet highly poetic hand. A dog, horses, a wolf, a stag, a goat, bears, a lamb and a wild boar appear alongside a camel, an elephant, a lion with a human face, a centaur, a creature that is half-bird, half-mammal, and a mermaid. **Adam** and **Eve** pass through the Gates of Heaven overwhelmed by grief. Note Adam's expression as he works and Eve's as she spins wool.

On the south wall, against the iconostasis, the depiction of the Last Supper has a definite Greek influence: note the table in the form of the letter omega. Also take a good look at the face of Christ: his eyes consumed by sadness.

● **The Lower Church★★** *(Biserica din Budeşti-Josani)*. *In the main street of the village.* A large gateway, dedicated in 1628, to Sfântu Nicoară leads you to the church. Unique to Maramureş, the steeple above the pronaos↪ is surrounded by four smaller spires. Inside, you can find part of the chain-mail coat of the famous haidouk (brigand) Pintea Viteazul *(p. 39)*, a local Robin Hood character who made a name for himself fighting against the imperial occupying authorities. The paintings inside, only partially preserved, have the hallmark colours and luminosity of **Alexandru Ponehalski's** work from 1762.

Sârbi★★

> *16 km S of Vadu Izei, 4 km N of Budeşti.*

● **The Upper Church★★** *(Biserica din Sârbi-Susani)*. *1 km from the entrance to the village, a signpost indicates "Biserica" to the left.* Climb a shaded pathway up the hill and through the graveyard. This is one of the most moving sites in Maramureş. During ceremonies, the congregation, too big for the tiny church, gathers outside, patches of colour scattered amongst the graves and trees. This is particularly true on 12 October, which is the festival of Saint Paraschiva, patron saint of the church.

The building was constructed in 1532 with dovetailed oak beams 60 cm wide. A sculpted wooden belt in the form of a twisted rope surrounds the building which contains some 18th-century icons on wood by Radu Munteanu.

● **The Lower Church★** *(Biserica din Sârbi-Josani)*. Between the river and old houses with worn wooden gateways, the road passes just below the lower church, which is in a superb position. The church was built in 1665 and is used today by Greco-Catholics.

At the edge of Sârbi, you will find an alembic still and a **washhouse** *(on the right of the road)*, in sight of the first houses of the next village.

Călineşti★

> *13 km S of Vadu Izei, 3 km N of Sârbi.*

● **The Upper Church★** *(Biserica din Călineşti-Susani)*. *Take a left from the main road.* The " upper *(Susani)* church" is found through a wooden gateway, down a sloping path which is frequented every Sunday by church-goers dressed in traditional costume.

● **Câieni Church★★** *(Biserica din Câieni)*. *From the road leading to Bârsana, take the path opposite house n° 385.* Built in 1663, the "lower *(Josani)* church", **Câieni Church★★**, was painted in 1754 by **Alexandru Ponehalski** who, lacking space, was forced to simplify his iconographic language. This has in no way reduced the expressiveness of most of the scenes, notably the **Way of the Cross**↪ scene (north wall of the naos↪) and the **Crucifixion**. In the middle of the **Last Judgement** scene on the east wall of the pronaos↪, there are three icons painted directly onto the wall depicting Christ, the Virgin Mary and the Baby Jesus, all radiating a supreme serenity.

From Călineşti to Vadu Izei *(p. 206)*, *via* **Corneşti** (church painted by Toader Hodor) and **Fereşti**, there is a 17km stretch of the most unspoilt rural landscape. ●

Iza Valley★

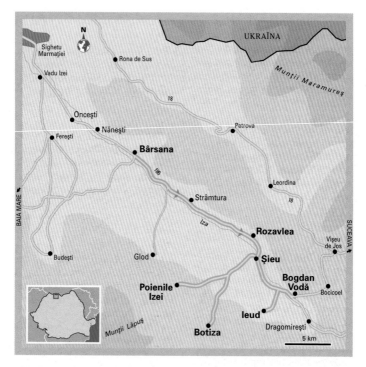

More exposed to outside influences, the traditional architecture of the Iza Valley is gradually being supplanted. Nonetheless, a stay in one of these villages will soon unearth some superb wooden churches and traditional houses, and a lively people keen to communicate.

From Vadu Izei (p. 206), take the DJ 186. You pass through **Onceşti★**, where there are some wonderful sculpted wooden gateways, and Năneşti, before arriving in Bârsana. ●

Bârsana Church★★

> *12 km S-E of Vadu Izei on the DJ 186. In the village centre, take a left turn leading up to the church. To visit the church, contact the priest Gheorghe Urda on ☎ 33. 10.06.*

A document dated 1391 records the existence of a monastery here which disappeared when Orthodox Roma-

exploring

Stay 2 or 3 nights in one of the villages in the tributary valleys: Ieud, Botiza or Poienile Izei are particularly charming.

Avoid road side offers of accommodation and so-called village information offices.

Address book p. 216. ●

nians were forced to switch to Greco-Catholicism (p. 54). In 1720, the town's wooden church was moved to this spot.

The wall paintings (1806) are the masterpiece of **Toader Hodor** who came from the neighbouring Vişeu Valley. He was responsible for the tentative and somewhat belated introduction of a Baroque style in the rural churches of Maramureş *(see inset p. 208)*. He was inspired not by the monumental, tragic aspect of the Baroque but rather its decorative flourishes and its sense of the spectacular. In places, the artist gives full reign to his creative fantasies, painting with free-spirited abandon. The dominant colours (white, blue and red) are vivid and contrasting. The iconostasis ↪ illuminates the naos ↪ with fresh colours while the imperial doors, covered in leafy scrolls, curves and counter curves, allow a glimpse of the sanctuary ↪ where, on the walls behind the altar there are seraphim and cherubim with bodies covered in eyes. On the vault Saint Elijah appears at the centre of a lively composition, while God the Father, the Archangels and the Evangelists are represented within Baroque-style medallions.

Return to the main road, lined with gateways *(p. 204)*. On the outskirts of the village, where an old convent used to stand, inspired by traditional wooden churches, there is now an ostentatious **monastic settlement**, which was built here in 1992.

Rozavlea Church★

> *25 km S-E of Vadu Izei, 12 km S-E of Bârsana on the DJ 186. Beyond the centre of the village, on the right. To visit, contact the priest, house n° 235 ☎ 33.32.11.*

Built between 1717 and 1720, the church of the Archangel-Saints Michael and Gabriel was constructed on the site of a church burnt down by the Tatars. The superb interior decor dates from between 1823 and 1825 and is the work of **Ion Plohod**, a painter from Dragomireşti, and who was assistant to Hodor in Bârsana.

Şieu Church★

> *29 km S-E of Vadu Izei, 4 km S-E of Rozavlea on the DJ 186. To visit, contact the priest, house n° 602 ☎ 33.30.25.*

This harmonious village church is decorated with paintings by **Ion Plohod** which enhance the evocative light of the interior.

A village in the Iza Valley.

© Pierre Soissons

Outdoor mass in Botiza.

Botiza★

> *39km S-E of Vadu Izei, 10 km S of Şieu on the DJ 186. From Şieu, turn right.* **Address book** *p. 216.*

Lying in the crux of two valleys, this village is famous for the roguishness and craftiness of its inhabitants. On the side of a hill, partly hidden by an ugly, concrete building, the **wooden church★**, dedicated to Saint Paraschiva, looks out over the graveyard. Sheep farming is still a major activity here, where the peasants remain very much attached to their pastoral customs *(see inset p. 198)*. Weaving carpets using vegetable-dyed wools is an ancient local tradition that is still being carried on today.

Poienile Izei★★

> *42km S-E of Vadu Izei, 15km S of Şieu on the DJ 186. From Botiza, make for Şieu; on the outskirts of the village, take a left turning.* **Address book** *p. 218.*

Amidst meadows and forests this village is particularly charming and harmonious, even if its ancient wooden houses are being gradually replaced by large, modern buildings.It is the birthplace of several renowned musicians including the Giurgs and the modest Ion de la Cruce.

More than the overly touristy Botiza, the village of Poienile Izei, with its superb natural surroundings and good quality guest houses *(p. 218)*, is a good place to base oneself for a few days. The small size of the village allows for greater immersion in village life.

● **Wooden Church★★**. *To visit, contact the priest, house n° 210,* ☎ *33. 43.21. Admission charge.* Standing resplendent in the cemetery where open air ceremonies are still held, this wooden church possesses a grace that the modern church nearby will never have. The interior paintings date from 1794 and are the work of a local artist. They are made up of large, framed scenes, three or four to each level. On the walls of the naos↪, the upper levels are dedicated to 18 episodes from the **Passion Cycle**.

On the south wall, above a small window next to the pronaos↪, the **Crown of Thorns** scene shows Jesus covered in bleeding wounds. On the north wall, a pelican is tearing at its own flesh to feed its young with blood: symbol of Christ crucified, his side pierced, to save the world. The walls of the pronaos are dedicated, in accordance with tradition, to the **Last Judgement**. In the centre of the west wall, above the entrance, Jesus, surrounded by his disciples, presides over the fate of man. From the entrance door to the middle of the north wall, crude and realistic images warn the sinner of what might await him in Hell: the liar is strung up by his tongue; he who ploughs on a Sunday is being ploughed by two devils; the woman

© Pierre Soissons

abortionist is swallowing a baby; the man who sleeps during mass is stretched out on a bed being tauted by a violin-playing devil; the blacksmith is being inflated by his own bellows; the dishonest boot-maker has a nail stuck in his bottom. Meanwhile, down below, Judas is disappearing into the mouth of the Leviathan.

Ieud**

> *40 km S-E of Vadu Izei, 4 km S-E of Șieu on the DJ 186. From Șieu, turn right.* **Address book** *p. 217.*

Ieud stretches for several kilometres along a pastoral valley dominated by the Țibleș massif (1,839 m).

● **The Church on the Hill**** *(Biserica din Deal). Before reaching the centre of the village, a signpost indicates a road to the left leading to the church. Open daily by appointment, contact the caretaker Gavrila Chindriș, house n° 598. Admission charge.* Built in 1364, near a wooden fortification belonging to Voivode Balc, son of Dragoș, this is the oldest church in Romanian Maramureș. The wall paintings date from 1782 and are the most accomplished work of **Alexandru Ponehalski** *(see inset p. 208).* Note the benign face of God the Father on the vault of the naos ↳ and the superb depiction of the **Passion Cycle**. As in other churches, the pronaos ↳ is dedicated to images of the **Last Judgement**: to the right of the entrance door, Hell and the punishments given out to sinners including those who sleep instead of going to church, drunkards, liars, innkeepers, murderers and many others, are graphically illustrated.

Next to this is Death, with scythe and pitch-fork. On the east door is **Saint Christopher**, the patron saint of travellers, who carried Jesus on his shoulders over a river – a recurrent theme of the Western Church, especially during the unsettling period of the Counter-Reformation.

Outside the church, on the edge of the cemetery, there is a cross adorned with a violin; this is the final resting place of **Gheorghe**

A funeral procession arrives at the Ieud valley church.

© Pierre Soissons

Covaci. He died a poor man in 2002, at the age of 80. A Roma violinist of great finesse, he kept the musical heritage of the village alive. Do not forget that **Bela Bartók** came to Ieud especially to record folk music (*p. 219*).

● **The Valley Church**★★ (*Biserica din Şes*). *In the main road of the village. Open daily by appointment, contact the caretaker Maria Chindriş a lui Nicoară, house n° 544. Admission charge.* The building that is sometimes described as "**Maramureş' wooden cathedral**" stands opposite the charmless modern concrete church.

The overgrown garden beckons you through the wooden gateway to explore this building, constructed in 1718. You must walk among the graves to the east cloister to appreciate the church's slender, elegant shape – the only one of its kind in Maramureş.

As you step inside, the atmosphere immediately bewitches you with the musky, dim lighting and that unique smell of old wooden churches. The walls are adorned with coloured hangings and a collection of icons on glass, many from the Transylvanian School in Nicula Monastery.

Bogdan Vodă

> *38 km S-E of Vadu Izei, 6 km S-E of Şieu on the DJ 186.*

The village of Bogdan Vodă was called **Cuhea** until a few decades ago. According to legend, Voivode ↬ **Bogdan I** left here to become the founder of Moldavia (1359).

The **wooden church**★, dedicated to Saint Nicholas, was built in 1718 on the site of a church burnt down by the Tatars the previous year. Its wall paintings are the work of an anonymous artist. The elegant profile of the building is now completely overpowered by the aggressive proximity of a concrete church, a typical example of religious building of the 1990s.

There is a fortnightly market on the outskirts of the village (*see inset p. 218*).

●●● **Suggested route:** From the Iza or Vişeu de Sus Valleys, you can reach **Bucovina** through the Prislop Pass. This route passes through some spectacular countryside, dominated, to the south, by the impressive **Rodna Mountains**★★ (*Munţii Rodnei*). As you emerge from the forest, the vast alpine landscape ahead of you contains much of ecological interest. ●

♥ The Vaser forest train★★

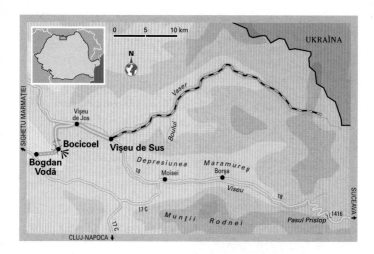

In Europe, steam engines are now virtually only ever used to pull tourists. A rare exception is right here in Mararmureş where a regular service transports wood, lumberjacks, forestry people and, of course, tourists.

Vişeu de Sus, Zipser town★

> *17 km N-E of Bogdan Vodă where you turn left for Vişeu de Jos (unpaved road for 3km). An exceptional view from* **Bocicoel Pass★★**. *After the village of the same name, turn right on the DN18 towards Borşa to reach Vişeu de Sus. 60km from Sighet by the DN18.* **Address book** *p. 220.*

The Zipsers were German workers who arrived in Vişeu de Sus in the 18th and 19th centuries. They mainly concentrated on the other side of the River Vaser, in a neighbourhood called the Zipserei, which has retained the tell-tale straight lines of houses from this time. They constituted a significant workforce of lumberjacks and woodmen. The name comes from "Zips", a Slovakian Tatras region, where some originally came from. They also originate from north-west Austria, Salzburg and the foothills of Bohemia. Today, most have emigrated to Germany so that the German language has all but disappeared from the area.

A journey through time

> *From the town centre, opposite the* Brad Hotel, *a road heads north towards the Vaser Valley. Continue along here to the forestry railway station (Caile ferate forestiere). In summer, at least 1 train daily except Sun. and bank holidays, 6am departure. Off season, random traffic.* **Address book** *(Vişeu) p. 220.*

Built in the 1930s, this narrow-gauge stretch of railway runs along the Vaser Valley for 45 km. The trains are pulled either by a steam or diesel engine and empty wagons are left all along the railway line ready to be loaded with wood. Once laden, the wagons are taken on to Vişeu. Shepherds, travelling doctors and frontier guards also use the railway line, often travelling on the weird and wonderfully improvised contraptions. Examples include the outer bodywork from Volkswagen or Ford minibuses mounted onto the chassis of track motor cars. The trains usually contain one passenger carriage. You can get off at any point, go for a walk and then jump back on a train or passing track motor car. ●

Address book

© Pierre Soissons

ℹ Maramureş Information Centre (*Centrul de Informare, Ţara Maramureş ului*) in **Vadu Izei**, 161 (next to the post office and town hall) ☎/fax (0262) 33.01.71. 6 km from Sighet, village centre, in a magnificently restored traditional building. An association representing Maramureş guest houses (*p. 206*).

Botiza

> *Dialling code* ☎ *262. See p. 212.*

Accommodation

Numerous accommodation possibilities of differing quality. Avoid the so-called information offices and head straight to a guest house.

In the village centre

▲▲ **Emilia Petreus**. n° 796 ☎ 33.40.33. *3 rooms, meals provided*. In the main street, look out for a small wooden gateway just after the Pensiunea Perţa Maria. Emilia's house is found through this, at the end of the path. Once you have found it you will be rewarded by a warm welcome.

▲▲ **Lucia and Şandor Suci**, n° 335 ☎ 33.40.36. *3 rooms, meals provided*. At the crossroads take a right along the river. The 4th house after the school. Spacious, with flowers everywhere and excellent food.

▲▲ **Casa Dorina Pătrăuş**, n° 678 ☎ 33.42.08. *3 rooms, meals provided*. From the centre, continue straight. 700 m further on, just after a bridge, the first house on the left. A good base for walking. Mr. Pătrăuş is a forest worker.

Valea Sasului

● **Getting there**. In the centre of Botiza, just after the bridge, turn right on the Valea Sasului and Poienile Izei road, along the river. After about 5 km of tarmac then earth road, you will reach the fork to Poienile Izei.

▲▲ **Aurica and Ion Costinar**, Valea Sasului ☎ 33.42.37. *6 rooms, meals provided*. Take the right fork towards Poienile Izei: the first white house on the right belongs to this most welcoming forestry family. There is a small covered balcony where you can eat outside in summer.

access

● **By train**: Botiza, Poienile Izei and Leud all use Iza station (*at Saliştea, 25 km E of Botiza and Poienile Izei, 15 km E of Ieud*). It is served by trains between Sighet and Bucharest or Cluj-Napoca.

No public transport out to the villages but, if you have a booking, your host may be able to come and fetch you (about € 10).

● **By bus**. Several daily departures from Sighet. ●

art and craft

Vegetable-dyed wool

© Pierre Soissons

To colour the wool for their famous rugs, the women from Botiza collect dyes from the surrounding countryside. The subtle colours are extracted from leaves, roots and flowers from local meadows and woods. In winter the age-old Maramureş motifs are woven forming a patchwork on the surface of the carpets. Images include fir trees, birds, sheep, women, a bridegroom on horseback and the village dance *(hora)*. The time and effort that goes into making just one of these rugs justifies the price, which can seem steep. This tradition would have disappeared altogether were it not for the wife of the village priest who encouraged the women to perpetuate and revitalise their skills. Sadly, under the false pretext of promoting tourism, this refined art is in the process of degenerating into the production of rather tacky carpets, with a mere outline of a church and the word " Botiza " emblazoned across them! ●

Traditional carpets

Victoria Berbecaru, n° 694 ☎ 33.42. 07. At the crossroads in the centre, take a left towards the church then a right just after the bridge. The first house belongs to Isador Berbecaru, the village priest. His wife has done much to revitalise the traditional use of vegetable dyes *(see above)*. *Guest rooms* also available.

Maria Costinar, n° 790 ☎ 33.40.44. Using traditional methods and designs, Maria Costinar spends her winters at the loom. Her daughter, Aurica Paşca, provides guest rooms.

Ana Trifoi, n° 861 ☎ 33.40.96. Probably the best carpets in the village and by far the cheapest.

Ieud

> Dialling code ☎ 262. See p. 213.

Accommodation

▲▲ **Casa Hotico** ♥ ☎ 33.61.33. *2 rooms. 1 km upstream from the valley church*. Take the second path on the right towards a school. At the end of the path, on the left is a sculpted gateway. Here you will find Gavrilo Hotico's house. This kindly, modest character is a renowned wood sculptor and church builder (see the new wooden church in Dragomireşti or the church built for the Romanian community in ... Chicago, USA!).

Poienile Izei

> *Dialling code* ☎ *262. See p. 212.*

Accommodation

▲▲ **Casa Bobocea** ♥ ☎ 33.43.95. *3 rooms, meals provided.* In the centre, take a right (towards the town hall). Continue for about 400 m until you get to a large white house on the right.

Do not be put off by the massive size of the house: your reception here will be exceptional; expect boozy evenings with neighbours and musician friends. The fabulous Ioana is a great cook; her roast chicken with polenta is a real delicacy...

Săpânţa

> *Dialling code* ☎ *262. See p. 197.*

Getting there

● **By bus**. Several daily bus links from Sighet.

Accommodation

▲▲ **Pensiunea Ileana** ♥, Maria Ileana Stetca ☎ 37.21.37. *3 rooms, meals provided.* A pleasant house opposite the cemetery. Quiet, efficient service and excellent cooking. Ask for the room with the dowry (*zestre*).

---

markets

● **Botiza**: Sat.

● **Bogdan Vodă**: Mon., alternating weekly with Dragomireşti.

● **Dragomireşti**: Mon., alternating weekly with Bogdan Vodă.

● **Ocna Şugatag**: Thu.

● **Rozavlea**: Tue.

● **Sighetu Marmaţiei**: Wed. and first Mon. of the month.

● **Stramtura**: Friday ●

Sighetu Marmatiei

> *Dialling code* ☎ *262. See p. 201.*

Getting there

● **By car**. 115 km from the Hungarian border via Satu Mare and the DN 1 C and DN 19. About 600 km from Bucharest, *via* Braşov, Târgu-Mureş, Bistriţa and the Iza valley.

● **By train**. From Bucharest, a night train leaves every afternoon and has one first class sleeping carriage (2 beds/compartment). It is a 14 hr journey! For the last 3 hrs, you have views of the Maramureş landscape. The **railway station** is 400 m from the central square. **Railways agency**: (*Agentia CFR*), piaţa Traian (central square) ☎ 952 or 31.26.66. *Open Mon.-Fri., 7am-2pm.*

● **By bus**. Buses from Baia Mare, Satu Mare and Cluj-Napoca provide daily links to the Maramureş villages. The **bus station** is near the railway station ☎ 31.15.12.

Festivals and Fairs

● **Cattle fair**. *1st Mon. and 2nd Wed. of every month, 7-11am.* Târgul de Animale: in the meadow next to the Petrom station, on the outskirts of town towards Baia Mare, are the monthly cattle fairs.

● **Winter festivals**: *2 days before New Year.* In the streets of Sighet groups from villages all over the region gather for the custom of the winter festival, equivalent to a western carnival (*p. 36*).

Accommodation

▲▲ **Motel Buţi**, str. Simion Barnutiu, 10 ☎ 31.10.35. *10 rooms.* Good accommodation in a quiet area. *Restaurant.*

▲▲ **Hotel Perla Sigheteană**, str. Avram Iancu, 65 ☎ 31.06.13. *8 rooms.* On the road to Săpânţa. *Restaurant.*

▲▲ **Hotel Tisa**, piaţa Libertăţii, 8 ☎ 31.33.41. *42 rooms.* This old hotel, typical of Sighet, is in the process of modernisation. *Restaurant.*

Wedding parties

The isolated position of Mararmureş goes perhaps some way to explaining why here, and nowhere else in Romania, has such a rich and unique musical heritage been preserved. The enchanting music is lively, fresh, and instantly recognisable for the nasal-like sound of the fiddle, or *cetera*, caused by a vertical groove carved out along the bridge. This is always accompanied by the *zongora*, a five-stringed guitar held vertically.

The big drum, or *doba*, echoes the stamping boots of the men who beat the rhythm, shouting out ritual incantations, often bawdy and provocative. The dancing couples twirl – everything centres around them – without a step out of place, flowery skirts flying prettily.

Musicians essentially play at weddings, be they for peasants, miners or woodmen. Sadly, the increasing popularity of discos at weddings has resulted in a serious decline in traditional weddings, at least for the time being. These village musicians will have to adapt.... or hang up their fiddles. •

Restaurants

As well as hotel restaurants there are several fast-food snack bars.

Vadu Izei

> Dialling code ☎ 262. See p. 206.

❶ **Maramureş information office** (*Centrul de Informare, Ţara Maramureş ului*), details p. 216. Organises accommodation in the village.

Getting there

● **By train**. Sighet station (6 km away).

● **By bus**. Several connections with Sighet, Baia Mare and the Mara, Cosău and Iza valleys.

Accommodation

▲▲ **Ioan Borlean** ♥, uliţa Batrâna, 704B ☎ 33.02.28. A traditional Maramureş house restored and thoughtfully refurbished by a man who is passionate about the heritage of his region. Traditional food is provided as well as a locally distilled plum brandy.

Restaurants

The information office can help you find a quick snack or traditional meal (by appointment).

Arts and crafts

● **Traditional waistcoats** (*pieptar*). Grigore Michnea, house n° 231.

● **Icons on glass**. Ioan Borlean (*see opposite*).

● **Traditional sculpted doorways**. Petru Bledea, house n° 603; Liviu Bledea house n° 603; Gavrila Arba, house n° 106; Petru Gogea known as Pupaza, valea Stejarului, n° 117, (a colourful character, well-known throughout Maramureş).

● **Leather sandals** (*opinci*). Vasile Arba, Valea Stejarului, n° 48.

● **Wood carving**, furniture. Vasile Apan, house n° 605.

● **Carpets**. Ileana Borlean, uliţa Batrâna, 704A ☎ 33.01.80.

● **Wickerwork**. Mihai Petreus, valea Cufundoasa, n° 92. This delightful man makes baskets that are carried to church on Easter Day.

© Pierre Soissons

The steam engine has to stop for 15 minutes every 8 km to fill up with water from the River Vaser. A round trip takes over 10 hours.

Festivals

Annual village festival *(Târg).* *End Aug. or Sept.* Local arts and crafts, music and dancing. Info. ❶

Vişeu de Sus

Dialling code ☎ *262. See p. 215.*

❶ **Provişeu**, str. Libertăţii 1 ☎/fax 35. 22.85, < www.viseu. mmnet. ro >. A friendly team help you organise your stay in the Vişeu valley and will tell you about the forest train.

Getting there

● **By bus.** Several links from Sighet.
● **By Vaser forestry train.** Holz Company.

Accommodation

▲▲▲ **Hotel Brad**, str. 22 Decembrie, 50 ☎ 35.29.99, fax 35.38.57. *11 rooms.* Hotel belonging to the Vaser forest sawmill. *Restaurant.*

▲▲ **Anastasia Bota-Schiesser** ☎ 35.42.33. Guest rooms in Zipserei.

▲▲ **Valea Vinului** ☎ 35.28.49. *Open Apr.-Oct.* Access: 500 m before the entrance sign to Vişeu de Sus, to the left, after approx. 4 km of rough road. This simple yet pleasing hostel is run by the very welcoming Björn and Florentina Reinhardt.

Eating

In the centre of Vişeu de Sus there are a few pizzerias and other fast food places where you can get the bare essentials. ●

Moldavia: Bucovina

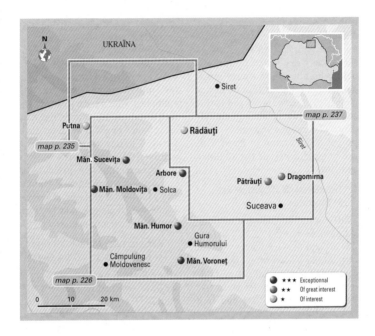

Tucked away in the north-east of Romania, on the furthest foothills of the Carpathian Mountains, is a land where diverse peoples have cohabited for centuries. Here lie Moldavia's origins, its most sacred and historically important sites.

Moldavia's golden age was during the 15th century *(p. 43)* under the long reigns of **Alexander the Good** (Alexandru cel Bun; 1400-1432) and **Stefan the Great** (Ştefan cel Mare; 1457-1504). It was finally subjugated by the Ottomans after fierce resistance which had long halted their progression into Europe. In 1775, the Turks relinquished the north-west portion of Moldavia to the Habsburg Empire; this was Bucovina (from the Slavic *bouk*, "the land of beech trees"). In 1918, this mythical land was returned to Romania. In 1944, the Soviet Union annexed the northern half of Bucovina including its capital, **Cernăuţi** (*Czernowitz in German* and *Tchernivtsy in Ukrainian*) which today lies in the Ukraine.

© Bernard Houliat

Although best known for its churches, Bucovina is an inexhaustible source of wonder. The rural landscape is alive with the colour and bustle of countless tiny villages with their beautifully and carefully decorated homes. Peasant society here has always put a high price on aesthetics, and even today, the curious and painstaking tradition of elaborately decorated household objects and buildings is very much alive. Multi-coloured houses, meticulously maintained wells and barns, and cosy interior furnishings are evidence of a refined peasant civilisation that goes hand in hand with the magnificence of the region's churches.

THE REVIVAL OF BYZANTINE ART IN MOLDAVIA

Shortly after the conquest of Constantinople in 1453 (p. 53), Byzantine art and the Orthodox world fell into a long period of apathy. Only Moldavia reacted against this, finding enough energy to revive its traditions. From mid-15th to mid-16th centuries, two waves of creative activity hit Moldavian churches. The first was architectural and the second, a flood of images.

Traditional Byzantine architecture influenced by Serbia (the tri-conch ↳ plan with three apses united by a central space) combined with certain Western elements, such as Gothic doorways, brought in through Transylvania or Poland. In the 15th century, Moldavian builders found new methods of complimenting the triconch plan: the tower lending height to the naos ↳, supported by an ingenious system of crossed arches. Roofs multiplied, with a separate roof over each section of the church, like hats being pulled upwards by an invisible string. Change also affected the insides: the exonarthex ↳ was added, sometimes enclosed, as at Voroneț, sometimes open, at Humor and Moldovița, and Chambers of Tombs were built, generally reserved for the sepulchres of princes.

ARCHITECTURE: MOLDAVIAN FUSION AT THE TIME OF STEFAN THE GREAT

When **Petru Rareș** (see inset opposite) was crowned in 1527, his first cousin **Grigore Roșca**, future Metropolitan ↳ of Moldavia was higoumena ↳ of Probota Monastery (p. 246). It was partly on his cousin's advice that the prince launched the

legends

The birth of Moldavia

In the neighbouring land of Maramureș there lived a young nobleman named **Dragoș**, renowned for his bravery. One day, he and his faithful companions, set off east to hunt in the mountains. Here, they found the footprints of an **aurochs** (an extinct European wild ox) and decided to follow them. Over mountaintops and through forests they went, until they reached a beautiful valley where the magnificent aurochs stood with a star on its forehead. They chased the beast to the shores of a pure and gentle river where they killed it. Dragoș named the river Molda after his dog, which had died of exhaustion. He and his friends were enchanted by this unknown land and decided to settle there with their families. Thus, on the banks of the **Moldova**, in these uninhabited lands where only nomad Tatars strayed with their flocks, they founded a State named after its river. Their emblem became the **aurochs with a starred forehead** and they made Dragoș their voivode ↳. ●

Prince and patron

Son of Stefan the Great *(p. 43)*, **Petru Rareş** is one of Moldavia's most fascinating characters. Once a fish-monger and a great trav-eller, he was an open-minded and cultivated man, surrounding himself with good advisors. His first reign lasted from 1527 to 1538, when he resisted Turkish domination of the region. Court rilvalries caused him to lose the throne but he came back, this time with Turkish support, from 1541 and 1546. Tirelessly ambitious, he was consumed by a sacred mission: to invigorate and protect the Church from the Turks and from the Refor-mation. With the help of his cousin, Metropolitan ↪ **Roşca**, he built monuments and had many others deco-rated by the greatest artists of the time. ●

Petru Rareş presents a scale model of the church to Christ by the intermediary of St Nicholas. Votive painting at Probata Monastery (p. 246).

great cycle of exterior wall paintings in Moldavia. Despite his immense culture and dynanism, Rareş would never have been able to undertake such a phenomenal artistic pro-gramme without the drive and sup-port of the monasteries.

STATE OF EMERGENCY

This dazzling campaign was actually an act of desperation. The Orthodox Church had been in decline since the Turkish conquest of Con-stantinople in 1453. Furthermore, at the beginning of the 1530s, Mol-davia was under pressure from three fronts: the Ottoman Empire, the Reformation and Poland.

Petru Rareş, who had land in Tran-sylvania (Cetatea de Balta; *p. 161*)

won over to the Lutheran cause, knew the havoc that the Reforma-tion would cause. This explains why the painted themes reassert the strength and purity of the "true (or "orthodox") faith", its legitimacy and long history. The frescoes accord a central role to the Virgin and the saints, which the Reforma-tion had brought into question.

The Turkish threat was different; its hold over the country was real. For several decades, Moldavia had been vassal of the Sublime Porte *(p. 54)*, which tolerated the Orthodox Church. The frescoes depicting the conquest of Constantinople, or the sinners in the Last Judgment *(p. 229)*, do seem, however, to con-tain an anti-Ottoman message.

Moldavian church iconography

Detail from an exterior fresco in Arbore Monastery illustrating Saint Demetrius (Dumitru), Patron Saint of soldiers.

© Pierre Soissons

Between 1530 and 1547, there was a massive campaign to decorate the outside walls of Moldavian churches. These vivid frescoes replayed the principal themes of Byzantine iconography.

An inspired campaign

This campaign was initiated by Voivode **Petru Rareş** *(see inset p. 223)* and his spiritual advisor, and cousin, Metropolitan **Grigore Roşca**. Before this time, in accordance with Byzantine tradition, only

South facade of Voroneţ Church, detail from Saint Nicholas' Akathist Hymn.

© Pierre Soissons

the interiors of churches were painted. In the space of only a few years – from the Church of Saint George in Hârlau in 1530 (p. 250) to Voroneț Church in 1547 – about fifteen churches were redecorated with frescoes – veritable icons. The movement stopped as suddenly as it had begun with two exceptions: Râșca Church in 1552 and Sucevița in 1596 (p. 232). Five churches have preserved their frescoes almost intact: Humor (p. 228), Moldovița (p. 231), Arbore (p. 226), Voroneț (p. 229) and Sucevița (p. 232). Only fragments remain at Probota (p. 246), Suceava (Church of Saint George at Sfântul Ioan cel Nou Monastery; p. 239) and Râșca.

Recess in the west facade of Arbore Church.

Tradition as creative inspiration

If the principal themes come from **Byzantine iconography**, the style of the frescoes is resolutely **Moldavian**. The most frequent scenes are: the Akathist Hymn to the Mother of God ↪, the Tree of Jesse ↪ (p. 231) and the Last Judgment ↪ (p. 229); less common are Genesis and the Akathist Hymn of Saint Nicholas. These themes developed in unusual ways, partly due to their displacement to the outside of the churches and partly to their specific instructive mission. Other themes, specific to Moldavian churches, include the procession of praying saints around the church apses (p. 233), the Ladder of Divine Ascent, the Celestial Customs, and the lives of Saint Paraschiva the Young and Saint John the New (see inset p. 236).

The Weighing of Souls, detail from a fresco at Arbore Church.

Standing up to the elements

Despite the rigours of Bucovina's climate, these exterior paintings have managed to survive reasonably intact for nearly five centuries. This resistance is due to the quality of the lime base and the other materials used so masterfully by the Moldavian painters. A **fresco** can only be painted onto a damp surface, hence the need to limit the painting to a small area at a time. The skill and speed of these artists enabled them, nonetheless, to execute large scenes within the optimum humidity conditions.

The red lines separating the paintings indicate the boundaries of each day's work.

Black is made from charcoal, ochres come from clays dyed with iron oxide, red is obtained from mercury sulphate or copper carbonate and blue comes from azurite or lapis-lazuli. Sometimes the colours become diluted in the lime wash, causing a ghostly transparency. ●

♥ The monastery trail★★★

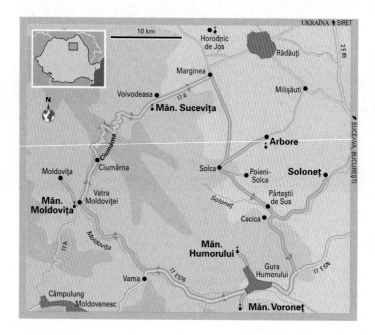

The five churches that have best preserved their exterior frescoes are found in one small region. **Humor**, **Moldoviţa**, **Voroneţ** and **Suceviţa** are all part of monasteries and **Arbore** is a village church. They are nearly all tucked away in secondary valleys which cut into the foothills of the Carpathian Mountains. The churches are all grouped in a 40 km radius, set in exceptionally beautiful countryside which has been meticulously toiled by Moldavian peasants.

Arbore Church★★★

> *28 km S-E of Suceviţa. From Suceviţa, head north. At Marginea, take a right until you reach Solca, then turn left. Open daily, 9am-6pm. Admission charge. Allow 1 hr.*

In a lovely bucolic setting, this church is dedicated to the decapitation of Saint John the Baptist. The frescoes here are particularly fresh and lively. Its founder, **Luca Arbore**, was not a prince but the spiritual advisor to Stefan the Great, and he intended the church and crypt for his own use. It was built in 1503 and painted four decades later by **Dragoş Coman**, one of the greatest 16th-century artists of the Orthodox East, and his assistants. Little is known about Coman, but this masterpiece indicates a familiarity with European art and the Renaissance.

● **The west wall**. A large recess built into the west facade of the church, shelters the frescoes from the wind and rain, thus helping to preserve them. This group of frescoes is particularly fluid, aided by the near-musical rhythm of both its compositions and colours: various shades of green, violet-pink, brick-red, crimson, blue and white. Precise draftsmanship lends an elegance and expressiveness to the figures in every scene. The inventive architectural features of the church provide a fantastic backdrop for the series.

This wall displays seven registers, each containing eleven scenes. The first three upper registers, now partly damaged, portray the **Life of Saint George** (*Sfântul Gheorghe; see photo p. 225*). On the second register, he stands before the Emperor Diocletian who orders him to renounce his faith. For refusing, the saint was plunged into a cauldron of boiling water then tied to a burning grill.

In the register below, he fights the famous dragon, tames it and presents it to the Emperor. Above the window, in a superb composition, the Imperial Court is paying him homage and offering him a banquet.

The fourth register recounts the life and martyrdom of **Saint Demetrius** (*Dumitru*), like Saint George, a protector of soldiers.

The fifth and sixth registers tell the life of **Saint Nikita** (*Nichita*). The seventh represents **Saint Paraschiva the Young**, in what is her first appearance in Orthodox iconography. At the beginning of the 16th century, the popularity of this saint in south-eastern Europe (*p. 256*) had only just begun to take hold.

● **The south wall**. This depicts the Akathist Hymn↬ about the Persian siege of Constantinople and the Last Judgment↬. It is in a poor state, as are the rest of the exterior paintings here.

On the walls of the apses only the blue remains, outlining the sun-bleached figures of the saints in their ghostly procession towards the rising sun.

●●● *En route* **to Humor**: beyond **Solca** and its church dating from 1614, you will pass through verdant countryside with long thin fields dotted with haystacks and copses.

Several **Polish villages★** (Cacica, Soloneţ) nestle here. About two-thirds of Polish Romanian citizens, approximately 3,000 people, live in Bucovina, perpetuating some beautiful rituals, especially the festivals around Easter and Assumption (15 August). Polish and Slovakian immigrants arrived here in the early 19th century at the invitation of the Austrian Empire which needed specialised workers for its salt mines. In the small village of **Pârteştii de Sus★**, many beautiful **traditional homes★** remain.

agenda

A 1-3 day trip covering about 120 km, starting from **Suceviţa**. If you wish to visit the monasteries in the chronological order in which their frescoes were painted, start at Humor and finish at Suceviţa.

At the height of summer, try to visit the monasteries early in the morning or late in the evening to avoid the throngs of tourists. If you are in Suceviţa, a visit at dawn or one hour before sunset is worth the effort.

There is parking available **at all the monasteries** and admission is charged; there is also a charge for taking photographs (please do not photograph the nuns). No smoking on site. Suitable dress and respectful behaviour are required at all times. At Moldoviţa and Suceviţa there are guided tours in English, French and German.

Accommodation at Suceviţa, Mănăstirea, Humorului, Poieni-Solca, Vama. Excellent meals in local guesthouses and in a few restaurants.

Address book p. 240. ●

Humor Monastery★★★

> *Mănăstirea Humorului.* 38 km S of Arbore. From Arbore, return to Solca then the DN17. In Gura Humorului, turn right to Mănăstirea Humorului. Open daily 8am-8pm. Admission charge. Allow 1 hr.

Under Prince Rareş' rule *(see inset p. 223)*, **Toader Bubuiog** and his wife Anastasia founded a monastery in 1530 which was closed down in 1775 by the Austrian authorities. The buildings slowly fell into disrepair, leaving only the north-east tower intact. Since the 1990s, life at the monastery has picked up with renewed vigour and enthusiasm.

Dedicated to the Assumption of the Virgin, the church was inaugurated on 15 August 1530. It was lengthened by an **exonarthex**↪, open on three sides and resting on four cross-arches. This was the first time such an architectural device had been used in Moldavia. The wall paintings all date from 1535 and are the work of a group led by **Toma de Suceava**, a man who appears to have frequented the West, particularly Mount Athos. According to a document dating from 1541, he was one of the official painters of Prince Rareş' court. A palette of reds, ochres, pinks, blues and oranges happily combine to brighten the walls. The **south wall** is a riot of images: the **Akathist Hymn to the Mother of God**↪ is followed, on the right, by that to Saint Nicholas.

The Akathist Hymn to the Mother of God

The ballet of colours and the musicality of the composition allow one to almost hear this hymn composed in the 6th century by Saint Romanus the Melodic, a Syrian monk who lived in Constantinople. Each tableau corresponds to one of the 24 stanzas of the hymn. Originally a Greek term, "akathist" means that one stays standing during the singing of the hymn. This hymn is sung in Moldavian monasteries every Saturday before the liturgy, except on important saints' days.

On the upper register, the first stanzas depict the Annunciation, the Visitation and the Nativity. Below these is a superb representation of the **cavalcade of the Three Kings**. A subsequent sequence recounts the Lives of the Virgin and Christ. By the window, there is a large icon depicting the Glorification of Mary (the **Theotokos**↪ "who carries God" in Greek) with the Child in her arms surrounded by angels and saints.

One stanza was added to the hymn at a later date, the **trope**, composed by Patriarch Sergius of Constantinople (610-638 AD) in thanks for the Virgin's help in lifting the Persian siege of Constantinople in 626 AD. This stanza is represented by the siege of the city and is depicted here, beneath the rest of the hymn.

It shows the besieged city, processions carrying the image of the Virgin and battles on the ramparts. The Turkish army is approaching. A rain of fire falls upon the enemy. A mounted knight pierces an Ottoman soldier with his lance; his name is written to the side: this is Toma, the artist. These images are most commonly interpreted as a message to the Moldavians of the time: the assailants being not the Persians of the 7th-century but the Turks of the 15th century.

The town looks much like Suceava, the capital of Moldavia, which followed the example of Constantinople in 626 AD, and sought patronage and salvation from the Virgin Mary. During Petru Rareş' first reign, frescoes would commonly depict the siege of Constantinople (Humor, Moldoviţa). After Rareş' return to power in 1541 with the support of the Sublime Porte *(p. 53)*, this scene was diplomatically withdrawn from the iconographic repertoire.

Voroneţ Monastery★★★

> *Mănăstirea Voroneţ. 9 km S of Mănăstirea Humorului. From Mănăstirea Humorului, return to the centre of Gura Humorului and turn right on the DN 17. After 1 km, on the edge of town, a road on the left leads to Voroneţ. Open daily, 8am-8pm. Admission charge. Allow 1 hr min.*

Between 26 May and 14 September 1488, Stefan the Great had the church of Voroneţ built on the site of the wooden hermitage of **Daniel the Hermit** *(Daniel Sihastru)*, his spiritual advisor. It has a triconch↘ plan, originally composed of a sanctuary↘, a naos↘ and a pronaos↘. The monastery was closed shortly after Bucovina was annexed (1775), becoming the parish church. Three nuns, Irina, Gabriela and Elena, brought the monastery back to life in 1991, establishing a convent here.

The frescoes around the altar and the naos are contemporary with the construction of the church. Those in the pronaos and exonarthex↘ were added later with the exterior frescoes. The **Passion Cycle** and a **votive painting** of the family of the founder-prince cover the naos. The walls and vault of the exonarthex are decorated with the 365 scenes from the **Menologium**↘. The **exterior frescoes**, completed in 1547, were the last to be commissioned by Petru Rareş. His mentor, Metropolitan↘ **Grigore Roşca**, oversaw their completion. The traditional themes stand out: the Prayer of All Saints *(p. 233)*, the Tree of Jesse↘ and the Akathist Hymn↘, but no siege of Constantinople *(p. 53)*.

The Last Judgment

The extraordinary **Last Judgment**, painted on five registers, fills the entire west wall.

● **First register**. Symbolising the end of time, angels are pictured rolling up the signs of the Zodiac. In the centre, archangels Michael and Gabriel open shutters revealing God the Father.

● **Second register**. Mary and John the Baptist intercede with Christ enthroned, beneath whose feet leaps the great fire which spreads through the following registers. Angels and apostles gather on either side.

● **Third register**. In the middle is the Throne of Etimasia (the empty throne), symbolising the wait for the second coming of Christ on Judgment Day. The Holy Spirit, repre-

The Last Judgment covering the west facade of Voroneţ Monastery.

© Pierre Soissons

sented by a dove, sits upon the throne. On either side, stand Adam and Eve. Under the throne are the Gospel and Chalice. On the far left, Saint Paul exhorts prophets, bishops and martyrs to come to the throne. On the right, Moses, holding the stone tablets, points out the throne to non-believers: Jews, Turks, Tatars, Armenians and Latins.

● **Fourth register**. The divine hand holds a set of scales. Below, a naked figure awaits judgment: will the scales tip him towards Heaven or Hell? Angels place rolls of parchment inscribed with good deeds committed by the deceased on one side of the scales. Scowling devils scrabble to pile lists of his sins on the other. With their tridents, the angels try to push the devils away. The damned stand in line, waiting to be thrown over the precipice to the fires below – unexpectedly, an angel is in the queue pulling Arius the Heretic by the beard (Arius denied Christ's divinity, thus provoking one of the first schisms in the Church (325 AD). On the right, the Resurrection of the Dead is depicted, to be continued on the register below. The Angel of the Apocalypse blows his horn, tombs are flung open, wild animals spit out the remains of devoured people. A woman wearing a fir-tree head-dress symbolises Earth. Near the Angel, a doe, symbol of purity, seems lost in this pack of wild beasts. Opposite, on the left, the procession of the righteous make their way towards Heaven.

● **Fifth register**. Overseen by the archangel, the Gates of Heaven open to welcome the righteous, all wearing halos. They are guided by Saint Peter who holds the key and who leads St Paul. Close by, one can spot the first of the Roman Emperors to be christened, Constantine, and his mother Helena, recognisable by their crowns. In Heaven, from left to right, Abraham, Isaac and Jacob are holding saved souls wrapped in scarves. The good thief, who was crucified with Christ, stands next to a seated Mary, flanked by the two archangels.

At the centre of the fresco, David is playing the *cobza*, a sort of lute still found in Moldavia. He seems to be playing for a figure dressed in white lying beside him: this is the symbol of the death of the just; a wisp of white floats from his mouth: this is the soul that the guardian angel will take to be judged. David has no interest in the scene taking place opposite him: the death of a sinner, where the devil, surrounded by flames, patiently looks on. The Resurrection of the Dead continues on the rest of the wall. The sea, symbolised by a woman, holds a boat and rides on the back of fish spitting out the drowned.

The other walls

The south wall is no less impressive, thanks to the sheer number of compositions and the excellent state of conservation of their colours. The western wall is taken up by the brightly painted **Akathist Hymn to Saint Nicholas** and below, the eleven paintings dedicated to the Martyrdom of **Saint John the New** (*see inset p. 236*). To the left of the door, the church's two "spiritual patrons" are depicted: the hermit Daniel Sihastru, who inspired the building of the church, and Metropolitan ↘ **Grigore Roşca** who initiated the campaign of fresco painting in Moldavian churches. The **Tree of Jesse** ↘ and, on the apses, the **Prayer of All Saints** (*p. 233*) are particularly arresting. The frescoes have almost completely faded from the north facade. You can, however, just make **Genesis** out. In the white light of Paradise, Adam and Eve commit the original sin and are thrown out by an archangel. Adam signs a pact with the devil, committing his descendants to damnation in exchange for the devil's help in toiling the land.

Moldoviţa Monastery★★★

> *Mănăstirea Moldoviţa. About 33 km N-W of Voroneţ. From Voroneţ, return to the DN 17 and turn left; at Vama, turn right to Moldoviţa. At Vatra Moldoviţei (the monastery is not in the village of Moldoviţa, 4 km further on), 200 m after a big junction, turn right. Open daily 8am-8pm. Admission charge. Allow 1 hr min.*

The first church founded here, by Alexander the Good in 1408, was carried away just a century later by a landslide. It was replaced, some 300 m downstream, by the present church which is dedicated to the Annunciation and was built in 1532. It was commissioned by Petru Rareş.

A monastery grew up around the church, defended by high ramparts and fortified towers. Today, around forty nuns maintain the harmonious atmosphere of the monastery. As soon as you step in the door, the bright, vivid colours captures one's attention.

This church has a lot in common with Humor (*p. 228*), built merely two years earlier, but here on a more princely scale: the dimensions are that much larger, and, like at Probota (*p. 246*), Voroneţ (*p. 229*), Pătrăuţi (*p. 237*) and Suceviţa (*p. 232*), the tower erected above the naos ↪ dominates the roof-line. The paintings date from 1537, and were probably the work of **Toma de Suceava** and his team, who produced the pictorial cycle at Humor. The frescoes are well-preserved and stunning. Inside, the most interesting compositions are the **Menologium** ↪ and the **Passion Cycle** ↪; and outside, the **Prayer of All Saints** (*p. 233*), and both on the south wall, probably Moldavia's finest **Akathist Hymn** ↪ and a particularly sumptuous version of the **Tree of Jesse** ↪.

The Tree of Jesse

The Tree of Jesse is a symbolic representation of **Christ's genealogy** in the form of a tree where **Jesse**, the father of King **David**, represents the root. This iconographical theme was widespread throughout Europe during the Middle Ages, but nowhere else did it reach the dimension and complexity of its Moldavian interpretations. In the Moldoviţa, Voroneţ and Suceviţa Monasteries, they cover vast surfaces of wall with up to a hundred brightly clothed characters depicted on hypnotic blue backgrounds.

At the base, Jesse is lying down. " A branch will come out of the trunk that is Jesse, and buds will burst from his roots. On him, will rest the Lord's Spirit", proclaimed the prophet Isaiah (11: 1-2). The tree rambles upwards over eight registers, its branches bearing flowers in the form of a chalice: each chalice holds one or more of Christ's ascendants. On the trunk, a row of kings is

© Pierre Soissons

The Tree of Jesse illustrates the continuity between the Old and New Testaments insisting on the earthly origins of Christ who, according to the Gospels of Matthew and Luke, was a descendent of David. Detail from a fresco at Moldoviţa.

Sucevița Monastery is maintained by a community of about 50 monks.

© Pierre Soissons

depicted, starting with David and his son Salomon, all the way to their descendant Joseph. The kinship is also spiritual: prophets adorn the peripheral branches, holding up their writings on the coming of the Saviour. The upper part of the composition presents scenes from the Lives of Mary and Christ, most notably the Nativity (right of the window) and the Crucifixion (above). Pagan philosophers of Antiquity are portrayed on the sides of the tree: Socrates, Plato, Aristotle, Pythagoras – whose spiritual searchings found their natural extension in Christian doctrine.

●●● *En route* to Sucevița: pass through **Ciumârna** *(from Moldovița Monastery, take the DN 17 A heading north)*, a village populated by Hutsuls *(see inset p. 241)*, then cross the **Ciumârna Pass★** (superb views at sunset over the sloping wooded landscape of Bucovina) and drop back

down into the small valley of Sucevița, fragrant with fir trees.

Sucevița Monastery★★★

> *Mănăstirea Sucevița. 34 km N-E from Moldovița. From the monastery, take the DN 17 A to Rădăuți. Open daily 8am-8pm. Admission charge. Allow 1 hr min. **Address book p. 240.***

Sucevița with its colourfully decorated farm buildings, stretches over 7 km of bucolic countryside. Some of the house facades here, and in the neighbouring village of Marginea, still bear the crest of the princely **Movila** family, who financed the monastery *(see inset opposite)*: two swords crossed like a pair of compasses.

In the middle of fir trees and meadows, towers and fortifications signal the presence of the monastery with a severity that is forgotten as soon as you enter. Due to its harmonious proportions, richly-coloured decoration and elegant architectural form, this is perhaps one of the most magnificent monastic complexes in Bucovina The church is of

© Bernard Houliat

The axis of the sanctuary at Sucevița.

Requiem to Moldavian art

The Movila brothers were great believers in the chivalric and sacred mission of Moldavia's sovereigns as guarantors of the unity of the Church. It was for this reason that they had the **Suceviţa** church frescoes painted. These were, however, to be the last exterior church frescoes to be painted for a long time. The flourishing period of 1530-1550 was over, the dazzling artistic drive burning itself out as quickly as it had begun. The state of emergency that had rallied church painters was over and Moldavia had become a powerless vassal of the Ottoman Empire. The brewing storm of the Reformation had passed and the Orthodox world had quietly withdrawn into the half-light of its churches. Suceviţa's lavish decoration is therefore a testament to the unattained goals of the period and, after this last effort, Moldavian churches would no longer be painted. This is why the church is sometimes referred to as a "**testament to Moldavian art**". This swan song was also sung by Vasile Lupu at Iaşi (p. 251 and inset p. 256). •

particular interest becaue of the founding family and for the late date of its frescoes. Built between 1582 and 1584, later fortified to become a princely residence, it is the only Moldavian church to have been decorated with external frescoes after 1552. They were commissioned between 1595 and 1596 by Metropolitan ↝ **Gheorge Movila** and the work carried out by his brothers Ion and Sofronie.

The north wall

As you enter the complex you first see the **Ladder of Divine Ascent**, the most famous of all the Suceviţa frescoes. This was inspired by the writings of **Saint John Climacus** who lived in Sinai in the 6th century, where he was Father Superior of Saint Catherine's Monastery. The east wall is split in two by a ladder whose 30 steps correspond to the 30 virtues a monk should possess. On either side, opposing universes are represented: on one side, angels fly in perfect synchronisation; on the other side, is a chaotic mass of gesticulating demons. Under the cornice, a heavenly white glow lights up the **Genesis** scenes. Below, the life of

Saint Pachomius is represented. This saint set out the rules of community life for the monks of Sinai in the 6th century. Between the two windows, you can see him demolishing a tower, symbol of pride, and so reinforcing the virtue of humility in monastic life.

The Prayer of All Saints

Moldavian iconography reaches its peak here, in this version of the procession of the saints which is found on all the painted churches in the region. Over eight registers, the characters, whose garments have been painted in scrupulous detail, move eastwards. On the first register, under the cornice, are the seraphim and cherubim. On the second, angels. These two registers recreate the **Heavenly Hierarchy of the Church**. Then comes the **Terrestrial Hierarchy**: prophets, apostles, the Church Fathers, martyrs and hermits. All move towards the central aisle, where are represented, from top to bottom, God the Father, Jesus Emmanuel ("God with us" in Hebrew), the icon of the Incarnation (Mary holding Jesus), Christ priest and judge and the **Eucharist** (Jesus in the chalice).

Detail of the Akathist Hymn to the Mother of God, Suceviţa.
The presence of the veil (Pokrov) above Mary's head shows Russian influence.

Lower down, on the buttress, Saint John the Baptist is depicted with angel's wings.

The south wall

The **Akathist Hymn to the Mother of God** ↪ and the **Tree of Jesse** ↪ fill the majority of the south wall. Instead of the siege of Constantinople, in the left-hand corner, the painters have depicted the martyrdom of the monks from Saint Catherine's Monastery in Sinai who were decapitated by Muslims. A porch, added much later, leads into the church.

The interior

Inside, there is a subtle play of light between the abundant gold and the very wide range of colours used in the paintings. The quality and delicacy of the execution reminds us that Ion and Sofronie were also painters of icons and miniatures. In the pronaos ↪, the east dome bears an image of the **Old Testament Holy Trinity**; the other dome shows **God the Father**. The pendentives depict dazzling representations of the **First Christian Councils**. The four walls carry the five registers of the **Menologium** ↪, the life of Saint George and, in particular, the life of Saint Nicholas, on the right; note the scene where the saint, in a boat, saves some sailors from the devil and a tempest.

The **Chamber of Tombs** ↪ contains the bodies of two of the Movila brothers, both respectively Voivodes ↪ of Moldavia: **Jeremy** (died 1606) and **Simion** (died 1609). A stone slab covering their tomb is engraved with the Moldavian coat of arms (head of a aurochs with a star on its forehead), and the crossed swords of the Movila family crest.

The **Passion Cycle** is spread around the naos ↪. A **votive painting** pictures Jeremy Movila being followed by his large family, offering a scale model of the church to Christ through the intermediary of the Virgin Mary. **Christ Pantocrator** ↪, with a captivating and benevolent face, shines down from the cupola of the naos tower.

Jeremy and Simion's **funerary cloths** are in the **Monastery Museum** along with life-size images of them dressed in ceremonial attire.

The **Monastery's feast day** is on 6 August (Transfiguration), and every year, crowds of pilgrims climb to the top of the mountain which overlooks the monastery from the opposite side of the valley *(climb: about. 40 min)*. Great panorama.

●●● **In the area**: the nearby village of **Voievodeasa**★ *(Fürstenthal in German)* has rows of gaily coloured wooden houses and neat gardens all laid out in rows. The village was inhabited by **Germans**, originally Sudetans drawn here by the Habsburgs in 1803, until the Second World War. ●

The northern edge of the Carpathians★★

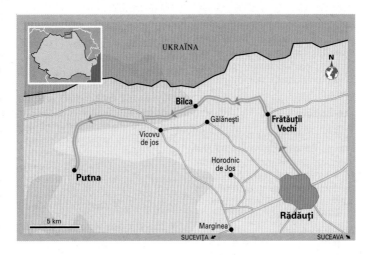

The Suceava Valley dominates this area, where a string of little villages stretches along both banks of the river, sometimes very close to the border with the Ukraine.

In the 15th century, the King of Moldavia, Stefan the Great, built one of his residences here. The site is in a tributary valley, no doubt chosen for its difficult access and the dense forests surrounding it – an ideal refuge from invading forces.

agenda

The route is approx. 34 km, starting in Rădăuți and finishing in Putna. Allow one day. Start in the morning by the market (Fri.) in **Rădăuți**.

Accommodation in Rădăuți and Sucevița.

Address book p. 240. ●

Rădăuți

> *16 km N-E Sucevița. From Sucevița, follow the main road which passes through Marginea before reaching Rădăuți.* **Address book** *p. 240.*

A market town, and one-time capital of Moldavia, Rădăuți became, at the beginning of the 20th century, home to one of the largest Jewish communities in Bucovina. The town is not immediately impressive, but there is plenty of activity when all the region's local farmers come to town on market day.

Bogdana Church★

> *Biserica Bogdana. Open daily 7am-7pm. Free admission. Allow about 20 mins.*

This 14th-century church is the work and resting place of Voivode→ **Bogdan** (1359-1365), founder of the Moldavian State (*p. 41*).

Dedicated to Saint Nicholas, it is the oldest stone church in Moldavia and the only one built on a Romanesque basilica plan: evidence of the lively competition between the Catholic and Orthodox Churches at the time.

The Ethnographic Museum★

> *Muzeul de Etnografie. Piața Unirii, 63,*
☎ *56.25.65. Open daily except Mon. 9am-*
5pm. Admission charge. Allow 30 mins.

The Rădăuți region was once a cultural crossroads which explains the
wealth of the museum's collections
including ceramics from Kuty and
Rădăuți, peasant furniture, household objects and richly varied costumes.

The bazaar★

The heart of the town lies in the
bazaar, a maze of passageways and
inner courtyards running from the
enclosed market to the far side of
the Sucevița road. It is filled with
market stands, piled high with
an unimaginable collection of
curiosities.

Putna★

> *50 km W of Sucevița, 34 km W of Rădăuți.*
At the Rădăuți synagogue, take the
Frătăuții Vechi road. In Frătăuții Vechi,
take a left. Cross Bilca to get back to the
main road. Take a left, after a bridge and a
junction, turn right.

From Rădăuți to Putna, *via*
Frătăuții Vechi★ and **Bilca★**, you
pass through some stunning typically
Bucovina villages: tightly-knit huddles of neat cottages with black roofs
and vegetable patches, flower beds
and orchards, where families eat outside in summer. Putna, larger than

most villages, is marked by the
memory of Stefan the Great, making
it an important site for Romanian
national identity.

Putna Monastery★

> *Mănăstirea Putna. Open daily 7am-*
8pm. Free admission. Allow about 15 mins.

The monastery church was founded
in 1468 by **Stefan the Great** *(p. 43)*
who designed it as his necropolis.
Pilgrims still flock to his tomb. The
ramparts were reinforced in the 18th
century. While the church itself is of
little interest having been restored
several times over, the monastery as
a whole is worth a visit. The **mu-**
seum★ *(open daily 10am-6pm;*
admission charge) displays a superb
collection of Byzantine embroidery.

♥ The Dragoş wooden church★

> *Biserica lui Dragoş. From Putna*
Monastery return on the same road. 400 m
from the monastery, turn left. Open daily
9am-5pm. Admission charge. Allow about
15 mins.

The church was supposedly first
built in Volovăț, near Rădăuți in
1346 on the initiative of Prince
Dragoş. Stefan the Great then had it
transported to this site to serve as a
church for the hermits scattered
around the forest while the
monastery itself was being built.
Built in oak, it has a pine wood
extension, giving it a fragrantly
woody and refreshing atmosphere
inside. ●

Saint John the New

In 1330, this merchant from Asia Minor was martyred by the Tatars in
Cetatea Albe (today Bielgorod Dniestrovski in the Ukraine) for refusing
to deny his Othodox faith. Canonised as Saint John the New, he was
immediately revered in Moldavia. A century later, his relics were
brought to Mirăuți in Suceava, on the orders of Alexander the Good,
and were later moved to the church of Saint George (Sfântu Gheorghe),
in the monastery named after him. On 24 June every year, pilgrims from
all over Romania gather in joyful celebration of the saint. Today, only
Saint Paraschiva of Iași *(p. 256)* is worshipped more. ●

From Rădăuți to Suceava★★

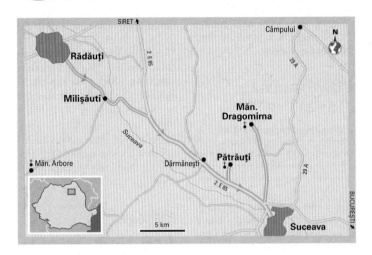

The Carpathian foothills give way to the strange world of the Moldavian hills with vast plains opening to the east. The villages around here are more modest but just as colourfully decorated and marked by a complex history.

From Rădăuți, follow the road to Suceava, passing through some beautiful villages such as **Milişăuti**, where large wooden tubs and a give-away smell reveals the local speciality: fermented cabbage. Beyond Dărmăneşti, a road on the left leads you to the long village of Pătrăuţi. On the outskirts, on the right, stands a gem of Moldavian art.

♥ Pătrăuţi Church★★

> *30 km S-E of Rădăuţi. To visit, ask at the house opposite the church. Admission charge. Allow about 20 mins.*

Built in 1487, this is the oldest surviving church built by Stefan the Great. Dedicated to the Holy Cross (beautiful festival on 14 September), this small marvel sums up the **Moldavian style**. The purity of its pro-

agenda

About 60 km. Allow half a day. The route focuses on the churches in Dragomirna and Pătrăuţi. Begin at Sucevița.

Accommodation at Sucevița and Pătrăuţi.

Address book p. 240. ●

portions is unmatched. Remains of exterior wall frescoes have been uncovered. The interior decoration, in bad condition, follows the Byzantine tradition, though some liberties have been taken with the traditional iconography, specifically with reference to historical events of the time.

At around this time, **votive painting** was becoming fashionable in princely foundations. Here, there is a rather flattering portrayal of **Stefan the Great** and his family. The Prince is offering a scale model of the church to Christ through the intermediary of **Constantine**, the first Roman Emperor to be christened, and a role-model for Stefan in his struggle to save Moldavia and his beloved Church. The same can be said of the **Procession of the Military Saints,** where the Archangel Michael, Defender of the Church, riding his white horse at the head of his celestial army, is followed by Emperor Constantine.

Dragomirna Monastery★★★

> *Mănăstirea Dragomirna. 17 km from Pătrăuți, 12 km N of Suceava. From Pătrăuți, return by the DN 2; at Suceava, turn left before a bridge over a railway line. Open daily 8am-8pm. Admission charge. Allow about 1 hr.*

North-east of Suceava is the site where, in 1602, **Anastasie Crimca** *(see below)* and the boyar ↪ **Luca Stroici** founded a monastic settlement based around a tiny **church★**, which today serves the cemetery. The larger church, inaugurated in 1609, has an unusual space-rocket shape whose elongated height seems completely out of proportion with its width.

The era of exterior wall painting had long past, but the **frescoes** inside the naos ↪ of the church perpetuate Moldavian traditions albeit with a penchant for ostentation and glitz. A sculpted band made up of three thick twisted ropes runs around the outside of the church. The **tower** was Moldavia's first example of Oriental-influenced carved stonework, later used in the construction of the Church of the Three Hierarchs in Iași *(p. 255)*. In 1627, Voivode ↪ **Miron Barnovski Movila** built high walls around the monastery to protect it against the permanent threat of attack in the region.

Under Crimca's patronage, in the first few decades of the 17th century, the monastery became a centre of cultural activity.

Suceava

> *12 km S of Dragomirna. From Dragomirna, take the DN 2 (S). Address book p. 240.*

Partially rebuilt, the former capital of Moldavia contains historically important landmarks that make a stay worthwhile.

● **The Ethnographic Museum★** *(Muzeul Etnografic). Str. Ciprian Porumbescu, 5 ☎ 21.40.81. Open daily except Mon. 10am-6pm. Admission charge.* This museum is installed in the former princely residence *(Hanul Domnesc)*, and has a fine

art

♥ The illuminations of Anastasie Crimca

Bishop of the Moldavian town of Roman, then Metropolitan of Moldavia, Anastasie Crimca is remembered as a generous and cultivated man. At **Dragomirna Monastery** he encouraged intense spiritual activity, notably setting up an illumination workshop, a particular passion of his.

While the themes and compositions of his miniatures diverge little from the Byzantine models, the freedom of his handwriting revolutionised the genre. His inimitable work is marked by vigourous parallel strokes, stylised outlining and vivid coloration. Magnificently composed, his texts are adorned with Oriental decorative elements.

In Dragomirna **monastery museum** you can admire some of the magnificent manuscripts he worked on. ●

© Pierre Soissons

The elegant church tower rises above the fortifications of Dragomirna Monastery, reflected in the lake where the monks breed carp.

collection of traditional carpets with animal motifs and some great traditional costumes.

● **The Monastery of Saint John the New**★ *(Mănăstirea Sfântul Ioan cel Nou). Opposite the central park, leave the main street (bd Ana Ipătescu) taking str. Mitropoliei towards Bosanci and Dolhasca (DJ 208 A); turn left 100 m further on. Open daily 8am-8pm. Admission charge. Allow 15 mins.* This settlement includes the **Church of Saint George** (Sfântu-Gheorghe), completed in 1522, built as the Metropolitan↪ church, hence its large size. Its roof was covered with glazed tiles in 1910 making it visible from afar. In 1534, the exterior walls were covered in frescoes: on the south facade are the remains of the Tree of Jesse↪ and an Akathist Hymn to the Mother of God ↪ with the famous verse about the siege of Constantinople *(p. 53).* The relics of Saint John the

New are buried in the church, under a stone canopy *(see inset p. 236).*

The monastery stands in quiet gardens, a haven away from the bustle of the town, which welcomes a flood of pilgrims each year on 24 of June.

The citadel★ *(Cetatea de Scaun). From the Monastery of Saint John the New, head out of town along the DJ 208 A, then turn left. Open daily 7am-6pm. Admission charge.* Built at the end of the 14th century, the citadel was renovated by Stefan the Great. He made it virtually impregnable. Indeed, it resisted attacks from Turks, Tatars and the Poles. Even Mehmed II, who conquered Constantinople, was not able, in 1476, to bring the walls down and had to beat a retreat.

In a pleasant wooded setting, you can see the remains of Stephen the Great's impressive fortifications with its seven defensive towers. ●

Address book

Pătrăuți Church typifies a form which became popular over the following century: the triconch plan, with a tower above the naos and lots of pointed roofs.

© Bernard Houliat

Mănăstirea Humorului

> *Dialling Code* ☎ *230. See p. 228.*

Accommodation

▲▲ **Casa Buburuzan** ☎0745.84.98.32 (mobile). *5 rooms.* Opposite the car park (200 m from the monastery). *Meals provided.* Wool carpets on sale.

▲▲ **Casa Bucovina** ☎ 0744.37.39.31 (mobile). *4 rooms.* Pass the monastery on the left and 200 m ahead. This is a basic yet comfortable and friendly home, on a farm with garden and large orchard. Wool carpets on sale.

Moldovița

> *Dialling code* ☎ *230. Visit p. 231.*

Folk art

▲▲ **Painted eggs, Semeniuc family** ☎ 33.63.81. In Moldovița, take a right after the village church, then after 100 m, take the path on the left. The house is 100 m ahead. Viorica, Violeta and Camelia (mother and daughters) keep the Hutsul *(pyssanka* in Ukrainian; *see opposite)* tradition of painting on eggs alive. The eggs are painted with bright coloured dyes, and given as Easter *(p. 35)* presents. Sale and demonstration on request. The house also has *2 guestrooms.*

Poieni Solca

> *Dialling code* ☎ *230. Map p. 226.*

Accommodation

▲▲ **Simion Jucan** ☎0745.02.11.51 (mobile). *3 rooms.* Deep in the bucolic setting of the Carpathian foothills, surrounded by meadows and orchards, this is a typcial, jovial farm and a comfortable guesthouse. Directions are complicated so it is best to ring Simion himself and let him guide you!

Rădăuți

> *Dialling code* ☎ *230. See p. 235.*

Accommodation

▲▲ **Pension Fast**, str. Ştefan cel Mare, 80 ☎ 56.00.60. *8 rooms.* Comfortable and well-priced. *Restaurant.*

Suceava

> *Dialling code* ☎ *230. See p. 238.*

Getting there

● **By plane**. 3 flights per week to Bucharest, with Angels Airlines, in collaboration with Tarom. Airport lies 6 km outside Suceava, towards Botoşani. **Tarom agency**, str. Nicolae Balcescu, 2 ☎21.46.86. *Open Mon.-Fri. 9am-5pm.*

● **By train**. Several daily connections with Bucharest and Suceava, including 2 daily Intercity trains.

minorities

The Hutsuls

© Antoine Schneck

The Hutsuls are a Slavonik people of enigmatic origin. They emerged from the north in the 17th century in what is now Bucovina, coming from the wildest outpost of the Carpathians, between Bucovina and Galicia.

They were invited here by the monasteries which, at the time, needed labour to work the forests. In exchange, the Hutsuls received land that they could cultivate for themselves. There are around 20,000 Hutsuls in Romania today, mainly in Bucovina, and maybe ten times this amount in the Ukraine. Their dialect, which is similar to Ukrainian with some Romanian words, has managed to survive due to their marginal existence in Romanian society. The Hutsuls carry on their tradition of **egg painting** which are given as presents on Easter day. •

Excellent night train (with sleeping carriages). Also lines to Iaşi and Timişoara. **Station** : Gara Suceava North, Iţcani district (on the road from Rădăuţi). **Railway company** (*Agenţia CFR*), str. Nicolae Balcescu, 8 ☎ 21.43.35. *Open Mon.-Fri. 7am-7pm.* Info. CFR ☎ 51.71.17.

• **By bus**. Regular buses run from Iaşi, Cluj, Bucarest, Rădăuţi and the Ukraine. Maxitaxis used in most towns (Târgu Mureş, Braşov, Bacşu, Piatra Neamţ, etc.). **Bus station** (*Autogara*): str. Vasile Alexandri, 9 ☎ 52.43.40, near the market.

Accommodation

▲▲▲ **Hotel Dava ♥**, str. Mitropoliei 3, ☎ 52.21.46, fax 52.00.87, < www.balada.ro >. *19 rooms. Restaurant.* The best hotel in Suceava.

▲▲ **Hotel Continental Arcaşul ♥**, str. Mihai Viteazul, 4-6 ☎ 21.09.44, fax 21.47.00. *96 rooms.* Comfortable, reasonable prices, well situated near the town centre. *Restaurant.*

▲▲ **Villa Alice**, str. bis Simion Florea Marian, 1 ☎ 52.22.54. *12 rooms.* Spacious and comfortable. Apart from breakfast, food has to be ordered.

Shopping

• **Bazaar**. Near the bridge in Suceava, take the direction of Botoşani. *Open every day except Mon. 6 am-12pm.*

• **Fresh Produce Market** (*piata agroalimentara*), str. Petru Rareş, 7, (near the bus station). Every day, all day.

Suceviţa

> *Dialling code* ☎ *230. See p. 232.*

❶ **Bucovina Reteaua Verde** ☎ 0745.33.34.02 (mobile), < inforeverde@yahoo.com >. Only 400 m from the monastery, towards Rădăuţi, on the right. Immediately after a hotel built in concrete. Small house that overlooks a communal pasture, the information bureau.

lifestyle

Winter at home with the soba

Winter is the season when one best understands the intimate pleasures of a Bucovina home. When villages disappear beneath a blanket of snow, the people huddle inside their cosy, brightly-coloured cottages. Tucked in under linen sheets and huge bed covers, the nights seem all too short. But nothing can beat the gentle warmth of the *soba*, huge stove-heaters made with fire bricks and covered with thick blue, green, or brown ceramic tiles that are also sometimes decorated. A fire in the morning and one at night heats these tiles that then gently release their heat throughout the day. Winter can be a blissful season, especially in Sucevița, where many guesthouses are equiped with a *soba*. •

Accommodation

▲▲▲ **Popas turistic Bucovina** ☎ 56.53.89. *About 60 places.* Modern hotel and villa on the edge of the forest, at the entrance of the village when coming from Moldovița. Comfortable. *Restaurant.*

▲▲ **Casa Felicia and Trandafir Cazac** ☎ 41.70.83 and 0745.56.02.53 (mobile). *5 rooms* et 2 bathrooms. A small and pleasant farm with large living quarters, chickens, a cat and a big garden. A renowned menu. Children can sleep in a little bungalow. Trandafir knows the region very well.

▲▲ **Casa Derevlean** ☎ 41.70.06. *5 comfortable rooms* and 2 bathrooms. When coming from Rădăuți, at the beginning of Sucevița, first st. on the right : you are in Voievodeasa, former German village (*Fürstenthal*). After about 200 m, on the left, there is a monumentous, traditional wooden door. A farm with a wooden structure, painted in the Bucovina trademark colours (green and white).

Restaurant

♦ **Gradina de Vara** ☎ 41.70.17. 1.5 km upstream from the Sucevița Monastery. Simple, tasty and reasonably priced food.

Vama

> *Dialling* ☎ *230. Map p. 226.*

Accommodation

▲▲ **Pensiunea Letiția Orșivschi** ☎ 23.92.12 and 0745.86.95.29 (mobile). *9 rooms* divided between two houses. *Meals provided.* 100 m from the train station. A friendly family of folkartists (specialising in embroidery).

▲▲ **Pensiunea Virginia**, str. Iorgu Toma, 192 ☎ 23.91.78 and 0723. 54.03.26 (mobile). *5 rooms* (soon to be more). *Meals provided;* Virginia is a great cook. Her enthusiastic husband Tică, is always willing to organise barbecue trips in the mountains! •

Mountains and hills of Moldavia

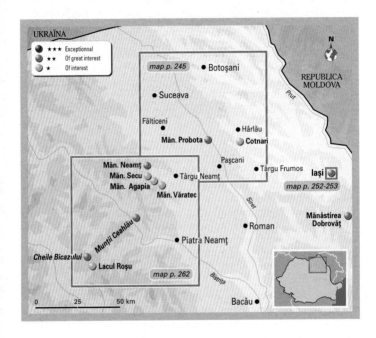

To the average westerner, Moldavia is something of an unknown entity. During the 16th and 17th centuries, this land, between the Black Sea and the Bucovine Carpathians, was considered a great country, governed by brilliant and cultivated hero-princes. Since this golden age, Moldavia has gradually slid into obscurity. Alienated and impoverished, the region – it is now merely a region – has reached something of a dead end which its future status as the eastern border of the European Union will do little to relieve. Historically, however, the country has survived far worse, and it knows that nostalgia for a once glorious past does not offer a solution. Today's Moldavian youth are particularly dynamic, realising salvation lies through relations with the wider world, and not just Bucharest, just as it did in the good old days of the voivodes.

history

The Republic of Moldova

Bessarabia, the eastern territory of Moldavia, situated between the Prut and Dniestr Rivers, was annexed by the Russian Empire in 1812. In 1918, it was reintegrated as part of Romania until Stalin established the **Moldavian Socialist Soviet Republic** (capital: **Chişinău** or Kichinev) in 1940. With the collapse of the USSR in 1991, this territory became the independent **Republic of Moldova**. The same language is spoken on each side of the border, although beyond the Prut river it is known officially as *moldovenesc*. During the Soviet era, this was the only Latin language to be written in the Cyrillic alphabet! •

Moldavia is divided in two by the Siret plain where, for hundreds of years, traders have passed through from as far afield as the Bosphorus and the Baltic countries. In the western half, tiny villages, monasteries and retreats are tucked away in the foothills of the gentle, forest-covered Carpathian Mountains. Refuge and shelter have always been sought and found here.

A great spiritual activity has been maintained around these mountains, making them one of the most important sites in the Orthodox world. To the east, lies the hills and the historically troubled side of Moldavia. Like many countries, times of adversity have resulted in a less open character. An almost frantic folk-music helps distract from the memory of more troubled times, as do the village: sort of oasis of modest clay houses painted with a blue or green limewash and lined with oriental-style balconies.

In summer, life disappears under the shade of great trelissed vines where elderly people and cats spend the hottest part of the day. The smell of peppers, ripe fruit and dill perfumes the laden air. It is in these intimate scenes that the real Moldavian art of living can be found: finding poetry and gentleness in everything however ephemeral. •

From Suceava to Iaşi

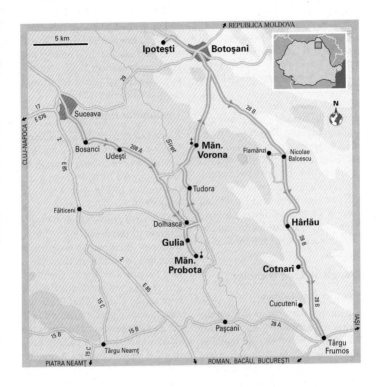

Moldavia was born in the mountains of Bucovina, but the Moldavian princes became increasingly distanced from this area as they built their residences further and further afield until their overstretched territory was difficult to control.

In the extreme north-east of Romania, the Botoşani and Iaşi hills are barren and of little interest despite the charm and tenderness which emanates from the region's villages.

The best times to go are in May, October and particularly during the winter months when the quality of the lights create strange sensations and primal feelings which explode into chaos at **New Year** (p. 36).

agenda

You will need **a full day** to follow in the footsteps of Voivode Alexandru Lăpuşneanu, who transferred the region's capital from Suceava (p. 238) to Iaşi (p. 251). *En route* visit Hârlău (p. 250), the Cotnari vineyards (p. 250) and Prince Petru Rareş' masterpiece: Probota Monastery (p. 246). From Suceava to Probota the roads are poor but they improve.

Accommodation available in Cotnari and Botoşani.

Address book p. 268. ●

Probota Monastery★★

> *Mănăstirea Probota. 40 km S-E of Suceava, 5 km S of Dolhasca. Leave Suceava towards Bosanci on the DJ 208 A. When you get to Dolhasca, take a right turn and then a left. Open daily from sunrise to sunset. Admission charge. Allow 1 and a half to 2 hrs.*

Take advantage of the poor condition of the road to drive slowly and really appreciate the atmosphere of the villages you pass through, such the Rom village of **Gulia** with its intensely blue, lime-washed houses. In the middle of lush green countryside, emerge the fortified walls and towers of the monastery whose name, Probota, has the meaning of "brotherhood" (of the monks) in Slavonic.

Church of Saint Nicholas

> *Biserica Sfântu Nicolae.*

The church was built in 1530 on the orders of **Petru Rareș**, son of Stefan the Great, who broke with tradition and designed this as his princely necropolis, instead of that at Putna Monastery *(p. 236)*. When he came to the throne in 1527, the higoumena↪ at Probata was none other that his first cousin **Grigore Roșca**, future Metropolitan of Moldavia. It was partly at his cousin's bidding that Petru Rareș initiated the cycle of exterior wall paintings on Moldavian churches *(p. 224)*. The first to have them were the Church of Saint George in Hârlău *(p. 250)* in 1530 and then Probota in 1532.

Over the following centuries, however, the monastery was neglected and its buildings gradually fell into ruin. The interior frescoes were painted over several times, while those on the exterior facades suffered irreparable damage. In the 1990s, however, a Japanese foundation financed some crucial research and restoration work in the church. The result was the unveiling of the magnificence of the original interior frescoes dating from 1532, which had, ironically, been preserved under the 19th-century academic paintings.

Although the building has the form of a traditional Moldavian church, the accentuated vertical proportions (the tower is 30 m high) and the large elongated openings show a more Gothic influence.

The interior frescoes★★★

Inside the church, the artists knew how to get the best from a fairly limited range of colours which in no way hampered their desire to bring the frescos to life with a host of lively detail.

● **The pridvor**↪. Evening light pours in through the huge Gothic windows illuminating the earliest example in a Moldavian church of a **Last Judgment**↪ fresco. The interplay of light and architectural forms here create a somewhat disturing atmosphere. The *pridvor* is not only the entrance porch, it also serves the symbolic function of a passage: bang in the middle of the Last Judgment, at the end of time itself, a door opens into the church, symbolically indicating the way to redemption.

● **The pronaos**↪. Topped with two domes, the height of the hall is accentuated by four tall windows. Note the hierarchical order of the pictorial programme: the **Virgin Mary** occupies the keystone, while the first **Councils** are found on the tympana; these were the early synods where Christian doctrine, dogma and liturgy were established. Further down the hierarchy, the saints are gathered on the **Menelogium**↪ registers. The Orthodox calendar begins here and is continued on the walls of the Chamber of Tombs.

● **The Chamber of Tombs**↪. The **Menelogium**↪ takes up almost all the wall space in the burial chamber. The massive series is never monotonous due to their inventiveness, tension and dynamism. The great

© Pierre Soissons

Each square of the pronaos' upper register in Probota depicts one day in the Orthodox calendar.

Prince Petru Rareş lies at rest on the south side, next to his wife Elena.

• **The naos**↳. On the west wall of the naos, the **votive painting** shows the founder of the church, Petru Rareş, presenting a model of the church to **Christ**, through the intercession of **Saint Nicholas**. A Turkish-looking figure stands behind him: **Iliaş**, Petru Rareş' son and successor who ruled Moldavia from 1546 to 1551. His name was erased and his face blackened after he converted to Islam!

The **Passion Cycle** fills a large portion of the walls. The narrative, lacking separation between the scenes, flows. The walls are peopled with jostling crowds and numerous details such as buildings of all shapes and sizes. The **Crucifixion** scene dominates the vault of the northern apse. Unfortunately, it is surrounded by some uninteresting remains of the 19th-century portraits which were painted over the original frescoes. The southern apse shows **Saint Nicholas**, the patron saint of the church, clad in his magnificent bishop's robes. On the west wall, the **Dormition of the Virgin**↳ is remarkable for the palpable emotion captured on the faces of those surrounding Mary, most notably on that of the angel leaning towards her. Under the south-east arch of the tower is the **Nativity** scene. On a south-west pendentive of the tower, **Saint**

portrait

Mihai Eminescu, national poet

Mihai Eminescu (1850-1889) has achieved cult status in Romania. With a rich, yet concise style, he wrote about the complexities of romantic love and its trail of pain and desperate solitude. He also sought inspiration in the traditional peasant repertoires and in the history of the Romanian nation's struggle against the invader, between the spiritual values of his people and the harmful effects of modern society.

Written in the very specific context of the 19th century and the emancipation of nations, his work has often been appropriated by Romanian nationalist groups. This great poet remains virtually unknown outside his native Romania and little of his work has been translated (p. 325). Wracked by fits of madness, Eminescu was eventually institutionalised in 1883, six years before his death. ●

Luke, the Evangelist, is pictured writing in the midst of a highly sophisticated setting. From the dome above the naos, the lofty figure of **Christ Pantocrator**↪ looks down benevolently on the gathered congregation.

Probota to Iaşi

> *From Probota head towards Dolhasca and Botoşani (N).*

Returning to Dolhasca, cross the River Siret to Tudora and Vorona. Both are renowned for their **ancient winter festivals** (p. 36), which still take place today.

Vorona Monastery

> *Mănăstirea Vorona. 2 km S-E from Vorona village, 35 km N of Probota.*

The road emerges from a dark forest into a vast clearing where lies the Vorona monastic complex. Lacking in historical or artistic interest, the monastery is still worth visiting for the refreshing, almost eerie peacefulness of the site.

In and around Botoşani

> *61 km N of Probota, 30 km N of Vorona.*
Address book p. 268.

At the heart of this modern town, bristling with high-rise blocks, a tiny island of the old jewish district has survived. It is typical of market towns of the past: eclectic houses overloaded with stucco and fleshy cornices surrounding lively inner courtyards which once bustled with transactions. Wooden stairs and walkways lead to appartments above. The **Ethnographic Museum** (**Muzeul Etnographic** : *str. Unirii, 3; open daily except Mon.; admission charge*) displays an assortment of local craft and costumes. The **Church of Saint Nicholas Popăuţi** (**Biserica Sf. Nicolae**), built in 1497 by Stefan the Great, is worth a visit.

The Botoşani hills are home to two of Romania's great cultural figures: the poet **Mihai Eminescu** *(see above)* and the composer **George Enescu** (*p. 325*). **Eminescu** spent his early childhood in **Ipoteşti** (*4 km W of Botoşani*) before leaving to pursue his studies in Vienna. He eventually returned to Iaşi, becoming an active member of its already intense cultural life. A memorial museum has been set up in a replica of his family home (**Casa Memorială**, *open Tue.-Sun. 10am-5pm; admission charge*).

The road meanders towards Iaşi through the treeless Botoşani hills covered with fields and pasture. Villages appear like welcome splashes of colour, alive with flowers, brightly painted houses, and orchards.

Moldavian brass bands

© Stephan Siedler/Piranha

Moldavian brass band music is a legacy of military music from the campaigns of the Ottoman army.

The **Ciocârlia** *(p. 324)* Brass Band is a particular favourite amongst the Westerners who have discovered the frantic rhythms of Moldavian dances. A brass band requires about ten musicians; flamboyant brass and clarinets are accompanied by a precise, breathless beat provided by helicons, tubas and percussion. This music was originally played by the Roms in the Ottoman army and subsequently became part of Moldavian village life, being played at weddings, festivals and other special occasions. The unrestrained inventiveness and virtuosity of the musicians enables them to permanently enrich their repertoire, introducing themes and arragements from elsewhere, without losing their soul. Some villages are famous for their brass bands, **Zece Prajini** for example, from where the Ciocârlia Brass Band originates. Some bands survive by playing every year at the Winter Festivals of **Vorona** *(p. 248)* and **Tudora**, but, sadly, more and more musicians are giving up. Soon, dancing the *sârba*, the *bătuta* or the ***ruseasca*** will be the exclusive reserve of tourists! ●

wine

Cotnari's golden nectar

Cotnari *grasă* owes its fine reputation to Stefan the Great. Although this is the northern limit for the cultivation of vines, some remarkable white wines are produced, some of which are similar to Tokay, Sauternes and the golden-yellow wines of the Jura. The ***grasă*** *cépage*, or grape variety, provides the bulk of Cotnari wines. *Grasă*, meaning, fleshy or full-bodied, aptly describes the qualities of this grape which imprints the wine with its own particular bouquet. The grapes are left on the vine as long as possible to shrivel and to be invaded by *Botrytis cinerea*, the "noble rot", before being hand-picked grape by grape, giving a wine with a high sugar content. You are unlikely to find the best examples of Cotnari wines in a supermarket. At the **Pension Bilius**, situated in the midst the vineyards, you can, however, enjoy the real thing. ●

Hârlău

> *109 km N of Probota via Botoşani, 48 km S of Botoşani on the DN 28 B.*

Stefan the Great had one of his favourite residences here. All that remain of the palace are a few ruins and the **Church of Saint George★**, consecrated in 1492. The first exterior wall frescoes in Moldavia were painted on this church. Sadly, they have disappeared over time, leaving the architecture exposed in all its elegant glory; the red brick makes a satisfying contrast with the white stone; and the cornice is brightly decorated with bricks glazed in different colours.

The Cotnari Vineyards★

> *119 km N of Probota via Botoşani, 58 km S from Botoşani, 10 km S of Hârlău on the DN 28 B. To reach the vineyards from the village, follow the signs for Bălceni.* **Address book** *p. 268.*

Stefan the Great was also responsible for making Cotnari wines famous *(see above)*. It is hard to imagine today that, during the 15th and 16th centuries, Cotnari was an important, commercial town.

From the hill overlooking the village, a harsh, sweeping landscape opens before you, a landscape which has been inhabited since prehistoric times. This amphitheatre of vineyards produces some delicious wines.

●●● **In the area**: the road to Cotnari passes close to the village of **Cucuteni** *(17 km S-W of Cotnari)* which has given its name to a civilisation dating back to around 4000 BC, famous for its anthropomorphic ceramics, coloured white, black and red which were discovered here and of which there is a good collection in the Iaşi History Museum *(Muzeul de Istorie al Moldovei p. 254).* ●

Iași★★

The outsize Palace of Culture stands like a statement of bravado of a capital clinging to the memories of a once glorious past.

Known as "Jassy" to some, but actually pronounced "yash", this city is blessed with a youthful population, a vibrant atmosphere and plenty of trees and green spaces. Nevertheless, Iași still seems completely worn out by its turbulent history.

BITTER-SWEET DESTINY
OF A CULTURAL BREEDING-GROUND

Although Iași has, for a long time, been in decline, it has always managed to maintained a rich and diverse cultural life. When, in 1565, the market town became the capital city of Moldavia, the latter was no longer the great kingdom it had been at the time of **Stefan the Great** *(p. 43)*, having lost much of its territory to the Ottoman Empire. With **Vasile Lupu** *(see inset p. 256)* at the helm from 1634 to 1653, Iași briefly had pretensions of being a second Byzantium: a sparkling, civilised town open to cultural influences and patron to the Orthodox world.

agenda

Allow **two full days** in and around Iași. Day 1: 6 hrs tour of the town on foot (inc. visits). Day 2: car or bus trip into the **Dobrovăț** countryside. Visit Iași's **Jewish cemetery A1** in the evening.

Accommodation available in Poiena and Iași.

***Address book** p. 268.* ●

All delusions of grandeur were quashed when the Sultan claimed Bucovina in 1775, and later Bessarabia. Iași hoped to become the capital of **Romania** when these principalities were integrated into the kingdom in 1812. When this failed to happen, Iași withdrew sulkily into a prolonged state of provincial exile, only to emerge during the **pogroms** of 1941, which left a numbing sense of suffering hanging over the town,

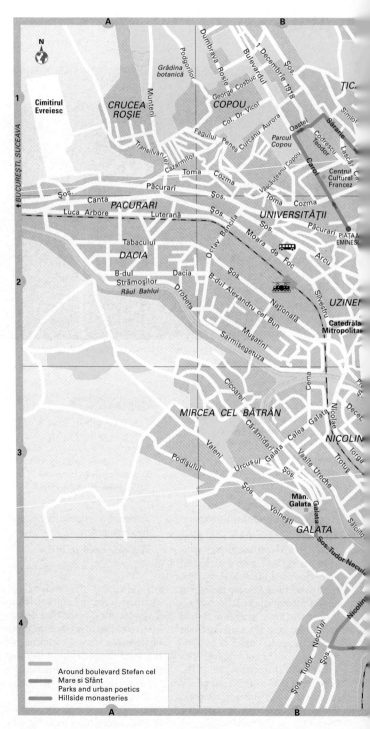

Around boulevard Stefan cel
Mare si Sfânt
Parks and urban poetics
Hillside monasteries

IAŞI

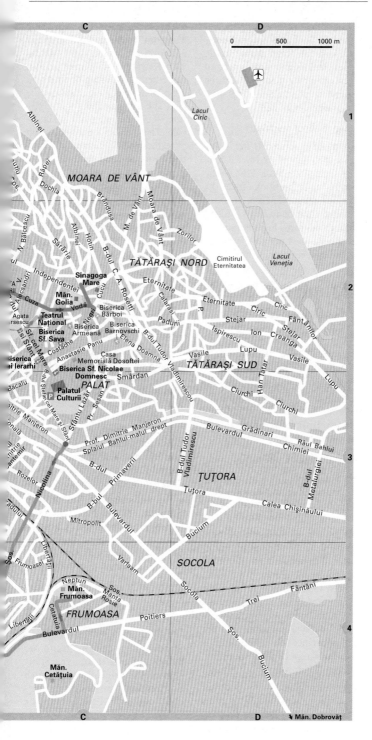

half of which was Jewish. Although in the middle of an economic wasteland and far from major trade routes, this is Romania's second largest university town (12% of the population are students). This, perhaps, is where hope lies.

THE TOWN OF SEVEN HILLS

Surrounded by seven hills, Iaşi is situated in the valley of the River Bahlui, a tributary of the River Prut. In the suburbs, ugly buildings from the Ceauşescu era stand next to a maze of low, semi-rural houses and gardens. Although destroyed in parts, much of the original town survives, including an impressive number of churches.

Around boulevard Ştefan cel Mare şi Sfânt

> *Bulevardul Ştefan cel Mare şi Sfânt. Parking available at the Palace of Culture.*

In the midst of a somewhat chaotic town centre, one street stands out: boulevard Ştefan cel Mare şi Sfânt, a magnificent avenue of parks and historic monuments.

The Palace of Culture*

> **C3** *Palatul Culturii. Piaţa Ştefan cel Mare şi Sfânt, 1* ☎ *21.83.83. Open daily except Mon. 10am-5pm. Admission charge, reduction for all four museums. Allow 2 hrs.*

This massive edifice blocks the eastern horizon of the town centre. Designed by architect **Ion Berindei**, who trained in Paris, it was built between 1896 and 1925 to house the administration of a town become provincial! The overly grandiose palace is like a monument to the self-importance of a capital which is unable to accept its fall from grace.

The **Voivode↪ Room,** on the first floor, is dominated by the portraits of almost all the Moldavian sovereigns, from Dragoş-Voda to King Michael. The palace today houses several museums.

● **The Moldavian Ethnographic Museum** (*Muzeul Etnografic al Moldovei*). If you miss the Moldavian New Year festivities (*p. 36*), come here for an idea of what you are missing: the masks, the bear, the goat and all the others – the only thing they have not got is the hullabalo! There is also a good collection of textiles and dyed carpets embroidered with bird and plant motifs.

● **The Museum of Science and Technology** (*Muzeul Ştiinţei şi Tehnicii*). A surprising collection of **musical instruments**: music boxes, mechanical accordions, Barbary organs, and a hilarious automated orchestra with three violins and a piano.

● **The Museum of Art** (*Muzeul de Artă*). The Romanian paintings in this museum are fascinating, not so much for their artistic value, but rather for their account of Moldavian rural life and its landscape. **N. Grigorescu** who painted Agapia Church (*p. 266*), shows a more down-to-earth style in his painting of an ox-cart (*Car cu boi*). **Th. Aman** invites us to a village dance (*Hora de peste Olt*). **O. Bancila** introduces us to an old Jewish tailor (*Batrân croitor*). Do not miss **Dimitrie Gavrielanu**'s Winter Festival scenes where monsters walk along a snow-covered path.

● **The Museum of Moldavian History** (*Muzeul de Istorie al Moldovei*). The famous **Cucuteni** ceramics (*p. 250*) are on display here. including some anthropomorphic statuettes, especially of women.

Princely Church of Saint Nicolas

> **C3** *Biserica Sfântul Nicolae Domnesc. Near (N) the Palace of Culture. Open daily 8am-sunset. Free admission.*

Standing between the grandiose Palace of Culture and the Stalinesque Hotel Moldova, this church is refreshingly modest. It is especially delightful during the sung liturgy, relayed outside by loudspeakers (*see inset p. 272*). Built by Stefan the Great in 1492, the coro-

religion

Who were the Three Hierarchs?

The Three Hierarch Saints were: **Basil the Great** (329-379 AD), organiser of monasticism and inspiration to Saint John Cassian and Saint Benedict; **Gregory of Nazianzus**, the "Theologian" (330-390 AD), philosopher and author of theological works; and **John Chrysostom** (Chrysostom meaning "Golden Mouth" in Greek) (345-407 AD), Patriarch of Constantinople, one of the most popular of Eastern preachers and a writer of numerous theological works: his liturgy remains the most widely used in the Orthodox Church. The three saints inspired such dedicated followers that their respective groups of zealots came to blows, bringng dissent to the Church. During the reign of the Byzantine Emperor, Alexius Comnenus (1081-1118), the three Saints appeared to **Saint John Mauropus**, Metropolitan of Eucheita in a dream. Speaking with one voice, they asked him to choose one day when all three saints could be celebrated so as to unite the rival groups in a yearly festival. John Mauropus chose 30 January, the end of the month in which their individual celebrations all fall: Basil the Great, 1 January; Gregory of Nazianzus, the 25th; and John Chrysostom, the 27th). ●

nations of many Moldavian have taken place here. The church was completely renovated by Lecomte du Noüy between 1884 and 1904.

●●● **In the area**: the colonnaded house where, in the 17th century, **Metropolitan ↝ Dosoftei** set up a printing house, producing some of the first texts to be printed in Romanian (*Casa Memorială Dosoftei* **C2**; *str. A. Panu, 69*).

The Church of the Three Hierarchs**

>**C2** *Biserica Trei Ierarhi*. *100 m along bd Ştefan cel Mare şi Sfânt on left.* ☎ *21.63.49. Open Tue.-Sun. 9am-12pm and 1pm-7pm. Admission charge. Allow 45 mins.*

Built between 1637 and 1639, the monastic **Church of the Three Hierarchs** lacks the harmonious silhouette of earlier Moldavian religious buildings. Its fame lies in its walls, covered in sculpted motifs spread over 30 friezes, one on top of the other, each one different: a **sumptuous stone lacework** made up of arabesques, flowers, scrolls and tracery which have undeniable Turkish, Caucasian or Persian links.

Some clumsy, late 19th-century restoration work by French architect Lecomte du Nouÿ had some regretful effects on the outside, but especially, on the inside of the church.

Once covered in gold and lapis-lazuli and richly endowed with

© Pierre Soissons

Church of the Three Hierarchs.

portrait

Byzantine dream of Vasile Lupu

In an age when voivodes rarely reigned for more than three years – sometimes only for a matter of weeks – the long reign (1634-1653) of **Vasile Lupu** (Basil the Wolf) was nothing short of miraculous. Originally Albanian, he was an enlightened, dynamic man and a skilled politician who inspired an unprecedented economic boom. Moldavia openly embraced the cultural developments of the time, including the Renaissance, and Vasile founded the **Academic College** in 1640, setting Iaşi's long university tradition in motion. However, it was with the **Church of the Three Hierarchs** (p. 235) that Vasile made his fatal mistake, shattering his dream of a Moldavian Byzantium and of returning his country to the glorious days of the Empire. He forgot that, ultimately, he was under the rule of the Sultan.

When he brought the remains of Saint Paraschiva to the Church, Vasile intended to instill his capital, and his reign, with prestige – a prestige that would be recognised by the Orthodox Christians of the former Eastern Empire. The Prince saw himself as protector and patron of the four great Patriarchs. This ambition was his downfall and he was removed from power by the Sultan. He was spared death by the sabre but was imprisoned for a year. On his release and return to grace, he bought the Moldavian throne for his son and became ambassador to the Sublime Porte. Vasile Lupu died in 1661, aged 64. ●

religious objects and tapestries, the church demonstrated the very best in Byzantine religious construction. It looks as if it was built in the form of a *chivot*, a silver tabernacle in the shape of a church placed on the altar to hold the Eucharist.

In 1641, the relics of **Saint Paraschiva the Young** (pronounced "paraskiva") were brought here. Born in Thrace, Saint Paraschiva died in the 11th century and is still revered in south-east Europe. Having been moved all around the Balkans, her remains ended up in Constantinople where Vasile Lupu, sensing the political benefits of possessing Paraschiva's remains, purchased them for a colossal sum (*see above*). In 1888, they were transferred to the nearby Metropolitan Cathedral.

The church contains the tomb of Vasile Lupu who was joined several years later by another important fig-

ure from Moldavian and European history: **Dimitrie Cantemir** (1673-1723), the short-lived sovereign Prince and luminary spirit.

The Metropolitan Cathedral of Saint Paraschiva

> **C2** *Catedrala Mitropolitana. From the Three Hierarchs, take the boulevard (N). Open daily 9am-8pm. Free admission.*

Built between 1833 and 1839, this huge monument is said to be the largest church in Romania. Not large enough, however, to hold the thousands of pilgrims who arrive each year from all over the country to celebrate Saint Paraschiva's feast day (14 October).

The church is the official sanctuary of the **Metropolitan** ↪ **of Moldavia** who, according to tradition, should also be Patriarch ↪ of Romania. The current Metropolitan, Daniel Ciobotea, was born in 1951.

The National Theatre*

> **C2** *Teatrul Național Vasile Alexandri.*
Opposite the Metropolitan Cathedral at the edge of the park. Str. Agatha Bârsescu, 18 ☎ *31.67.7818. Opening hours vary according to rehearsals and performances.*

The National Theatre was completed in 1896 according to designs by Viennese architects. Lavishly decorated, it is one of the most splendid theatres in Romania. In the park opposite, there used to be a summer theatre: the beginnings of the region's famous Yiddish Theatre *(see inset p. 258).*

●●● **Suggested routes:** Golia Monastery *(see below)* is not far from the National Theatre. Alternatively head back on boulevard Ștefan cel Mare și Sfânt to piața Eminescu.

Parks and urban poetry

> *From piața Eminescu to Golia Monastery and the Palace of Culture via the Copou Park and Țicău hill. On foot allow about 2 hrs.*

To appreciate the charm of Iași's old town, you must (as with so many Romanian towns) try and look beyond the Communist-era concrete monstrosities. Many hidden gems can be found in their shadows. The following route is a suggested 2-3 hour walk through the city. It can be cut short by taking tram-line 1 to **Copou Park.**

Copou Park*

> **B1** *Parcul Copou. From piața Eminescu, head back up bd Carol I. The main entrance is off the boulevard. Open daily from 8am-sunset. Free admission.*

Brightly coloured trams hurtle down bd Carol I, commonly known as Copou. Walk past the **University C2** *(Universității)* and the **French Cultural Centre B1.** Copou Park was built in 1834 by Prince Mihai Sturdza. Today, it is a great place for a Sunday stroll or to meet friends on a summer's evening.

The Țicău district*

> **B1** *Opposite Copou Park, str. Oastei brings you to șos. Sărărie.*

If you are a fan of quaint old towns, you will be love this area spread out over the hilly Țicău district with its sleepy roads, vine-choked houses and little courtyards.

Stroll back along the peaceful str. Dimitrie Ralet, Lascăr Catargiu and Vasile Conta, the main student district, to get back to the piața Eminescu. Take the scenic route along str. Alexandru Lăpușneanu, piața Unirii and the beautiful **str. Cuza Vodă,** which passes behind the National Theatre, bringing you to the station where trams from all over town meet beneath the fortified walls of Golia Monastery. In the proximity of this busy market area you will find a monastery, a synagogue and four churches, one of which is Armenian.

Golia Monastery*

> **C2** *Mănăstirea Golia. str. Cuza Voda, 51. Open daily from sunrise to sunset. Free admission.*

The massive gate tower heralds the monastery, founded in 1546 by Chancellor Golia. In 1650, **Vasile Lupu** *(see inset opposite)* rebuilt the church. Having paid tribute to Byzantium in the Church of the Three Hierarchs *(p. 255)*, this time, Vasile looked to the West for inspiration, employing Italian master-craftsmen. The exterior walls show **Renaissance** influence, namely in the Corinthian pilasters with acanthus-leaf capitals, wide archways and triangular pediments, and a cornice supported by scrolled brackets. The entrance porch is framed with delicate motifs and surmounted by the Moldavian aurochs upheld by two lions. Ștefaniță, son of Vasile Lupu *(see inset opposite)*, added a host of towers and domes to the roof, clearly influenced by Russian architecture. Inside, however, the church remains classically

culture

Yiddish theatre

After touring all over Eastern Europe, a troup of travelling musicians and actors, the **Broder Zinger**, settled in Iaşi in 1868. Their encounter with **Avram Goldfaden** resulted in the world's first professional Yiddish language theatre. On the stage of the summer theatre, the **Pomul Verde** ("the Green Tree"), one after another, musicals, plays and other theatrical pieces from the classical Yiddish repertoire were performed by the Goldfaden troup and other theatre groups from all over Europe. In reply to the demand for more exacting theatre, new names appeared who, today, are points of reference of Yiddish culture: Sholem Aleikhem, I. L. Peretz, Shalom Asch. At the Pomul Verde, Jewish and Moldavian cultures mixed.

In 1883, however, in Moscow, where anti-Semitic laws had just been passed, the troup's European tour turned sour. Goldfaden crossed the Atlantic and founded the first Jewish theatre in New York. After World War II, Communist rulers tolerated the Bucharest and Iaşi troupes. The former is still performing; the Iaşi troup, however, did not survive the closure of the Pomul Verde theatre in 1963. •

Byzantine, down to the ghostly dim lighting. Close to the stall where the voivode ↪ sat, the heart of Prince **Potemkine** is apparently buried. He died near Iaşi in 1791 whence he had come on behalf of Catherine II of Russia to parley with the Turks.

In the monastery's peaceful courtyard, the memory of **Ion Creangă** (see inset p. 264), a deacon unlike any other, lives on. One day, a superior, come to inspect the monastery, surprised him shooting at the crows sitting on the church's cross. This incident is merely one of the The Improper Actions of Deacon Ion Creangă: going to the theatre, hunting and drinking in taverns. Eventually, the Metropolitan expelled him from the monastery. The defrocked deacon went on to become the famous storyteller that we know and love.

The Great Synagogue*

> **C2** *Sinagoga Mare. Opposite Golia Monastary, take str. Cucu (towards the airport). The synagogue is about 100 m along on the left, str. Sinagogilor, 7. To visit, contact Pincu Kaisermannk, representative of the Jewish community,* ☎ 25.97.87.

Iaşi is the birthplace of **Yiddish theatre** *(see inset above)* and the **Israeli national anthem**. In 1878, Naftali Herz Imber wrote the Hebrew poem *Hatikvah* (Hope), which was set to a Moldavian folk tune by Samuel Cohen. Jews have lived in Moldavia since the 15th century, and, in 1940, the Jewish community made up half of Iaşi's population with over one hundred synagogues in the city. Today, only the Great Synagogue of 1671, the oldest remaining in Romania, still functions.

●●● **In the area C2**: near Golia Monastery, the white silhouettes of **Barnovschi Church** *(Biserica Barnovschi)* and the monumental **Bărboi Church** *(Biserica Bărboi)* rise up. A walk around the **market** *(every morning)*, past the **Armenian Church** *(Biserica Armeană)* will bring you to str. Costache Negri.

Saint Sava Church*

> **C2** *Biserica Sf. Sava. From Golia Monastary and the Great Synagogue, take str. Costache Negri. Str. Costache Negri. Open daily. Free admission.*

Built in 1583, this church is dramatically different from any other church in Moldavia: thick walls, wide low towers and massive form, crowned with two Ottomanesque domes. In 1746, an Arabic language **printing house** was set up for the use of those of Orthodox faith from Asia or Sinai.

The Iaşi Jewish Cemetery★★★

> **A 1** *Cimitirul Evreiesc. Towards Bucharest on şos. Păcurari (bus or trolley-buses from piaţa Eminescu). Before leaving Iaşi, about 400 m after traffic lights and before a bend, turn right. Open daily. To visit, contact Pincu Kaisermann, representative of the Jewish community ☎ 25 97 87. Admission charge. Allow about 1 hr.*

A small, discreet road climbs uphill between concrete apartment blocks to the Jewish cemetery. Over 100,000 tombs stretch across an immense hillside with a broad view of the town. Near the entrance gates, a heavy concrete slab covers the communal grave where some of the victims of the 1941 pogrom are buried.

Walk up to the top of the hill along paths overgrown with weeds, through forests of tomb-stones leaning every which way.

The hillside monasteries

> *From the Jewish Cemetery, make for the Palace of Culture, then turn right onto şos Nicolina. You will need a car.*

Returning from the Bosphorus, armed with the Sultan's *(p. 45) firman* (decree) of investiture, the Moldavian voivodes↪ would make their triumphant entry to Iaşi through this valley. The Monasteries of Cetăţuia *(p. 260)* and Galata *(p. 260)* are perched on the surrounding hilltops. Galata, in fact, has the same name as the district of Constantinople where the princes would stay while waiting for their precious nomination. ●

The Iaşi Jewish Cemetery poignantly recalls a large community, which has all but disappeared.

© Pierre Soissons

Galata Monastery*

> **B3** *Mănăstirea Galata. On the şoş Nicolina, after a "Mol" service-station and a modern church. After a cemetery, take a small road off to the right to the monastery. Open daily 8am-sunset. Free admission. Allow about 30 mins.*

Completed in 1582 by **Peter the Lame** (Petru Şchiopul), this ample two-tower church is faithful to traditional Moldavian architecture. There are, however, traces of Byzantine-Wallachian influence such as the thick twisted belt surrounding the building. Also, the traditional wall separating the naos ↪ from the Chamber of Tombs ↪ has been replaced here by three arches, creating a far more spacious interior. From an architectural point of view, the church is thus a transition between the 15th-century, somewhat rational architecture of Stefan the Great, and the more emphatic architecture of the 17th and 18th centuries.

From the hill outside the ramparts, you can count all the towers and bells of Iaşi (be sure to bring your binoculars) as well as the factory chimneys and other eyesores stretching away to the east.

A path winds down the hillside between little houses where chickens and cats wander happily about among the trelissed vines.

Cetăţuia Monastery**

> **C4** *Mănăstirea Cetăţuia. From Galata Monastery, return to şos Nicolina and continue until you get to a blue factory; then turn left onto bd. Poitiers which passes over the railway. 300 m futher on, take a small road right near the trolleybus 43 station. Open daily from 8am to sunset. Free admission. Allow 30 mins.*

The road climbs through a wood to a vast plateau where you'll find this fortress (*cetăţuia* means fortress in Romanian). You could also brave the climb through the forest on foot.

Built by Voivode ↪ Gheorghe Duca (1668-1672), who is buried here, the church was laid out to the same plan as the Church of the Three Hierarchs (*p. 255*). This, however, is a less grandiose example. The proportions are put into perspective by the vast, light-filled space that surrounds it.

Frumoasa Church*

> **C4** *Biserica Frumoasa. From the Monastery, return to the bottom of the hill, cross the bd and take a (bad) road for 200 m. Open daily 8am-sunset. Free adm.*

This church was rebuilt in the 19th century and presided over a prestigious monastery which saw such important guests as members of the Sublime Porte (the Ottoman government) stay within its walls. This once obviously glorious church (*frumoasa* means "beautiful") is today surrounded by railway lines, concrete blocks, wasteland and crumbling roads. The Neoclassical porch remains with a rigid beauty sadly incongruous amidst the weeds.

Dobrovăţ Monastery**

> *Mănăstirea Dobrovăţ. 34 km S of Iaşi on the DN 24. From Iaşi, head for Vaslui. In Poiana, 4 km beyond Schitu Duca, turn right (signalled) and take a badly-surfaced road for 12 km. Open daily from sunrise to sunset. Admission charge. Allow about 1 hr.*

The road passes through a forest before coming out into a small valley where the village of **Dobrovăţ** is situated. You can see the church and its bell tower on the other side of the valley. At the centre of the village, turn right for the monastery, re-inhabited by monks since 1990.

The church

The understated outline of the church is similar to the one at Humor (*p. 228*). Built in 1503-4, it was the final achievement of **Stefan the Great**. In 1529, **Petru Rareş** (*see inset p. 223*) commissioned the interior wall paintings. These frescoes form the link between Stefan the

The piercing, almost unnatural autumn light in Moldavia.

© Bernard Houliat

Great's era and the visionary work of Rareş who, as early as 1530 in Hârlău *(p. 250)*, brought life and colour to the external walls of churches. The frescoes are faded and difficult to see, but once your eyes are accustomed to the dim light, you will be able to discern the density and refinement of each scene.

The interior frescoes★★

In the naos ↳, the **Passion Cycle** occurs amidst a profusion of architectural details including distorted building, palaces, porticos, domes, pediments, staircases, canopies, rocks and high walls. On the south wall, to the left of the window, **Christ's arrest** and the **Denial of Saint Peter** are depicted complete with a cockerel looking on ("Before the cock crows, you will deny me three times"). Between the window and the west wall, the **Trial of Christ** is shown in an extravagant semi-circular edifice. The series continues on the west wall: the Crown of Thorns, the Mocking of Christ, Judas hanging himself, and the casting of lots for Christ's clothes. Throughout, the backdrop is intricately detailed. The **Way of the Cross** unfolds on the north wall up to the window, overlooked by the **Crucifixion**.

Below the Passion Cycle, the decoration continues on both sides of the door. To the left, an unusual **votive painting**: **Stefan the Great**, the founder, presents Jesus with a miniature model of the church; behind him stands **Bogdan**, half-brother and predecessor of **Petru Rareş**. No other figure is depicted here. Painted two years after Petru, Stefan the Great's illegitimate son, came to power, the paintings are undoubtedly an attempt to stamp his royal mark on this church, the last to be constructed by his father. The three characters, dressed in all their finery, appear like Byzantine emperors whose successors the Moldavian princes always claimed to be. To the right of the door are the figures of the Emperor Saints **Constantin** and **Elena**, two other symbols of Byzantine glory. ●

Neamţ mountains and monasteries★★

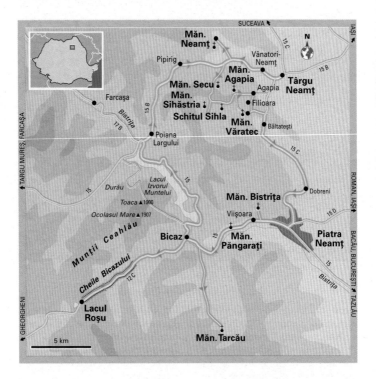

From Bucovina, the forest-clad flanks of the Carpathians slope south. Pastures and valleys are dotted with villages with brightly coloured, wooden-slatted houses. In the **Neamţ** (meaning "German") region, the scenery becomes wilder; rivers gush in spectacular torrents through the Bicaz Gorges and the legendary Ceahlău massif, Moldavia's very own Mount Olympus, looms up through the trees.

Although less well-known than the monasteries of Bucovina, a prosperous and ancient monastic tradition has made this area a centre of Romanian Orthodoxy. The great **Neamţ Monastery** is the most famous, but other smaller monasteries are also worth a visit. Of little architectural value, these are nonetheless, beautifully integrated with the peaceful forest landscape.

agenda

You can visit the Neamţ monasteries (p. 263) in **one day** including some good walks. On your **second day** you could pass through the Bicaz Gorges (p. 267), the gateway to Transylvania, or return to Târgu Neamţ (p. 263). **Accommodation** is available in monasteries or there are hotels and guesthouses in Târgu Neamţ, Piatra Neamţ, Farcaşa and Vânatori Neamţ. Staying in a guesthouse in **Tazlău** (p. 271) is a great base for forest walks. There are hiking trails all over the **Ceahlău** massif. Further information on < www.neamt.ro >.

***Address book** p. 268.* ●

In and around Târgu Neamţ

> *103 km W of Iaşi on the DN28, DN28A, DN28B and DN15B. 60 km S of Suceava on the DN2 and DN15C.* **Address book** *p. 271.*

This small, run-down town with its badly surfaced roads was a famous market town at the end of the 14th century. Apart from the citadel, there is not much here but its makes for a good base for visiting the region.

Neamţ Citadel

> *Cetatea Neamţului. 1 km W of Târgu Neamţ. Open daily except Mon. 10am-4pm. Admission charge.*

Perched on a rocky outcrop of the first foothills, the citadel has over-looked this opening in the for no less than six centuries. Built by Petru Musat in 1391, it was reinforced by Stefan the Great *(p. 43)* for whom it played a vital role in his defensive strategy. In 1476, the citadel resisted a siege of 200,000 led by Mehmet II, the conqueror of Constantinople in 1453. As its strategic importance diminished, it gradually fell to ruin.

The locals make free use of use of wood and zinc to decorate their houses.

© Pierre Soissons

Ion Creangă's house

> *Casa Memorială Ion Creangă. At Humuleşti (district S of Târgu Neamţ). At the first crossroads out of town (towards for Piatra Neamţ), take a left towards Tupilaţi. The house is 200 m further along. Str. Ion Creangă, 8.* ☎ *66.33.20. Open daily 9am-5pm. Admission charge.*

This great Moldavian storywriter immortalized the vibrant village life of his childhood *(see inset p. 264).* The house he was born in, built by his grandfather, has been turned into a museum which attempts to recreate the era through traditional decor, books, photographs and other piecemeal souvenirs.

The Neamţ monasteries★★

> *From Iaşi or Târgu Neamţ, take the DN15B (W).* **Address book** *p. 271.*

If 18th-century voyagers were to return to these forests today, they would scarcely notice the difference. The sacred Neamţ Mountains are home to some 20 monasteries or hermitages *(skites)*, guardians of a spiritual tradition, which has, since 1990, enjoyed a renewed vigour with pilgrims from all over Romania making their way to these forests.

Neamţ Monastery★★

> *Mănăstirea Neamţ. 16 km W of Târgu Neamţ by the DN15B then turn right. Open daily from 8am-sunset. Admission Charge. Allow approx. 30 mins.* **Address book** *p. 271.*

Tucked away in a tiny valley full of sanctuaries (including a miserable 19th-century baptistry), Neamţ is the largest monastery of its kind in Romania. A brotherhood has existed here since at least the 14th century but it was in 1497, that **Stefan the Great** completed the largest of his religious foundations. It was the pinnacle of Moldavian architecture. Both the form and the proportion are perfect, as the silhouette of the charch and its apses shows. Green,

portrait

The liveliest of all Romanian writers

Ion Creangă's (1837-1889) work was inspired by a childhood spent running about the streets of his native village which he left to join Iaşi Seminary. After becoming a deacon, he was defrocked for lack of discipline. He was also dismissed from his post as a schoolteacher. Eventually, it was **Mihai Eminescu** *(p. 248)* who discovered his wonderful talent for storytelling. These two became inseparable, putting the world to rights in Creangă's house or on trips to Iaşi's local taverns; the two men even died in the same year.

Written in local Moldavian dialect, full of evocative sounds and imagery, Ion Creangă's work is based on his childhood memories and the goings-on in the local Neamţ villages. Unfortunately, his work is rarely translated, and, when it is, the language is so diluted as to be unrecognisable! •

brown, blue and red glazed bricks adorn the full height of the walls, culminating in a row of arches. Above these, just beneath the roof, two further rows of small blind arches are inset with glazed bricks and discs. Admire the three Gothic windows on the west side of the church which form perfect patterns of stone, brick and glazed brick.

Of great cultural importance, this church was home to the country's best Romanian chroniclers, calligraphers and miniaturists. Its library still contains over 11,000 volumes. The name Neamţ remains linked to **Païsie Velitchkovsky** *(see inset opposite)* who, together with a huge team of monks, translated the key **hesychast** ↪ texts, thus keeping this monastic tradition alive in the Orthodox world.

Secu Monastery*

> *Mănăstirea Secu. 17 km W of Târgu Neamţ, 11 km S-W of Neamţ Monastery. From Neamţ Monastery, return to the DN 15 B and turn right, then 3 km further, turn left. Open daily 8am-sunset. Free admission.* **Address book** *p. 271.*

In August 1821, following the failure of the Heteria uprising *(p. 105)*, the Ottomans took a bloody revenge.

Retreating to the mountains, the conspirators (380 to 500 men) sought refuge withing the walls of Secu Monastery. A 14-day siege ensued, resulting in their surrendering to the Salih Pacha's army. Despite assurances to the contrary, they, along with the monks, were all massacred and the monastery burnt down. Other monasteries in the area also suffered considerable damage. Built in 1602 on the site of an ancient hermitage, the church was restored in 1830.

Sihăstria Monastery*

> *Mănăstirea Sihăstria. 20 km S-W of Târgu Neamţ. From Secu Monastery, keep on road for 4 km. Open daily 8am-sunset. Free admission.* **Address book** *p. 271.*

Nestling in the bottom of the valley, the Sihăstria Monastery was originally a hermitage attached to Secu *(see above)*. **Father Cleopa** (1912-1998), resided here. This man's lively spirit and wisdom made him one of the spiritual guides of Romanian Orthodoxy today. Persecuted by the Communists, he hid between 1958 and 1964, in a tannery deep in the forest, known only to a local woodcutter who brought him food and supplies.

religion

Romanian monasticism

The Neamţ Monastery was at the origin of a revival in hesychasm (17th century).

© Bernard Houliat

Romanian monasticism can be traced back to the very beginnings of Christianity in Dobrogea *(see inset p. 274)* and Muntenia *(p. 90)*. From these early times, hermits were scattered throughout the countryside. They shared the fate of the local population, moving around to escape invading forces. Thus an enduring bond was forged between them. When the Wallachian and Moldavian States were formed in the 14th century, the voivodes looked to the monks and this bond for support. In return, the voivodes founded and restored monasteries, as well as protecting them, enabling them to be central to Romanian culture for many centuries. The Romanian States were granted relative liberty under Ottoman rule unlike their Balkan counterparts; Romanian princes were permitted to spend colossal sums on maintaining the monasteries of Mount Athos and Constantinople. Wallachia and Moldavia provided asylum for countless religious exiles from the Balkans and even from the Russian Empire. **Païsie Velitchkovsky** was one such asylum seeker, fleeing Russia, who became Father-Superior of **Neamţ Monastery**, where the renowned intellectual activity was to have repercussions throughout the Orthodox world. Since 1990, hermitages have been springing up throughout Moldavia – pilgrims continue to seek spiritual guidance from their spiritual fathers *(duhovnici)* and the monastic world is still an integral part in the lives of many ordinary Romanian people. ●

Saint Theodora's Cave and Sihla Hermitage★

> *Peştera Sfinţei Teodora* and *Schitul Sihla*. *26 km S-W of Târgu Neamţ, 6 km from Sihăstria. From Sihăstria, go back for 1 km (3 km from Secu). Turn right onto a dirt track. Car park (supervised) at the pass. From here, it is 15 mins easy walking.*

On the ridge between Sihăstria and the Agapia Valley, the path meanders down between large accumulations of sandstone.

● **Saint Theodora's Cave**. A smell of candlewax reaches you as you start to make out a flickering light at

the entrance to a cave. It was here at the end of the 17th century that "Theodora the Pious" lived for around 20 years on a diet of grass, and bits of bread brought to her by birds from Sihăstria.

● **The Chapel**★★. *Free admission.* Continue along the path and you come out above the Sihla Hermitage where a community of monks has recently grown up. The tiny chapel, built in 1763, barely holds five people. Remove your shoes before entering the silent room, fragrant with incense burning in the miniature iconostasis ↪.

Agapia Monastery*

> **Mănăstirea Agapia**. *12 km S-W of Târgu Neamţ. From the pass: continue along the dirt track for 7 km. From Târgu Neamţ: take the DN 15 C (towards Piatra Neamţ), after 5 km, turn right and pass through Agapia village. The monastery is 4 km upstream.* **Address book** *p. 271.*

A collection of small, white houses and chapels, dominated by the profile of the main church, make up the monastic village of Agapia ("love" in Greek) which, together with Văratec *(see below)*, unites over 800 nuns. Five or six live in each house and are supervised by an elder. Each household has its own routine. The church, founded by **Vasile Lupu's** brother, was consecrated in 1647. Between 1859 and 1862, the interior was painted in the Academic style of the time by **Nicolae Grigorescu** (1838-1907) before he left for Paris and the Barbizon school where he was to become a painter of rural scenes. Some of his work is displayed in the Iaşi Art Museum *(p. 254)* and the Bucharest National Art Museum *(p. 69)*.

● **The Museum**. *Open daily 9am-5pm.* It displays icons, superb rugs and other religious objects.

● **The Old Agapia** *Skite (Schitul Agapia din Deal)*. *30mins on foot from the monastery.* Far from the bustle of the valley, in the midst of a green and tranquil haven, lies the original site of Agapia, mentioned as early as the 14th century.

Văratec Monastery*

> **Mănăstirea Văratec**. *15 km S-W of Târgu Neamţ, 7 km S of Agapia Monastery from where, about 500 m from the monastery, take a right on a delicious forest road. Access is also possible from Filioara and Agapia. Open daily 8am-sunset. Admission charge. Museum open daily, 9am-5pm.* **Address book** *p. 271.*

At the edge of the "silver forest", as **Mihai Eminescu** *(p. 248)* described it in his poem, there is a wooden church built in 1785 by Mother Olimpiada, a local nun. Dedicated to the Assumption of the Virgin, it was replaced in 1812 by the current Neoclassical church, which was completed a few years later by the addition of the surrounding wall and the nuns' cells. The courtyard is a bloom of flowers.

The Neamţ Mountains**

> *From Târgu Neamţ or Văratec, head towards Piatra Neamţ on the DN 15 C.*

Compared to the lush settings of the monasteries, **Piatra Neamţ** and its surroundings appear somewhat insipid. Luckily, the Ceahlău massif and the beautiful Bicaz Gorges are only 40 km away.

Piatra Neamţ

> *44 km S of Târgu Neamţ on the DN 15 C.* **Address book** *p. 271.*

In this village where he had a residence, Stefan the Great founded the imposing **Church of Saint John the Baptist** (*Biserica Sf. Ioan Botezătorul*) in 1498. Nearby, the **Ethnographic Museum** (*Muzeul de Etnografie; piaţa Libertăţii,1* ☎ *21.68.08; open daily 10am-5pm; admission charge*) offers an insight into the wealth of the local folkculture.

From Piatra Neamţ to the heart of the Carpathians

> *From Piatra Neamţ, head for Bicaz on the DN 15.*

● **Bistriţa Monastery*** (*Mănăstirea Bistriţa*). *9 km W of Piatra Neamţ.* Just beyond the town, on the right, this monastery has existed since the 14th century. Voivode Alexander the Good is buried here.

● **Pângaraţi Monastery*** (*Mănăstirea Pângaraţi*). *15 km W of Piatra Neamţ.* The present church, dating from 1642, has two sanctuaries, one on top of the other, which explains its height. The upper level contains a beautiful late 18th-century iconostasis ↪.

● **Tarcău Monastery*** (*Mănăstirea Tarcău*). *42 km S-W of Piatra Neamţ*. A valley opens on the left, 2 km before Bicaz, leading to the monastery, almost completely engulfed by the forest. The wooden church dates from 1833 but hermits lived in these mountains long before.

● **Bicaz**. *26 km W of Piatra Neamţ*. At a height of 127 m, the Bicaz dam has retained the 40 km-long **Lake Izvorul Muntelui** (*Lacul Izvorul Muntelui*) since 1960.

●●● **Suggested routes:** you can reach Poiana Largului and get back to the **Târgu Neamţ** region (*89 km N-E of Bicaz*) from here. The Bicaz Gorges are also the gateway to nearby Transylvania.

The Ceahlău massif**

> *From Bicaz, take the DN 15; after 3 km turn right towards Durău.*

Moldavia's very own Mount Olympus, crowned by eroded limestone ridges, grasses and rocky outcrops, is the **Ceahlău** massif (pronounced "tchek-lao"). Its name comes from the Bearded Vulture, long since disappeared from the region. The mountain (1,907 m) has been a sacred place since Antiquity. Neighbouring Dacian tribes believed that their gods lived here. For centuries, the massif has been home to thousands of hermits, which is why Moldavians often compare it to Mount Athos or Mount Thibor. Like these, it has a **chapel** dedicated to the Transfiguration (1,800 m, founded in 1993, feast day 6 August). One of its summits, **Toaca,** is named after the Romanian name for the board that, until the end of the 19th century, the hermits would beat to call to prayer to their brothers lost deep in the mountain forests.

The Ceahlău massif is ideal for hikers although it can get rather crowded in summer. September is the best time to visit, the spectacular autumn light and colours adding to the spirituality of the place. By car,

Bicaz Gorges.

© Pierre Soissons

you can reach the heart of the massif and the Durău resort, which is built around the monastery. Lots of hiking trails begin here (*Info: <www.neamt.ro>*).

The Bicaz Gorges** and Lake Roşu*

> *Cheile Bicazului and Lacul Roşu. From Bicaz, take the DN 12 C heading S-E towards Gheorgheni.*

The road leading to Transylvania (*p. 183*) runs through this spectacular gorge, at times very narrow with cliff faces rising to 1,200 m. The area is quite touristy, but you can head off the main road for a chance to see some wilder scenery. Upstream from the gorge, a natural dam was formed after a landslide in 1838, creating **Lacul Roşu*** (Red Lake). All that remains of the forest which once grew here are a few ghostly stumps that appear through the surface of the water, petrified by time and by the limestone contained in the water

From Lacul Roşu you enter the mysterious Transylvanian **Szekely Land** (*p. 180*). ●

Address book

Izvorul Muntelui lake in the Bicaz region.

Botoșani

> *Dialling code* ☎ *231. See p. 248.*

Accommodation

▲▲ **Rapsodia Hotel**, str. Cuza Vodă, 4 ☎ 51.49.25, Fax: 51.80.54. *166 rooms.* A basic but clean and comfortable hotel. *Restaurant.*

Cotnari

> *Dialling code* ☎ *232. See p. 250.*

Accommodation

▲▲ **Casa Bilius** ♥ ☎ 73.01.54. *3 rooms.* Climb back up to the Cotnari village and near the top, on the right, Casa Bilius is next to the manor (well with a large wheel). A family of Cotnari wine specialists. Delicious meals are provided on request (Mrs Bilius is one of the region's best cooks) and you can sample some of the oldest Cotnari wine vintages (at western prices!).

Farcașa

> *Dialling code* ☎ *233. See p. 262.*

Accommodation

▲▲▲ **Pensiunea Orizont** ☎ 0744.70. 24.08 (mobile). *6 rooms and 2 suites with bathroom.* 12 km at the northern most point of Lake Izvorul Muntelui, located on the road which follows the Bistrița valley and leads to Vatra Dornei. *Small hotel-restaurant.*

Iași

> *Dialling code* ☎ *233. See p. 251. Map p. 252.*

Getting there

● **By air**: **Tarom** provides direct flights between Bucharest-Otopeni to Iași daily except Sat. **Angel Airlines** offers links *via* Suceava Mon.-Fri. **Airport**: N of the town, E of Ciric Park **D1** ☎ 27 85 10.

• **By train**: The very practical Bucharest-Iaşi Intercity train unfortunately does not run on weekends. An overnight train with cabins runs *via* Timişoara (Cluj\Oradea\Suceava) to Iaşi. **Train Station B2** ☎ 21.56.00. Built in 1871, at the end of the Lvov-Czernowitz (Cernăuţi)-Iaşi line. An attractive building whose main entrance is raised on a Venetian loggia.

• **By bus**: Daily connections to Bucharest, and main towns. There are also regular services to Chişinău, Istanbul, Athens and western Europe. **Bus station** *(Autogara)*, şoş. Moara de Foc, **B2** ☎ 21.47.20. From the CFR station minibuses are located all along the şoş. Moara de Foc and provide services to the local area and towns in eastern Romania. The bus station is around 400 m along the same avenue.

Accommodation

▲▲▲▲ **Traian Hotel** ♥, piaţa Unirii, 1 **C2** ☎ 26.66.66, fax 21.28.62. *137 rooms.* Gustave Eiffel's team designed this building and its metal framework. The somewhat run-down restaurant fills with tourists and the Moldavian jet-set. It has a pleasant view of the surrounding streets. Good quality and reasonably priced.

▲▲▲▲ **Pensiunea Little Texas** ♥, str. Moara de Vânt, 31 **C2** ☎/fax 27.18.33. *8 impeccable rooms* with good views of the town. Don't let the flags and portrait of the American president put you off! This small hotel is the best in town. *Excellent restaurant.*

▲▲ **Orizont Hotel**, str. Grigore Ureche, 27 **C3** ☎ 25.65.70, fax 25.60.70. *50 rooms.* Five minutes from the Palace of Culture, behind the *Moldova* hotel. Reasonably priced. Very quiet, despite a basement disco.

▲ **Sf Nicolae Ecumenical Institute Hostel**, str. Agatha Bârsescu, 9 **C2** ☎ 27.60.77, fax 21.30.34. *Several appartments and around 30 rooms.* Hostel for pilgrims situated right next to the national theatre.

Restaurants

♦♦♦ **Bolta Rece**, str. Rece, 10 ☎ 21.22.55. Built at the turn of the 18th century, this tavern with its vaulted wine cellar has always welcomed intellectuals and members of the Junimea. Indifferent menu.

♦♦ **Club RS** ♥, str. Fatu, 2A (Râpa Galbenă) ☎ 21.30.60. Greek and Romanian dishes.

♦♦ **Expo**, parcul Exposißiei **B1** ☎ 21.36.55. In Copou park.

♦♦ **Ginger Ale** ♥, str. Săulescu, 23 **B2** ☎ 27.60.17. The Irish Pub in Iaşi serves some of the best food in town.

♦♦ **Hanul Trei Sarmale**, şos. Bucium, 50 **D4** ☎ 23.72.55. Take the exit for Vaslui and find this restaurant at the foot of the Bucium hill. Another of Iaşi's institutions, well known in the 17th century, frequented by Eminescu and Creangă *(see inset p. 248 and p. 264).* The food is not a strong point but it is a very pleasant place to have a drink and try some *mititei (p. 27).*

♦♦ **Pinocchio**, şos. Bucium, 24 **D4** ☎ 24.20.98. A roomy restaurant serving Italian cuisine and ice cream.

♦ **Anita**. Found in a street which does not appear on any map (the local Palestinians call it "Jerusalem" street!), which leads the university's *Institut Medico Farmaceutic.* A small middle-eastern restaurant with excellent food and very reasonable prices.

Shopping

Piaţa Agroalimentară Market *(Hala Centrala)*, between str. Costache Negri and Stada Barboi **C2**. Good for fruit and veg. Open every morning from 7am. There are also some lively markets in the Tătăraşi and Nicolina areas.

Bazar Nicolina ♥. In the S of the town, bd Nicolae Iorga and aleea Rozelor and part of the **C3** şos Nicolina. Admission charge. New or second hand you can find just about everything you could need among

transport

Some great tram routes offer an original way to see Iaşi's sights.

© Pierre Soissons

By **car** from Bucharest *(393 km S-W)* or from Suceava *(150 km N-W)*: a vast avenue lined with modern buildings leads you to the city centre and **piaţa Eminescu B2**. On Sundays and holidays part of **bd Ştefan cel Mare şi Sfân** is closed to vehicles. To explore the centre on foot, it is best to park in one of the paying car parks near the *Traian* Hotel or the **Palace of Culture C3**.

Trams and **buses** run all over town. Tickets can be purchased from kiosks at any of the larger bus or tram stops, particularly at Golia (no transport map is available). For an unusual yet pleasant way to see the city, take tram lines. Both routes 1 (Copou-Copou) and 3 (Gara-Dancu) offer interesting circuits. ●

the bric-a-brac from Istanbul and further a-field. It has a typical Moldavian bazaar atmosphere .

Bars and nightlife

Biblos B1/2, bd Carol I, 27. Traditional decor and it stays open until the small hours.

Corso B2, str. Lăpuşneanu, 13. In the pedestrian street near piaţa Unirii.

Ethos B2, str. Vasile Conta, 30. The most popular student haunt.

La Georgel C/D2, str. Pădurii, 24. A friendly place, owned by a musician.

Events

● **October**. European Festival of Yiddish Culture; info. at the French Cultural Centre *(see below)*. **13-15** The great Iaşi St Paraschiva Festivals *(p. 256)*.

● **20 June**. Music Festival. Info.: French Cultural Centre *(see below)*.

Useful addresses

● **British Council library**. Str. Păcurari, 4 ☎/fax 11.61.59.

● **French Cultural Centre ♥** (Centre culturel français). Bd Carol I, 26 **B1** ☎ 26.76.37, fax 21.

10.26, <www.ccf.tuiasi.ro>. An important institution in Iaşi which organised exhibitions, concerts, and the Festival of Yiddish Culture *(see inset p. 258)*. You can also get useful info. on cultural events in Iaşi. *Open Mon.-Thur. 9am-noon, 1pm-6pm, Fri. 9am-4pm.*

● **Railways**. CFR Agency **C2**, piaţa Unirii, 10 ☎ 24.26.20.

● **Airlines**. Angel Airlines, **B2** ☎ 0721.27.04.57 (mobile), fax 27. 85.10. **Tarom**: str. Arcu, 3-5 ☎ 21. 70.27 , Fax 26.77.68 or 11.52.39.

● **Coach companies**. Atlassib ☎/fax 21.34.91. Services to Germany, France, Italy, Spain. **Eurolines C2**, 2 piaţa Unirii, ☎/fax 21. 78.22, coaches to France, Germany, Belgium, Switzerland, Portugal and Greece.

● **Pharmacy**. *farmacia n° 2* **C2** piaţa Unirii, 3 ☎ 11.60.29. *Open Mon.-Fri. 7am-8pm, Sat. and Sun. 24hr/24.*

Neamţ Monasteries

> *Dialling code* ☎ *233. See p. 263.*

Accommodation

Pilgrims and travellers can find lodging at most monasteries.

Agapia Monestary ☎ 24.47.36. *Around 60 rooms* divided between two small houses with often only the most basic conveniences. Book by telephone or upon arrival. Don't expect a peaceful stay; there is always a bustle of activity going on here!

Sihăstria Monastary ☎ 25.18.97. *Around 20 rooms.* A cosy and well situated place, great for meditative walks… Beware, it is not easy to reserve a room here.

Văratec Monastary ☎ 24.47.41. Much the same set up as at Agapia, but quieter.

Accommodation is also available at **Secu and Neamţ monasteries**.

Piatra Neamţ

> *Dialling code* ☎ *233. See p. 266.*

Accommodation

▲▲▲ **Central hotel**, piaţa Petrodava, 1 ☎ 21.62.30, fax 21.45.32. *132 rooms.* Basic but comfortable, in a well-situated town. *Restaurant.*

Poiana

> *Dialling code* ☎ *232. See p. 266.*

Accommodation

▲▲ **Pensiunea Quattro-Route** ☎ 29. 47.20. *6 double rooms.* 22 km along the DN 24 heading for Vaslui. Near the Dobrovăţ Monastery. *Restaurant.*

Târgu Neamţ

> *Dialling code* ☎ *233. See p. 263.*

Accommodation

▲▲▲ **Doïna Trust** ☎ 79.02.70 or 79. 16.10, fax 79.08.43. *10 double rooms, 2 apartments.* Breakfast is not included. A small, quiet hotel with modern architecture and a strange orange interior décor, but with pleasant, comfortable rooms. A good base for exploring the local area. *Restaurant.*

▲ **Statiunea Oglinzi** ☎ 79.03.17. *Around 25 rooms.* Decent rooms in a calm and relaxing location. Reasonably priced. *Restaurant.*

Tazlău

> *Dialling code* ☎ *233. See p. 262.*

Accommodation

▲▲ **Casa Florean** ☎ 29.82.57. *6 rooms.* 35 km S of Piatra Neamţ. Off the beaten track, this is a very friendly French family home. Produce from the forest and neighbouring farms is used in all meals here (including the famous Angelica jam!).

music

Where to hear Orthodox choirs

During Sunday mass or at important celebrations, the Seminary Choir performs at the **Church of the Three Hierarchs C2** *(p. 255).*

The Sanctus choir perform at the **Metropolitan Cathedral C2** *(p. 256).*

Perhaps the most beautiful choir is the mixed, secular Mira Choir, who sing at the **Church of Saint Nicholas** *(p. 254)* near the Palace of Culture. **Recordings** can be bought at the church entrance. •

Make sure that you telephone first for directions however because you'll definately need them! Its worth finding though, being good place for forest walks. A great place to stay several nights.

Vânatori Neamţ

> *Dialling code* ☎ *233. See p. 262.*

Restaurant

Popas Branişte, also known as "Han Maria". On the road between Târgu Neamţ and Neamţ Monastery. Good traditional fare.

Vorona

> *Dialling code* ☎ *231. See p. 248.*

Accommodation

Familia Petru Popa ♥, str. Poiana, 111 ☎ 58.86.64. *2 guest rooms, shared bathroom.* From Tudora, the Poiana road is the road heading left just before you reach Vorona town centre. The house is covered in bright flowers. A generous welcome awaits from this simple family, who rarely takes in tourists. Food is delicious and healthy. A home from home!

Events

• **31 December**. Vorona and Tudora **Winter Festivals** *(p. 36)*. •

Dobrogea

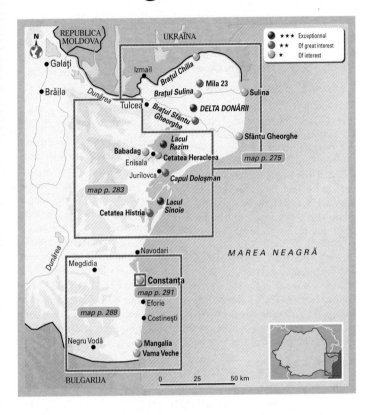

I n Dobrogea, Europe's youngest stretch of land, the Danube Delta, lies in the shadow of one of the oldest mountains in the world, the Măcin massif (467 m). At the frontier between Europe and the Middle East, meeting point for the migrating birds of Europe and Asia, this area is an ancient cross-roads of civilisations.

THE WONDERS OF NATURE

There is a strange feeling to the **Măcin Mountains** *(Munţii Măcin)*, the eroded remains of ancient Hercynian mountains. To the east, they give way, first to a range of smaller hills, covered in forests of oak, hornbeam and lime, then to a gently undulating grassy plateau, dotted with sheep and small shrubs which gradually slopes down to the sea. The vast open spaces of this area are the most arid all Romania. It rarely rains here, and tempera-

© Ministry of Transport, Construction and Tourism of Romania tures in summer can exceed 40 °C (104°F), whereas in winter they can drop below -30 °C (-22°F). During the autumn and winter months this bleak, open landscape has an almost mystical austerity to it in sharp contrast to the lush tangle of that other wonder of nature: the **Danube Delta**.

A LAND OF ANCIENT CIVILISATIONS

This harshness has not, however, halted the development of civilisations in this area. It is, in fact, one of the oldest inhabited regions in Europe; ancient remains can be found all over Dobrogea, some dating back to the Stone Age. Set between the Black Sea, the Danube and Carpathians, the area is ideally situated for trade and exchange. Ionian Greeks established flourishing cities here in the 7th century BC, later occupied and expanded by the Romans. Dobrogea was also one of the first Christianised lands in Europe (see below), supposedly evangelised by the Apostle Andrew. The flip side of the coin is that it was often the first region to be ravaged by invading civilisations that would later spread through Europe. One civilisation left a strong mark: the Turks settled in Babadag (p. 286) as early as 1262, relayed by the Ottoman Empire, which annexed Dobrogea 150 years later. This dependency only came to an end in 1878 when the region joined the Romanian state (p. 49).

THE COASTLINE BEACHES

At the end of the 19th century, Dobrogea became the holiday destination for Bucharest society, including the royal family, largely because it is the only stretch of coastline in Romania. During the Ceaușescu era, mass tourism developed the area to accommodate thousands of Romanians and citizens of other Communist countries wishing to have a seaside holiday. After 1990, this enthusiasm waned but there is no reason why the Black Sea resorts should not, once again, become a major holiday destination. ●

religion

One of the first Christianised lands in Europe

Dobrogea is scattered with crypts, tombs and rupestrian basilicas, evidence of intense and ancient spiritual activity. A large number of martyrs came from in this area, some still revered by Orthodox Romanians today. It was the **Apostle Andrew** who brought Christianity to Dobrogea. The cave where he lived for five years is about 4 km south-east of the main road (60 km W of Constanța), at the edge of the forest near the village Ion Corvin and close to today's border with Bulgaria. The former hermitage became a monastery in 1990 and today the liturgy is worshipped on the very stone which served as the apostle's altar.

Towards Ostrov (15 km W of Saint Andrew's cave), **Dervent Monastery** was founded in the 10th century, at the point where three stone crosses mark the site where nine of Saint Andrew's disciples were martyred. **Saint John Cassian**, one of the fathers of eastern and western monasticism, who died at Marseilles, originated from **Casimcea** (48 km S-W of Babadag). This region teemed with ascetics and hermits who, fleeing invaders, took refuge in the Carpathians, mostly around Buzău (p. 88), bringing Christianity to communities further inland. ●

The Danube Delta★★★

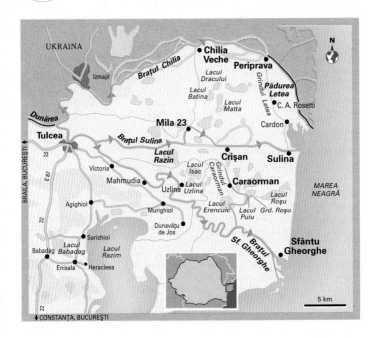

Companion of some of the most startling civilisations of Europe, the River Danube runs out to the sea in rather a disorderly fashion. Water lilies and a multitude of birds and fish feed among the vast silt deposits and stagnating backwaters. This delta is the second-largest of its kind in Europe (after the Volga) and covers over 5,600 km² (twice the size of Luxembourg, and nearly four times the size of the Camargue delta in France).

The Danube Delta generally refers to a geographical expense which not only includes the actual delta – a basic triangle of 80 km – but also the surrounding areas which are intimately linked to it. Miles upstream for example, there is a succession of stagnating backwaters, lakes and marshland. To the south, you'll find **Lake Razim** *(p. 286)*, which used to be one of the main outlets of the Danube, and the **Sinoie lagoon**. This

agenda

A boat trip is essential. Allow **two days for each arm of the Danube**. Boats regularly set off from **Tulcea** (supervised car park), for the delta villages. Most hotels and guesthouses offer motor boat trips to the more remote locations. If you have a tight schedule, it is easier to let a travel agency organise everything for you (transport, permits, etc). The **floating hotel** is an original and fun way to see the delta *(see inset p. 296)*.

Accommodation available in Crişan, Dunavăţ de Jos, Mila 23, Sf. Gheorghe, Sulina, Tulcea, Uzlina.

Don't forget your bird-watching equipment *(p. 309)*.

Address book *p. 293.* ●

A bird's paradise

Flapping wings, squawks, high-pitched trills, cackles, screeches and diving splashes: in the Danube Delta silence does not exist. Its geographical position, diversity of natural habitats and lack of human interference explain why this area is populated with the highest concentration of bird colonies in Europe.

An extraordinary crossroads

The Northern hemisphere is crossed by many of the great bird migration paths. Five of them intersect in Dobrogea, coming from Central Europe, north of the Black Sea, the Caucasus and Iran, and from the arctic regions of Europe and Asia. The 45th parallel also goes through the Danube Delta making it the perfect mid-way stopping-off point between the Equator and the North Pole. It has therefore become essential for breeding, hibernation and migration for a large number of species of bird. Certain stay for the winter whereas others begin or carry on their journey to warmer climes in the Mediterranean, the Middle-East or Africa. Pelicans, ibis and egrets return to nest here every spring. The geographical position does not explain everything, however. If millions of birds flock to the region it is also because they find ideal living conditions: forests, marshland, steppes, reed beds, lakes, lagoons and water courses offer infinite possibilities for shelter, an abundant food supply and undisturbed peace.

Glossy ibis

Recognisable for its ccurved beak and dark colouring which shimmers with purple and green, the glossy ibis *(Plegadis falcinellus)* nests in the reed beds of the delta (30 % of the European population of this wader live here).

A labyrinth teeming with life

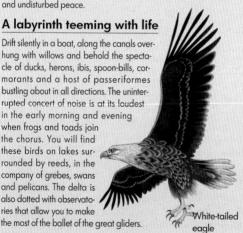

Drift silently in a boat, along the canals overhung with willows and behold the spectacle of ducks, herons, ibis, spoon-bills, cormorants and a host of passeriformes bustling about in all directions. The uninterrupted concert of noise is at its loudest in the early morning and evening when frogs and toads join the chorus. You will find these birds on lakes surrounded by reeds, in the company of grebes, swans and pelicans. The delta is also dotted with observatories that allow you to make the most of the ballet of the great gliders.

White-tailed eagle

Early in the morning, this large bird of prey skims the surface of the water, hunting for big fish, which it grabs with its talons and, after a fierce struggle, carries off to be eaten elsewhere. This fishing eagle sometimes catches ducks, geese, small birds and small mammals. The rest of the day it recuperates, perched in a tree by one of the many canals and backwaters of the River Danube.

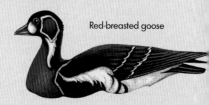

A white stripe down the flanks identifies the red-breasted goose *(Branta ruficolis)*. Approximately 20,000 of these birds (or 50 % of their worldwide population) winter in the southern part of the delta, between the prairies and Razim and Sinoie Lakes. In summer, they nest in the Siberian tundra, not far from the arctic coast.

Red-breasted goose

The Pelicans' Ballet

In March, great flights of white pelican leave the Nile delta and the Red Sea to come and nest in the Danube Delta, totalling 50 % of their total European and Asian population. These huge birds (the wingspan of the grey-feathered Dalmatian pelican can reach 3.20 m) live in both fresh and salt water environments. In the delta, you will find them mostly on Lakes Babina, Dracului, Matiţa, Roşca, Uzlina, Isac and Roşu. Always in perfect synchronisation, they take off in groups of several dozen, fly around, land and swim. Feeding is also a group activity, which only takes place in the mornings: between 7am and 9am, groups of about ten birds each set out onto the lake and, forming a semi-circle, drive the fish to shallow waters by beating their wings on the water. They then dive in unison and scoop up their prey in the pouch they have under their beak. Big fish like carp make up their staple diet, each bird consuming about one kilogram of fish per day (multiply that by the 11,000 pelicans in the delta and that's a lot of fish!). ●

White pelican

Dalmatian pelican

Red-crested pochard

Artwork by Gaëtan du Chatenet

The vast spaces around the Danube offer a seasonal habitat.

complex environment has always attracted exiles and refugees, like the Russian "old believers" *(rashkolniks, p. 284)*, the Zaporizhzhya Cossacks or the Tatars. It could be an even older tradition, because, according to Greek myth, Jason and the Argonauts fled to **Ister** (former name for the Danube) after they seized the Golden Fleece from Colchis (probably Georgia).

THE YOUNGEST LAND IN EUROPE

Huge silt deposits (50 million tons a year, or 20 times more than the Rhine) mean the Danube Delta is constantly pushing out into the Black Sea. This giant area of outwash is structured around the three main arms of the Danube: the Chilia *(p. 280)*, the Sulina *(p. 280)* and the Sfântu Gheorghe *(p. 282)*. There are also some 400 lakes (10% of the delta) and countless smaller branches that are inter-connected by hundreds of kilometres of channels and man-made canals. Areas that are either constantly or periodically submerged make up 80% of the delta.

From the Black Sea to dry hills, over a a distance of few dozen kilometres, is a condensed mosaic of permanently evolving ecosystems, unique in Europe, and largely undisturbed by human activity.

FROM THE SEA TO THE STEPPES

A sand bank separates the sea from vast floodable spaces which, being neither land nor water, are the most interesting parts of the delta. The delta lakes are gradually filling up with silt and vegetation; water lilies and huge reed beds (2,700 km²) increase their suffocating grip. Thanks to their hollow rhizomes, the reed beds are able to lie on the surface like a kind of living raft (or *plaur* to the locals). These floating islands are a mish-mash of mulch, organic debris and tangled roots.

Around 13,000 years ago, the **Caraorman** *(p. 281)* and **Letea** *(p. 280)* **sand dunes** formed the Black Sea coastline; today, they lie at right angles to the river, isolated inside the delta. These strips of land, along with the sand banks, and the river and canal banks are just about the only bits of land permanently above water; this is where the odd habitation has grown up. Vast expanses of water spread out behind these dunes which used to impede the river's path. Alluvial deposits are, however, filling these expanses up bit by bit and sealing them off, leaving a string of small lakes which are slowly turning into

© Pierre Soissons

bog. Further upstream, water turns first to mud and then firm, dry land. The landscape quickly dries out. Without any transition, from the river bed, the land becomes vast, arid plains similar to the Russian steppes: scattered clumps of grasses, shrubs (hawthorn, blackthorn) and other plants, which can survive the dry, and sometimes freezing, conditions.

THE DANUBE DELTA BIOSPHERE RESERVE

As well as fascinating scenery, the Danube Delta is also blessed with exceptional biodiversity. Over 1,700 species of plant have been recorded around 3,450 animal species, of which 160 are fish *(see inset p. 282)* and 300 birds, including 166 nesting species *(p. 276)*.

This fragile environment has enormous ecological importance and, since 1990, has officially been part of the world's network of **Biosphere Reserves** *(see inset p. 280)*. In 1998, the site expanded across the border to encompass the Ukrainian part of the delta in this protective scheme. On the Romanian side, 18 sites, or 8.7% of the delta's surface area, are strictly protected: all human activity is prohibited. Access permits are, in principle, only granted to specialists and researchers. The "buffer zones", 38.5% of the surface area, allow traditional activities and tourism, insofar as they respect the environment. All visitors, however, must have a permit. The remaining area (52.7%) is given over to economic development zones where preservation of the area's biodiversity goes hand in hand with its sustainable exploitation. Access permits are issued by the Danube Delta Biosphere Reserve Office *(see Address book p. 295)* but they are usually included in package tours *(p. 296)*, and are also available at travel agents and hotels. Special permits are also required for fishing and camping in the wild.

Tulcea

> *279 km N-E of Bucharest, 125 km N of Constanţa, on the DN 22.* **Address book** *p. 295.*

Tulcea *(Castrum Aegyssus* to the Romans), is the main access point for the Danube Delta. Nearly all boats and ferries set off from here. In fact, the town would be of little interest if it wasn't for the port and the vast promenade along the river bank, lined with the delta boat landing stages.

nature

Biosphere Reserves

Biosphere Reserves are coastal and inland areas that are internationally recognised by UNESCO as territories of **outstanding ecological importance**. The programme for man and the biosphere (MAB, Man and the Biosphere) aims to promote ecological equilibrium between human beings and the natural world. These reserves are certified by UNESCO at the request of the countries concerned. The areas continue, however, to be the responsibility of the country concerned and therefore remain subject to its legislation.

There is an international network of Biosphere Reserves which have to satisfy three priority functions. These are: to contribute to the conservation of the landscape and ecosystem; to favour economic and human development respectful of socio-cultural and environmental particularities and to encourage systems of environmental control, research, education and the information exchange. Info: < www.unesco.org >. ●

● **The Ethnographic and Folk Art Museum** (*Muzeul de Artă Populară și Etnografie*). *Str. 9 mai, 4,* ☎ *51.62.04. Open Tue.-Sun. 9am-5pm. Admission charge.* A good introduction to the Danube Delta. Highlights include a section on traditional fishing and a good collection of local weaving.

The Chilia arm★

> *Brațul Chilia. Length: 120 km. From Tulcea by boat p. 294.*

The youngest arm of the Danube branches off to the north 11 km upstream from Tulcea, forming a natural frontier with the Ukraine. It carries 58% of the river flow before, in its turn, branching off to create its own delta, (mainly in the Ukraine). The Chilia arm has the least traffic and very little tourist infrastructure, bar a few private guesthouses.

● **Chilia Veche**. *80 km E of Tulcea.* Passenger boats run to this village which, under Stefan the Great of Moldavia (p. 43) in the 15th century, was a hive of activity. Save for some sturgeon fishing, the village is now all but forgotten about.

● **Periprava and the Letea sand dune★**. *103 km E of Tulcea.* Further downstream from Chilia Veche, **Periprava★**, one of the most isolated places in the delta, is only served by the occasional boat (*see inset p. 294*). South from here, you can walk or drive a 4WD along the **Letea sand dune★** (*Pădurea Letea*).

The sand is fixed by an impenetrable and strictly protected forest: oak trees sevearl centuries old and black poplars, elms, ash and thorny shrubs are smothered in creepers, some over 25 m long. Wild boar, black bellied foxes, and snakes inhabit the area.

The Sulina arm★

> *Brațul Sulina. Length: 64 km. From Tulcea, by boat p. 294.*

The other two arms of the Danube separate 17 km downstream from Tulcea: the Sfântu Gheorghe arm (*p. 282*) runs south-east while the Sulina flows to the east. The Sulina arm only carries 18% of the total flow of the Danube, but transports most of the commercial traffic. Cutting right through the middle of the delta, it has always been the shortest route across. The **European Danube Commission**, based in Sulina, was founded in 1856 to manage the interests of neighbouring countries, as well as those of France and Great Britain. Considerable developments to facilitate river traffic have been made: a **canal** was dug out between 1880 and 1902 to cut a passage through the main bends of the river, shortening the route by 21 km. Easier to navigate than the two other arms, this route allows for quick access to the villages at the heart of the delta.

Mila 23**

> *34 km E of Tulcea. By boat p. 294.* **Address book** *p. 294.*

English engineers used to measure the course of the Danube in miles, mile 0 being a point on the Black See coast at Sulina. The milestones have remained a part of the topography. Hence, at 23 miles inland you find a village called **Mila 23**, lying on a bend known as the "Old Danube" (*Dunarea Veche*). This village of Russian "old-believers", or Lipovani (*p. 284*), huddles on a strip of land around its church. Wandering

around the tiny streets is the best way to observe the cob walled houses with their reed roofs and blue or green painted woodwork.

Little black fishing boats (*lotca*) are pulled up all along the banks of the river; these belong to the dying breed of Lipovani fishermen. The rules of the **Biosphere Reserve** impose overwhelming constraints on these fishermen who have survived three centuries as a perfectly integrated part of this ecosystem their ancient fishing methods making little impact on fish populations.

Around Crişan*

> *47 km E of Tulcea by boat.* **Address book** *p. 293.*

Crişan is the main stopping off point between Tulcea and Sulina. The village stretches along the south bank of the Danube for about a kilometre and is an excellent base for exploring the surrounding lakes and canals. There are private guest rooms and boarding houses available.

Boats run to the village of **Caraorman**** ("black forest" in Turkish), a 3.5 km strip of houses with beau-

A typical Dobrogean house.

© Pierre Soissons

fishing

The fish of the delta

Whether fresh or saltwater, fish abound in the delta (about 160 species). Despite a general decrease in population, certain species are still found in great numbers including pikeperch (*şalău*), bream (*plătică*), carp (*crap*), perch (*biban*), rudd (*rosioara*) and crucian carp (*caracuda*). You can also find pike (*stiucă*), tench (*lin*) and catfish (*somn*). Migrating fish come to breed here in the spring, including the pontic shad (*scrumbie*) and some sturgeon, including the three main suppliers of caviar: sevruga (*păstrugă*), ossetre (*nisetru*) and beluga (*morun*). The **Biosphere Reserve** (*see inset p. 280*) office issues fishing permits and levies a tax of about €6 per day's fishing; this is usually included in the set price offered by specialist agencies. ***Address book*** *p. 296.* ●

tiful gardens back onto the **Pădurea sand dune** (*Pădurea Caraorman*), 18 km long and resembling that of Letea.

Sulina★

> *71 km E of Tulcea by boat.* ***Address book*** *p. 295.*

Mentioned in Byzantine documentation around 950, **Sulina** was, for a while, the hideout for ruthless Black Sea pirates. There are six main roads, numbered in Roman numerals, from I to VI.

Bordering the river as it opens out to the sea, you can find a few pretty, early 20th-century houses, cafés and restaurants along road I.

Facing the river, the former headquarters of the **European Danube Commission** recalls bygone times when this end-of-the-world town bustled with engineers, adventurers and traders from all over Europe and the Middle East.

The **lighthouse,** (18.5 m tall) built in 1802 is now a long way from the sea, and the town is gradually sinking into oblivion. The juxtaposition of the town's **cemeteries** are a poignant record of Sulina's more colourful times. Between the town and the beach you can find Orthodox, Lipoveni Orthodox (*p. 284*),

Catholic, Anglican, Jewish and Muslim cemeteries. On the seafront, Europe comes to an end in a long, fine sandy beach.

The Sfântu Gheorghe arm★★

> *Braţul Sfântu Gheorghe. 109 km in length. From Tulcea, by boat p. 294.* ***Address book*** *p. 295.*

Absorbing 23 % of the river flow, the oldest arm of the Danube is also the most sinuous. The distance from Tulcea to Sfântu Gheorghe has, however, been greatly reduced by canals which cut across six of the main bends in the river.

● **Sfântu Gheorghe★**. *81 km E of Tulcea.* This little port was mentioned as early as 1318. Its sandy streets lead to one of the longest beaches on the coast. Opposite the landing stage, on the other side of the Danube, is **Sacaline Island**, a sand bank that appeared around 1897. Access is strictly controlled due to the high concentration of bird colonies found there.

Several canals connect the Sfântu arm to Lake Razim (*Lacul Razim, p. 286*) but, in order to explore the region properly, you need to return to Tulcea. ●

Tulcea to Constanţa

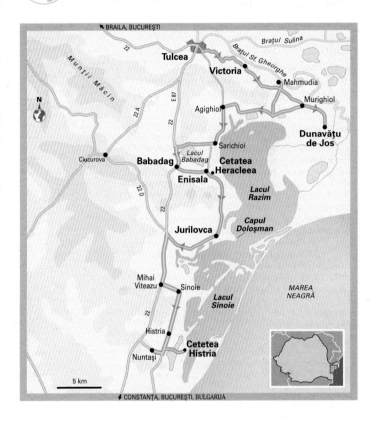

A trip down the Danube past Lake Razim and Lake Sinoie provides a further glimpse of the incredible natural surroundings while following in the footsteps of a remarkable ancient civilisation as well as those of the Turkish invaders.

Final glimpse of the Danube

>*Murighiol: 36 km S-E of Tulcea. From Tulcea, take the road to Murighiol.*

The road runs set back and parallel to the Sfântu Gheorghe arm (*p. 282*). You pass bronzed peasants with black eyes, others with beards and blue eyes, women with blond hair and pale skin, others with Ori-

agenda

The route is about 225 km long. Although the DN 22 is excellent, the state of secondary roads varies. Allow **one day**. Don't forget your bird watching equipment (*p. 309*).

***Address book** p. 293.* ●

ental features. Most of the Dobrogea villages are Romanian, but some are inhabited by Russians, Greeks, Bulgarians, Turk and Tatars.

In the centre of **Victoria** (*15 km S-E of Tulcea*), an abandoned Catholic church recalls a time when the vil-

Russian delta fishermen

Long-bearded, blue-eyed men can be found piloting their black fishing boats around the Danube Delta, crossing themselves ostentatiously. The peaceful, remote air of the Lipovani fishermen conceals the bitter memory of one of the most terrible periods in Russian history.

The Lipovani fishermen preserve the mysterious traditions of the 17th-century Russian Church.

From "raskol" to Peter the Great

In the 17th century, Tsar **Alexis Mikhaïlovitch** instructed the Patriarch of Moscow, **Nikon,** to tackle the lax practices that had, over the centuries, crept into the daily rituals of the Russian Church. In 1652, a synod undertook a reform. Millions of believers, led by the **priest Avvakoum,** refused to change their traditions, and so schism (**raskol** in Russian) became inevitable. The Church and Russian society were torn in two. The "old-believers", or *raskolniks*, were excommunicated and suffered ferocious persecution over the following decades, resulting in tens of thousands of deaths. Pushed to the point of mass hysteria, they committed acts of collective suicide by burning. For them the Apocalypse and the coming of the Antichrist were imminent, to such an extent that, a few years later, they recognised the Antichrist in the figure of Peter the Great, who merely intensified the terror. Fascinated by Western European lifestyle, he tried to impose it on Russian society, with decrees *(oukases)* forcing men to cut off their beards and to exchange their traditional dress for Western clothing.

The double origin of the Lipovani

The majority of the *raskolniks* fled north to the Urals and Siberia, and on to Alaska, Canada and Australia, where their descendents still live. Another group went west, settling mainly in Moldavia, around Iași, Suceava and Rădăuți. In the 18th century, a second wave of Russian fugitives arrived. These were the old-believers, Cossacks who fished on the Don and had participated in the uprising of Russian peasants under Ataman **Nekrassov.** When these uprisings were quashed by tsarist armies, they fled to Turkey and Dobrogea.

Below: Saint's day procession around the church.

© Bernard Houliat

© Bernard Houliat

This explains the double origin of the Russian old-believers now living in Romania known as the "Lipovani", a term only used in Romania. The uncertain etymology of this word (Lipovani might come from *lipa*, "lime tree" in Russian; or there's a certain Filipov who immolated himself in the north of Russia at the time of the *raskol*...) only contributes to the mystery surrounding these people.

The last of the bearded

Today the Lipovani are mainly concentrated in Moldavia and Dobrogea, and, while nurturing their own strong community spirit, are, for the most part, well integrated into Romanian society. Younger generations, however, are beginning to abandon the old traditions of a culture which is moving inexorably towards the bulging graveyard of civilisations. Meanwhile, there are still a few old men with long beards who continue to spit on the ground whenever Nikon or Peter the Great are mentioned. ●

Below left: according to ancient Russian tradition, church-goers cross themselves ostentatiously several times before entering.

Below right: Lipovani priests do not study theology; they are elected by the community.

© Bernard Houliat

© Bernard Houliat

lage was populated by Germans. Just on the outskirts, on the right, some holes in the slope indicate the presence of **bee-eaters**. This magnificent bird arrives here at the end of April and is easily recognisable for its metallic shriek and bright turquoise and orange plumage.

From **Murighiol** (*36 km S-E of Tulcea, boats to Uzlina Island p. 296*), a 10 km dirt track leads to **Dunavăţu de Jos★**, a beautiful traditional village (the furthest point in the delta accessible by road). Return to Murighiol then head S-W to Lake Razim.

Lakes Razim and Sinoie★★★

> *Lacul Razim, Lacul Sinoie. From Tulcea, head for Babadag (S).*

The road circles Lake Razim, once a bay on the Black Sea known as the **Gulf of Halmyris**. Today it is enclosed by a thin coastal strip of land. In the past, when freshwater mixed with sea water, the lake's rich fish-life provided a living for the Lipovani fishing villages (*p. 284*).

Now overgrown with plankton, the lake is slowly suffocating; fish are dying out and the fishermen are reduced to unemployment. Lake Sinoie is an extension of Lake Razim, a vast lagoon that is also gradually being cut off from the Black Sea by an expanding sand bank.

Babadag★

> *92 km from Tulcea via Murighiol, 36 km S of Tulcea on the DN 22.*

Babadag is intimately linked to the history of Turkish presence in Dobrogea. Between 1262 and 1264, 12,000 Seljuq Turks, who preceded the Ottoman Turks, were led by **Sara Saltuk Baba** at the request of the Byzantine Emperor Michael VIII, to settle around Babadag.

In the shadow of the **Ali Ghazi Pacha mosque★** (*Mosheia Ali Ghazi Pacha*), the oldest in Romania (1522), Sara Saltuk's tomb is a sacred site for all Romanian Muslims. At the entrance to the town (on the Tulcea side) is the Rom Muslim district (or *horahane* "those who read the Koran") where the women wear superbly coloured clothes.

From Babadag to Histria

> *Head east from Babadag towards Enisala et Jurilovca.*

● **Enisala Peasant Museum** (*Muzeul "Gospodăria Tărănească"*). *Open daily except Tue. 10am-6pm in summer, 8am-4pm in winter. Admission charge.* At the entrance to Enisala, a road on the left, towards Sarchioi (N), leads back to the marshes and a traditional fisherman's house that has been converted into a museum.

● **Heracleea citadel★** (*Cetatea Heracleea*). Returning to Enisala, take the road which heads to Jurilovca alongside Lake Razim. After 2 km and, on a promontory, you can make out the ruins of Heracleea; an old Roman, then Byzantine and Genoese citadel.

● **Cape Doloşman★★** (*Capul Doloşman*). Before reaching Jurilovca, to the left, you can make out the silhouette of Cape Doloşman, one of the strictly protected areas of the Biosphere Reserve (*see inset p. 280*).

Known to ornithologists all over the globe, this sumptuous site is one of the major resting point on the great migratory routes (observatories available). In November, thousands of red-breasted geese (*p. 276*) touch down here amongst the ruins of a 6th century BC Greek colony.

● **Jurilovca**. Huge fishing warehouses recall the time not so long ago when there were abundant populations of fish in Lake Razim.

●●● **Suggested route:** From Jurilovca, take the DN 22 and return straight back to Constanţa.

Histria**

> *151 km from Tulcea via Murighiol, 77 km S of Tulcea and 42 km S of Jurilovca on the DN 22. From Jurilovca, take the DN 22. Turn left to Mihai Viteazu, then left again to Sinoie, where again you turn left.*

A thorough lesson in ancient history lies about 3 km beyond the village of Histria, on the desolate banks of **Lake Sinoie**** *(p. 286)*. Towards the middle of the 7th century BC, Greek navigators from Milet, the richest city in Ionia (Asia Minor), established a trading post in this sheltered anchorage. The hinterland, inhabited by the Getae, was rich in supplies of cereals, wood, cattle, skins and honey. It did not take long for the trading post to become the main Greek port in Dobrogea, a magnificent city with numerous temples. Histria brought all the splendours of Milet to the shores of the Black Sea: shining out across the Greek world, the Ionian civilisation was at its most glorious, thanks to its close ties with the Orient, source of wisdom and riches.

The city existed for fourteen centuries, thriving under both the Roman and Byzantine civilisations. The gradual silting-up of the bay led to the town's decline and to the rise of Tomis *(Constanţa, p. 289)* and Callatis *(Mangalia, p. 292)*. In the 7th century, invading forces wiped it off the map altogether.

Excavation work, begun in 1914, has turned up some fascinating objects, many of which are on display in the **museum**** *(☎ 0241.61.87.63, open daily except Mon. 9am-8pm in summer, 9am-5pm in winter; admission charge for the museum and the site; allow one and a half hours)*. This is a worthwhile preliminary to visiting the site itself, which you access by foot, and where you will find remains of temples, baths and Byzantine basilicas. If you visit in late afternoon, stand in the old forum – where only a few columns still stand – and watch the spectacular flights of pelicans and swans illuminated by the setting sun. You might get a chance to see the White-Tailed Eagle, or sea eagle *(p. 276)*, which was the emblem of Histria, featured on its coins.

From Histria, head back to Constanţa on the DN 22, *via* Nuntaşi. ●

The Black Sea coast★

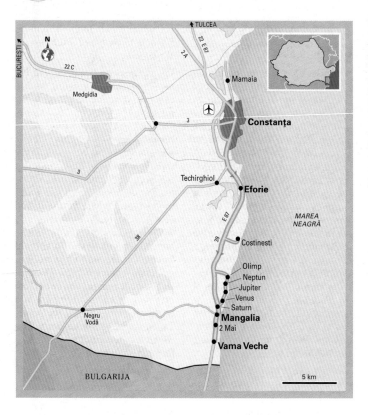

A string of seaside resorts stretches along the 82 km of coastline, from north of Constanța to the frontier with Bulgaria. They account for 41% of Romania's hotel business. Some already existed at the end of the 19th century, but many were constructed in the 1970s and 1980s.

The lush countryside, the quality of the sandy beaches and, of course, the sunshine more than compensate for some miserable urban development and intrusive loudspeakers.

The towns at both extremities of this coastline are worth a visit. These are the former Greek trading posts of Tomis (*Constanța; p. 289*) and Callatis (*Mangalia; p. 292*).

agenda

Take a **day tour** of the region of about 80 km. The fine sandy beaches are ideal for kids, the water is warm, and tides negligible. In summer, the temperature can reach 25 °C (77°F), and the water 26 °C (79°F).

Services are gradually improving. You can now find hotels for all budgets. It is best to reserve in advance through specialised travel agencies *(p. 297)*. Constanța *(p. 298)* has particularly good restaurants.

***Address book** p. 297.* ●

portrait

Ovid's melancholy

Born in 43 BC, Ovid (Publius Naso) was a contemporary of Virgil and Horace. His poetry was highly regarded in Rome. For some unknown reason, Emperor Augustus exiled him, in 9 BC, to **Tomis**, at the very limits of the Empire. Inconsolable, Ovid composed poems inspired by the bitterness of exile. These are united in a collection evocatively entitled **Tristia**. "... under stars which never set in the ocean, I am existing still, here in a barbarous land. Fierce Sarmatians encompass me round, and the Bessi and Getae; names how unworthy to be sung by a genius like mine!" He also wrote narratives in prose called **Pontics**. After eight years in exile ,he died on the shores of the Black Sea.

In 1887, a statue designed by the Italian Ettore Ferrari was erected on **piaţa Ovidiu**; there is a replica in Sulmona, Ovid's home town in Italy, twinned with Constanţa. Ovidiu is a commonly used first name – a sign of respect for the poet as well as for Romania's attachment to its Latin roots. ●

Constanţa★

> 266 km E of Bucharest, 125 km S of Tulcea and 44 km S of Histria on the DN 22. Allow about 4 hrs. **Addresss book** p. 297.

Constanţa, Romania's third biggest town, is worth exploring for its archaeological treasures and for the atmosphere of the old town centre.

ANCIENT TOMIS

This site has been inhabited since the 5th millennium BC. In the 6th century BC, Greeks founded the colony of **Tomis**, on the peninsula where the old town is today. The Roman Empire reached Dobrogea in 29 BC, settling for six centuries. Until then, Tomis had struggled along in the shadow of its neighbours **Histria** (p. 287) and **Callatis** (Mangalia; p. 292), but it gradually became the seat of Roman military command. Taking advantage of Histria's decline, Tomis developed its port, but from the 3rd century, it was repeatedly sacked by invaders.

It was renamed Constantiana in the 6th century in honour of Emperor Constantin's sister; this shortened to Constanţa (or Küstendje during the Ottoman era).

THE OTTOMAN PRESENCE

By the 10th century, the once beautiful city had been reduced to a fishing village, to which Genoese merchants added a slight shine, but the Ottoman conquest of Dobrogea in the 15th century began a long period of lethargy, from which Constanţa only emerged in 1878 (p. 49). The town regained its dynamism, becoming the port that Romania so badly needed.

Archaeological and National History Museum★★

> **B2** *Muzeul Naţional de Istorie şi Arheologie. Piaţa Ovidiu, 12* ☎ 61.45.62. *Open Wed.-Sun. 9am-5pm (9am-8pm in summer). Admission charge. Allow 2 hrs.*

The museum presents the history of Dobrogea from the Stone Age (100,000-35,000 BC) to the present day. The most interesting objects are on the ground floor. These include some Greek and Roman remains which were uncovered when the old railway station was demolished in 1962.

● **The Glykon★★**. This 3rd-century masterpiece is carved from a block of marble. Protector of the home, the Glykon has the muzzle of a

getting around

The old town is concentrated on a promontory. Allow 4 hrs to tour the town on foot, including visiting the museums. By car, head towards the centre and down to the **marina B2** *(Portul turistic Tomis; paying car park)*. From the car park, steps lead to the upper town. You come out near **piața Ovidiu B2** where there is a statue of Ovid and the **Archaeological Museum**★★. You can also get here by **train** or **maxi-taxi** from the Black Sea beach resorts: from Mangalia *(p. 292)*, the coastal train serves all the resorts. From the station, take a taxi to piața Ovidiu.

Address book p. 295. ●

sheep, human eyes and ears, and long hair which seem to be still wet. Its serpent's body, coiled around itself, ends with a lion's tail.

● **Fortuna and Pontos**. The goddess **Fortuna** stands with **Pontos,** the god of the Black Sea, at her feet. They are protectors of the city and its port.

● **Nemesis**. A small room in the form of a temple porchway contains two identical statuettes representing **Nemesis**, goddess of Revenge and Universal Harmony.

Roman remains★

> *Behind the National History and Archaeological Museum.*

The city's Roman remains are found down an alleyway lined with altars and Roman tombstones.

● **B2 Roman mosaics★** *(Edificiul roman cu mozaic)*. *Open daily except Mon. 9am-8pm in summer, 10am-6pm in winter. Admission charge. Allow approx. 30 mins.* A vast complex on three levels once linked

the upper town to the harbour. A modern building protects the 850 m² of this colourful mosaic (discovered in 1959), inset with geometric and plant motifs. The original edifice (over 2,000 m²) was built towards the end of the 4th century AD and enlarged over the centuries. It was the town's commercial centre until the 7th century with several levels of workshops, warehouses and shops (anchors, amphora, resin) reached down to the harbour.

● **B2 The Roman baths** *(Terme Roman)*. Further on, near the cliff, are the remains of some Roman public baths. Aqueducts ten kilometres long brought water to the town and a sophisticated system of pipes took the waste waters to the sea.

Tomis boulevard

> *Bulevardul Tomis. Back to piața Ovidiu.*

Bd Tomis begins on the north side of **piața Ovidiu B2**, a bustling pedestrian street full of bars. At n° 39, the small Hunchiar Mosque **B2** *(Geamia Hunchiar)* was built in 1867-1868 with stone taken from an Ottoman bridge destroyed in 1828. The delightful building at n° 32, built in 1893, houses the **Folk Art Museum★ B2** *(Muzeul de Artă Populară* ☎ *61.61.33; open daily 9am-7pm in summer, 10am-6pm in winter; admission charge; allow 1 hr)* which contains, among other ethnographic treasures, some wonderful collections of woven fabrics.

Through the streets to the sea

> **B2** *From bd Tomis, return to piața Ovidiu via str Mircea cel Batrân.*

● **B2 The Mahmudiye Mosque** *(Moscheia Mahmoud II)*. *Cross piața Ovidiu and take str. Muzeelor. Str. Crângului, 1. Open daily 9am-6pm. Admission charge.* On the corner of the first road to the right, lies the huge Mahmudiye Mosque, built in 1910 as a gift from King Carol I to the Dobrogea Muslim community.

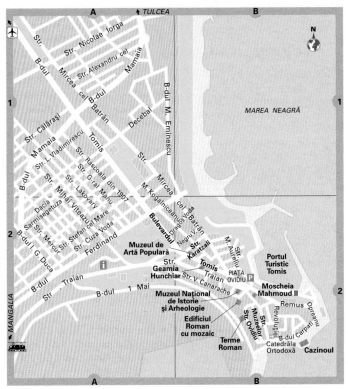

CONSTANȚA

Having climbed the 140 steps of the minaret (47 m), you will be rewarded by an **unparalleled panoramic view** of the town and sea. All along the streets of Muzeelor, Titulescu and Ovidiu are interesting examples of 1900-1920s architecture sometimes sober, sometimes extravagant.

● **B2 The casino★** *(Cazinoul)*. Down on the seafront, the casino is plumb in the middle of a vast semi-circular promenade that links the commercial port with the marina. This theatrical building, inaugurated in 1910, is the work of architects Daniel Renard (French) and Petre Antonescu, (Romanian). It combines great imagination with Art Nouveau influences and elements from traditional Romanian architecture. The best thing about the restaurant here is the seafront terrace.

Arriving at the marina **B2** *(Portul turistic Tomis)*, you cannot miss the incongruous form of the "On Plonge" restaurant *(p. 298)* where a plate of freshly cooked fish on the seafront terrace would not be a bad way to end the day.

Constanța to the Bulgarian border

> *Bulgarian border: 56 km S of Constanța on the DN 39.*

On leaving Constanța, the coast road crosses the Danube canal *(see inset p. 292)*.

From Eforie to Mangalia

> *Eforie: 35 km N of Mangalia, 9 km S of Constanța on the DN 39.*

Between lake **Techirghiol** (famous for its therapeutic mud) and the sea

history

The Danube canal

The Romans dreamt of linking the Danube to Tomis to avoid the tricky delta area. Over the centuries, the idea resurfaced several times, but it was not until 1949 that any action was seriously taken. Political prisoners, deportees and "volunteers" (300,000 people in 1951) worked on the canal in terrible conditions. It was an insane project that was abandoned in 1953, with only 7 km of canal dug. It was taken up again in 1975, using modern methods and a modified course. Work lasted more than eight years. In 1984, Ceaușescu inaugurated the canal: over 65 km long, crossing Dobrogea from west to east, made to the highest European standards. The canal cut 400 km off the route from Cernavoda to Constanța, from where it is now possible to sail on to Rotterdam and the rest of Europe. •

Romania's southern-most town is a renowned centre of thalassotherapy (p. 298), but it is also known for its ship building yards. The Greeks apparently founded the Collatis colony (future Mangalia) at about the same time as Tomis (Constanța).

● **Archaeological Museum**★ *(Muzeul de Arheologie Callatis)* ☎ 75.35.80. Open Tue.-Sun. 9am-8pm Jun-Sept., 9am-5pm Oct-May. *Admission charge.* Collections of prehistoric, Getae, Greek, Roman and Byzantine remains. In 1994, digs uncovered 1,000 m^2 of a Romano-Byzantine district of Callatis.

● **Sultan Esmahan Mosque**★ *(Moscheia Esmahan Sultan)*. Str. Oituz. Significant Turkish and Tatar communities still use this mosque, a throwback to the Ottoman Empire built in 1590, surrounded by a picturesque cemetery.

● **The bazaar**★ *(Bazar)*. Between str. Eminescu and str. Vasile Pârvan, the bazaar would not look out of place on the Bosphorous.

Vama Veche★

> *176 km S of Tulcea, 54 km from Constanța, 8 km S of Mangalia and 2 km N of the Bulgarian border on the DN 22 then the DN 39. Address book p. 299.*

On the southern outskirts of Mangalia, you pass through **2 Mai**, a fishing village which is overrun with tourists in the summer. Since the 1970s, **Vama Veche**★, has become a meeting place for non-conformists. The early "settlers" built cabins which have never ceased to expand through inspired and bizarre extensions that somehow fit in with the madcap charm of the place. Today, Vama Veche is the place to be seen: villas and large cars are multiplying.

●●● **A quick trip into Bulgaria:** With the border so close, all you need is a passport for a trip to **Bulgaria,** into "Southern Dobrogea", which was part of Romania between the two World Wars. •

lies the town of **Eforie**, which was a fashionable holiday resort until the late 1930s. In those days, it was known as **Carmen Sylva** – a pseudonym chosen by Queen Elisabeth, wife of Ferdinand, herself a poet.

After the resorts of **Olimp** and **Neptun,** built in the 1960s, came **Jupiter, Venus** and **Saturn,** have the reputation of being favourite holiday destinations for families on a budget. Covered in lush cool greenery, they are indeed very pleasant.

Mangalia★

> *168 km S of Tulcea, 43 km S of Constanța on the DN 22 then the DN 39. Allow about 1 hr. Address book p. 298.*

Address book

Reed beds create a fragile foundation for other species to grow on.

The Danube Delta

Crișan

> Dialling code ☎ 240. See p. 281.

Accommodation

▲▲▲ **Pensiunea Delia** ☎ 54.70.18. *14 rooms*. Near the landing stage. *Restaurant*.

▲▲ **Pensiunea Gherasim Gabriel**, str. Principala, 115 ☎ 54.70.20. *2 double rooms*. 1 shared bathroom. *Meals provided.* From the landing stage, go left along the riverside for 350 m (the str. Principala is the river bank road).

▲▲ **Pensiunea Maria**, str. Principala, 119 ☎ 54.70.21 or 0744.95.71.48 (mobile). *2 rooms* with 1 double and 1 single bed each. *1 room* with bunk beds. 2 bathrooms. *Meals provided.* 50 m further along from Pensiunea Gherasim (same directions as above). Sheltered terrace area and courtyard. Boat trips in to the delta.

Dunavățu de Jos

>Dialling code ☎ 240. See p. 286.

Accommodation

▲▲▲ **Hotel Egreta** ♥ ☎ 51.71.03 or 0722.64.40.27 (mobile), <www. delta-group.ro >. *24 rooms* with all modern conveniences. Well signed-posted directions. Situated on a canal bank, private landing stage. Swimming pool, private parking. Excellent *restaurant*.

▲▲▲ **Pensiunea Solinia** ☎ 0744 65.41.51 (mobile). *12 rooms*, some with air conditioning and private bathrooms. Boats of all sizes available to hire and fishing equipment to help you make the most of your trip into the delta. Private parking. *Restaurant*.

▲▲ **Pensiunea Pelican** ☎ 0744 56.88.78 (mobile) or 0745.08.07.38 (mobile). *14 beds* with private bathrooms, 1 small suite. There are also *14 beds* available in more basic rooms (which are therefore cheaper), with a shared bathroom at their disposal. The *Pelican* is plain, simple and functional. Boats and private parking available. *Restaurant*.

River transport in the delta

Travelling by river is essential for exploring the Danube Delta. What follows is a list of the main routes and destinations (allow €5-€10 for a return ticket). Board at Tulcea (p. 279) at the Navrom terminal (boats and hydrofoils) or at the AZL landing stage (Colanda boats)

ROUTE	DEPARTURE TIME	LENGTH	VIA
Tulcea-Sulina			
Hydrofoil			
TULCEA-SULINA	daily 2pm	1.30hrs	Crişan
SULINA-TULCEA	Wed., Fri., Sun. 7am	1.30hrs	Crişan
Navrom			
TULCEA-SULINA	Mon.-Fri. 1.30pm	4hrs	Maliuc, Gorgova, Crişan
SULINA-TULCEA	Tue.-Sat. 7am	4.30hrs	Crişan, Gorgova, Maliuc
Tulcea-Mila 23			
Colanda 1			
TULCEA-MILA 23	daily 1pm	15 hrs	
MILA 23-TULCEA	daily 6am	9 hrs	
Tulcea-Sf. Gheorghe			
Navrom			
TULCEA-SF. GHEORGHE	Mon.-Fri. excl. Tue.1.30pm	4.30 hrs	Mahmudia, Murighiol
SF. GHEORGHE-TULCEA	Tue.-Sat. excl. Wed. 6.30am	5 hrs	Mahmudia, Bălteni
Tulcea-Chilia Veche			
Navrom			
TULCEA-CHILIA VECHE (PERIPRAVA)	Mon.-Fri. excl. Thur. 1.30pm	5.30 hrs	Patlangeanga, Ceatalchioi, Plaur, Pardina, Tatanir
CHILIA VECHE-TULCEA (PERIPRAVA)	Tue.-Sat. excl. Fri. 6.30am	6hrs	Tatanir, Pardina, Plaur, Ceatalchioi, Patlangeanga

Mahmudia

> *Dialling code* ☎ *240. See p. 277.*

Accommodation

▲▲▲ **Hotel Teo** ☎ 54.55.50, 0722.21.33.34 (mobile). *18 rooms.* An excellent hotel near a typical regional village. *Restaurant.*

See Basics p. 300

Mila 23

> *Dialling code* ☎ *0240. See p. 281.*

Accommodation

▲▲▲ **Pension La Vica** ☎ 54.64.42 or 0744.42.24.73 (mobile), < www.la-vica.go.ro >. *4 double rooms, meals provided.* From the landing stage, head straight towards the water tower (400 m), for this conveniently situated family home.

▲▲ **Pension Valodea** ☎ 54.63.93 or 0721.98.05.21 (mobile). *4 rooms, meals provided.* A fishing family.

Sfântu Gheorghe

> *Dialling code* ☎ *240. See p. 282.*

Accommodation

▲▲▲ **Pension Mareea** ☎ 54.68.75 or 0744.30.63.89 (mobile), < www. mareea.go.ro >. *10 double rooms* (all modern conveniences, air con.). From the landing stage, head right for 250 m. The owner has three landing stages. *Restaurant*, bar and terrace.

Sulina

> *Dialling code* ☎ *240. See p. 282.*

Accommodation

▲▲▲ **Pension Coral ♥**, str I ☎ 54.37.77 or 0742.97.40.16 (mobile), *6 rooms* (all modern conveniences, air conditioned). Landing stage. Excellent *restaurant*, terrace overlooking the Danube.

▲▲ **Pension Jean Bart**, str. I ☎ 54.31.28 or 0723.63.33.53 (mobile). *Rooms with 2, 3, or 4 beds* at reasonable prices. On the banks of the Danube. The owner, Aurel, or Aurică, can organise boat and fishing trips. *Restaurant.*

Tulcea

> *Dialling code* ☎ *240. See p. 279.*

❶ **Antrec/Deltaturism Information and Reservation office ♥**, str. Portului, 34A ☎ 51.12.79, 0721. 09.21. 50 (mobile), < www. deltaturism.ro >. *Open daily 7.30am -7pm.* In the same building as the Danube Delta Biosphere Reserve office. English is spoken at reception. Paula Mihailov and Doina Pinic make a remarkable team, they can tell you anything you need to know about the delta, including boat times, hotel reservation, boat hire and how to pay the visitor's tax in exchange for a hotel bill.

❶ **Danube Delta Biosphere Reserve office** (*ARBDD, Administratia Rezervatiei Biosferei " Delta Dunarii "*), str Portului, 34A ☎ 51.89.45, fax 51. 89.75, < www.ddbra.ro >. *Open Mon.-Fri. 9am-4pm.* The reception desk and information office is in a building overlooking the port, between the *Delta* hotel and the station. Information on wildlife in the delta, exhibitions, visitor's tax, sale of detailed maps *(see inset p. 280)*. If the office is closed, go to the Antrec office (same hall, see above), which has more regular opening hours.

Getting there

● **By car**. From Bucharest: take the DN 2A (E 60) to Hârşova, then the DN 22 A to Tulcea. From Moldavia and Buzău: cross the Danube at Brăila or Galaţo, then the DN 22 to Tulcea.

● **By train**. Several trains daily from Bucharest and Constanţa, *via* Medgidia. An unpractical and time consuming way to travel. **Railway station**, str. Gării (at the harbour, W end of town). The station is an interesting example of Ceauşescu-era architecture. **Railways agency** (*Agenţia CFR*), str. Unirii 4 ☎ 51. 33.60. Ticket reservation.

● **By bus**. Bucharest-Tulcea. 8 microbus/day. Departure from Bucharest, Calea Plevnei, 236 (compagnie SC Augustina ☎ 0723.82.38. 46 [mobile]). 4.30 hrs journey. In Tulcea, get off at the bus station or the Delta hotel. **Constanţa-Tulcea** and return. Every 30 mins between 5.30am and 7.30pm. Info at Tulcea ☎ 0722.60.23.05 (mobile). Links with other towns. Local links include: Tulcea-Dunavătu de Jos, 6.30am, 1.30pm, 6.30pm; Tulcea-Babadag, 1 morning bus and 1 evening. Bus station (*Autogara*), str. Gării ☎ 51.33.04 (at the harbour, W end of town, next to the railway station).

♥ Floating hotel *(hotel plutitor)*

On the first level of this **converted barge,** there are twin cabins with *en suite* shower rooms, air-conditioning and, if necessary, heating. On the upper level, there is a large restaurant with a bar extending onto a terrace. The hotel is pulled along the main canals by a tug boat and ,unlike hotels on dry land , it can be moored in wild, remote locations. Thus, it can be used as a "base camp" for trips of 3-4 hours through the labyrinth of lesser canals in smaller boats – of which the hotel tows several. Enquire at the travel agencies in Tulcea. ●

Accommodation

▲▲▲▲ **Hotel Delta**, str. Isaccei, 2 ☎ 51. 47.20. *117 rooms.* Expensive but comfortable and directly on the port esplanade. *Restaurant.*

▲▲▲ **Hotel Europolis**, str. Pǎcii, 20 ☎ 51.24.43. *75 rooms.* Less expensive than the Delta hotel, but equal in service. Good quality. *Restaurant.*

Restaurants

Apart from hotel restaurants there are fast food stands in strada Pǎcii.

Useful addresses

● **Travel agency. Atbad**, str. Babadag, 11 ☎ 51.41.14, fax 51.76. 25, < www.atbad.hypermart.net >. Ask for Marilena Apolon, who speaks English. This professional (and expensive) agency offers accommodation in some high-quality floating hotels *(see inset above)* as well as a superbly isolated guesthouse in the S-W of the delta (near Lake Razim). The agency also runs the holiday village on Lake Roşu *(map p. 275)*. Speedboat travel (at about € 300 a day!).

Ibis Tours, str. Griviţei, 1, bl. C1, ap. 9 ☎ 51.27.87 or 0722.38.13.98 (mobile). A specialist in bird-spotting trips in Dobrogea.

Simpaturism, str. Isaccei, 2 ☎ 51.57.53, < www.simpaturism. ro >. On the ground floor of the *Delta* hotel. This agency manages the Uzlina Cormoran Complex, but can also reserve rooms for you throughout Romania, especially on the Black Sea coast.

● **Ferry terminal and landing stages.** Ferry terminal *(Gara Fluvialǎ)*, str. Gǎrii ☎ 51.15.53. On the waterfront, to the W of the town, adjoining the bus station. This is the boarding point *(ponton)* for **Navron** boats and the **hydrofoils** *(navǎ rapidǎ)*. Parking is secure and supervised, at the entrance to the ferry terminal, on the right. (approx. € 1.20/day). *Timetable p. 294.* **Landing stage for AZL boats** *(ponton AZL)* ☎ 51.11.54 or 0744.18.98.80 (Vladimir Cravtov's mobile). Next to the arts centre, 300 m upstream from the ferry terminal. Departure point for daily services to Mila 23 (by boat *Colanda 1*). Supervised parking. *Timetable p. 294.*

● **Post Office** *(Poşta)*, str. Pǎcii, 6. *Open daily except Sun. 8am-6pm.*

Uzlina

> *Dialling code* ☎ *240. Map p. 277.*

Accommodation

▲▲▲▲ **Cormoran Complex** ☎ 0744. 73.63.72 (mobile), < www.cor moran. ro >. *84 places.* Divided between a hotel ***, chalets, and a floating hotel *(see inset above)*.

Access by boat only from Murighiol (*p. 283*). Supervised parking. Uzlina island has been turned into a little paradise thanks to the imagination of Cornel Gaină. Boat trips to see pelicans on Lake Uzlina (observatories). *Restaurant.*

▲▲▲▲ **Pension Tamarin** ☎ 0744.21 58.85 (mobile). *44 places* in very comfortable rooms. *Restaurant.* Access by boat only (10 km) from Murighiol (*p. 283*). Fast boat crossing guaranteed (boarding point at S.C Tamarin with private parking).

The Black Sea coast

Constanţa

> *Dialling code* ☎ *241. Map p. 291. See p. 289.*

❶ **Coastal information** ♥, **Tourist information centre** (*Centru de Informare Turistica*) **A2** ☎ 55.50.00, fax 55.51.11, < www.infolitoral.ro >. Information on the coastline (hotels, restaurants, transport), hotel reservation, etc. A very efficient service.

Getting there

● **By car**. From Bucharest, the most direct route is on the DN 3 *via* Feteşti, and on a few sections of the future Bucharest-coast motorway. Alternative route: DN 2A *via* Urziceni, Slobozia and Hârşova. From Tulcea, DN 22. From Bulgaria follow the fast coast road.

● **By air**. Regular flights from Bucharest, Greece and Turkey. From the airport, take a Tarom bus to the town centre. **Mihail Kogalniceanu International Airport** ☎ 25.83.78. 25 km N-W of Constanţa. **Tarom agency** (*Agenţia Tarom*), str. Ştefan cel Mare, 15 ☎ 66.26.32 or 61.40.66. Information and reservation.

● **By train**. From Bucharest, about ten trains daily, more in summer. **Station** (*Gara*), str. Gării **Off map by A2**. Continue down bd Ferdi-

nand, in the S-W of the town for str. Gării, take trolleybus 40 from the town centre. **The railways agency** (*Agenţia CFR*), aleea Vasile Canarache, 4 **B2** ☎ 61.46.90. Information and ticket reservation.

● **By bus**. Daily connections by bus or maxitaxi to Bucharest and Constanţa. **South Bus Station** (*Autogara Sud*), str. Burada Teodor, 1 **Off map by A2** ☎ 66.52.89 is next to the railway station. Regular shuttles to Bucharest (and other big towns) and a constant service (in summer) to seaside resort towns. Beware: there is also a bus station in the north of the town (*Autogara Nord*) **Off map by A1** for local services (Mamaia). **Eurolines**, str. Ştefan cel Mare, 71 **A1** ☎ 66.27.04. Provides connections all over Europe.

Accommodation

▲▲▲▲ **Hotel Capri** ♥, str. Mircea cel Batrân, 109 **B2** ☎ 021.55.30.90 (mobile), < www.capri.ro >. *16 rooms, 8 suites.* Very comfortable.

▲▲▲▲ **Hotel Dali**, str. Smardan, 6A **A1** ☎/fax 61.61.14, < www.hotel-dali.ro >. *8 suites, 7 rooms* each with a balcony.

▲▲▲▲ **Hotel Guci**, str. Răscoala 1907, 23 ☎ 69.55.00, fax 63.84.26. *20 rooms.* On the top floor of the hotel there is a good Mexican *Restaurant.*

---

directions

Coming from Bucharest on the DN 3, you enter town on bd Brătianu, which takes you to bd Ferdinand **A2** and the old town centre. From **Bucharest** and **Tulcea** on the DN 2 follow the main artery road, bd Tomis **B2**, which brings you out in the old town. To get to **Mangalia** (well signed), leave town on bd Ferdinand **A2** and bd 1 Mai **A2**. Constanţa's old town is built on the peninsula which overlooks the port. ●

▲▲▲ **New Safari** ♥, str. Karatzali, 1 ☎ 0722.32.24.61 (mobile). *10 rooms.* Superb panoramic view of the Moderne beach. Good *restaurant* which mixes traditional Romanian and international cuisine. Some fish specialities. Sea view.

Restaurants

Crama Veche, str. Călăraşi, 1 **A1** ☎ 66.00.73. Macedonian and Romanian cuisine.

El Greco ♥, str. Decebal, 18 **A1** ☎ 0722.41.40.10 (mobile). As if to remember the close links between Constanţa and Greece, this restaurant, situated in a quiet street produces good quality and varied cuisine. The interior courtyard is particularly pleasant.

Gavroche ☎ 54.44.48. On the marina, in a boat on the quayside. Fish *restaurant.*

Joie de Vivre, str. Decebal, 24 **A1** ☎ 61.44.48. French influenced menu.

Les Marins, str. Ştefan cel Mare, 19 **A2** ☎ 61.47.97. A bar serving Romanian and international food.

On Plonge ♥, ☎ 60.19.05. On the sea wall of the marina. Interesting architecture. A sea food and fish *restaurant.* Go for the fish rather than sea food.

Shopping

Market, piaţa Griviţei **A2**. S of str. Ştefan cel Mare. Local cheeses and fruit here. *Open daily from 7am.*

Vinoteca Antoniadis, str. Ştefan cel Mare, 72 **A2**. Wine specialist. Bottles from vintages dating back to 1952.

Night life

There are cafés and fast food restaurants along bd Tomis.

Useful addresses

● **Travel Agency. Latina**, str. Primăverii, 6 **Off map by A1** ☎ 63.97.13. Seaside Hotel reservation, transfers from Constanţa airport. Excursions. Car hire. **Simpaturism A1**, str. Răs-coala 1907, 9 ☎ 66.04.68, < www. simpaturism.ro >. Useful for hotel reservation on the coast. Car-hire.

Jupiter

> *Dialling code* ☎ *241. See p. 292.*

Accommodation

▲▲▲ **Hotel Capitol** ☎ 73.13.05. *221 rooms.* The family suite is particularly good value.

Mamaia

> *Dialling code* ☎ *241. Map p. 288.*

Accommodation

▲▲▲▲▲ **Hotel Iaki-Bucureşti** ☎ 83. 13.60 or 83.10.25, fax 83.11.69. *60 rooms.* Luxury but relatively affordable hotel. *Restaurant.*

▲▲▲▲ **Hotel Caraiman II** ☎ 83.13.81, fax 83.13.46. *53 rooms.* 50 m from the beach, an excellent modestly-sized hotel/*restaurant.* Fairly expensive in high season. *Restaurant.*

▲▲▲ **Hotel Briza** ♥, ☎ 021.83.10.12 (mobile), < www.capri.ro >. *13 rooms and 3 suites.* A pleasant hotel with high-quality rooms at a reasonable price. *Restaurant.*

Mangalia

> *Dialling code* ☎ *241. See p. 292.*

Accommodation

▲▲▲▲▲ **Hotel President**, str. Teilor, 6 ☎ 75.58.61, fax 75.56.95, < www. hpresident.com >. *65 rooms.* When this hotel was being build some remains from the time of the ancient city were restored inside the building. *Restaurant.* Car hire.

▲▲▲ **Hotel Astra** ♥, str. Teilor, 9 ☎ 75.16.73, fax 75.20.52. *50 rooms.* A good quality deal near to the sea.

▲▲▲ **Hotel Mangalia**, str. Rozelor, 35 ☎ 75.20.52, fax 75.35.10. *268 rooms.* With a reputed **thalassotherapy** centre, open all year. *Restaurant.*

Restaurant
Captain Mondy's, bd 1 Decembrie 1918 ☎75.31.68. Near the Mangalia marina. The Irish pub in Callatis.

Vama Veche

> *Dialling code* ☎ *241. See p. 292.*

Accommodation
▲▲▲ **Hotel Ca'Bianca** ♥. *21 rooms en suite.* Restaurant overlooking the beach.

▲▲ **Pensiune Golden Sea.** *15 double rooms en suite.* A green and yellow painted wooden house at the entrance to the village.

Bar-restaurants
Bibi Bistro ☎ 0722.24.12.16 (mobile). Pleasant, fairly pricey restaurant that can get noisy.

Zapata ☎ 0722.34.10.66 (mobile), < www.zapata.ro >. Spot the sombrero and you've found this lively night spot.

Useful address
● **Vama Veche Reservation Centre** (*Dispecerat Vama Veche*) ☎ 0722.88.90.87 (mobile), < rezervari@vamavecheholidays.ro >. Essential for hotel reservation in Vama Veche or 2 Mai.

Venus

> *Dialling code* ☎ *241. See p. 292.*

Accommodation
▲▲▲▲ **Hotel Carmen** ☎ 73.10.08, fax 73.11.10, < www.hotelcarmen.

---

gastronomy

Tasty winter dishes

Every September, houses in this region are infused with the the smell of vegetables, mushrooms and spices being chopped together and cooked down to makes conserves for the lean times of winter. These vegetable purées are called **zacuscă** and each home prepares its own version. You might therefore find a homemade purée of wild mushrooms, tomatoes and onions.

There is vegetable paté made from tomato, peppers, onion, dill, bay leaves and celery. Or mushrooms chopped withbay leaves, carrots and water onions. In the mountains of Bucovina, they make stunning cep patés. These aromatic patés are served cold, spread onto bread, toast or, as an alternative, as a filling for flaky pastry. ●

---

ro >. *99 rooms.* Conference centre, indoor swimming pool, private beach, sauna.

▲▲ **Hotel Florica** ♥ ☎ 73.14.06, fax 73.12.66. *180 rooms.* A cheap and cheerful option. There is a very pleasant interior courtyard where you can have a drink among the plants. Ask for room 217, which has a great view. You can eat at the restaurant **Esplanada** (very reasonable). ●

basics

Organising your Trip

© Pierre Soissons

Useful information

Tourist Offices

● **In Romania**.
National Authority for Tourism, Str Dinicu Golescu 38, Bucharest, Romania
☎ +40-21-314.9957, fax +40-21-314.9960,
< www.mtromania.ro >,
< romaniatravel.com >,
< promovare@mturism.ro >.

● **In the UK**.
Romanian National Tourist Office, 22 New Cavendish Street, London, WIG 8TT ☎ +44 (0) 20.7224.3692, fax +44 (0) 20.7935.6435,
< www. romaniatourism.

Above: anything can be found in Romanian small shops.

Previous page: painted eggs, a Bucovina's speciality.

com > or < visitromania. com >, < romaniatravel@ btconnect.com >.

● **In the US**.
Romanian Tourism Office, 14 East 38th Street, Floor 12, New York, NY 10016
☎ +1.212.545.8484, fax +1.212.251.0429,
< www.romania tourism.com >, < romania@ romania-tourism.com >.

Embassies and consulates

● **In the US**.
Romanian Embassy,
< www.roembus.org/ english >.
Romanian Consulate, 1607 23rd Street, NW, Washington D.C., 20008; Mr. Cristian Gaginsky, Consul
☎ +1.202.332.2879 ext. 117/118, fax +1.202.232.4748. Open Mon.-Fri. 10am-1pm.

● **In the UK**.
Arundel House, 4 Palace Green, London W8 4QD, UK ☎ +44 (0) 20.7937.9666, fax +44 (0) 20.7937.8069,
< www. roemb.co.uk >,
< roemb@copperstream. co.uk >. Open Mon.-Fri. 9am-5pm.

Romania online

● **General info**.
< www.romanian tourism.com >: website with a search engine to help you find accommodation, transport, maps and other important information when planning your trip.

< www.turism.ro/ english/index.php >: a nicely planned website with useful addresses, ideas and photos to help you plan your trip with links

to the same information in several languages.

< www.romaniatourism. com >: official website for Romanian Travel and Tourism; includes practical information, vacation ideas, literature and links to other sites.

< www.romaniatravel. com >: contains good information about travelling to the country; sponsored by the Romanian Tourism Promotion Office.

● **Current events, news.** < www.nineoclock.ro > or < www.romanian-daily.ro >: English-speaking online newspaper updated daily with politics, weather and entertainment.

< www.centraleurope. com/romaniatoday >: updated daily by The Central European Review, this site has the latest in breaking news and analysis.

● **History and Culture.** < www.ici.ro/romania/ traditii/romania.html >: general information about the country, its history, customs and traditions.

Romanian culture in the UK

The Romanian Cultural Centre, 7-8th floor, 54 - 62 Regent Street, London W1R 5PJ ☎ +44 (0) 20.7439.4052, < www. romanianculturalcentre.org. uk > or < www.radur. demon.co.uk/rcc.html >,

< mail@romanian culturalcentre.org.uk > or < romaniancentre@rhplon don.freeserve.co.uk >.

Romanian culture in the US

Romanian-American Network, 7847 N. Caldwell Ave., Unit D, Niles, IL 60714 ☎ +1.847. 663.0950, +1.847.663.0960, < www.romanian-american.net >, < publisher@ameritech. net >.

Romanian Churches in the US, a list can be found at < www.roembus. org/english/communi ties/Romanian_churches _in_US.htm >.

When to go?

The climate in Romania is continental temperate. The hills and mountains of the country are marked by long, raw winters with snowstorms common. Spring and fall are milder, but are short-lived. Summer tends to be hot, especially in the plains and hills.

●●● Weather Reports: < weather.yahoo.com/ regional/ROXX.html >.

● **Springtime**. This is the ideal time to explore the Danube delta and bird watch. May and June are the best months for strolling Bucharest or Timişoara. In May,

orchards in Oradea, Moldavia and in Transylvania are covered with flowers. Agro-pastoral festivals are held in Maramureş (p.).

● **Summer**. From July 15 to August 15 is high season in Bucovina, Maramureş, Sighişoara, the Black Sea and the Danube Delta so be sure to book well in advance. Heavy heat weighs in Bucharest during this time yet the mountain climate is ideal for hiking.

● **Autumn**. In Transylvania, the orchards turn and lose their fruit and the mountains are at their peak beauty. It is the ideal time to visit the monasteries of Bucovina: light, beautiful forest foliage and complete serenity.

● **Winter**. Romania is known for hard winters with a rigorous dry cold and blinding snow conditions, which often lasts three months in the mountains. The New Year is celebrated according to Moldavian tradition (including in Bucovina). Spectacular lights create an unusual ambiance in the hills of Moldavia and on the Danube delta. Skiers can bank on good snow conditions in the Carpathians. The Apuseni and the Szekler country (the places where record

weather		
Average temperatures in °F (in °C)	**Summer**	**Winter**
WALLACHIA, BANAT	72 (22)	34 (1)
BLACK SEA	70 (21)	38 (3)
BUCOVINA, MARAMUREŞ, HARGHITA, APUSENI	58-61 (14-16)	25 (-4)
TRANSYLVANIA	61-64 (16-18)	28 (-2)

temperatures have touched -48 °F; -44 °C) are favourable to off-trail skiing.

Individual travel

Airlines

The best prices for flights to Bucharest between € 320 and € 380 can be found with Tarom (Transporturile Aeriene Române), Romania's state-owned air carrier. If your point of embarkation is outside the EU, you will most likely have to change planes in a European capital before landing in Romania. Bucharest is no more than two hours by plane from most cities in Western Europe.

Tarom offers a daily flight between London and Bucharest and the other cities in Romania can be reached with flights via Bucharest.

The best itinerary coming from the UK and Ireland is to fly via another European airport such as London's Heathrow or Gatwick, which can set you back approximately € 315 to € 465.

Austrian Airlines via Vienna < www.austrian airlines.com >. This is the preferred airline to Romania from North America and offers daily connections to Bucharest, Timişoara and Cluj from several cities in the USA and Canada.

British Airways < www. britishairways.com >. Direct flights to Bucharest, fares vary and begin from about € 335 from London for a roundtrip (maximum return date is one month after departure).

Tarom Airlines
< www.tarom.ro >
In the UK, 27 New Cavendish Street, London, W1G 9TX ☎ +44 (0) 20.7224.3693/7935. 3600, fax +44 (0) 20.7487.2913, < lonoffice@ taromuk.co.uk >.
In the USA, Empire State Building 350, Fifth Ave. 1410, NY 10118 ☎ +1.212.687.6013/6014, fax +1.212.661.6056, < taromnyc@tarom.us >.

Other carriers such as Air France <www.airfrance. com >, Alitalia < www. alitalia.com >, Czech Airlines < www.czechairlines.com >, CSA < www.csa.cz >, Delta Air Lines < www.delta.com >, JAT Airways < www.jat.com >, KLM-Royal Dutch Airlines < www.klm.com >, Lufthansa via Frankfurt < www.lufthansa.com > or Malev-Hungarian Airlines < www.malev.hu >, Olympic Airlines < www.olympicairlines. com >, Swiss International Airlines < www.swiss. com >, and Turkish Airlines < www. turkishairlines.com > offer flights to Bucharest Otopeni airport via other cities.

For in/outbound flights from Bucharest Otopeni Airport, schedules can be found on their website < www.otp-airport.ro >.

●●● **Flights possible to provincial cities** such as Cluj, Timişoara and Sibiu. Go to Tarom's website or those of Austrian Airlines, Lufthansa or Carpatair < www.carpatair.com >.

Travel agencies

A good bet for finding discounted fares is through brand-name agencies such as those based in the US and Canada. Such agencies include:

STA Travel < www.sta-travel.com >
☎ 1.800.226.8624.

Travel CUTS
< www.travelcuts.com >
☎ 1.888.835.2887.

Additionally, you might try **USIT** based in Ireland < www.usit.ie >.

Visit Romania, Blvd Ion Mihalache 62, Sector 1, Bucharest 011195 ☎ +40-21-223.1818/ 223.20.40/223.20.03, fax +40-21-223.1810, < www.visit-romania.ro >, < office@visit-romania.ro > is a locally based travel agency run in association with Carlson Wagonlit. They offer a full range of services and competitive ticket prices.

Charter flights

If you are diligent in your research, you may be rewarded with a 20% discount on official fares. It's worth checking out charter flights that fly during the summer to Constanfla on the Black Sea.

Tarom operates charter flights through Viaclub from Arad, Bucharest, Cluj-Napoca and Timişoara, among others.

The most comprehensive list of charter flights leaving the UK can be found at Just the Flight < www. justtheflight.co.uk >.

By train

Considering the train can take about 46 hours from London (33 from Paris) with several stops and changes along the way, compounded by the price of a ticket 30% more than that of a flight, this method of transportation might seem lacking in practicality. That said, it is the best way to see the countryside and the best way to go if you want to make stopovers in such cities as Budapest or Vienna.

For train schedules, a helpful tool is the Thomas Cook European Time Table (L11), updated monthly and available in bookstores in the UK.

You can also visit < www.cfr.ro > for information on train schedules and fares.

Austrian rail website

< www.oebb.at > (in German and English) offers practical information and is probably the best European site of its genre. Easy to use and fast, the site has a reservation capacity and there you can plan your voyage from a selected departure city.

Romanian National Railways (SNCFR)

operate service from Bucharest to many European cities. First and second-class couchettes are available for journeys of 10-hours or longer.

For advanced ticket reservations, go to RailEurope < www.raileurope.com >. The best place to get EurRail passes, travel specials and deals.

● From Budapest to Banat and Transylvania.

BUDAPEST - BANAT. Several trains per day. Trip time: approx. 4 hours 30 minutes for Arad and 6 hours for Timişoara.

BUDAPEST - NYUHATI - CLUJ. Two trains per day.

Going towards Cluj-Budapest: Night train with couchettes. Trip time: approx 8 hours 30 minutes. One of the trains offers connections for Bucovine and Maramureş.

By car

The majority of travellers originating from Western Europe who choose to travel to Romania by car have the luxury of lengthier holidays (often two weeks or more). Though it is a good option for some, the journey takes approximately two to four days. Certain regions, such as those in the west (Transylvania, Apuseni) and in the north (Maramureş, Bucovina) are easier to access.

When renting a car in Europe, don't forget to check with the car hire agency about its policy regarding taking the car across national borders.

> Border patrol.

The main access points are through the Danube valley, Switzerland or Italy. They all connect to Hungary, where there are five different border patrols open 24 hours a day, 7 days a week.

●●● Good idea: the

Borş-Oradea and Naedlac-Arad borders are often heavily congested. Consider the three other passage-ways, especially the rural Valea lui Mihai border.

● Main points of entry.

HUNGARY. If you are travelling from the west, you may enter the country at one of four points of entry in Petea (11 km NW of Satu Mare), Borş (14 km NW of Oradea), Vărşand (66 km N of Arad) and Nădlac (between Szeged and Arad). Petea, Borş

and Nădlac link up with major highways from Budapest.

SERBIA AND MONTENEGRO. Points of entry are Jimbolia (45 km W of Timişoara), Moraviţa (between Timişoara and Belgrade), Naidăş (120 km E of Belgrade) and at Portile de Fier (10 km W of Drobeta-Turnu Severin).

BULGARIA. The main border crossing is Giurgiu (opposite Ruse) with a 4 km-long toll bridge spanning the Danube. Calafat (opposite Vidin) is another point of entry, as are Ostrov-Silistra (opposite Călăraşi), Negru Vodă (37 km NE of Tolbuhin) as well as Vama Veche (S of Mangalia).

●●● To make your own itinerary: < www.via michelin.com >.

● Taxes and fuel.

> Highways.

In Germany: free. In Hungary: € 10 for 10 days (April 2003).

> Road tax.

In Austria: € 7.6 for 10 days (April 2003). These can be bought at the border and in Bavarian gas stations. In Hungary: the *matrica* can be purchased at the border and in gas stations.

> Fuel.

The average prices in Austria and Hungary are comparable: € 0.95 for super unleaded and € 0.7 for gas-oil, less expensive than in Bavaria (€ 1.12 and € 0.89).

●●● See Domestic transport, p. 311.

By motor coach

Beginning in 2001, the elimination of visas for Romanian carriers in Western Europe paved the way for an explosion of cheap transportation to the country.

Regular routes offer service to the four corners of Europe several times per week. The trip, a comfortable one, lasts approximately 40 hours. Aside from the motor coach companies, agencies specialising in Romania offer tickets for the ride.

> **Western Europe - Bucharest.**

Eurolines, Europe's largest bus conglomerate, is the best option and offers frequent service and connection to most cities in Scandanavia, Western and Central Europe. Check their website < www.eurolines. com > for complete schedules and fares. The office in Bucharest is headed by Touring Blvd Alexandru Ioan Cuza 5a, Sector 1 ☎ +40-21-210.0890, fax +40-21-210.0812, < office@touring.ro >.

●●● **Note:** Eurolines services 24 Romanian cities including Sibiu, Sighişoara and Braşov.

border

The main routes all end up in Hungary, where one can choose between 5 checkpoints (open 24 h/24), from south to north: Nădlac (Arad, Timişoara, Sibiu, Bucharest); Gyula-Vărşand (Banat, Apuseni mountains); Borş (Oradea, Apuseni mountains, Cluj, Transylvania, then Bucovina or Bucharest); Valea lui Mihai (Satu Mare, Maramureş, Bucovina); Csenger-Petea (Satu Mare, Maramureş, Bucovina). ●

Organised tours

The natural diversity of Romania opens the possibility for original touring itineraries to suit every traveler. Thanks to the internet, you can even take advantage of offers in Romanian travel agencies (see visiting address book).

Romanian specialists

Canada Adventures Abroad Worldwide Travel Ltd, 2148-20800 Westminster Highway, Richmond BC V6V 2W3 ☎ 1800.665.3998, fax +1.604.303.1099, < www. adventures-abroad.com >.

UK Worldwide Adventures Abroad Ltd, Unit M Staniforth Estates, Main Street, Hackenthorpe, Sheffield S12 4LB ☎ +44.114.247.3400.

USA Adventures Abroad Worldwide Travel Ltd, PMB 101, 1124 Fir Ave, Blaine, WA, 98240 ☎ 1800.665.3998, fax +1.604.303.1099.

Transylvania Uncovered (UK), 24A Middle Street South, Driffield, East Yorkshire, UK YO25 6PS ☎ +44 (0) 1377.200.118, fax +44 (0) 1377.254.779 < www.beyondthe forest.com >, < travel@ beyondtheforest.com >. Adventure tourism; organises trips for kayaking, hiking, caving and photo safaris.

Explore Worldwide (UK), 1 Frederick Street, Aldershot, Hants GU11 1LQ ☎ +44 (0) 1252.760.000, fax +44 (0) 1252.760.001, < www. exploreworldwide.

com >, < info@explore worldwide.com >. Worth contacting if you are interested in walking tours of the country; itineraries exploring "village folklore" can take you through the famous to more remote spots of the country.

Footloose Adventure Travel (UK), 3 Springs Pavement, Ilkley, West Yorkshire, LS29 8HD ☎ +44 (0) 1943.604.030, fax +44 (0) 1943.604.070, < www.footloose adventure.co.uk >, < info@footlooseadventure. co.uk >. Walking tours in the Carpathians and other picturesque spots in the country.

Romania Travel Centre (UK), Pack Your Bags, 39 Mount Pleasant, Turnbridge Wells, Kent, TN1 1PN ☎ +44 (0) 1892.515.524, fax +44 (0) 1892.511.579, < www.packyourbags.com/ romania >, < enquiry@ romaniatravelcentre.com >. A good source for cheap tickets to Romania, excursions in the Carpathians and spa tours.

Scenic Romania (USA), ☎ +1.239.495.5076, fax +1.239.495.5092, < www.tradescotours.com/ tours/scenic_romania. htm >. Provides visitors with a deluxe escorted tours. One includes an 8-day car or motor coach tour of Bucharest, Sibiu, Baia Mare, Cluj, Brasov, Count Dracula's Bran Castle and Sinaia for $ 1,543 for single occupancy, $ 1,295 for double.

Quest Tours & Adventures (USA), 700 SE 39th Avenue, Portland, OR 97214 ☎ +1.800.621.8687, fax

+1.503.234.5332, < www.romtour. com >, < tour@romtour. com >. Their menu includes trips to monasteries and spas, and, of course, Dracula tours.

Cultural tours

For a more interesting trip, these agencies offer intellectual and stimulating voyages for those who prefer to travel off the beaten-path. These trips are for groups, they may require you to be a part of a larger group even though they respect the will of the solo traveller.

Atlantic Tours, Calea Victoriei 202, Sector 1, Bucharest, ☎ +40-21-312.7689, < www.atlantic. ro >, < office@atlantic.ro >. For about € 986, you can take an all-inclusive trip to see the best of Romania with this tour operator.

RoCultours/CTI, Blvd Primaverii 50, Bucharest 1, ☎/fax +40.21.223.2619/ 40.21.230.2292, < www.cti@rotravel.com >, < cti@pcnet.ro >. Activities are coordinated by the local nonprofit academic association of Bucharest's European Cultural Centre. Included on the menu are wine tours, four-day study tours of Transylvania (from € 275 per person), five-day tours of the Bucovina monasatries (€ 495 per person). Also on offer is a two- or four-day Greatest Hits tour of Transylvania and Wallachia (€ 165/€ 395). Tours may be organised for 2 to 25 people.

Green Mountain Holidays, Str Principala 305, Izvorul Crisului, Judetul Cluj, Romania ☎ +40-26-441.8691, < www.dntcj.ro/gmh >,

< gmh@mail.dntcj.ro >. Puts together adventure tours such as kayaking, hiking, caving and photo safaris.

Kron-Tour, Str Baritiu 12G, 500025 Braşov, ☎ +40-26-841.0515/0715, < www.krontour.ro >, < office@krontour.ro >. Organises ski packages and lift passes and is also an agent for most private German bus companies.

Mara Tours, Calea Victoriei 87-89, Sector 1 Bucharest ☎ +40-21-324.5626, < www.mara.ro >, < maratour@mara.ro >. If a relaxation trip is in order, call on this travel agency specialising in spa tours. For about € 436, you can spend one week in a spa-hotel, full pension with accommodation and treatment.

Micomis Agenţie de Turism, Str Republicii 53, Braşov 500030 ☎ +40-268-470.472/475.658, fax +40-268-410.321, < www.micomis.ro >, < office@micomis.ro >. A generalist travel agency which offers ski packages, cheap regional tours as well as the standard Dracula visit.

Roving Romania, Str Toammei 13, Bloc 4, Sc D, Apt 13, 2200 Braşov ☎ +40-744-212.065, < www.roving-romania.co.uk >, < roving@deltanet.ro >. A comprehensive agency, RR will tailor a 4WD Landrover, foot or bike experience for the most specific of travellers. Special interests include bird-watching, botany, photography, local traditions and customs and painted monasteries. They also cater to the

mainstream adventure-traveller who seeks the thrill of hiking and skiing.

Money

The national currency unit is the leu ("lion"), in plural, lei. In 1990, 1 € bought you 2 lei, compared to 41,000 today… Bills of 2,000; 10,000; 50,000; 100,000; and 500,000 lei; coins in denominations of 1,000 or 5,000 lei.

●●● See **Exchange**, p.310.

● **Credit/Debit Cards**. ATM machines (bancomat) are in every Romanian city. Paying on a card (Visa, Eurocard, Mastercard, etc.) is acceptable in most hotels and certain restaurants (surely in Bucharest), in upscale boutiques and supermarkets (except the Metro) and in gas stations such as MOL and ÖMV. Card logos will normally be displayed in shop windows and glass doors which accept card payment, though it is always best to ask first.

● **Western Union Money Transfer**. In case of an emergency, you can securely receive cash without a local bank account. The sender brings cash (limited to $ 5,000) to one of many Western Union branches (oftentimes in local post offices), fills out the necessary paperwork and pays about 10-20% commission. Then, they inform (by telephone or mail) the recipient of the exact amount and the 10-digit pin code. About 10 minutes later, the recipient can retrieve the money at a participating Western Union counter in their area. What you need to bring is a valid photo ID and the 10-digit pin code.

Western Union correspondents are present in most Romanian towns; generally they can be found in banks (where the WU logo is posted) or at main post offices in main towns.

 For more information:
< www.westernunion.com >.

Formalities

Papers

For a stay of 30 days (maximum), travellers from the European Union don't need a visa, nor do Americans. Presenting a valid passport or photo ID is sufficient at border points. Its validity must extend six months beyond the date of entry if you wish to apply for a visa should you choose to stay longer. Those residing in countries outside of the European Union and certain Eastern European countries may also need a visa to gain entry into the country.

Car

In order to drive in Romania, you must be in possession of a driver's license, car registration, proof of insurance (you should be sure it covers damage occurred in Romania), as well as the car rental agreement. An international Driving Permit (IDP) is a good thing to have, but not necessary. If the vehicle does not belong to you, a letter of agreement on the owner's behalf should suffice should you have a run-in with a nit-picky police officer.

Customs

You may legally enter Romania with a maximum of $ 10,000 US in pocket money. Importation of tobacco and alcohol is restricted. You may also carry across objects for personal use such as a camera, video camera, etc. They must be declared upon entry and exit as a practical and cautionary measure. Officially, the exportation of antiques is possible with an authorisation from the local cultural authority.

Animals

Dogs and cats (2 domestic animals per person, maximum) must procure medical certificates of health and rabies vaccinations with a legal translation and must be more than one month and

less than one year old. Cats' vaccinations should be not older than six months.

 # Sanitary precautions

● **Vaccinations**.
Though there is no obligatory vaccination to enter the country, it is always a good idea to update general ones such as tetanus, polio, hepatitis B and diphtheria. The vaccination for Hepatitis A is recommended as no visitor is spared from poor hygiene.

● **Tick-borne encephalitis**.
The risk is slight (p.312); however, if you plan on staying for more then 30 days in a rural wooded area in spring or summer, the Ticovac vaccination is a precaution to consider. One injection repels ticks for 30 days, a second lasts between 9 and 12 months and a third for three years.

●●● See **Health**, p.313.

Packing your bags

Maps

A map of Europe (1/3000000) should give you space to visualise your trip. Covering the whole of the country, road maps are not exempt from error. Your best bet is the IGN/Marco Polo map (1/750000) for sale in travel bookstores. Though the indispensable remains the Road Tourist Atlas (p.) for sale in Romania. The backpacker will find the few available maps to vary dramatically in quality. At 1/15000 or 1/20000, maps of the major cities are sold in gas

budget

● **Transportation**. For flights and organised tours (p.304). One litre of gasoline goes for about €0.7 for premium (super) and €0.6 for motorină (gas-oil). Bucharest-Iaşi in a first-class sleeping car runs about €22. A plane ride between Bucharest-Cluj: €90.

● **Lodging**. Per person, per night, expect to pay about €9 to €20 for shared rooms with communal bathrooms (with half-board); €10 to €28 in a double room with breakfast in a hotel **; €18 to €105 in a ***; €70 to €450 in a **** or *****.

● **Meals**. A placîntă (stuffed crepe with cheese and fennel) costs about €0.2; a pizza between 1.5 and €3; a meal in someone's home (bed and breakfast) between €3 and €7; an all-out dinner in Bucharest for about €25.

● **Museums and monuments**. For such excursions, admission prices vary between €0.5 to €6. Taxes for photo and video taken at the door of monuments can run between €1.5 and €8.5.

● **Daily expenses**. To give an idea: a postal stamp for Western Europe (€0.4), telephone card (€4.8), espresso (€0.4), 50 cl draught beer (€0.24), a litre of Maramureş plum brandy (€2.4), a simple gentleman's haircut (€0.4 to €1), parking fees (€0.3), gala concert at the Bucharest Roman Athenaeum (€15.5 to €24,5), 1 kilo of tomatoes in the middle of summer (€0.75) and automobile oil change (€2.5). ●

stations and bookstores in the country.

Automobile equipment

If you drive to Romania between November and April, keep the snow chains in the trunk should the occasional storms leave the roads impassable. Snow tires are extremely handy and can be bought on your trip for about €90 a pair.

●●● Caution: triangular hazard signs are obligatory and tyres with nails prohibited.

Travelling pharmacy

The ideal medical case: insect repellent (p.314), sun screen with high SPF, anti-diarrhoeal tablets, local antiseptic, Biafine® (for burns), a bit of ether (kills ticks before extraction), tweezers, eye disinfectant, Paracetamol or equivalent (for headaches and pains), general antiobiotic. You should also include bandages and compresses, an elastic band such as Elastoplast®. A small case of Aspivenin® is always useful in cases of insect bites or a bad run-in with a horned viper (in the Banat).

Clothing

In the middle of summer, you should prepare for indecisive weather: one day of heat may be followed by a cool evening's breeze. Think of bringing something appropriately dressy (you never know when you'll be invited to a wedding; p.) and covered to visit the churches (p.). In winter, expect a frigid cold; bring warm waterproof shoes and non-skid soles (and thick socks) or boots. If it rains and you are in the countryside, you won't regret it! House slippers are recommended for inside houses.

The range of the ornithologist

The Danube Delta region threatens to awaken even the most dormant ornithologist: bring a pair of high-quality binoculars, muted clothing and your Petersons's Guide (p.).

For the amateur fresco-watcher

Binoculars are equally useful for getting closer to magnificent frescoes on church ceilings. A pocket torch will allow you to see them better as well. ●

Keys to a successful stay

© Pierre Soissons

Arrival

● **By plane.**
The majority of air traffic is routed through **Bucharest-Otopeni** (20 km north of the centre on the DN 1 towards Ploiești). For domestic flights, make connections either at this airport or at Bucharest-Banesa (5 km from the city centre on the DN 1). There are car hire agencies at the airport. To get to the city centre or to Banesa airport, take either the bus or a taxi (p. 84). Other international airports include Cluj (p. 191), Sibu (p. 176), Timișoara (p. 119), and Constanța (p. 297).

●●● **Note**: At the airport, the porters who kindly carry your luggage to a taxi are commissioned by them!

● **By train.**
International trains (p. 303) from Western Europe, Hungary, Moscow, Istanbul or Sofia all connect at Bucharest north station, which is linked to the city centre by subway (p. 83). Certain trains (originating from Vienna and Budapest) pass through Cluj (p. 191), Târgu Mureș (p. 193), Brașov (p. 174) or Timișoara (p. 119).

● **By car.**
Romanian border checkpoints are open 24 hours a day (p. 313).

● **By bus.**
International coaches serve most Romanian cities, either directly or via other connections.

●●● See **regional address books**.

Currency exchange

You can buy *lei*, in banks and bureaux de change (casă de schimb or schimb valutar) in most towns. There are no standard opening hours but most establishments are open Mon.-Fri. 8am-4pm, some on Sat. There are cash machines and bureaux de change in the airport (bad rates). Major hotels offer a 24-hour bureau de change service, but commission is high. Don't try to exchange money on the black market in the street. It's against the law, without gain (same fees as the bureaux) and risky, dealers being renowned for pulling tricks on gullible tourists. In 1990, 2 *lei* bought 1 €, compared to 41,000 in 2003. Your pockets will not be big enough to stash all the notes and coins you will need.

●●● See **Money**, p. 307.

 Dining out

Romanians do not dine at specific times, they eat at any time, when they come home from work, before they go or, even during.

Breakfast are big while **lunch** is lighter to allow room hearty **dinner**.

In general, **restaurants** open late-morning. They serve non-stop throughout the day and late in the evening. You can get fixed menus that are a quick and cheaper option. There are pizzerias everywhere.

 Domestic transport

By car

Car is still the best means to get around remote areas of the country. Main roads are generally well-maintained, but secondary roads can be potholed and rough. Roadworks are not always fore-warned and local roads are often not surfaced at all.

● **Rules of the road.** The **speed limit** is reduced to 50 km/hr in urban areas, on major roads it is 80 km/hr and on motorways 90 km/hr. **Fines** are charged for speeding.

The legal blood-alcohol level is 0.00%!

● **Finding your way.** Road maps are on sale in petrol stations. An indispensable tool for travellers who like exploring by car is the *Atlas Turistic Rutier* (sold in petrol stations and bookshops), or one of the

---

holidays

● **January 1ˢᵗ and 2ⁿᵈ:** New Year.

● **March 1ˢᵗ:** Spring solstice. On this day, women are given flowers and small gifts.

● **Easter:** two days, the date varies depending on the calendar. In 2005: May 1ˢᵗ and 2ⁿᵈ, in 2006: April 23ʳᵈ and 24ᵗʰ.

● **May 1ˢᵗ:** May Day. This day is not universally celebrated: most Romanians work and, for the most part, shops are open.

● **December 1ˢᵗ:** National Holiday. This day celebrates the union of Romania declared in Alba Iulia in 1918 *(p. 50)*.

● **December 25ᵗʰ and 26ᵗʰ:** Christmas. ●

---

dozens of roadmaps of Romania which include city plans.

In order to navigate the network of roads, learning the **nomenclature** is important: **E** for European highway, **DN** *(drum naţional)* for a national motorway, **DJ** *(drum judeţean)* for a departmental road. *Drum nemodernizat:* non-surfaced track, *Drum forestier:* forest track, usually for private access only.

● **Fuel.** Fuel is cheap (about 25% cheaper than in Western Europe). You should have no problem finding unleaded petrol *(benzină fără plumb)*. You can also

---

find two standards of diesel *(motorină)*: diesel and *eurodiesel* (more refined and reliable for temperatures below -25°C; 77°F).

In cities, major petrol stations are open 24hr/24. For guaranteed quality choose the national brand, **PETROM**, or well-known international brands (such as **MIL** or **OMV**, which accept credit cards).

● **Precautions.** More than anywhere else, cars here are a symbol of virility! Watch out for arrogant manoeuvres.

Beware of carts on the roads too, especially at night as they often do not have lights! Drive carefully!

● **Maintenance.** Garages are commonplace. For small repairs, inventive mechanics *(inset p. 318)* can perform wonders. The majority of major European brands are available at dealers should you need a part replaced.

Secondary roads are muddy and dusty, major service-stations have **carwash** equipment. Certain garages offer a complete cleaning service of the interior and exterior.

● **Parking.** Car parks are few. Pay (expect € 0,2 per hour) on site.

● **Car hire.** The main car hire agencies have offices in some of the main cities (at airports or near to major hotels). Drivers must be over 21 and have held a valid license for more than a year. You will be asked for your passport number or identity card, as well as a security deposit (between

€ 250 and € 500). In Cluj (automobile delivery is possible anywhere in Romania), **Pan Travel** agency (p. 191) offers unbeatable deals for Dacias in perfect condition.

By plane

Tarom airlines (p. 304) offers daily flights from the capital to Cluj and Timişoara. Other main cities in the country are served two to three times per week (about € 80 per person for a one-way Bucharest-Cluj). The equipment is relatively new (ATR 42-500) and is maintained in excellent condition.

Tarom company agencies are available in major cities (see **regional address books**) and are open from Mon. to Fri. from 9am to 5pm. They also handle international bookings. Visit < www.tarom.ro >.

By train

A national institution, the **CFR** (Compania Naţională de Căi Ferate Române), pronounced "chefaerae", has an extensive network covering about 11,000 km (p. 17).

● **Information**. There is a CFR agency (agenţia de voiaj CFR) in most cities served by train. (open Mon. to Fri. from 7am to 7pm). A telephone service ☎ 952 gives information and time tables which are also available on their website: < www.cfr.ro >.

● **Connections**. Major cities are connected by **Intercity** trains (IC), or **Rapid** (R), as well as **Accelerated** trains (A). The intercity trains are fast and comfortable, and

have a restaurant car; however, they do not run on weekends.

On the regional level, **Personal** trains, the Romanian version of the local train, link cities in the same region, stopping in each village and sometimes in isolated stations in the countryside. Often crowded and very slow (about 30 km/hr, sometimes less), the Personal can be unbearable when they are packed in the height of summer and they are freezing (unheated) in winter… nevertheless this is the best way to immerse yourself in local colour especially on market or festival days.

● **Reserving and purchasing tickets**. Get your ticket at a CFR agency (see **regional address books**) or at the station ticket counters (casa de bilete).

RAPID. You will be issued with 2 tickets: the ticket for the trip, with carriage and seat number marked on the back, and the "*supliment de viteză*" ticket, but don't be misled by this false promise of speed! There are ticket counters for each class. In major train stations, the train number and destination are marked above the counters.

PERSONAL. No reservation necessary. Tickets can be bought just before you board or on the train.

●●● **Note**: When buying your ticket on the train, you may find yourself being offered a reduced price by the ticket inspector without giving you a ticket. Accept this offer at your own risk!

NIGHT TRAINS. Reserve in a CFR agency between 10 days to 24 hrs before travel. As well as your two train tickets you will be issued with a third "night train" ticket.

Night trains heading deep into the countryside have 1st class sleeping cars *(vagon de dormit)*. The prices are reasonable (about € 22 one-way Bucharest-Suceava, 450 km, 7 hours) for a cabin with two bunks. For a supplementary fee, you can reserve an entire cabin for one person.

In each car, train staff, or the conductor, will watch over the security and comfort of the passengers. Someone will pass among the cabins selling bottled water, beer, sodas and coffee in the morning. As soon as you board the train, your ticket will be taken and kept until you disembark.

In 2nd class, compartments have 6 beds.

By bus

Every city has a bus station *(autogară)*, often close to the railway station. Romania is well served by a vast network of reliable coach routes between cities within the country and abroad, there are daily buses to Istanbul from Bucharest for example, for approximately € 45 a return trip.

At the *autogară*, you can find information on destinations and timetables. For a reasonable fee (about € 17 from Suceava to Cluj for example), coaches are a comfortable way to travel. Local buses are not well-kept, nor are their emissions standards on a par with western Europe. However, this practical service is beginning to disappear little by little and is being replaced by 15-seat mini-coaches (referred to as *maxitaxis* in cities), which provide shuttle links between provincial areas and Bucharest. Generally, such services wait for clients near railway stations, bazaars or city exits and leave as soon as the seats are filled.

By boat

A common mode of transport on the Danube *(see inset p. 294)*, from Tulcea to the mouth of the river: Periprava, Sfântu Gheorghe and Sulina. Ferries make trips in the Danube from Calafat to Vidin. There are also organised cruises which depart from Vienna and Budapest and sail to the Black Sea.

Emergencies

Police ☎ 955.
Fire Department ☎ 981.
Complaints: Ministry of Tourism ☎ 021-410.12.95.
Telegrams ☎ 957.
Medical Emergencies: ambulance ☎ 961; emergency doctor ☎ 975.

Festivals & holidays

Most holidays coincide with the religious calendar *(p. 33)*. The **Orthodox calendar** is still followed: it is actually against the law to work on Sundays and some other designated holidays. There are many local festivals, organised by towns or villages but national festivals are rare.

In the countryside, agro-pastoral festivals are a cause for great celebration.

Equally Romanians of other faiths (Muslim, Judiasm, etc) follow their own traditions.

Health

You are unlikely to return from your trip with a bug, but taking certain precautions is advisable.

Each city has a well-equipped hospital *(spital)* and pharmacy *(farmacia)*.

In rural areas, basic health care can be administered at a clinic *(dispensar)*. Clinic staff are well-trained and often multi-lingual.

● **Beware of ticks**.... Be careful when spending time in forest areas: avoid lounging on the ground, it is advisable to wear socks and check your skin from time to time. In the case of a suspect tick, seek medical advice within 24 hours; a doctor can identify and remove ticks safely. The ticks in question are found all over Central Europe, from the Vosges to

Russia and beyond. There is little risk: only one *caepuşœ* out of 70,000 is infected with Encephalitis, and cases of Lyme's disease, for which there is no vaccination as of yet, are even rarer.

● **... and mosquitoes**. In the Danube delta, the Banat and on the Wallachian or Moldavian plains, mosquitoes can be infected with minor viruses, but do not spread serious illness. To avoid being bitten, wear a repellent (p. 309).

● **Hospital Risks**. Even if doctors are well-trained, hygiene standards in hospitals leave a lot to be desired. It is best to avoid them completely... and obtain a good health insurance that will pay for you to get back to your home country if the case arises (p. 308). If you are in dire need of emergency treatment, try at least to avoid blood transfusions.

● **Drinking water**. Avoid drinking tap water and stick to bottled mineral water, which is becoming standard in most restaurants. Bottled water can be found in most shops.

● **Food**. Be wary of processed sausages and canned meats: food manufacture is poorly regulated, and in any case, they are practically inedible. To avoid gastro-intestinal infections be wary of *mititei* (small grilled sausages) prepared in open-air bazaars, along highways in markets, or even in restaurants as they are often served undercooked.

● **Emergency services**. Each village usually has one resident doctor and community clinic. Major cities have hospitals and private clinics as well as several pharmacies, some of which are open 24 hrs/24 (p. 312).

●●● See **Sanitary precautions**, p. 308.

Hotels and guesthouses

Hotels

Classification for hotels follows the star-rating system, from one to five. The hotel industry is slowly rising to meet European standards. Deluxe 5-star hotels in Bucharest, for example, will be well equipped (p. 83). Some one- and two-star hotels, fortunately less and less so, have shockingly low standards of cleanliness, service and water works. In Bucharest, expect to pay between € 120 and € 390 for a double room in a four or five star hotel (▲▲▲▲), € 35 to € 210 in a three-star hotel (▲▲▲); and € 30 to € 95 in a two-star hotel (▲▲). Outside of the city, you can expect to be able to reduce this amount by about 10 to 30 %.

You should **reserve** well in advance of arrival, especially in Bucharest. The majority of hotels now have e-mail addresses and often staff will speak several foreign languages.

●●● See **regional address books** or go to < www.cazari.ro > and < www.hotels.ro >.

Motels and guesthouses

These establishments, with 4 to 20 rooms, have been appearing in recent years, mostly near big cities, on major motorways and near tourist sites. The quality varies greatly, but on the whole, this is a cheap and reliable option (from € 20 for bed and breakfast).

In a *cabană*

Mainly found in the mountains, these are great bases for hiking in the wilds. Cabins may be dirty and uncomfortable, but the scenery usually makes up for it. Prices vary according to comfort: between € 3.5 a night in a mountain refuge to € 45 for a room in a chalet.

Home stays

Through chance encounters or word-of-mouth, you might be able to find a room in a Romanian's private home. People in the outer-regions of Romania are more hospitable and are more likely to open their doors to a visitor. This is, on the whole, a rich experience as hosts are often very friendly (p. 20). The minister of tourism has established a ranking system from one to three "daisies". A 1-daisy establishment means washing facilities can be basic (but functional), sometimes the lavatory is in the garden; 2 daisies indicates a good level of washing facility (shared bathroom) and level 3 means there will be en-suite bathrooms in every room.

The cost of a **bed and breakfast** with en-suite bathroom and WC varies between € 11 to € 22 per person, the more expensive does not necessarily mean the highest quality. Certain homes give the price of a room (e.g. € 11 for two people) and count breakfast and dinner

loss or theft

Should you lose your passport or have it stolen, you must take the following steps: make a declaration of theft or loss at the nearest police station. With this document and three passport-sized photos, go to your country's embassy consulate in Bucharest to demand a replacement and an emergency temporary pass. The consulate will inform you of the steps necessary to complete the process.

Take the precaution of keeping a photocopy of your passport. ●

separately (expect to pay between € 3.5 and € 5) .

●●● **A good idea**: Many monasteries offer lodging to travellers at fairly reasonable prices *(p. 118 and 271)*.

Floating hotels

Along the main banks of the Danube delta *(inset p. 294 and p. 296)*, you can stay the night on a barge that has been transformed into a hotel *(ponton dormitor)*. This is a unique but sometimes fairly expensive option (€ 50 to € 90 per day with full board).

Caravaning

There are lots of farmland areas and forest clearings where you can park up. To find the best spots, often it's enough to ask around, especially hotel owners, who will gladly give you addresses in the local area. People living in the countryside are often happy to let you park on

their land for a night or two. Here, your vehicle will be safe, allowing you to further explore on foot. It is polite to have meals in the owner's home (it will be suggested by your hosts). Also, you may be able to use their bathroom if they have one. Even if the owners ask for nothing in return, you should give a donation: € 2 per person for a night, € 3 to € 4 for dinner and breakfast, € 1 for use of their bathroom facilities *(see regional address books)*.

Camping

Open-air camping is not regulated, apart from few protected areas such as the Danube delta. It is possible to **camp on a farm** (same rules as for caravaning).

Romania used to have an excellent network of camp sites *(popaș)*; unfortunately, few have remained in good condition. Though communal bathroom facilities leave something to be desired, these campgrounds have wooden cabins *(căsuță;* plural: *căsuțe)* with two beds which means you do not need a tent. When they are clean, this can be a really picturesque and cheap option (€ 2 to € 3.5 per night). Certain sites have developed into quality holiday villages with all services and conveniences *(p. 118)*.

You can get camp site maps in tourist offices in most countries, although they are often incomplete. *(p. 302)*.

●●● See **Hotels and guesthouses** p. 310 and **regional address books**.

Internet

Cybercafés are found in all cities. Prices shouldn't exceed € 1 per hour in Bucharest, € 0.5 in the countryside.

Language

Romanian is the national language which all citizens must understand and speak *(see Language guide p. 329)*.

Each minority, however, has the right to speak their own dialect. Certain languages are even taught in school (Hungarian, Romanès, German, Polish, Ukrainian, Russian, etc) alongside the obligatory Romanian.

French, the former second language of choice for Romanians, is still spoken despite an increase in the use of **English** by younger generations drawn by the language and culture of anglophone countries. Subtitled American television series have been introduced into the Romanian home. **German** is still widely spoken in Transylvania.

Local time

Romania is two hours ahead of GMT. At 2pm local time in Bucharest, it is noon in London.

Opening hours

● **Banks**.
Mon.-Fri. 8.30am-3pm (sometimes 5pm); certain banks open on Sat. from 8.30am to noon (Bank Post, Bancă Comercială Română).

transport

Vulcanizare

This word is indispensable for anyone considering making a voyage by car in Romania: it designates the tiny repair workshops where breakdowns or flat tyres can be fixed in record time. Rough, unsurfaced roads, loose horseshoe nails, bald tyres and patched-up inner tubes mean these mechanics, who set up shop on highway verges, are never out of work. They make their presence known by a roadside sign which may be a tyre tacked to a tree or propped on a pot. In these Ali Baba-style shacks, the walls are covered with cover-girl posters, calendars and, of course, religious images. Each customer here receives equally attentive treatment from the grease-covered mechanic, he will take as much time and care over the businessman's Mercedes as he will fixing the farmer's cartwheel. •

● **Administrative offices**.
Mon.-Fri. 8am-4pm; on Fridays, offices often close after midday.

● **Shops**.
In the city, many small food shops stay open 24 hours a day (marked on windows "non-stop"). In the countryside, there are no standard hours, owners often living above or just nearby to the shop. Supermarkets are open Mon.-Fri. 8am-9pm; Sat. 8am-6pm. In the city, shops are open Mon.-Fri. 9am-6pm; sometimes Sat. morning.

● **Museums**.
Most museums are open every day except Mon., generally 9am-5pm. For smaller museums, hours are less predictable.

● **Pharmacies**.
Opening hours vary greatly. However, in major cities, the main pharmacy (or n° 1) is open either 24 hrs a day ("non-stop") or daily from 7am-9pm. Other pharmacies: Mon.-Fri. 8am-8pm, Sat-Sun. 8am-4pm.

● **Post offices**.
In major cities: Mon.-Fri. 8am-8pm, Sat. 8am-noon,
closed Sun. Note: the telephone *(Romtelecom, p. 315)* and the post *(Poştă româna)* are two separate services, administrated by different companies, even if they often share the same office.

● **Frontier post offices**.
Open 24 hrs/24.

● **Petrol stations**.
In all cities, there will be at least one 24-hr petrol station ("non-stop"). Stations often have mini-markets selling food and drinks.

 ## Post

● **Stamps**.
Stamps can be bought in all post offices. Allow 3 to 12 days for post to go between Romania and Western Europe; a letter will cost about € 0.40 to send. Allow approximately 10 days for a letter to reach North America, which costs around € 0.80.

● **Express mail**.
Expedited mail services, such as DHL, have offices in Bucharest and in most big towns.

 ## Security

Romania is a safe country, the proof of which, as always, is the lack of visible police presence. However, you should be wary of pick-pockets at airports, in markets and bazaars, in stations and on public transport. Also, credit card fraud is becoming more widespread; watch out when withdrawing cash from cash machines in the street. Verify credit card print-outs and the total being charged before signing a bill. Always keep these in case of a dispute or in case of loss or theft *(inset p. 308)*.

 ## Sports and leisure

Romania offers countless outdoor sporting activities.

● **Hiking**.
It's not always easy when you find yourself alone on a poorly-marked trail. Some travel agencies at home and in Romania *(p. 307)* organise walking holidays for beginners to intermediates, with itineraries that will take

you to the heart of rural life and will point out that sites of cultural interest along your way.

● Caving.
For all you need to know about speleology in Romania, contact: Cristian Ciubotarescu at the Sfinx association, Gârda de Sus (p. 143) ☎ 0744-331.672 <cristigarda@yahoo.com>.

● Winter Sports.
The Carpathian mountains are home to some quality ski resorts much less expensive than in Western Europe. Resorts offer good range of services and accommodation (see *regional address books*).

Telephone

Use

● Telephoning Romania from abroad.
Dial 00.40, then the department code and the corresponding number (6 digits in provincial areas, 7 in Bucharest). For example, if you are calling someone in the province of Alba dial: 00.40.258 followed by the 6 digits of their number.

● From Romania.
Dial 00 followed by the country code (44 for Britain, 1 for the United States and Canada).

● In Romania.
Dial the department code and the 6 digits of your correspondent. If you are calling within the same department, dial the 6 digits of your correspondent.

Public Telephones
In each major city there is an official Romtelecom

office (open Mon.-Fri. 6am-8pm, Sun. 8am-1pm). In smaller cities and villages, service is more limited (closed Sat.-Sun.).

Public telephone booths are attached to walls and take orange-coloured phone cards sold at Romtelecom outlets.

The cost of a one minute call from a booth or land line is about € 0.50 (to Western Europe) to € 0.60 (to the USA and Canada).

Romtelecom phone cards (cartelă telefonică) are sold in Romtelecom outlets, at post offices and in kiosks bearing the Romtelecom logo.

If you wish to call abroad, a card with 150,000 lei lasts about six minutes. Note that for international calls, the card must be charged with at least 500,000 lei.

Mobile phones
The *mobil* is widely used, thanks, for the most part, to a good coverage by different service providers. If you subscribe to international roaming services before you leave, you should be able to use your mobile.

A Romanian mobile phone call is billed at the same rate as a local call. However, calls abroad are costly. Also keep in mind that when you receive phone calls from abroad, you will still be paying approximately half the cost of the call.

If, during your stay, you wish to use a Romanian mobile network you can buy a phone card on the Orange network in kiosks

bearing the Orange logo (news stands, telephone boutiques, etc.). There are several cards to choose from, from about € 12 to € 35.

Tipping

It is not in the culture to tip, and is not expected, but don't let that stop you if you are pleased with service…

Toilets

Avoid public toilets unless they are paying ones.

In the city, restaurant and café toilets will not always be clean.

In the countryside, despite great development in plumbing networks, you may find yourself confronted with an outhouse loo at the bottom of a garden or in a field, which, at least, contributes to the ecosystem!

Tourist information

With some exceptions (see *regional address books*), public tourist information does not really exist. This kind of information is often given out by agencies in hotels or private establishments which call themselves "information offices" but are actually quite limited and unreliable.

Websites (inset p. 312) are a good alternative.

If you are staying in a guesthouse, the staff will probably offer good local information. ●

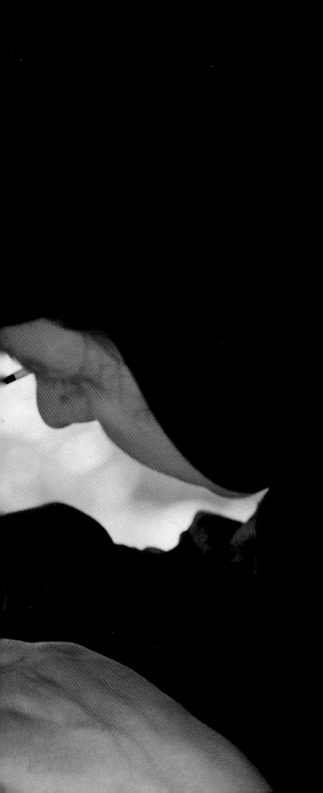

Important dates in Romanian history

Antiquity

Around 1000 BC The Geto-Dacians, descendants of Thracians, settle between the Carpathians and the Danube.

Mid-7th century BC Greek colonists settle along the Black Sea coast *(p. 288)*.

87-106 Reign of Decebal, King of the Dacians.

Roman Dacia

101-106 The Emperor Trajan conquers Dacia, which becomes a province of the Roman Empire.

271-272 The Roman Empire withdraws from Dacia under pressure from barbarian invasions.

Romanian Principalities

4th-6th century Invasions of Huns, Gepidae, Avars, Goths and Slavs *(p.39)*.

9th century The Magyars arrive in Transylvania.

11th-13th century Invasions of Pechenegs and Cumans.

Around 1150 Germanic settlers arrive in Transylvania.

1241 Mongolian invasion.

Around 1324 Basarab I founds the Principality of Wallachia.

1359 The Principality of Moldavia is founded by Dragoş, prince of Maramureş *(p. 222)*.

1395 The Ottomans take control of Wallachia *(p. 41)*.

1441-1456 Iancu of Hunedoara reigns in Transylvania *(see inset p. 137)*.

1456-1462 Vlad Tepes, prince of Wallachia *(see inset p. 43)*.

1457-1504 Stephen the Great reigns in Moldavia.

1541 After the Hungarian defeat by the Ottomans at Mohacs (1526), Transylvania becomes a vassal of Istanbul.

1600 The short-lived union between Wallachia, Moldavia, and Transylvania during the reign of Michael the Brave.

1688-1714 Constantin Brâncoveanu reigns in Wallachia *(p. 102)*.

1697 A portion of the Romanian Orthodox Church joins the Uniate Church.

1699 The Ottomans lose Hungary and Transylvania to the Austrians (Karlowitz Treaty).

1711-1821 In Wallachia and Moldavia, Phanariot regime, princes of Greek origin, installed by the Ottomans *(p. 45)*.

From 1718 Swabian colonists settle in the Banat (Banater Schwaben).

1775 Bucovina is annexed by Austria.

1784 Peasant uprising in the Apuseni *(see inset p. 135)*.

1812 Bessarabia is annexed by Russia.

1821 The Pandors uprising led by Tudor Vladimirescu.

1829-1856 The Treaty of Adrianople (1829) establishes a Russian protectorate over Wallachia and Moldavia.

Independence

1848 Revolutionary activity in Moldavia and Wallachia quelled by the Russians and Ottomans. In Transylvania: support for the insurrection against the Habsburgs followed by a violent reaction against the Hungarians who wanted to annex the province.

1859 The representative assemblies of both Principalities elect Alexandru Cuza as leader. Union is formed.

1866 The Union of the Principalities becomes Romania.

1878 Romania becomes independent and the Ottoman empire cedes Dobrogea (Berlin congress).

1881 Charles Hohenzollern-Sigmaringen becomes King Carol I, the first Romanian king.

1907 Peasants' revolts violently suppressed.

1914 Ferdinand I, King of Romania.

1916 Romania takes part in the war on the side of the Allies.

December 1st 1918 At Alba Iulia, Romanians from Transylvania and Banat vote for the re-unification of their province with Romania *(p. 50)*.

1919-1920 As a result of the Treaties of Saint-Germain, Neuilly and Trianon, the regions of Bucovina, Southern Dobrogea, Transylvania, Crişana, Maramureş and Northern Banat become part of Romania.

A struggle for the Kingdom of Romania

1925 Patriarchate of Bucharest created.

1930 Carol II's accession to the throne (see inset below). Corneliu Codreanu creates the Iron Guard, a fascist and anti-semitic political movement.

1938 King Carol II proclaims a royal dictatorship and eliminates Codreanu.

1939 Romania proclaims its neutrality at the beginning of World War II.

1940 The country is carved up according to the German-Soviet secret pact. June: northern Bucovina and Bessarabia are annexed by the USSR. August: The Germans yield the north of Transylvania to admiral Horthy of fascist Hungary. September: Carol II calls General Antonescu, a fascist sympathiser, to power and abdicates in favour of his son Michael.

June 1941 Romania joins the war, helping the Nazis in their offensive against Russia.

August 1944 The Soviet Army invades Romania; King Michael arrests Antenescu and declares war against Germany and Hungary.

Communist Romania

1945-1946 The USSR integrates northern Bucovina into the Ukraine and annexes Bessarabia, which becomes the Socialist Soviet Republic of Moldavia. The south of Dobrogea is returned to Bulgaria. Romania reclaims the part of Transylvania annexed by Hungary in 1940. A coalition government led by Petru Groza, pro-communist head of the Ploughmen's Front, comes to power.

1947 The monarchy is abolished and King Michael is forced into exile. The opposition parties are systematically eliminated.

December 1947 Proclamation of the Romanian People's Republic with a constitution modelled on the Soviet version.

March 1948 The Communists take power.

1949-1952 Collectivisation of agriculture; development of heavy industries .

1952 Gheorghiu-Dej replaces Petru Groza as head of government. Repressive purges follow.

1955 Romania adheres to the Warsaw Pact. Nicolae Ceauşescu (1918-1989) joins the Communist Party's Political Office.

The escapades of King Carol II

© Photothèque Hachette

Scandal in the Romanian court: in August 1918, Carol, the heir apparent, hides in Odessa in order to marry a certain Zizi Lambrino who bears him a son in 1920. The royal court refuses to accept the liaison and annuls the marriage. Carol submits and, conforming to his parents' wishes, marries Helen of Greece. Their son Michael is born in 1921. But a new scandal erupts: Carol falls in love with Elena Lupescu-Wolf, the granddaughter of a Bessarabian rabbi. In Paris, where the two lovers take refuge, he tells his father, King Ferdinand, that he renounces the throne. In 1927, when the King passes on, the crown thus goes to his grandson Michael. Carol , however, returns from exile in 1930 to recover the throne. Despite his royal undertakings, he sends for his mistress and Queen Helen is forced to leave. In 1940, having returned the crown to Michael, he leaves Romania for new adventures. The couple seeks asylum in Latin America, then in Portugal. At his death, Carol is buried in Lisbon. His remains are eventually transferred to Romania in 2003. ●

development

The European Union

Started in 1993 with an agreement of association, the process of Romania's acceptance into the European Union could lead to her being admitted by January 1st 2007, at the same time as Bulgaria. Since the end of 2000, the government of Prime Minister Adrian Nastase, has introduced a series of pragmatic measures with encouraging results: GNP has grown from 1.5% in 1993 to 5.3% in 2001 while inflation has decreased from 256% in 1993 to 34.5% in 2001. Thorough structural reforms due to harmonisation with European standards and industrial restructuring are underway with financial support from the European Union and international bodies such as the World Bank and the IMF. The State is progressively demantling the nationalised sector (40% in 1999, down from 74% in 1992) in favour of an expansion into a more liberal market-based economy.

The EU is therefore preparing to welcome an country vital for regional stability . Romania is seventh in Europe in terms of population (22.5 million inhabitants). •

1958 Soviet occupation army leaves Romanian territory. The government distances itself from Moscow. Gheorghiu-Dej calls on patriotic ardour and gives the signal for a "Romanianisation" of the party. Political prisoners start to be released and trade with the West increases.

1965 Death of Gheorghiu-Dej. The party's central committee designates Ceauşescu as his successor.

May 1968 Romania refuses to participate in the Soviet-led invasion of Czechoslovakia.

1974 Ceauşescu creates the position of president of the republic and appoints himself as such.

1980 Ceauşescu appoints his wife Elena as Vice Prime-Minister.

1987 Ceauşescu's son becomes minister for Youth. November: riots at the Braşov factories repressed (p. 171).

1989 While the communist regimes collapse in Eastern Europe, communist power in Romania is strengthened. November: during the 14th Congress of the Romanian Communist Party, Ceauşescu is massively re-elected. December: the Timişoara riots spread to Bucharest. Dec 22: Ceauşescu decrees a state of urgency. Dec 25: Ceauşescu and his wife are tried and executed.

The return of democracy

May 1990 The National Salvation Front wins the first free democratic elections; Ion Iliescu is elected president and appoints Petre Roman as Prime Minister.

1991 Property laws lead to the return of lands to their former owners.

1992 Re-elected, Ion Iliescu appoints Nicolae Vacaroiu as Prime Minister.

1993 Protests against the government. Romania is admitted into the Council of Europe.

September 1996 Treaty between Romania and Hungary guarantees the inviolability of their borders and the rights of minority groups in each country. November: legislative and presidential elections. The opposition wins. Emil Constantinescu is elected as president and Victor Ciorbea is appointed Prime Minister.

1999 Beginning of negotiations to enter the European Union.

2000 Ion Iliescu returns to power, Adrian Nastase is appointed as Prime Minister.

2002 Romania is admitted to NATO.

2003 Carol II's remains are returned to Romania (see inset p.321). October: revision of the Constitution to adapt to the demands of NATO and the European Union (see inset above). •

Books, CD's and films

Romanian literature is rarely translated and sadly, great names such as Mihai Eminescu and Ion Creanga remain unknown to an international public.

Stories, essays and novels

● **CARTARESCU**, Mihai, *Orbitor*, Gallimard, 2002. Often compared to Kafka or Borges, this novelist "writes about the quiet inhumanity of things" with irony.

● **CIORAN**, Emil, *On the Heights of Despair*, Chicago University Press, 1987.

● **ELIADE**, Mircea, *Le Roman de l'adolescent myope*, Actes Sud, 1996. A philosopher and historian who has left a few autobiographical texts and novels *(p. 325)*.

● **GHEORGHIU**, Virgil, *Les Immortels d'Agapia*, Gallimard, 1998 *(see inset p. 325)*.

● **GOMA**, Paul, *Gherla*, Gallimard, 1976. The bestial universe of political prisoners in the 1950's.

● **ISTRATI**, Panaït, *Les Chardons du Baragan*, Grasset, 2003.

● **MÜLLER**, Herta, *The Appointment*, Metropolitan Books, 2001. German writer originally from Banat, who relates her experience of the dictatorship, humiliation and fear.

● **REZZORI**, von Gregor, *Snows of Yesteryear*, Vintage, 1991. Austro-Italo-Romanian writer (1914-1999) who evokes his childhood in Bucovina ruined by the Hapsburg empire.

● **MIHAI**, Sebastian, *Journal 1935-1944: The Fascist Years*, Ivan R. Dee Inc, 2000.

Poetry and theatre

● **CELAN**, Paul, *Selected Poems and Prose of Paul Celan*, W.W Norton & Co. 2001.

● **IONESCO**, Eugène, *Rhinoceros and other plays*, Grove Press, 1969.

● **OVID**, *Sorrows of Exile*: *Tristia*, Clarendon Pr, 1992.

● **VISNIEC**, Matei, *Théâtre décomposé, ou l'homme poubelle*, L'Harmattan, 1996.

Travel texts

● **FERNANDEZ**, Dominique, *Romanian Rhapsody: An overlooked Corner of Europe*, Algora Pub, 2000.

● **LEIGH FERMOR**, Patrick, *Between the Woods and the Water*, Penguin, 1987.

● **LONDRES**, Albert, *Le Juif errant est arrivé*, Le Serpent à Plumes, 1998.

● **MAGRIS**, Claudio, *Danube*, Vintage, 1989.

History

● **DURANDIN**, Catherine, *Histoire des Roumains*, Fayard, 1995.

● **GILLET**, Olivier, *Religion et Nationalisme. L'idéologie de l'Église orthodoxe roumaine sous le régime communiste*, Éd. de l'Université de Bruxelles, 1997.

● **IOANID**, Radu, *La Roumanie et la Shoah*, Maison des sciences de l'homme, 2002.

● **LE BRETON**, Jean-Marie, *La Fin de Ceauşescu. Histoire d'une révolution*, L'Harmattan, 1996.

Art, culture and society

● **CUISENIER**, Jean, *Mémoires des Carpathes*, Plon coll. Terre Humaine, 2000.

● **DURANDIN**, Catherine, *La Roumanie, un piège ?*, Hesse, 2000.

● **NITESCO**, Sanda, *Un brin d'aneth et de ciel bleu. Imprécis de cuisine roumaine*, L'Harmattan, 2000.

● **PACHET**, Pierre, *Conversations à Jassy*, Maurice Nadeau, 1997.

● **TABARD**, Marielle, *Brancusi, L'inventeur de la sculpture moderne*, Gallimard, coll. Découvertes, 1995.

Classical music

● **ENESCO** George, *Oedipus* (with Lawrence Foster, Barbara Hendricks, Jose Van Dam), Emi classics, 1990. The Greatest Romanian Composer's Masterpiece unjustly unknown.

● **LIPATTI**, Dinu, Sonates for piano: pieces by Chopin, Enescu, Ravel and Liszt, Emi classics, 2001 *(see inset p. 326)*.

● **G**HEORGHIU, Angela, **Tosca**, DVD Emi classics, 2001. Music from Benoit Jacquot's film, from Puccini's piece (with Roberto Alagna and Antonio Pappano).

Traditional music

No other European country holds such a rich and lively music.

● **F**ANFARE **C**IOCÂRLA, Radio Pascani, Piranha, 2000 (see inset p. 249).

● **G**UTSA, Nicolae, Today's great gypsy voice, Silva Screen, 1996. The gypsy idol and her unique style are inspired from the Banat tradition to invent new musical forms at times extraordinary at times less so.

● **N**ETI **S**ANDOR **F**ODOr, **Popular Hungarian music from Transylvania**, Hungaroton, 1999. A wonderful man and a fabulous violinist undiscovered in his own country.

● **Marriage music from Maramureş**, Ocora, Harmonia Mundi, 1993.

● **T**ARAF DE **H**AÏDOUKS, **Dumbala dumba**, Wagram, 1999. An international star, the dizzying "lautari" musicians from the Clejani village have developed a repertoire destined to seduce western audiences.

Films

● **P**INTILLÉ, Lucian, **The Cedar**, DVD, mk2 (p. 326).

● **G**ATLIF, Tony, **Gadjo Dilo**, DVD. ●

Famous Romanians

● **Brâncusi**, Constantin. Sculptor of Romanian origin (Pertisani 1876-Paris 1957); he frequented Max Jacob in Paris, Apollinaire, Picasso, Modigliani... Influenced by the peasant world of his childhood in Oltenia, he progressively abandoned naturalistic representation in favour of primordial forms with symbolic value.

● **Brassaï**. Naturalised French, the photographer Halasz Gulya (1899-1984) was connected with Paris and the surrealists whose strangeness he captured on film. Brassaï came from Braşov (Brassò in Hungarian), hence the pseudonym.

● **Brauner**, Victor. Born at Piatra Neamţ in Moldavia in 1903, he grew up with a father fascinated by the occult. Linked to the surrealists as early as 1932, he settled in France in 1938. Considered as one of the great surrealist painters, he translated dreams into images, mixing human, animal and vegetable before tapping into primitive art. He died in Paris in 1966.

● **Caragiale**, Ion Luca. (1852-1912) A monument of Romanian theatre. He observed and mocked with remarkable finesse the Balkano-Romanian petty bourgeoisie: rogue lawyers, bureaucrats, journalists, politicians, demagogues and arrivistes. Though his comedies are vignettes of the mores of his time, they also have a universal and timeless appeal. Still regularly performed, his plays are often adapted for the television.

● **Celan**, Paul. Born in 1920 at Cernăuţi (Czernowitz), he took part in the tragic destiny of Bucovina, wiped out by the madness of war: "It was a place where men and books lived". He arrived in Paris in 1948. He is one of the great poets of the 20th century. He wrote in German, the language of the Jews from Bucovina and also the language of death. In 1970, he threw himself into the Seine.

● **Celibidache**, Sergiu. One of the world's greatest conductors. He studied music and philosophy at Bucharest and then in Berlin where, in 1946, he became the conductor of the Berlin Philharmonic before handing over to Herbert von Karajan in 1954. He went on to work with La Scala in Milan, the French National Orchestra and the Munich Philharmonic. A rigorous perfectionist, he made precious few recordings which, along with a strong personality has given him a near legendary status.

● **Cioran**, Emil. Born at Raşinari (*p. 147*) in 1911, he settled in France in 1937 where he died in 1995. He scathingly attacked "doctrines, ideologies and bloody farces" and the derisory destiny of man and of his illusions. His books include *A Short History of Decomposition* and *Tears and Saints*.

● **Comaneci**, Nadia. Five medals of which three gold at the Montreal Olympics and four medals at the Moscow Olympics: a gymnast prodigy. Born in Oneşti in Moldavia in 1961.

● **Eliade**, Mircea. (1907-1986) A historian of religious studies, an anti-semite and fervent nationalist in Romania between the two world wars.

● **Enescu**, George. Born in 1881 near Botoşani in Moldavia, Enescu was a violinist before becoming a great composer (*Romanian Rhapsodies*, several works for strings, the opera *Oedipus*). He exiled himself to Paris in 1945 where he died in 1955.

● **Fondane**, Benjamin. Writer and poet, born Benjamin Wechsler in 1898 at Iaşi. He emigrated to Paris in 1923 where he continued to write in French. He died in Auschwitz in 1944.

● **Gheorghiu**, Angela. Since making her name and international reputation at Covent Garden in 1992, this soprano has become one of the greatest divas of our time. Two of her best recordings are *La Traviata* and *Tosca* (*p. 324*) accompanied by the tenor, Roberto Alagna, also her husband. She was born in Adjud in Moldavia in 1965.

● **Gheorghiu**, Virgil. Writer. (Războieni Neamţ 1916-Paris 1992) Little published in English, Gheorghiu is best known for the film version of his novel *The Twenty-fifth Hour* directed by Henry Verneuil. An anti-communist, he was exiled to France in 1948 and became an Orthodox priest in 1963. Accused of anti-semitism in some of his earliest texts, which he only indirectly denies, this writer with an astonishing style remains a complex and controversial personality.

● **Goma**, Paul. Writer born in Bessarabia in 1935. His work is inspired by his personal experience in communist prisons (*p. 323*) and of his aversion to the regime. He has lived in Paris since 1977.

● **Hagi**, Gheorghe. Footballing genius, one of the world's best players of his generation. Hagi was born in 1965.

● **IONESCO**, Eugène. (1909-1994) A French playwright of Romanian descent who developed a "theatre of the absurd" which denounces and mocks conventions, drawing on the impotence of a humanity which is both painful and entangled in the apocalyptic historical context of the aftermath of the Second World War.

● **ISTRATI**, Panaït. Writer (1884-1835). The son of a Greek smuggler and a Romanian washerwoman, he spent his childhood between his mother's village and the great port of the Danube. A life of wandering lead him to France where his storytelling talents were discovered by Romain Rolland. In 1924, he published *Kyra Kyralina*. He became passionately involved in the communist movement before denouncing its abuses in *Vers l'autre flamme* (To the Other Flame) in 1929. Considered as a red agitator by the reactionaries and as a reactionary by the left, Istrati died of tuberculosis in Bucharest in 1935. Spontaneous, generous and full of verve, he is, above all, a great storyteller worthy of the eastern tradition. Undiscovered in his country of birth, he is, for many, one of the greatest Romanian writers.

● **LIPATTI**, Dinu. The spiritual son of George Enescu *(p.96)*, of a precocious talent and great sensibility, Dinu Lipatti (1917-1950) blossomed, first on the violin then on the piano which he studied in Bucharest. Before the Second World War, his renown spread throughout Europe. His audiences were enraptured by his interpretations of Bach, Chopin, Schumann, Schubert, Ravel and George Enescu. At the end of the War, he left Romania to settle in Geneva. On 16 September 1950 at Besançon, he gave his last recital, playing Chopin, Mozart, Bach and Schubert; the concert was recorded and continues to captivate to this day. On 2 December he died of leukaemia. He was only 33.

● **LUCA**, Gherasim. Surrealist poet, born in 1913 in the Jewish quarter of Bucharest. In 1952, Salman Locker (his real name) escaped to Paris. A friend of André Breton and Victor Brauner, this spellbinding personality, always dressed in black, remained a solitary and a rebel. His books are rare but explosive. He gave recitals where his mere presence left the audience in shock and awe. Like his friend Paul Celan, he ended his life by throwing himself into the Seine in 1994.

● **MÜLLER**, Herta. Writer born in 1953 in Banat, a member of the Swabian minority *(see inset p. 110)*. She has lived in Berlin since 1987. Her works recount the horror of daily life during the dictatorship.

● **NASTASE**, Ilie. Born in 1946, one of the heroes of international tennis in the 1970s (best player in 1973). Known and loved by those who had the chance to see him for his humour, non-conformism and talent on the tennis court.

● **NAUM**, Gellu. Surrealist poet (1915-2001). His masterpiece is a long prose poem, *Zenobia*.

● **NOAILLES**, Anna de. (1876-1933) Born princess Brâncoveanu, the countess of Noailles spent her entire life in France where she made a name for herself as a poet.

● **OBERTH**, Hermann (Sibiu-1894, Nuremberg-1989). Pioneer of space travel, he was one of the originators, along with Wernher von Braun, of the German V-2 flying bomb and later worked on the US space program which led to man's first visit to the moon.

● **PINTILLÉ**, Lucian. The most famous Romanian filmmaker (born in 1933).

● **REZZORI**, (von) Gregor. Writer (in German), born in 1914 in Czernowitz, in the mythical Bucovina which haunts much of his work.

● **ŢIRIAC**, Ion. Born in 1939, tennis player then partner and manager of Ilie Nastase. After 1990, his dynamic personality has played a key role in Romania's economy.

● **TZARA**, Tristan. Dadaist writer, born in Moineşti, Moldavia, in 1896, died in Paris in 1963.

● **VISNIEC**, Matei. Born in 1956 at Rădăuţi, Bukovina; has lived in Paris since 1987; writer and theater director.

● **WEISSMULLER**, Johnny. Actor. (1904-1984) Tarzan was born in Timişoara!

● **WIESEL**, Elie. American francophone writer, born in Sighetu Marmaţiei *(p. 201)* in 1928; wrote *The Night*, a memoir of his experiences at Auschwitz; Nobel Peace Prize (1986); founded the Elie Wiesel Foundation for Humanity. ●

Glossary

● **The Akathist Hymn** (from the Greek "not sitting"). A hymn is a sung prayer. Akathist means that one has to remain standing during the hymn. (*See p.228*).

● **Autocephalus** (from the Greek "who has his own head"). Designates the independence of the Russian, Bulgarian, Serb and Romanian Churches.

● **The boyars.** High ranking nobles in Slavonic countries, particularly Russia.

● **The Calendar.** The Orthodox Churches use both the Julian (ancient) and the Gregorian (new) calendars. Today, the Julian calendar is thirteen days behind the Gregorian one.

● **The Chamber of Tombs.** A room in the princely churches of Moldavia, between the naos and the pronaos, where the sepulchres of the church's founders are placed.

● **Council** (from the Latin *concilium*: "assembly"). Meeting of all the bishops. The first Council met in Jerusalem, around 50 AD. Councils decide dogma: the incontestable truths in matters of faith, liturgy or the evolution of Christianity in history. A Synod differs from a Council in that the former applies to a meeting of bishops on a strictly regional or national scale.

● **Deicis** (from the Greek "prayer, intercession"). The intercession of the church for the salvation of the world. The icon of the Deicis is often portrayed on top of the central door of the iconostasis: it shows Christ enthroned, with Mary on his right and John the Baptist on his left, with the representatives of the Church on either side.

● **The Dormition of the Virgin** (from the Latin "sleep"). The Orthodox term for the Virgin's death. The Dormition (Assumption for Catholics), is celebrated on 15 August.

● **Exonarthex**. See pridvor.

● **Filioque**. Term given to the dogmatic dispute which led, in 1054, to the Great Schism between the Orthodox Church and the Roman Church. Faithful to the credo established during the Council of Nicaea (325 AD), the Orthodox Church professes that the Holy Spirit emanates from the Father through the Son. In the 7th century, the Roman Church modified the credo so that the Holy Spirit emanates from the Father and from the Son (in Latin "*ex patre filioque procedit*").

● **The inscribed Greek cross.** Common architectural church plan in Constantinople. Two barrel vaults supported by central pillars in the naos intersect to form a cross with equal-length arms. At the intersection, four pendentives support a tower.

● **Hesychasm** (from the Greek *hesychos* "quiet"). Spiritual tradition specific to monastic Orthodoxy consisting of intensive invocation of Christ by a repetitive prayer in order to attain inner peace.

Detail from an exterior fresco in Moldoviţa Monastery illustrating the Tree of Jesse

● **Higoumena.** Superior of a monastery.

● **Icon** (from the Greek *eikona* "image"). A sacred image most commonly painted on wood, sometimes on glass, portraying Christ, Mary or the saints. The themes and execution of icons follow strict rules. The icon is above all a liturgical object with an important religious role.

● **Iconostasis**. A feature of Orthodox churches, the iconostasis is a partition covered with icons separating the divine world (the sanctuary, where the Eucharist is celebrated) from the human world (the naos where the faithful congregate). In the centre, the **imperial doors**, on which the Annunciation and the four Evangelists are represented, open onto to the altar. Only the officiating priests were allowed through and, at the time of the Byzantine Empire, the Emperor, hence their name. At certain moments of the liturgy, during Easter for instance, they are opened and the altar is visible. The diaconal doors, on each side, allow access for the deacons and their assistants.

● **Imperial doors.** See iconostasis.

● **The Ladder of Divine Ascent.** A ladder of thirty rungs, each representing a virtue which a monk must possess to reach the next level. At the top of the ladder: Paradise. It is described in the writings of Saint John Climacus (16th century, the Superior of the Monastery of Saint Catherine, Sinai). See Sucevița (p. 232).

● **The Last Judgment.** For Christianity, Jesus must return at the end of time to judge mankind. The good shall be rewarded with eternal life in God's Kingdom; the evil shall suffer in eternal flames. This theme was introduced in the exterior frescoes of Moldavia's and Bucovina's churches at the beginning of 16th century. See Voroneț (p. 229).

● **The Menelogium** (or menelogion or synaxarion). A lection containing, for each day of the liturgy, the account of the appropriate saint's life.

● **Metropolis**. The capital of an ecclesiastical province.

● **Metropolitan**. Bishop of a metropolis or of an autocephalous church.

● **Naos**. Part of the church separating the sanctuary from the iconostasis. Sometimes reserved for men during the liturgy, it is prolonged to the west by the pronaos.

● **Orthodox** (from the Greek "true faith".) Name given to the Uniate Church which separated from the Roman, or Catholic Church in 1054.

● **The Pantocrator** (from the Greek "all powerful"). Term most often used for Christ. In Byzantine iconography, the Christ Pantocrator is often represented seated, with his right hand raised and his left hand holding the Gospel.

● **The Patriarch.** The title of the leading hierarchs of the first four autocephalus churches or patriarchates (Constantinople, Alexandria, Antioch, Jerusalem), elected by the synod. Also said of the heads of the autocephalous churches (Moscow, Belgrade, Bucharest and Sofia).

● **Post.** Fast, Lent. See inset p. 34

● **Pridvor** (or exonarthex). A section sometimes added to the western side of a church, forming a transition between the profane and sacred worlds. Those who are not pure stand here during the liturgy.

● **Pronaos.** Part of a church lengthening the naos towards the west (except in Bucovina, see p. 221). The pronaos used to be reserved for women during the liturgy. Nowadays, women stand on the left of the pronaos and men on the right.

● **Sanctuary.** Eastern part of the church where the altar is placed.

● **Schism**. A split between factions of a Church, often over a question of dogma, such as The Great Schism of 1054, between the Orthodox Church and the Roman Church.

● **Theotokos** (from the Greek "God bearer" or "Mother of God"). A qualifying term given to Mary at the Council of Ephesus (431 AD). Theotokos is often represented on icons and in frescoes. See Moldovița (p. 231).

● **Tree of Jesse**. Jesse was the father of David, King of Israel (1010-970 BC). According to the Bible, David was to be the ancestor of the Messiah, saviour of the Jews. For the Christians, Jesus *is* the Messiah: his genealogy is represented by a tree whose roots spring from Jesse's loins. See Moldovița (p. 231).

● **Triconch**. A church plan with three apses united by a central space, the summit of each apse forming a conch.

● **Uniate** (Church). See p. 54.

● **Voivode** (or hospodar). The former title of princes in Moldavia and Wallachia. Also the title of governors in Eastern European countries. ●

Some Romanian words

Romanian is a Romance language: its structure and the majority of its vocabulary have recognisable Latin origins. A third of the words, however, are Slavonic with further inputs from Turkish, Hungarian, Albanian and Greek. The traveller who is already familiar with another romance language such as French, Italian, Spanish or Portuguese will not be lost in Romania.

pronunciation

If the written word is understandable, pronunciation isn't as easy:

e	«a»	ş	«ch»
u	«oo»	ţ	«ts»
ă	«uh»	c	«k» before a, ă, â, î, o, u
ai	«i»		
oi	«oye»	ch	«k» before e and i
au	«ao»		
â et î	«uy»	c	«tch» before e and i

> the **ii** group is pronounced as an **e** at the end of a word.

> an **i** at the end of a word is silent.

ge	«jay»
gi	«jee»
ghe	«gay»
ghi	«ghee»

Conversation

How are you?	ce faceţi?
What is it?	ce este?
How much?	cât costă?
I don't speak Romanian.	nu vorbesc româneşte
What does it mean?	ce înseamnă?
How do you say?	cum se spune?
What time is it?	cât este ora?
Yes	da
No	nu
Hello	bună ziua
Good evening	bună seara
Good night	noapte bună
Thank you	mulţumesc
Please	vă rog/ te rog
Good bye	la revedere
See you soon	pe curând
Miss	domnişoară
Mister	domn
Girl	fată
Boy	băiat
Excuse me	vă rog să mă scuzaţi
Today	astăzi / azi
Yesterday	ieri
Tomorrow	mâine
Open	deschis
Closed	închis
Expensive	scump
A good deal	ieftin
Happy trails	drum bun
Go away!	du-te!
My name is...	Mo appelle

Orientation

Where is...?	unde este?
Is it far?	este departe?
Here	aici
There	acolo
Next door	lângă
Far	departe
In front of	în faţa
To the right of	la dreapta
To the left of	la stânga
Straight ahead	tot înainte
Before	înainte
Behind	înapoi
Entrance	intrare
Exit	ieşire
Village	sat
City	oraş
Street	stradă
Place	piaţă
Boulevard	bulevard
Bridge	pod
House	casă
Fair	târg
Market	piaţă
Chemist/Pharmacy	farmacie
Hospital	spital
Police Station	poliţie
Toilets/ WC	toaletă
Hostel	han
Train	tren
Boat	vapor
Bus	autobuz
Handcart	căruţă
Car	maşină
Route	drum
Petrol/Gas Station	benzinărie
Ticket	bilet
Sleeping compartment	vagon de dormit
Departure	plecare
Arrival	sosire
Information Desk	birou de informaţii

Sleeping and eating

Is there a room available?	aveţi o cameră liberă?
What's the price?	care este preţul?
– per person	de persoană?
– per night	pe noapte?
Half board	demi-pensiune
Full board	pensiune completă

numbers

0	zero	11	unsprezece
1	unu	12	doisprezece
2	doi	20	douăzeci
3	trei	30	treizeci
4	patru	40	patruzeci
5	cinci	50	cincizeci
6	șase	100	o sută
7	șapte	500	cinci sute
8	opt	1 000	o mie
9	nouă	1 000 000	un million
10	zece		

Room .... cameră
One/ two beds .... un pat /două paturi
Bathroom .... baie
Meals .... masă
Breakfast .... mic dejun
Lunch .... prânz
Dinner .... masă de seară / cină
The bill .... notă de plată
Bottle .... sticlă
Water .... apă plată
Beer .... bere
Wine: white/red .... vin alb/ roșu
Eau-de-vie .... țuică/palincă/horincă
Coffee .... cafea
Tea .... ceai
Milk .... lapte
Sugar .... zahăr
Jam .... dulceață
Honey .... miere de albine
Bread .... pâine

Butter .... unt
Oil .... ulei
Meat .... carne
Porc .... porc
Cow .... vacă
Veal .... vițel
Chicken .... pui
Lamb .... miel
Fish .... pește
Mushrooms .... ciuperci
Egg .... ou
Soup .... supă/ciorbă
Cheese .... brânză
Cake .... prăjitură
Ice-cream .... înghețată
Fruit .... fructe

The calender

Monday .... luni
Tuesday .... marți
Wednesday .... miercuri
Thursday .... joi
Friday .... vineri
Saturday .... sâmbătă
Sunday .... duminică
January .... ianuarie
February .... februarie
March .... martie
April .... aprilie
May .... mai
June .... iunie
July .... iulie
August .... august
September .... septembrie
October .... octombrie
November .... noiembrie
December .... decembriel ●

Index

Bucharest : place name

Brâncuşi, Constantin (1876-1957) : person

SHEPHERDS : KEY WORD

Bold text refers to the most detailed items.

Bold italic text refers to address books and directory.

Abbreviations : Apus. = Apuseni Mountains; Buch. = Bucharest; Buc. = Bucovina; Heart Trans. = Heart of Transylvania; Dob. = Dobrogea; Mara. = Maramureş; Mold. = Moldavia; South Trans. = Southern Transylvania; Wall. = Wallachia.

336 • In brief

Imprimé en France par I.M.E. 25110 Baume-les-dames
dépôt légal : 48211 - N° imprimeur : 17561
24/0023/2